Fodor's

OAHU

Welcome to Oahu

Little did we realize that the emergence of a novel coronavirus in early 2020 would abruptly bring almost all travel to a halt. Although our Fodor's writers around the world have continued working to bring you the best of the destinations they cover, we still anticipate that more than the usual number of businesses will close permanently in the coming months, perhaps with little advance notice. We don't expect things to return to "normal" for some time. As you plan your upcoming travels to Oahu, please confirm that places are still open and let us know when we need to make updates by writing to us at editors@fodors.com.

TOP REASONS TO GO

★ **Pearl Harbor:** This historic memorial in Honolulu is a sobering, don't-miss sight.

★ **Waikiki:** Busy but beautiful, with a perfect beach for first-time surfers.

★ **Great Food:** Simple plate lunches, fresh sushi, creative Hawaii regional cuisine.

★ **Polynesian Cultural Center:** The famous luau provides insight into island culture.

★ **Nightlife:** From upscale jazz bars to local hangouts, Honolulu comes alive after dark.

★ **North Shore:** Shave ice, big waves, pro surfers, and a slower pace add appeal here.

Contents

Fodor's Features

Chapter 1

EXPERIENCE OAHU

25 ULTIMATE EXPERIENCES

Oahu offers terrific experiences that should be on every traveler's list. Here are Fodor's top picks for a memorable trip.

1 Explore North Shore

Spend a day on the North Shore. Start off in Kaneohe and drive up Kamehameha Highway all the way to Haleiwa, stopping along the way at fruit stands, shrimp trucks, beaches, world-famous surfing spots (don't miss Waimea Bay), and scenic overlooks. *(Ch. 5)*

2 Watch a Hula Show

For a more traditional, less touristy introduction to hula and Hawaiian music, go to the free hula show that's held several nights a week on Kuhio Beach. *(Ch. 3)*

3 Learn to Surf

Waikiki is popular, but White Plains has fewer crowds and better conditions for beginner surfers; you can rent gear or sign up for lessons at the recreation stand. *(Ch. 4)*

4 Have a Plate lunch

Everyone should try this bargain-priced Hawaii lunch tradition: an entrée with white rice and a scoop of macaroni salad. It's an island favorite. *(Ch. 3, 4, 5, 6)*

5 Relax at Kailua Beach

Looking for that idyllic, unpopulated stretch of white sandy beach and Technicolor blue water? Visit Kailua Beach for easy swimming waves and maximum sand. *(Ch. 6)*

6 Paradise Cove Luau

Let's face it. There is no non-touristy luau, but Paradise Cove is where locals like to take visitors for traditional Hawaiian foods (give *poi* a chance) and a genuinely fun experience. *(Ch. 4)*

7 Munch on Malasadas

A must-eat, these deep-fried, sugar-coated doughnuts without holes (first brought to the islands by Portuguese immigrants) are an island fixture. *(Ch. 3, 4, 5, 6)*

8 Byodo-In Temple

Part of the Valley of the Temples cemetery complex, Byodo-In is a smaller version of the 11th-century original in Uji, Japan, but it's every bit as beautiful and peaceful. *(Ch. 6)*

9 Makapuu Lighthouse Trail

Less crowded than Diamond Head, Makapuu (popular with families because of the paved trail) offers an equally beautiful panorama of a different part of Oahu's coastline. *(Ch. 6)*

10 Seek a Waterfall on the Manoa Falls Trail

Manoa Falls is an easy (though occasionally muddy), 1½-mile rain-forest hike in Manoa Valley with the reward of a 150-foot waterfall at its end. *(Ch. 3)*

11 Explore Chinatown

Oahu's Chinatown is a jumble of the historic and hip, with a revitalized dining scene, plus a mix of galleries, shops, and cultural sites. *(Ch. 3)*

12 Snorkel at Hanauma Bay

This nature preserve nestled in a volcanic crater with a vibrant reef is a phenomenal, family-friendly place to see colorful fish and other sea life. *(Ch. 6, 7)*

13 Enjoy Kitsch at La Mariana Sailing Club

Hawaii's tiki era may be over, but La Mariana, a throwback restaurant and tiki bar, carries on the tradition. *(Ch. 3)*

14 Walk Through Waikiki

The best way to enjoy Waikiki's famed tourist strip is by foot: skip the traffic, burn off some mai tai calories, and catch the sights you might otherwise miss. *(Ch. 3)*

15 Take a Cruise or Kayak Trip

You've got to get out on the water, whether it's on a sunset catamaran cruise, a whale-watching trip, or a kayak excursion in the Mokulua Islands. *(Ch. 6, 7)*

16 Take Tea at the Moana

Relaxed and refined at the same time, the Moana Surfrider offers high tea on its oceanfront Banyan Veranda, complete with dainty sandwiches, desserts, and a dose of glamour. *(Ch. 3)*

17 Visit Iolani Palace

The only royal residence in the U.S. gives you an introduction to Hawaii's monarchy era, which ended with the overthrow of Queen Liliuokalani in 1893. *(Ch. 3)*

18 Eat out in Kaimuki

This unassuming neighborhood east of Waikiki and north of Diamond Head offers a diverse array of restaurants (both upscale and local) in a hip (but not-too-hip) part of town. *(Ch. 3)*

19 Explore the nature preserve at Kaena Point

Striking, stark, solitary: Kaena Point requires an easy (though not shaded) hike out to the island's westernmost point, which is considered a sacred spot. *(Ch. 5, 7)*

20 Relive History at Pearl Harbor

You can't go to Oahu and skip a visit to Pearl Harbor National Memorial, which preserves four different World War II sites, including the USS *Arizona* Memorial. *(Ch. 3)*

21 Treat Yourself to Shave Ice at Island Snow

Matsumoto's on the North Shore may be the most well-known, but we (and former president Barack Obama) prefer Island Snow in Kailua. *(Ch. 6)*

22 Try a Spam Musubi

If you want to eat like a local, you've got to try what is basically Spam sushi—sticky rice with seasoned, fried Spam wrapped up in seaweed. It's surprisingly tasty. *(Ch. 3, 4, 5, 6)*

23 Visit Doris Duke's Shangri-La

Tobacco heiress Doris Duke's waterfront mansion here was inspired by the Middle East, South Asia, and North Africa. Don't miss it. *(Ch. 3, 6)*

24 Feel the Wind at Nuuana Pali Lookout

On especially windy days, you can actually lean up against the wind, and on most days, you get spectacular views. *(Ch. 6)*

25 Watch the Pros Surf at Waimea Bay

During winter, when waves can crest past 20 feet, Waimea Bay is one of the best places in the world to watch the pros catch the big ones. *(Ch. 5)*

WHAT'S WHERE

1 Honolulu. The vibrant capital city holds the nation's only royal palace; free concerts under the tamarind trees in the financial district; and the art galleries, hipster bars, and open markets of Nuuanu and Chinatown. It also encompasses Waikiki—dressed in lights at the base of Diamond Head, famous for its world-class shopping, restaurants, and surf—and Pearl Harbor, Hawaii's largest natural harbor and the resting place of the USS *Arizona*, sunk on December 7, 1941.

2 West (Leeward) and Central Oahu. This rugged western side of the island is finding a new identity as a "second city" of suburban homes, golf courses, and major resorts surrounding lagoons in the Ko Olina area. Although the interstate cuts through the area, fertile Central Oahu is an integral part of Hawaii's rich cultural history. This valley, between the Waianae and Koolau mountain ranges, is an eclectic mix of farms, planned communities, and strip malls.

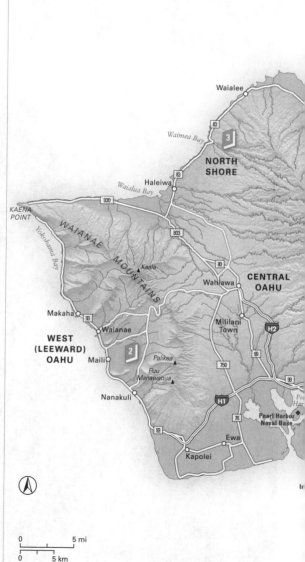

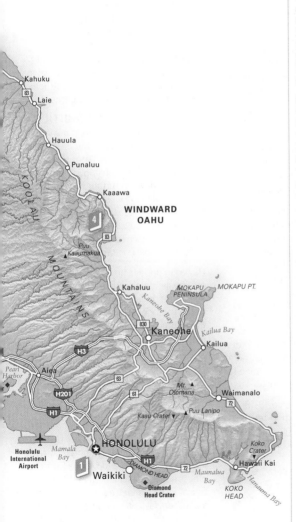

3 **North Shore.** Best known for its miles of world-class surf breaks and green sea-turtle sightings, the North Shore is home to the legendary laid-back surf town of Haleiwa. This plantation area also boasts farms, restaurants, and hiking trails.

4 **Windward (East) Oahu.** The sleepy neighborhoods at the base of the majestic Koolau Mountains offer a respite from the bustling city, with long stretches of sandy beaches, charming eateries, ancient Hawaiian fishponds, and offshore islands to explore. On the southeastern corner of Oahu, Honolulu's main bedroom communities crawl up the steep-sided valleys that flow into Maunalua Bay. Also here are snorkelers' favorite Hanauma Bay and a string of wild and often hidden beaches.

Oahu Today

The third-largest Hawaiian island, Oahu is also the most densely populated, with about 75% of the state's residents. Often called "The Gathering Place," Oahu is usually the first stop in Hawaii for visitors.

TOURISM AND THE ECONOMY

Tourism is Hawaii's primary industry, relying heavily on international travelers and generating $17 billion in revenue from some 10 million visitors in 2019. About a half million tourists arrive on Oahu every month, the majority staying in Waikiki.

Hawaii's "shelter in place" order, issued in response to the COVID-19 pandemic, was lifted slowly starting in June 2020, but by then many businesses had been closed for several weeks, and there was growing concern about a longer-term strategy for reopening Hawaii's economy.

As the most developed island, Oahu's on-going dependence on tourism has resulted in hardship for locals, including traffic problems, elevated housing prices, and general overcrowding that has strained the island's natural resources for years. Hawaii's average salaries don't offer enough economic stability for middle-to-low income residents due to the state's high cost of living. Most people who live here have a long commute to their work in Honolulu (or they may hold multiple jobs), and it's not uncommon for many to live with extended family.

In late 2019, Bill 89 (Ordinance 19-18) passed, prohibiting illegal short-term rentals. Some residents argue that the new law has unfairly limited an income stream they have relied on to make ends meet. At this writing, short-term rentals are allowed only in Waikiki, Ko Olina, and Turtle Bay, with most others being prohibited.

SUSTAINABILITY

Oahu has begun educating the community on the importance of keeping beaches and oceans clean and ensuring that marine life and reefs remain healthy. You won't find plastic straws in your cocktails on Oahu, and all sunblock sold here is mandated to be reef-safe by January 2021. Plastic shopping bags are also prohibited, so bring your own reusable bag. The city of Honolulu has committed to create a carbon-neutral economy, using renewable energy, a green infrastructure, and sustainable waste management.

EMBRACING LOCAL TRADITION

The arrival of Western Europeans in the late 1700s nearly caused the eradication of the Hawaiian culture. After Hawaii became a U.S. state in 1959, a process of Americanization further silenced some of the remaining Hawaiian cultural traditions: the Hawaiian language was banned from schools, cultural celebrations were forbidden, and children were distanced from their local customs.

Hawaiian pride is now resurgent as native islanders rediscover their heritage—from hula, lei-making, and music to the methods for pounding poi and the nutritional and healing properties of native herbs, flowers, and other plants. There's also a renewed interest in building authentic Polynesian wooden canoes and learning traditional navigation. Several major educational facilities, such as Windward Community College, offer free Hawaiian language courses.

Visitors to Waikiki will experience Oahu's history as well. Landmark hotels such as the Royal Hawaiian and Moana Surfrider offer free (and fascinating) in-depth historical tours, as well as weekly lei-making and other Hawaiian ceremonies on site. Tourists can also learn to catch waves on a surfboard or a wooden outrigger canoe.

Most notably, the Native Hawaiian population is also on the rise in Oahu for the first time since the 18th century. Considered the first of its kind, the local settlement Puuhonua o Waimanalo—developed in partnership with the state in 1994 on the windward side of Oahu—is home to more than 200 mostly native residents, who live on nearly 50 acres of land and support the culture and traditions of Hawaii.

NEIGHBORHOOD DEVELOPMENT
In recent years, Oahu's gritty Kakaako neighborhood, a former industrial area, has become rather hip and trendy, filled with bars, restaurants, breweries, and stores. It's also known for its colorful street art. However, while it's a tourist magnet, most of the area's luxury high-rises are owned by non-residents.

Ko Olina, 40 minutes west of Waikiki, is another area that's seen a great deal of recent development. It is now home to major resorts and several picturesque man-made lagoons. It's a busy spot, especially on weekends, when locals and tourists arrive. The Windward beach town of Kailua is also seeing an influx of visitors; what was once a quiet community is now a popular spot for tourists, who drive from Waikiki to spend the day on the beach at the evening at the towns local restaurants. It's increasingly crowded, so attempts have been made to restrict parking to control the crowds.

HOMELESSNESS
Unfortunately, homelessness is a very real and challenging situation on Oahu, which has the state's largest homeless population. (In fact, Hawaii has the highest per capita rate of homelessness in the country.) An assistance plan has moved as many as 600 individuals per month off the street and into permanent housing but isn't keeping pace with the increasing needs. Everyone agrees that this is a complex problem that requires ongoing attention.

TRANSPORTATION
The Honolulu Rail Transit system has been in development for over 40 years and is expected to cost more than $9 billion dollars (far more than originally budgeted) before it's eventually finished. This elevated rail line will span 20 miles—from East Kapolei to the Ala Moana Center, with several extensions, including a station in Waikiki. Half of the train line (from Kapolei to Aloha stadium) is slated to open in late 2020, and the entire system is scheduled to be ready in December 2025.

AGRICULTURE AND OAHU'S CULINARY SCENE
Years ago, the major crops grown on Hawaii were sugarcane and pineapple, but those have nearly disappeared, at least commercially. Although most of Hawaii's food is still imported, a statewide movement to create a more sustainable food-supply chain has rekindled interest in local agriculture and inspired restaurants to emphasize farm-to-table cuisine. In several of Oahu's neighborhoods, weekly farmers' markets offer everything from fresh papaya or mango to small-batch honey, jam, and chocolate. Chefs and restaurateurs have partnered with the Hawaii Restaurant Association to ensure they are serving the freshest produce, meat, and seafood.

Until COVID-19 shut down the state, restaurants on Oahu—especially in Waikiki and Kakaako—were thriving. You'll find every cuisine imaginable (and at every price point), from casual beach fare to multi-course tasting menus. These days, it's not unusual to see local, indigenous ingredients on menus, and chefs (some home-grown) who introduce a blending of culinary styles, such as Italian or French with a distinctive Hawaiian twist.

Oahu's Best Beaches

HALEIWA ALII BEACH PARK, NORTH SHORE

A world-famous surfing spot, Haleiwa Beach Park is the center of the North Shore's surf community and hosts the Vans Triple Crown of Surfing each November. Adjacent is Alii Beach Park, a popular (and often busy) spot, with lots of shade, picnic tables, showers, and other amenities. Considered one of the few safe areas for swimming on the North Shore, it's a great beach for snorkeling and where beginners can try surfing. Be sure to soak in some authentic island vibes by checking out the town of Haleiwa's shops and surf culture.

SUNSET BEACH, NORTH SHORE

As beautiful as its name implies, Sunset Beach, just down the road from the world-famous Bonzai Pipeline, is a favorite gathering spot to enjoy the day's last brilliant rays before the sun dips below the horizon. It offers calm waters and fun snorkeling in summer and big waves in winter.

ALA MOANA REGIONAL PARK, HONOLULU

Just a few steps away from the Ala Moana Center's shops and restaurants, this beach offers extraordinarily fine sand and smaller crowds than Waikiki, which is about 20 minutes away. With lifeguards and amenities (though little shade), this is a family-friendly spot with plenty of activity in and out of the water, including stand-up paddle boarding and snorkeling, as well as bicycling and picnicking. It's also a favorite surfing spot for locals, with several popular breaks just offshore.

BELLOWS BEACH, HAWAII KAI

Lovely and picturesque, Bellows Beach is on the island's windward coast and known for its striking stretch of wide, white sand and shimmering shades of sapphire blue water. Near Waimanalo Beach Park and Bellows Air Force Station, it's usually open to the public on weekends and a favorite spot for body boarders and surfers. A fun place for camping, this eastward-facing crescent is famous for spectacular sunrises, shady ironwood trees, and strong afternoon breezes.

KO OLINA, LEEWARD (WEST) OAHU

Situated in front of several major resorts on the island's western coast, picture-perfect man-made lagoons are totally protected and offer soft sand and calm, turquoise water. This area was truly made for family-friendly fun, with kayaks, SUPs, and snorkel gear readily available for rent. There's plenty of room here for everyone, with grassy areas for relaxing and enjoying a pleasant beach day. If you're traveling with kids, you'll feel at home … steps away is Disney's incredible Aulani resort.

KUALOA REGIONAL PARK, WINDWARD OAHU

This expansive park with lots of shade and green space gives campers and other beachgoers plenty of room to spread out. The sand itself isn't very wide, but the waves are gentle, and it's a great spot for

Ko Olina, Leeward (West) Oahu

swimming and especially kayaking and paddle boarding. If the wind is kicking up, you may see locals flying large, two-handed kites. The scenery here is particularly lovely, as the Koolau Mountains are a distant backdrop. Mokolii Island is visible offshore.

LANIKAI BEACH PARK, WINDWARD OAHU

Tucked away in a quiet residential neighborhood, this beach offers powdery white sand and crystal-clear water but very limited shade. If you're an early riser, it's worth getting here before dawn, as it's a gorgeous place to catch the sunrise. Unlike the nearby Kailua Beach Park, there's no food, water, or facilities here, so bring whatever you think you will need to enjoy this tranquil setting. Access to this beach is through several narrow pedestrian walkways that you can see from the street, but parking is very limited.

SANDY BEACH, HAWAII KAI

Spacious and stunning, Sandy Beach offers plenty of room to spread out atop the fine golden sand and enjoy the scenery, including a glimpse of the nearby Halona Blowhole if the tides are right. Popular with locals, this south shore beach is known for its crashing shorebreak and has lifeguards and facilities. If the waves are rough, retire to the shoreline and watch the beach activity from your lounge chair, including kites performing acrobatics in the gusts.

WHITE PLAINS, LEEWARD (WEST) OAHU

A go-to beach for surfing, stand-up paddle boarding, and body boarding, White Plains is a favorite spot among locals and known to be less crowded than Waikiki. It's also the spot to enjoy beautiful azure water and a smooth, sandy bottom, unlike the other

(rockier) beaches in the area. The currents and wind can be unpredictable and get a bit strong at times, but there are lifeguards watching over the swimmers. It's not unusual to see seals. You'll find abundant parking, showers, restrooms, barbecue grills, and picnic tables here.

WAIMEA BAY, NORTH SHORE

During the summer, the snorkeling is simply magical at this popular, jaw-droppingly beautiful beach. But in winter, surf's up, so be careful if you don't know what you're doing. Major contests are held here as waves frequently reach 20 feet. "The Eddie" surf competition honors big-wave-surfer Eddie Aikau, attracting fans from across the islands, so arrive early in the morning and claim your seat on the dunes.

Oahu's Most Incredible Natural Wonders

WAIMEA BAY AND VALLEY, NORTH SHORE

The scenic and legendary Waimea Bay is famous for powerful, big waves in winter and calm water in summer. Nearby is the lush and expansive Waimea Valley, with exquisite scenery, including waterfalls (there's an admission charge, though).

HALONA BLOWHOLE, WINDWARD (EAST) OAHU

North of the picturesque Hanauma Bay, the Halona Blowhole can be viewed easily from a lookout just off the Kalanianaole Highway. Formed by ancient lava tubes, this blowhole blasts a forceful spray about 30 feet in the air when the tide is right.

MANOA FALLS, HONOLULU

In the lush Manoa Valley, the beautiful and ancient waterfall drops 150 feet into a pool that's surrounded by a tropical rain forest with soaring bamboo, trees, and flowers. It will come as no surprise that the cascade is a popular filming location.

DIAMOND HEAD, HONOLULU

Legendary and majestic, Oahu's breathtaking Diamond Head Crater is an iconic symbol of the island. Looming large above Waikiki's coastline, the former military outpost is now a popular place to hike. Panoramic views from the top are truly splendid, but it's a steep climb.

KAENA POINT, WEST (LEEWARD) OAHU

Wild and remote, Kaena Point is the westernmost point on Oahu. Featuring picturesque coves and sweeping ocean views, this spot can only be reached by hiking a rocky (and often muddy) trail along the rough coastline that offers extraordinary vistas. It's home to a bird sanctuary and nature reserve. The point has two entrances (Kaena State Park and Mokuleia), so if you're feeling inspired, you can trek for about 5 miles round-trip.

HANAUMA BAY, SOUTH-EAST OAHU

On the island's southeast coast, Hanauma Bay is considered one of the most popular snorkeling spots here. With brilliant white sand and shallow, calm water, this stunning nature preserve is teeming with many species of colorful tropical fish and marine life. Over the years, it's become increasingly crowded, so visitors are now capped at 3,000 per day.

Diamond Head

NUUANU PALI LOOKOUT, WINDWARD (EAST) OAHU

As part of the Koolau mountain range, the legendary Nuuanu Pali lookout is situated inside of Nuuanu State Park and offers a spectacular panoramic view of Oahu. At nearly 1,000 feet high, this notoriously windy spot offers views far across the island's windward coast and the ocean beyond. It also played a major role in King Kamehameha I's epic victory over the troops of Oahu, which killed hundreds of warriors.

KOOLAU MOUNTAINS, WINDWARD (EAST) OAHU

Stretching nearly 40 miles, this majestic volcanic mountain formation features an abundance of steep trails that lead to gorgeous waterfalls and streams. The most recognizable section of this mountain is the Pali Cliff that rises to about 2,000 feet on the eastern side.

MAKAPUU LOOKOUT POINT, WINDWARD (EAST) OAHU

On the island's south-eastern tip, the Makapuu Lookout Point is located just off the side of the Kalanianaole Highway. A paved walkway leads to an overlook with a breathtaking panoramic view of Windward Oahu's dramatic sea cliffs and lovely Makapuu Beach Park (or take a short hike to the lighthouse nearby). It's also known as a great spot for whale-watching.

MAKAPUU TIDEPOOLS, WINDWARD (EAST) OAHU

Adjacent to the Makapuu Lookout Point are the Makapuu tidepools. Usually filled with incredible and colorful marine life, they are easily reached via a paved trail from the lookout's parking area. It's an easy 30-minute stroll on a clearly marked path.

Flora and Fauna in Hawaii

KUKUI

The kukui, or candlenut, is Hawaii's state tree. Hawaiians had many uses for kukui. Oil was extracted from its nuts and burned as a light source and also rubbed on fishing nets to preserve them. The juice from the husk's fruit was used as a dye. The small kukui blossoms and nuts also had medicinal purposes.

PLUMERIA

This fragrant flower is named after Charles Plumier, the noted French botanist who discovered it in Central America in the late 1600s. Plumeria come in shades of white, yellow, pink, red, and orange. The hearty, plentiful blossoms are frequently used in lei.

GARDENIA

The gardenia is a favorite for lei makers because of its sweet smell. The plant is native to tropical regions throughout China and Africa, but there are also endemic gardenia in Hawaii. The nanu gardenia are found only in the Islands and have petite white blossoms.

HONU

The honu, or Hawaiian green sea turtle, is a magical sight. The graceful reptile is an endangered and protected species in Hawaii. It's easier to run across honu during a snorkeling or scuba diving excursion, but they occasionally can be spotted coming to the ocean's surface.

HUMPBACK WHALES

Each year, North Pacific humpback whales make the long journey to Hawaii from Alaska. With its warm waters, Hawaii's shores provide the ideal place for the marine mammals to mate, birth, and nurse their young. They arrive between November and May, and their presence is an anticipated event for many. You can see them up close during whale-watching boat tours.

MONK SEAL

Known as the *ilio holo I ka uaua*, or, "dog that runs in rough water," monk seals are endemic to Hawaii and critically endangered. Most of these mammals, which can grow more than seven feet long and weigh more than 600 pounds, live in remote, uninhabited Northwestern Hawaiian Islands.

TROPICAL FISH

Approximately 25% of the fish species in the Islands are endemic. Snorkeling in Hawaii is a unique, fun opportunity to see colorful fish, big and small. Interestingly, Hawaii's state fish, the tongue-twister *humuhumunukunukuapuaa*, or reef trigger, is not endemic to the state.

NENE GOOSE

Pronounced *nay-nay*, the endemic nene goose (the state bird) is the rarest in the world. Thanks to preservation efforts, the goose, which is a descendent of the Canadian goose, has been bred back from the edge of extinction and reintroduced into the wild.

HIBISCUS

In 1923, the Territory of Hawaii passed a law designating hibiscus as Hawaii's official flower. While there are more than 30 introduced species of the large, colorful flowers throughout the Islands, there are five endemic types. In Hawaiian, the endemic hibiscus has yellow blossoms and is known as mao hau hele, which means the "traveling green tree."

PIKAKE

These small, delicate blossoms are known for their hypnotic sweet scent. The jasmine flower was introduced from India and was a favorite of Princess Kaiulani. Pikake, which is the Hawaiian word for the blossom as well as peacock—another favorite of the princess—is the subject of many mele or Hawaiian songs.

What to Eat and Drink in Hawaii

SHAVE ICE

Shave ice is simple in its composition—fluffy ice drizzled in Technicolor syrups. Shave ice traces its roots to Hawaii's plantation past. Japanese laborers would use the machetes from their field work to finely shave ice from large frozen blocks and then pour fruit juice over it.

MUSUBI

Musubi are Hawaii's answer to the perfect snack. Portable, handheld, and salty, musubi are a great go-to any time of day. The local comfort food is a slice of Spam encased in packed white rice and snugly wrapped with nori, or dried seaweed. Available everywhere, musubi are usually just a few dollars.

MAI TAI

When people think of a Hawaiian cocktail, the colorful Mai Tai often comes to mind. It's the unofficial drink to imbibe at a luau and refreshingly tropical. This potent concoction has a rum base and is traditionally made with orange curaçao, orgeat, fresh squeezed lime juice, and simple syrup.

HAWAIIAN PLATE

The Hawaiian plate comprises the delicious, traditional foods of Hawaii, all on one heaping plate. You can find these combo meals anywhere from roadside lunch wagons to five-star restaurants. Get yours with the melt-in-your-mouth shredded kalua pig, pork, or chicken *laulau* (cooked in ti leaves) with *lomi* salmon (diced salmon with tomatoes and onions) on the side and the coconut-milk haupia for dessert. Most Hawaiian plates come with the requisite two scoops of white rice. Don't forget to try *poi*, or pounded and cooked taro. For an authentic plate, visit Helena's Hawaiian Food on Oahu; just be sure to get there early.

POKE

In Hawaiian, *poke* is a verb that means to slice and cut into pieces. It perfectly describes the technique Hawaiians have used for centuries to prepare poke the dish. The cubed raw fish, most commonly ahi, or tuna, is traditionally tossed with Hawaiian sea salt, imu kohu, seaweed, inamona, or crushed, roasted kukui nuts. Today, there are countless varieties of poke across the Islands. It's a must try when visiting Hawaii. On Oahu, Ono Seafood, a no-frills, take-out eatery serves made-to-order poke.

MANAPUA

When *kamaaina*, or Hawaii residents, are invited to a potluck, business meeting, or even an impromptu party, you'll inevitably see a box filled with manapua.

Poke

Inside these airy white buns are pockets of sweet char siu pork. Head to Oahu's Chinatown in Honolulu, and you'll find Chinese restaurants with manapua on their menus, as well as manapua take-out places serving a variety of fillings. There's sweet potato, curry chicken, *lup cheong* (or Chinese sausage), even sweet flavors such as custard and ube, a purple yam popular in Filipino desserts.

SAIMIN
This only-in-Hawaii noodle dish is the culinary innovation of Hawaii plantation workers in the late 1800s who created a new comfort food with ingredients and traditions from their home countries.

MALASADA
Malasadas are a beloved treat in Hawaii. The Portuguese pastries are about the size of a baseball and are airy, deep-fried, and dusted with sugar. In Honolulu, on Oahu, Lenard's Bakery is a well-known purveyor of these delicious desserts.

LOCO MOCO
Loco moco is one of Hawaii's classic comfort-food dishes. The traditional loco moco consists of white rice topped with a hamburger patty and fried eggs and generously blanketed in rich, brown gravy. Cafe 100 in Hilo on Hawaii Island is renowned as the home of the loco moco. The 74-year-old café's original loco moco is one of the most popular, and at the amazing price of $4.35.

KONA COFFEE
In Kona, on Hawaii Island, coffee reigns supreme. There are roughly 600 coffee farms dotting the west side of the island, each producing flavorful coffee grown in the rich, volcanic soil. Kona coffee is typically harvested from August to December.

What to Buy in Hawaii

MACADAMIA NUT CANDY
Macadamia are native to Australia, but the gumball-sized nut remains an important crop in Hawaii. It was first introduced in the late 1880s as a windbreak for sugar cane crops. Today, mac nuts, as they are colloquially known, are a popular local food, especially in desserts. They are easily found at convenience and grocery stores.

LEI
As a visitor to Hawaii, you will likely receive a lei, either a shell, kukui nut, or the fragrant flower variety, as a welcome to the Islands. Kamaaina or Hawaii residents mark special occasions by gifting lei.

LAUHALA
The hala tree is most known for its long, thin leaves and the masterful crafts that are created from them. Lauhala weavers make baskets, hats, mats, jewelry, and more, using intricate patterns.

JEWELRY
Island-inspired jewelry is a unique and personalized gift. There are several styles from which to choose, including pieces featuring Tahitian pearls, shells like the dainty orange and pink sunrise shell, and gold Hawaiian heirloom necklaces and bangles with black Old English lettering.

ALOHA WEAR
Aloha wear in Hawaii has come a long way from the cheap fabrics with the too bright and kitsch patterns (although those still exist). Local designers have been creating stylish, modern Aloha shirts, dresses, and more with soft, sleek prints that evoke Island botanicals, heritage, and tradition. Hawaii residents sport Aloha wear for everything from work to weddings.

KONA COFFEE
Reminiscence about your wonderful Hawaii getaway each time you brew a cup of Kona coffee. Authentic Kona coffee is renowned throughout the world for its heady aroma and full-bodied flavor. Stores and cafés sell bags of varying sizes.

HAWAIIAN SEA SALT
A long tradition of harvesting salt beds by hand continues today on the islands of Kauai and Molokai. The salt comes in various colors, including inky black and brick red; these distinctive colors come from the salt reacting and mixing with activated charcoal and alaea, or volcanic clay.

BIG ISLAND HONEY
With its temperate climate and bountiful foliage, honey-bees love Hawaii. The island's unique ecosystem results in robust honey flavors, including the nutty macadamia nut blossom honey or the ohia lehua variety, made from the endemic tree.

UKULELE
In Hawaiian, *ukulele* means "the jumping flea." The small instrument made its way to the Islands in the 1880s via Portuguese immigrants who brought with them the four-string, guitar-like machete. It is renowned as a solo instrument today, with artists like Jake Shimabukuro and Taimane Gardner popularizing it.

KOA WOOD
If you're looking for an heirloom keepsake from the Islands, consider a Koa wood product. Grown only in Hawaii, the valuable Koa wood is some of the world's rarest and hardest wood. Hawaiians traditionally made surfboards and canoes from Koa trees.

What to Read and Watch

HAWAIIAN MYTHOLOGY, BY MARTHA BECKWITH

This exhaustive work of ethnology and folklore was researched and collected by Martha Beckwith over decades and published when she was 69. *Hawaiian Mythology* is a comprehensive look at the Hawaiian ancestral deities and their importance throughout history.

HAWAII'S STORY BY HAWAII'S QUEEN, BY LILIUOKALANI

This poignant book, by Queen Liliuokalani, chronicles the 1893 overthrow of the Hawaiian monarchy and her plea for her people. It's an essential read to understand the political undercurrent and the push for sovereignty that exists in the Islands more than 125 years later.

MARK TWAIN'S LETTERS FROM HAWAII, BY MARK TWAIN

In 1866, when Samuel Clemens was 31, he sailed from California and spent four months in Hawaii. He eventually mailed 25 letters to the *Sacramento Union* newspaper about his experiences. Along the way, Twain sheds some cultural biases as he visits the Kilauea volcano, meets with Hawaii's newly formed legislators, and examines the sugar trade.

SHOAL OF TIME: A HISTORY OF THE HAWAIIAN ISLANDS, BY GAVAN DAWS

Perhaps the most popular book of this best-selling Honolulu author is *Shoal of Time*. Published in 1974, this account of modern Hawaiian history details the colonization of Hawaii and everything that was lost in the process.

MOLOKAI, BY ALAN BRENNERT

Alan Brennert's debut novel, set in the 1890s, follows a Hawaiian woman who contracts leprosy as a child and is sent to the remote, quarantined community of Kalaupapa on the island of Molokai where she then lives. The Southern California–based author was inspired to write the book during his visits to Hawaii.

THE DESCENDANTS

Based on the book by local author, Kaui Hart Hemmings, the film adaptation starring George Clooney and directed by Alexander Payne was filmed on Oahu and Kauai. It spotlights a contemporary, if not upper-class, family in Hawaii as they deal with family grief and landholdings in flux.

50 FIRST DATES

The majority of this 2004 Drew Barrymore–Adam Sandler rom-com was shot on Oahu. While the plot is simultaneously cute and cheesy, *50 First Dates* highlights the beauty of Hawaii. You can pick out several picturesque island places, including the rolling Kualoa Ranch and Waimanalo, Makapuu, and Kaneohe Bay, all on Oahu's rustic east side.

BLUE HAWAII

The 1961 musical features the hip-shaking songs and moves by Elvis Presley, who plays tour guide Chadwick Gates. Elvis famously sings *Ke Kali Nei Au*, or *The Hawaiian Wedding Song*, at the iconic and now-shuttered Coco Palms Resort on Kauai. (The resort has remained closed since 1992 following Hurricane Iniki.)

MOANA

The release of *Moana* in 2016 was celebrated by many in Hawaii and the Pacific for showcasing Polynesian culture. The now-beloved animated movie, which includes the story of the demigod Maui, features the voice talents of Aulii Cravalho and Dwayne Johnson. In 2018, *Moana* was re-recorded and distributed in Olelo Hawaii, or the Hawaiian language, with Cravalho reprising her role. It marked the first time a Disney movie was available in Hawaiian.

Kids and Families

CHOOSING A PLACE TO STAY

Resorts: All the big resorts make kids' programs a priority. When booking your room, ask about *keiki* (children's) menus at restaurants, free activities on the property, and pools and water parks built specifically for the younger set.

In Waikiki, your best bet for kids is the Hilton Hawaiian Village, where there's a large beach and loads of kids' programs. Also good choices: Alohilani Resort's Monkeypod Kids' Club, Waikiki Beach Marriott Resort, and the Aston Waikiki Beach Hotel.

Condos: You can cook your own food and get twice the space of a hotel room for much less. Be sure to ask about the size of the complex's pool and barbecue availability. For the ultimate family condo experience on Oahu, Marriott's Ko Olina Beach Club can't be beat with its sheltered beaches, four pools, barbecues, children's play areas, large kitchens, and an on-site grocery store. In Waikiki, try the Waikiki Shore and Luana Waikiki.

OCEAN ACTIVITIES

On the Beach: In Waikiki, your best beach bets for young children are Kuhio Beach Park and Fort DeRussy Beach Park, both protected from a strong shore break and with a wide stretch of sand, with lifeguards on duty. On the windward side, try Kailua Beach Park, with its shady trees and good bathroom/shower facilities. North Shore beaches are recommended for children only in the summer months, and of these, Waimea Bay, with its wide stretch of sand and good facilities, is best for kids. On the leeward side, Ko Olina's protected coves are great for families with small children.

On the Waves: Waikiki is *the* place for everyone to learn to surf, including kids. Some hotels, including the Royal Hawaiian, a Luxury Collection Resort,

Queen Kapiolani, and the Outrigger Waikiki Beach Resort, offer in-house surf schools. Or, for a less crowded surfing experience, head to Barber's Point.

The Underwater World: Hawaii is a great place to introduce your kids to snorkeling. Even without the mask and snorkel, they'll be able to see colorful fish darting around coral reefs, and they may also spot endangered Hawaiian green sea turtles and dolphins. On Oahu the quintessential snorkeling experience can be had at Hanauma Bay, where kids can see hundreds of species of fish in protected waters and enjoy a wide stretch of beach. In summer months only, Shark's Cove on the North Shore is an interesting experience for older kids who already have snorkeling basics.

LAND ACTIVITIES

Oahu is fortunate to have the largest variety of land-based experiences in the Islands. Kids can visit the Honolulu Zoo for twilight tours, explore the undersea world at the Waikiki Aquarium, or husk a coconut at the Polynesian Culture Center. Hoomaluhia Botanical Garden offers wide-open spaces and a duck pond, while Kualoa Ranch is the place for horseback riding.

AFTER DARK

At night, younger kids get a kick out of a luau, and many of the shows incorporate young audience members, adding to the fun. Older kids are more likely to enjoy the handful of more modern luau, incorporating acrobatics, lively music, and fire dancers. On Friday, don't miss watching the Hilton Hawaiian Village's free fireworks show at 7:45 pm or 8 pm (varies seasonally) from your beachfront seat.

Weddings and Honeymoons

There's no question that Hawaii is one of the country's foremost honeymoon destinations, but it's also popular for destination weddings.

THE BIG DAY

Choosing the Perfect Place. You really have two choices to make: the ceremony location and where to have the reception. For the former, Oahu offers beaches, sea-hugging bluffs, gardens, private residences, resort lawns, and, of course, places of worship. As for the reception, there are these same choices, as well as restaurants and even a luau. If you decide to go outdoors, make sure to have a back-up plan for inclement weather.

Finding a Wedding Planner. If you're planning to invite more than an officiant and your loved one, seriously consider hiring a wedding planner who can help select a location, design the floral scheme, and recommend a florist and photographer. They can also plan the menu and choose a restaurant, caterer, or resort, and suggest Hawaiian traditions to incorporate into your ceremony.

If it's a resort wedding, most have on-site wedding coordinators who can provide guidance and one-stop shopping. Resorts also have indoor-outdoor space for ceremonies, private dining areas for any size reception, and stunning photography spots on property. However, many independent wedding planners around Oahu specialize in certain types of ceremonies—by locale, size, religious affiliation, and so on. Share your budget, and get a detailed written proposal before you proceed.

Getting Your License. There's no waiting period in Hawaii, no residency or citizenship requirements, and no required blood test or shots. You can apply and pay the fee online; however, both the bride and groom must appear together in person before a marriage-license agent to receive the marriage license at the State Department of Health in Honolulu. You'll need proof of age—the legal age to marry is 18. Upon approval, a marriage license is immediately issued and costs $60. After the ceremony, your officiant—who must be licensed by the Hawaii Department of Health—will mail the marriage certificate (proof of marriage) to the state, and you'll get your copy about four months later. There's an informative instructional video on the state's official website. For more detailed information, visit ⊕ *marriage.ehawaii.gov.*

Wedding Attire. In Hawaii, basically anything goes, from long, formal dresses with trains to casual attire—even bathing suits! For men, a pair of solid-color trousers with a nice aloha shirt is appropriate. If you're planning a wedding on the beach, barefoot is the way to go.

Local Customs. The most obvious traditional Hawaiian wedding custom is the lei exchange in which the bride and groom take turns placing a lei around the neck of the other—with a kiss. Bridal lei are usually floral, whereas the groom's is typically made of *maile,* a green leafy garland that drapes the neck. Brides often also wear a *lei poo*—a circular floral headpiece. Other Hawaiian customs include the blowing of the conch shell, hula, chanting, and Hawaiian music.

THE HONEYMOON

Do you want Champagne and strawberries delivered to your room each morning? A breathtaking swimming pool in which to float? A five-star restaurant in which to dine? Then a resort is ideal. A small inn or condominium is also good if you're on a tight budget or don't plan to spend much time in your room. The good news is that Waikiki's accommodations are almost as plentiful as the beaches.

HAWAIIAN CULTURAL
TRADITIONS HULA, LEI, AND LUAU

HULA: MORE THAN A FOLK DANCE

Hula has been called "the heartbeat of the Hawaiian people" and also "the world's best-known, most misunderstood dance." Both are true. Hula isn't just dance. It is storytelling.

Chanter Edith McKinzie calls it "an extension of a piece of poetry." In its adornments, implements, and customs, hula integrates every important Hawaiian cultural practice: poetry, history, genealogy, craft, plant cultivation, martial arts, religion, protocol. So when 19th-century Christian missionaries sought to eradicate a practice they considered depraved, they threatened more than just a folk dance.

With public performance outlawed and private hula practice discouraged, hula went underground for a generation. The fragile verbal link by which culture was transmitted from teacher to student hung by a thread. Even increasing literacy did not help because hula's practitioners were a secretive and protected circle.

As if that weren't bad enough, vaudeville, Broadway, and Hollywood got hold of the hula, giving it the glitz treatment in an unbroken line from "Oh, How She Could Wicky Wacky Woo" to "Rock-A-Hula Baby." Hula became shorthand for paradise: fragrant flowers, lazy hours. Ironically, this development assured that hundreds of Hawaiians could make a living performing and teaching hula. Many danced *auana* (modern form) in performance; but taught *kahiko* (traditional), quietly, at home or in hula schools.

Today, decades after the cultural revival known as the Hawaiian Renaissance, language immersion programs have assured a new generation of proficient chanters, songwriters, and translators. Visitors can see more, and more authentic, traditional hula than at any other time in the last 200 years.

Like the culture of which it is the beating heart, hula has survived.

Lei *poo*. Head lei. In *kahiko*, greenery only. In auana, flowers.

Face emotes appropriate expression. Dancer should not be a smiling automaton.

Shoulders remain relaxed and still, never hunched, even with arms raised. No bouncing.

Eyes always follow leading hand.

Lei. Hula is rarely performed without a shoulder lei.

Arms and hands remain loose, relaxed, below shoulder level—except as required by interpretive movements.

Traditional hula skirt is loose fabric, smocked and gathered at the waist.

Hip is canted over weight-bearing foot.

Knees are always slightly bent, accentuating hip sway.

Kupee. Ankle bracelet of flowers, shells, or foliage.

In kahiko, feet are flat. In auana, they may be more arched, but not tiptoes or bouncing.

BASIC MOTIONS

Speak or Sing

Moon or Sun

Grass Shack or House

Mountains or Heights

Love or Caress

At backyard parties, hula is performed in bare feet and street clothes, but in performance, adornments play a key role, as do rhythm-keeping implements such as the pahu drum and the *ipu* (gourd).

In hula *kahiko* (traditional style), the usual dress is multiple layers of stiff fabric (often with a pellom lining, which most closely resembles *kapa*, the paperlike bark cloth of the Hawaiians). These wrap tightly around the bosom but flare below the waist to form a skirt. In pre-contact times, dancers wore only kapa skirts. Men traditionally wear loincloths.

Monarchy-period hula is performed in voluminous muumuu or high-necked muslin blouses and gathered skirts. Men wear white or gingham shirts and black pants.

In hula *auana* (modern), dress for women can range from grass skirts and strapless tops to contemporary tea-length dresses. Men generally wear aloha shirts, but sometimes grass skirts over pants or even everyday gear.

SURPRISING HULA FACTS

■ Grass skirts are not traditional; workers from Kiribati (the Gilbert Islands) brought this custom to Hawaii.

■ In olden-day Hawaii, *mele* (songs) for hula were composed for every occasion—name songs for babies, dirges for funerals, welcome songs for visitors, celebrations of favorite pursuits.

■ Hula *mai* is a traditional hula form in praise of a noble's genitals; the power of the *alii* (royalty) to procreate gave mana (spiritual power) to the entire culture.

■ Hula students in old Hawaii adhered to high standards: scrupulous cleanliness, no sex, daily cleansing rituals, certain food prohibitions, and no contact with the dead. They were fined if they broke the rules.

WHERE TO WATCH

If you're interested in "the real thing," there are annual hula festivals on each island. Check the individual island visitors' bureaus websites at ⊕ *www.gohawaii.com*.

If you can't make it to a festival, there are plenty of other hula shows—at most resorts, many lounges, and even at certain shopping centers. Ask your hotel concierge for performance information.

ALL ABOUT LEI

Lei brighten every occasion in Hawaii, from birthdays to bar mitzvahs to baptisms. Creative artisans weave nature's bounty—flowers, ferns, vines, and seeds—into gorgeous creations that convey an array of heartfelt messages: "Welcome," "Congratulations," "Good luck," "Farewell," "Thank you," "I love you." When it's difficult to find the right words, a lei expresses exactly the right sentiment.

WHERE TO BUY THE BEST LEI

Most airports in Hawaii have lei stands where you can buy a fragrant garland upon arrival. Every florist shop in the Islands sells lei; you can also treat yourself to a lei while shopping for provisions at any supermarket or box store. And you'll always find lei sellers at crafts fairs and outdoor festivals.

LEI ETIQUETTE

■ To wear a closed lei, drape it over your shoulders, half in front and half in back. Open lei are worn around the neck, with the ends draped over the front in equal lengths.

■ Pikake, ginger, and other sweet, delicate blossoms are "feminine" lei. Men opt for cigar, crown flower, and ti leaf lei, which are sturdier and don't emit as much fragrance.

■ Lei are always presented with a kiss, a custom that supposedly dates back to World War II when a hula dancer fancied an officer at a U.S.O. show. Taking a dare from members of her troupe, she took off her lei, placed it around his neck, and kissed him on the cheek.

■ You shouldn't wear a lei before you give it to someone else. Hawaiians believe the lei absorbs your mana (spirit); if you give your lei away, you'll be giving away part of your essence.

ORCHID

Growing wild on every continent except Antarctica, orchids—which range in color from yellow to green to purple—comprise the largest family of plants in the world. There are more than 20,000 species of orchids, but only three are native to Hawaii—and they are very rare. The pretty lavender vanda you see hanging by the dozens at local lei stands has probably been imported from Thailand.

MAILE

Maile, an endemic twining vine with a heady aroma, is sacred to Laka, goddess of the hula. In ancient times, dancers wore maile and decorated hula altars with it to honor Laka. Today, "open" maile lei usually are given to men. Instead of ribbon, interwoven lengths of maile are used at dedications of new businesses. The maile is untied, never snipped, for doing so would symbolically "cut" the company's success.

ILIMA

Designated by Hawaii's Territorial Legislature in 1923 as the official flower of the island of Oahu, the golden ilima is so delicate it lasts for just a day. Five to seven hundred blossoms are needed to make one garland. Queen Emma, wife of King Kamehameha IV, preferred ilima over all other lei, which may have led to the incorrect belief that they were reserved only for royalty.

PLUMERIA

This ubiquitous flower is named after Charles Plumier, the noted French botanist who discovered it in Central America in the late 1600s. Plumeria ranks among the most popular lei in Hawaii because it's fragrant, hardy, plentiful, inexpensive, and requires very little care. Although yellow is the most common color, you'll also find plumeria lei in shades of pink, red, orange, and "rainbow" blends.

PIKAKE

Favored for its fragile beauty and sweet scent, pikake was introduced from India. In lieu of pearls, many brides in Hawaii adorn themselves with long, multiple strands of white pikake. Princess Kaiulani enjoyed showing guests her beloved pikake and peacocks at Ainahau, her Waikiki home. Interestingly, pikake is the Hawaiian word for both the bird and the blossom.

KUKUI

The kukui (candlenut) is Hawaii's state tree. Early Hawaiians strung kukui nuts (which are quite oily) together and burned them for light; mixed burned nuts with oil to make an indelible dye; and mashed roasted nuts to consume as a laxative. Kukui nut lei may not have been made until after Western contact, when the Hawaiians saw black beads from Europe and wanted to imitate them.

LUAU: A TASTE OF HAWAII

The best place to sample Hawaiian food is at a backyard luau. Aunts and uncles are cooking, the pig is from a cousin's farm, and the fish is from a brother's boat.

But even locals have to angle for invitations to those rare occasions. So your choice is most likely between a commercial luau and a Hawaiian restaurant.

Some commercial luau are less authentic; they offer little of the traditional diet and are more about umbrella drinks, spectacle, and fun.

For greater culinary authenticity, folksy experiences, and rock-bottom prices, visit a Hawaiian restaurant (most are in anonymous storefronts in residential neighborhoods). Expect rough edges and some effort negotiating the menu.

In either case, much of what is known today as Hawaiian food would be as foreign to a 16th-century Hawaiian as risotto or chow mien. The pre-contact diet was simple and healthy—mainly raw and steamed seafood and vegetables. Early Hawaiians used earth ovens and heated stones to cook seafood, taro, sweet potatoes, and breadfruit and seasoned their food with sea salt and ground kukui nuts. Seaweed, fern shoots, sweet potato vines, coconut, banana, sugarcane, and select greens and roots rounded out the diet.

Successive waves of immigrants added their favorites to the ti leaf–lined table. So it is that foods as disparate as salt salmon and chicken long rice are now Hawaiian— even though there is no salmon in Hawaiian waters and long rice (cellophane noodles) is Chinese.

AT THE LUAU: KALUA PORK

The heart of any luau is the *imu*, the earth oven in which a whole pig is roasted. The preparation of an imu is an arduous affair for most families, who tackle it only once a year or so, for a baby's first birthday or at Thanksgiving, when many Islanders prefer to imu their turkeys. Commercial luau operations have it down to a science, however.

THE ART OF THE STONE
The key to a proper imu is the *pohaku*, the stones. Imu cook by means of long, slow, moist heat released by special stones that can withstand a hot fire without exploding. Many Hawaiian families treasure their imu stones, keeping them in a pile in the backyard and passing them on through generations.

PIT COOKING
The imu makers first dig a pit about the size of a refrigerator, then lay down *kiawe* (mesquite) wood and stones, and build a white-hot fire that is allowed to burn itself out. The ashes are raked away, and the hot stones covered with banana and ti leaves. Well-wrapped in ti or banana leaves and a net of chicken wire, the pig is lowered onto the leaf-covered stones. Laulau (leaf-wrapped bundles of meats, fish, and taro leaves) may also be placed inside. Leaves—ti, banana, even ginger—cover the pig followed by wet burlap sacks (to create steam). The whole is topped with a canvas tarp and left to steam for the better part of a day.

OPENING THE IMU
This is the moment everyone waits for: The imu is unwrapped like a giant present and the imu keepers gingerly wrestle out the steaming pig. When it's unwrapped, the meat falls moist and smoky-flavored from the bone, looking just like Southern-style pulled pork, but without the barbecue sauce.

WHICH LUAU?
Most resort hotels have luau on their grounds that include hula, music, and, of course, lots of food and drink. Each island also has at least one "authentic" luau. For lists of the best luau on each island, visit the Hawaii Visitors and Convention Bureau website at ⊕ *www.gohawaii.com*.

MEA AI ONO: GOOD THINGS TO EAT.

LAULAU
Steamed meats, fish, and taro leaf in ti-leaf bundles: fork-tender, a medley of flavors; the taro resembles spinach.

Laulau

LOMI LOMI SALMON
Salt salmon in a piquant salad or relish with onions and tomatoes.

POI
Poi, a paste made of pounded taro root, may be an acquired taste, but it's a must-try during your visit.

Consider: The Hawaiian Adam is descended from *kalo* (taro). Young taro plants are called "keiki"–children. Poi is the first food after mother's milk for many Islanders. Ai, the word for food, is synonymous with poi in many contexts.

Lomi Lomi Salmon

Not only that, we love it. "There is no meat that doesn't taste good with poi," the old Hawaiians said.

But you have to know how to eat it: with something rich or powerfully flavored. "It is salt that makes the poi go in," is another adage. When you're served poi, try it with a mouthful of smoky kalua pork or salty lomi lomi salmon. Its slightly sour blandness cleanses the palate. And if you don't like it, smile and say something polite. (And slide that bowl over to a local.)

Poi

E HELE MAI AI! COME AND EAT!

Local-style Hawaiian restaurants tend to be inconveniently located in well-worn storefronts with little or no parking, outfitted with battered tables and clattering Melmac dishes, but they personify aloha, invariably run by local families who welcome tourists who take the trouble to find them.

Many are cash-only operations and combination plates, known as "plate lunch," are a standard feature: one or two entrées, two scoops of steamed rice, one scoop of macaroni salad, and—if the place is really old-style—a tiny portion of coarse Hawaiian salt and some raw onions for relish.

Most serve some foods that aren't, strictly speaking, Hawaiian, but are beloved of ka-maaina, such as salt meat with watercress (preserved meat in a tasty broth), or *akubone* (skipjack tuna fried in a tangy vinegar sauce).

The History of Hawaii

Hawaiian history is long and complex; a brief survey can put into context the ongoing renaissance of native arts and culture.

THE POLYNESIANS

Long before both Christopher Columbus and the Vikings, Polynesian seafarers set out to explore the vast stretches of the open ocean in double-hulled canoes. They didn't just flail around and land here by accident; they understood the deep nuances of celestial navigation and were masters of the craft. From western Polynesia, they traveled back and forth between Samoa, Fiji, Tahiti, the Marquesas, and the Society Isles, settling on the outer reaches of the Pacific, Hawaii and Easter Island, as early as AD 300. The golden era of Polynesian voyaging peaked around AD 1200, after which the distant Hawaiian Islands were left to develop their own unique cultural practices and subsistence in relative isolation.

The Islands' symbiotic society was deeply intertwined with religion, mythology, science, and artistry. Ruled by an *alii*, or chief, each settlement was nestled in an *ahupuaa*, a pie-shaped land division from the uplands, through the valleys, and down to the shores. Everyone contributed, whether it was by building canoes, catching fish, making tools, or farming land, thereby developing a sustainable society.

A UNITED KINGDOM

When the British explorer Captain James Cook arrived in Kealakekua Bay in 1778, he was greeted by the Hawaiians as a person of important stature. With guns and ammunition purchased from subsequent foreign trading ships, the Big Island chief, Kamehameha the Great, gained a significant advantage over the other *alii* (chiefs). He united Hawaii into one kingdom in 1810, bringing an end to the frequent interisland battles that dominated Hawaiian life.

Tragically, the new kingdom was beset with troubles. Native religion was abandoned, and *kapu* (laws and regulations) were eventually abolished. The European explorers brought diseases with them, and within a few decades the Native Hawaiian population was decimated.

New laws regarding land ownership and religious practices eroded the underpinnings of pre-contact Hawaii. Each successor to the Hawaiian throne sacrificed more control over the Island kingdom. As Westerners permeated Hawaiian culture, so did social unrest.

MODERN HAWAII

In 1893, the last Hawaiian monarch, Queen Liliuokalani, was overthrown by a group of Americans and European businessmen and government officials, aided by an armed militia. This led to the creation of the Republic of Hawaii, and it became a U.S. territory for the next 60 years. The loss of Hawaiian sovereignty and the conditions of annexation have haunted the Hawaiian people since the monarchy was deposed.

Pearl Harbor was attacked in 1941, which engaged the United States immediately into World War II. Tourism, from its beginnings in the early 1900s, flourished after the war and naturally inspired rapid real estate development in Waikiki. In 1959, Hawaii officially became the 50th state.

TRAVEL SMART

2

Updated by
Tiffany Hill

★ **CAPITAL:**
Honolulu

👥 **POPULATION:**
980,000

💬 **LANGUAGE:**
English, Hawaiian

$ **CURRENCY:**
U.S. dollar

📠 **AREA CODE:**
808

⚠ **EMERGENCIES:**
911

🚗 **DRIVING:**
On the right

⚡ **ELECTRICITY:**
120–220 v/60 cycles; plugs
have two or three rectangu-
lar prongs

🕐 **TIME:**
Hawaii-Aleutian Standard
time, five hours behind New
York

🌐 **WEB RESOURCES:**
www.gohawaii.com
www.hawaii.com
www.hawaii-guide.com

✈ **AIRPORT:**
HNL

Know Before You Go

Planning a trip to Oahu? It's better to be prepared. Here are some important pieces of information you should know while making your plans.

GETTING TO YOUR HOTEL

Honolulu International Airport is 20 minutes (60 minutes during rush hour) from Waikiki. Car-rental companies have booths at baggage claim; shuttle buses then take you to the car-pickup areas. An inefficient airport taxi system requires you to line up for a taxi wrangler who radios for cars (about $40–$45 to Waikiki). Other options include Lyft or Uber rideshares, the city's reliable bus system ($2.75) with stops throughout Honolulu and Waikiki, or the Roberts Hawaii shuttle ($18), which transports you to any hotel in Waikiki. Ask drivers to take Interstate H1, not Nimitz Highway, or your introduction to paradise will be via Honolulu's industrial back side.

SHOULD YOU RENT A CAR?

You can get away without renting a car if you plan on staying in Waikiki. But if you want to explore the rest of the island, there's no substitute for having your own wheels. Avoid the obvious tourist cars—candy-color convertibles, for example—and never leave anything valuable inside, even if you've locked the car. Get a portable GPS navigator or make sure your phone has a navigation app, as Oahu's streets can be confusing.

Reserve your vehicle in advance, especially when traveling during the holidays and summer breaks. This will not only ensure that you get a car but also that you get the best rates. (Cars do sell out during busy periods.)

DRIVING ALWAYS TAKES LONGER THAN YOU EXPECT

Don't let maps fool you. Although the distance between Waikiki and, say, the North Shore is roughly 40 miles, it may take more than an hour to get there, thanks to heavy traffic, construction, and other factors. Many of Oahu's main roads are a single lane in each direction, with no alternate routes. So if you're stuck behind a slow-moving vehicle, you may have no other choice than to hope it turns soon. Heavy traffic moving toward downtown can begin as early as 6 am, with after-work traffic starting at 3 pm.

OAHU IS EXPENSIVE, BUT THERE ARE WAYS TO SAVE

A vacation to Hawaii doesn't have to break the bank. Take advantage of coupons in the free publications stacked at the airport and in racks all over Waikiki. Online sources like Groupon offer discounted rates for everything from dinner cruises to massages. Buy your souvenirs at Longs or ABC Stores rather than at shops catering solely to tourists, and you'll likely get the same goods for less money.

You don't need to stay at a pricier waterfront hotel when, in Waikiki, almost all hotels are a short walk to the shore. Access to beaches and most hiking trails on the island is free to the public. For inexpensive fresh fruit and produce, check out farmers markets and farm stands along the road—they'll often let you try before you buy.

For cheap and quick lunches, consider a food truck. Part of the culinary landscape of Oahu for generations, these lunch wagons—which rove around downtown and other areas—charge less than restaurants. Take advantage of *pau hana* time (happy hour) for cheaper drinks and appetizers at many establishments.

SEEING PEARL HARBOR REQUIRES SOME PLANNING

Pearl Harbor is a must-see for many, but there are things to know before you go.

Consider whether you want to see only the USS *Arizona* Memorial, or the USS *Bowfin* and USS *Missouri* as well. You can also visit the Pacific Aviation Museum on Ford Island. Allow approximately 1 hour 15 minutes for the USS *Arizona* tour, which includes a 25-minute documentary of the Pearl Harbor attack and a ferry ride to the memorial itself.

You can now reserve USS *Arizona* Memorial tickets online for a certain day for a $1 processing fee. If you don't reserve tickets ahead of time, plan to arrive early—same-day tickets for the USS *Arizona* Memorial are free and given out on a first-come, first-served basis. They can disappear within an hour, and your entire party must be present to receive same-day tickets. Take some time to enjoy the upgraded visitor center, which houses two exhibits using state-of-the-art technology to tell the story of the attack on December 7, 1941.

Strict security measures prohibit any sort of bag (purses, backpacks, diaper bags, camera cases—even small ones), although cameras are allowed. Strollers are allowed in the visitor center but not in the theaters or on the shuttle boats. Baggage storage is available for a $5 fee. Also, don't forget your ID.

Children under four years of age are not allowed on the USS *Bowfin* for safety reasons, and they may not enjoy the crowds or waiting in line at other sights.

Older kids are likely to find the more experiential, hands-on history of the USS *Bowfin* and USS *Missouri* memorable. The Pacific Aviation Museum's vintage planes are bonus attractions if you have the time.

DON'T JUST STAY IN WAIKIKI

While Waikiki is a great place to stay, especially for first-time visitors, be sure to leave the hustle and bustle of Oahu's most popular neighborhood and explore the island's other notable areas. Take a day trip to the North Shore, home to 10- to 20-foot monster swells in the winter. Another must-visit neighborhood is Kailua, on Oahu's windward side. Over the last 20 years, Kailua has transformed from a tranquil neighborhood to a buzzing beach town complete with hip boutiques and restaurants with locally sourced menus.

STAY SAFE WHILE EXPLORING OAHU'S OUTDOORS

Hawaii's natural wonders, while beautiful, can also be perilous if you're not careful. When you're at the beach, don't turn your back to the ocean; waves can often be unpredictable. When you're swimming, snorkeling, or surfing, check for hazardous conditions, such as shorebreaks and rip currents beforehand. It's also a good idea to swim

and snorkel with a buddy. Remember the adage: when in doubt, don't go out.

AVOID MOSQUITOES

To protect against mosquitoes, which are most abundant during the summer months, apply repellent containing DEET, and wear long sleeve shirts and pants during outdoor activities such as hiking.

RESPECT LOCAL CULTURE

Hawaii is a unique place with a vibrant, rich culture. Your visit to the islands will be that much more rewarding if you take the time to learn about the history and culture of Hawaii and its peoples. Places such as the Bishop Museum and Iolani Palace offer an interesting, educational glimpse into Hawaii's storied past.

When you're exploring the outdoors, look out for cultural sites such as the rock wall remains of a temple or Hawaiian petroglyphs, and treat the area with respect.

Getting Here and Around

Visitors to Oahu can navigate by orienting themselves to a few major landmarks. Oahu is made up of three extinct shield volcanoes, which form the island's two mountain ranges: Waianae and Koolau. The Waianae range curves from Kaena State Park, on the island's western-most point, past Makaha, Waianae, and Nanakuli to Ko Olina on the sunny leeward shore. The extinct craters of Diamond Head and Koko Head are usually visible from anywhere along the island's Leeward Coast. The Koolau range forms a jagged spine that runs from the island's eastern tip along the Windward Coast to the famous surfing center on the North Shore.

✈ Air

Flying time to Oahu is about 10 hours from New York, 8 hours from Chicago, and 5 hours from Los Angeles.

From the U.S. mainland, Alaska Airlines, American, Delta, Hawaiian, Southwest, and United are the primary U.S. carriers to serve Honolulu.

All the major airline carriers serving Hawaii fly direct to Honolulu; some also offer nonstops to Maui, Kauai, and the Big Island, though most flights to the latter two come from the West Coast only. Honolulu International Airport, although open-air and seemingly more casual than most major airports, can be very busy. Allow extra travel time during busy mornings and afternoons.

Plants and plant products are subject to regulation by the Department of Agriculture, both on entering and leaving Hawaii. Upon leaving, you'll have to have your bags X-rayed and tagged at the airport's agricultural inspection station before you proceed to check-in. Pineapples and coconuts with the packer's agricultural inspection stamp pass freely; papayas and certain other fruits must be treated, inspected, and stamped. But most other fruits are banned for export to the U.S. mainland. Flowers pass except for citrus-related flowers, fruits, or parts; jade vine; and mauna loa. Also banned are insects, snails, soil, cotton, cacti, sugarcane, and all berry plants.

Bringing your dog or cat with you is a tricky process and not something to be done lightly. Hawaii is a rabies-free state and requires animals to pass strict quarantine rules, which you can find online at ⊕ *hdoa.hawaii.gov/ai/aqs*. Most airlines do not allow pets to travel in the cabin on flights to Hawaii (though Alaska Airlines and Hawaiian Airlines are notable exceptions). If specific pre- and postarrival requirements are met, most animals qualify for a five-day-or-less quarantine.

AIRPORT

Honolulu International Airport (HNL) is roughly 20 minutes (9 miles) west of Waikiki (60 minutes during rush hour) and is served by most of the major domestic and international carriers. To travel to other islands from Honolulu, you can depart from either the interisland terminal or the commuter terminal, located in two separate structures adjacent to the main overseas terminal building. A free Wiki-Wiki shuttle bus operates between terminals.

AIRPORT TRANSFERS

Some hotels have their own pickup and drop-off service, though they may charge a fee, so check when you book accommodations.

Taxi service is available on the center median just outside baggage-claim areas. Look for the taxi dispatchers wearing yellow shirts, who will radio for a taxi. The fare to Waikiki runs approximately $40–$45 plus 40¢ to 45¢ per bag, and tip, with a maximum of four passengers. An oversize baggage fee may apply. Uber and Lyft also serve the airport.

Another option is to take a private shuttle service like Roberts Hawaii. The company will greet you at the arrival gate, escort you to baggage claim, and take you to your hotel. Call ahead for the service, which costs $18 per person for one-way service, $34 round-trip.

TheBus, the municipal bus, will take you into Waikiki for only $2.75, but all bags must fit on your lap or under your legs.

INTERISLAND FLIGHTS

If you've allotted more than a week for your vacation, you may want to consider visiting one of the other Hawaii Islands. From Honolulu, flights depart almost hourly from early morning until evening. Since each flight lasts only 30–60 minutes, you can watch the sun rise on Oahu and set on the Big Island, Kauai, Lanai, Maui, or Molokai. To simplify your vacation, schedule your return flight to Oahu so that it coincides with your flight home.

In addition to Hawaiian Airlines, Southwest Airlines and Mokulele Airlines operate regular service between the islands as well as charters, so be sure to compare prices. All have frequent-flyer programs that entitle you to rewards and upgrades. A number of wholesalers offer Neighbor Islands packages including air, hotel, rental car, and even visitor attractions or activities.

🚲 Bicycle

If you're need to get around Waikiki and Honolulu, there's a relatively low-cost, zero-emissions transportation option: bikeshare. Biki Bikeshare Hawaii (⊕ www.gobiki.org) has 1,300 aqua,

cruiser-style bicycles at 130 solar-powered stations dotting the Waikiki and Honolulu corridor. You can unlock a bike from a station using your credit or debit card, without having to sign up for the member pass. A one-way fare costs $4 for 30 minutes. There's also a multistop pass for $25, which gets you 300 minutes of riding time. ■TIP→ **There is a $50 security hold placed on your card when you check out a bike.**

🚌 Bus

Getting around by bus is an affordable option on Oahu, particularly in the most heavily touristed areas of Waikiki. In addition to TheBus and the Waikiki Trolley, Waikiki has brightly painted private buses, many of them free, that shuttle you to such commercial attractions as dinner cruises, shopping centers, and the like.

You can travel around the island or just down Kalakaua Avenue for $2.75 on Honolulu's municipal transportation system, affectionately known as TheBus. It's one of the island's best bargains. Buses make stops in Waikiki every 10–15 minutes to take passengers to nearby shopping areas.

Free transfers have been discontinued, but you can purchase a one-day pass for $5.50. Just ask the driver as you're boarding. Exact change is required, and dollar bills are accepted. Monthly passes cost $70.

The company's website has timetables, route maps, and real-time bus tracking, or you can download the free DaBus2 app for your smartphone. You can call to speak with a representative for route advice. Or you also can find privately published booklets at most drugstores and other convenience outlets.

Getting Here and Around

The Waikiki Trolley has six lines and dozens of stops that allow you to plan your own itinerary while riding on brass-trimmed, open-air buses that look like trolleys. The Cultural Honolulu Tour (Red Line) travels between Waikiki and Chinatown and includes stops at the State Capitol, Iolani Palace, and the King Kamehameha statue. The Waikiki Shopping Shuttle (Pink Line) runs from the T Galleria by DFS to Eggs 'n Things, stopping at various Waikiki locations and the Ala Moana Center. The Scenic Diamond Head Tour (Green Line) runs through Waikiki and down around Diamond Head. The Honolulu Dining Express (Yellow Line) makes stops at the city's iconic restaurants, including Rainbow Drive-In, Leonard's Bakery, and Haili's Hawaiian Food. There's also a south shore coastline tour (Blue Line) and a line that runs to Bishop Museum, Aloha Stadium, Pearl Harbor (Purple Line). A one-day pass costs $25 to $45, four-day passes start at $65, and seven-day passes start at $70

🚗 Car

You can get away without renting a car if you plan on staying in Waikiki. But if you want to explore the rest of the island, there's no substitute for having your own wheels. Avoid the obvious tourist cars—candy-color convertibles, for example—and never leave anything valuable inside, even if you've locked the car. A GPS will save you on phone data and guide you through Oahu's sometimes-confusing streets.

If you are renting a car, reserve your vehicle in advance, especially when traveling during the holidays and summer breaks. This will not only ensure that you get a car but also that you get the best rates. Also, be prepared to pay for parking;

almost all hotels in Honolulu (and many outside of Honolulu) charge for parking.

Except for one area around Kaena Point, major highways follow Oahu's shoreline and traverse the island at two points. Rush-hour traffic (6:30–9:30 am and 3:30–6 pm) can be frustrating around Honolulu and the outlying areas. Winter swells also bring traffic to the North Shore, as people hoping to catch some of the surfing action clog the two-lane Kamehameha Highway. Parking along many streets is curtailed during these times, and tow-away zones are strictly enforced. Read curbside signs before leaving your vehicle, even at a meter.

Asking for directions will almost always produce a helpful explanation from the locals, but you should be prepared for an island term or two. Instead of using compass directions, remember that Hawaii residents refer to places as being either *mauka* (toward the mountains) or *makai* (toward the ocean). Other directions depend on your location: in Honolulu, for example, people say to "go Diamond Head," which means toward that famous landmark, or to "go *ewa*," meaning in the opposite direction. A shop on the *mauka*–Diamond Head corner of a street is on the mountain side of the street on the corner closest to Diamond Head. It all makes perfect sense once you get the lay of the land.

CAR RENTALS

Hotel parking garages charge upwards of $40 per day, so if you're staying in Waikiki you may want to rent a car only when you plan to sightsee around the island. You can easily walk or take public transportation to many of the attractions in and around the area.

If you are staying outside Waikiki, your best bet is to rent a car. Even though the

Car Rental Resources

Automobile Associations

AAA	☎ 800/222–4357 for roadside assistance	⊕ www.aaa.com
National Automobile Club	☎ 650/294–7000	⊕ www.nacroadservice.com (CA residents only)

Major Agencies

Alamo	☎ 888/233–8749	⊕ www.alamo.com
Avis	☎ 800/633–3469	⊕ www.avis.com
Budget	☎ 800/218–7992	⊕ www.budget.com
Hertz	☎ 800/654–3131	⊕ www.hertz.com
National Car Rental	☎ 884/382–6875	⊕ www.nationalcar.com
Thrifty Car Rental	☎ 800/334–1705	⊕ www.thrifty.com

city bus is a wonderfully affordable way to get around the island, you'll want the flexibility of having your own transportation, especially if you're planning lots of stops.

■ TIP→ **Make sure that a confirmed reservation guarantees you a car. Agencies sometimes overbook, particularly for busy weekends and holiday periods.**

You can rent anything from an econobox and motorcycle to a Ferrari while on Oahu. Rates are usually better if you reserve through a rental agency's website. It's wise to make reservations far in advance, especially if visiting during peak seasons.

Rates in Honolulu begin at about $25 a day for an economy car with air-conditioning, automatic transmission, and unlimited mileage. This does not include the airport concession fee, general excise tax, rental-vehicle surcharge, or vehicle-license fee. When you reserve a car, ask about cancellation penalties and drop-off charges, should you plan to pick up the car in one location and return it to another. Many rental companies offer coupons for discounts at various attractions that could save you money later on in your trip.

In Hawaii you must be 21 years of age to rent a car, and you must have a valid driver's license and a major credit card. Those under 25 will pay a daily surcharge of about $15 to $35. Request car seats and extras such as GPS when you make your reservation. Hawaii's Child Restraint Law requires that all children under four be in an approved child safety seat in the backseat of a vehicle. Children ages four to seven must be seated in a rear booster seat or child safety seat with restraint such as a lap and shoulder belt. Car seats and boosters run about $13 per day.

In Hawaii your unexpired mainland driver's license is valid for rental for up to 90 days.

Be sure to allow plenty of time to return your vehicle so that you can make your flight. Traffic in Honolulu is terrible during

Getting Here and Around

morning and afternoon rush hours. Give yourself about 3½–4 hours before departure time to return your vehicle if you're traveling during these peak times; otherwise, plan on about 2½–3 hours.

DRIVING

Driving on Oahu is a mix of one-way country roads and congested city streets. As in most major cities, traffic in and around Honolulu is bad, especially during rush-hour. The H1 highway travels from Kapolei on the west side to Kahala in east Oahu. Weekday rush-hour traffic on the H1 tends to run from 6 to 9 am and again from 3 to 7 pm. During these times, it may take 45 minutes to travel only 10 miles, so plan ahead. But Hawaii drivers are generally friendlier than their Mainland counterparts. You'll seldom hear car horns.

GASOLINE

Gasoline is noticeably more expensive on Oahu than on the U.S. mainland.

PARKING

In Honolulu's densest neighborhoods (Chinatown, Kakaako, Ala Moana, Kaimuki, and downtown), parking is often limited and can be expensive. While there are a variety of parking lots, parking structures, and street parking, you will always have to pay. The same goes for nearly everywhere in Waikiki. Some businesses validate for parking, so it's always a good idea to ask in advance. As you head out west to Kapolei or Haleiwa or northeast to Kailua, parking is generally easier to come by and more often free.

ROAD CONDITIONS

Oahu is relatively easy to navigate. Roads, although their names are often a challenge for the tongue, are well marked; just watch out for the many one-way streets in Waikiki and downtown Honolulu. Keep an eye open for the Hawaii Visitors and Convention Bureau's red-caped King Kamehameha signs, which mark major attractions and scenic spots. Ask for a map at the car-rental counter. Free publications containing helpful maps are found at most hotels throughout Waikiki.

ROADSIDE EMERGENCIES

In case of an accident, pull over if you can. If you have a cell phone, call the roadside assistance number on your car-rental contract or AAA Help. If your car has been broken into or stolen, report it immediately to your rental-car company. If it's an emergency and someone is hurt, call 911 immediately.

RULES OF THE ROAD

Be sure to buckle up, as Hawaii has a strictly enforced mandatory seat-belt law for front- and backseat passengers. Children under four must be in a car seat (available from car-rental agencies), and children ages four to seven must be seated in a booster seat or child safety seat with restraint such as a lap and shoulder belt. Hawaii also prohibits texting or talking on the phone (unless you are over 18 and using a hands-free device) while driving. The highway speed limit is usually 55 mph. In-town traffic travels 25–40 mph. Jaywalking is not uncommon, so watch for pedestrians, especially in congested areas such as Waikiki and downtown Honolulu. Unauthorized use of a parking space reserved for persons with disabilities can net you a $250–$500 fine.

Oahu's drivers are generally courteous, and you rarely hear a horn. People will slow down and let you into traffic with a wave of the hand. A friendly wave back is customary. If a driver sticks a hand out the window in a fist with the thumb and pinky sticking straight out, this is a good thing: it's the *shaka,* the Hawaiian symbol for "hang loose," and is often used to say "thanks."

🚢 Cruise

When Pan Am's amphibious *Hawaii Clipper* touched down on Pearl Harbor's waters in 1936, it marked the beginning of the end of regular passenger-ship travel to the Islands. From that point on, the predominant means of transporting visitors would be by air, not by sea. Today, however, cruising to Hawaii is a delightful way to experience the beauty and majesty of the Pacific Ocean and Hawaiian Islands. Several major cruise lines offer seasonal cruises to and from the Hawaiian Islands (typically from Los Angeles, San Francisco, or San Diego) with interisland cruise components. But you can also hop aboard a strictly interisland cruise with Norwegian Cruise Line's ship *Pride of America,* or Un-Cruise Adventures' smaller yacht.

🚗 Ride-Sharing

Both Uber and Lyft are an available and convenient way to get around while you're visiting Oahu. Although you may still want to rent a car while you're on island—especially if you're staying in or visiting the North Shore or towns on the east side of Oahu—ride-shares are especially good for quick trips and evenings out when you want avoid parking or imbibe. Both Uber and Lyft pick-ups are allowed at designated locations at the airport.

🛵 Scooter

You might hear them before you see them: the *vroom* of the engine as they zip past traffic. Mopeds and scooters are a common form of transportation in the islands, both for locals and visitors. They're easier and sometimes cheaper than renting a car and can be checked out for around $25 to $30 a day (daily rates are lower for multiday rentals.) Some companies event rent to people as young as 18. But these freedoms come with a few caveats. Mopeds and scooters aren't allowed on any highways, and renting a scooter requires a valid motorcycle license.

🚕 Taxi

Taxis cost $3.10 at the drop of the flag and each additional mile is $3.60. Taxi and limousine companies can provide a car and driver for half-day or daylong island tours, and a number of companies also offer personal guides. Remember, however, the rates are quite steep for these services, running $100 to $200 or more per day. Uber and Lyft also serve Oahu, including for airport pick-ups.

Essentials

Dining

Oahu is undergoing a renaissance at both ends of the dining spectrum. You may wish to budget for a pricey dining experience at the very top of the restaurant food chain, where chefs Alan Wong, Roy Yamaguchi, George Mavrothalassitis, Chris Kajioka, and others you've seen on the Food Network and Travel Channel put a sophisticated spin on local foods and flavors. Dishes that take cues from Japan, China, Korea, the Philippines, the United States, and Europe are often filtered through an Island sensibility. Take advantage of the location, and order the superb local fish—mahimahi, opakaka, ono, and opah.

Spend the rest of your food dollars where budget-conscious locals do: in plate-lunch places and small ethnic eateries, at roadside stands and lunch wagons, or at window-in-the-wall delis. Snack on a *musubi* (a handheld rice ball wrapped with seaweed and topped with Spam), slurp shave ice with red-bean paste, or order Filipino pork adobo with two scoops of rice and macaroni salad.

In Waikiki, where most visitors stay, you can find everything from upscale dining rooms with a view to Japanese noodle shops. When you're ready to explore, hop in the car, or on the trolley or bus—by going just a few miles in any direction, you can save money and eat like a local.

Kaimuki's Waialae Avenue, for example, is a critical mass of good eats and drinks. There you'll find an espresso bar, a Chinese bakery, a patisserie, an Italian bistro, a dim-sum restaurant, elevated Hawaiian food, Mexican food, and a Hawaii regional-cuisine standout (3660 on the Rise)—all in three blocks, and 10 minutes from Waikiki. Chinatown, 15 minutes in the other direction and easily reached by the Waikiki Trolley, is another dining (and shopping) treasure, not only for Chinese but also Vietnamese, Filipino, Burmese, Mexican food, and even a chic little tea shop. Kakaako, the developing urban area between Waikiki and Chinatown, also offers a mix of local eateries, upscale restaurants, and ethnic takeout.

Outside Honolulu and Waikiki there are fewer dining options, but restaurants tend to be filled with locals and are cheaper and more casual. Windward Oahu's dining scene has improved greatly in recent years due to the visitors to Kailua and Lanikai beaches, so everything from plate lunches to creative regional offerings can be found there. Kapolei has also witnessed an increase in variety and upgrade in both the number and quality of eateries; previously the area had predominantly Mainland chains and fast-food joints.

DISCOUNTS AND DEALS

If you eat early or late you may be able to take advantage of prix-fixe deals not offered at peak hours. Many upscale restaurants offer great lunch deals with special menus at cut-rate prices designed to give customers a true taste of the place.

PARKING

In Waikiki, downtown Honolulu, or Chinatown, walk, take a cab, or call Lyft or Uber when you are going out for dinner; it can be cheaper than parking or valet rates. Elsewhere on Oahu, free or reasonably priced parking is available.

PAYING

Most restaurants take credit cards, but some smaller places do not. It's worth asking. Servers expect a 20% tip at restaurants; some add an automatic gratuity for groups of six or more.

RESERVATIONS AND DRESS

At Honolulu's top upscale restaurants, book your table from home weeks in advance. Otherwise, you can usually reserve when you get into town. Even some of the most coveted tables can be had at the last minute if you can be flexible.

Casual still reigns supreme; most top restaurants abide by the dressy casual (i.e., "aloha wear") standard, where dark jeans are acceptable. A select few of Honolulu's nicest spots ask men to wear a jacket.

MEALS AND MEALTIMES

People dine early here—the most sought-after dinner reservations are between 6 and 8. Exceptions: sushi bars and Japanese taverns, a few 24-hour diners, and new, popular restaurants. Takeout places still open at dawn and close shortly after midday.

SMOKING

Smoking is prohibited in enclosed areas open to the public, including restaurants, bars, and clubs.

WHAT IT COSTS in U.S. dollars			
$	$$	$$$	$$$$
AT DINNER			
under $17	$17–$26	$27–$35	over $35

➕ Health and Safety

Hawaii is known not only as the Aloha State, but also as the Health State. The life expectancy here is 81.3 years, the longest in the nation. Balmy weather makes it easy to remain active year-round, and the low-stress attitude seems to contribute to the general well-being.

When visiting the Islands, however, there are a few health issues to keep in mind.

COVID-19

A new novel coronavirus brought all travel to a virtual standstill in the first half of 2020. Although the illness is mild in most people, some experience severe and even life-threatening complications. Once travel started up again, albeit slowly and cautiously, travelers were asked to be particularly careful about hygiene and to avoid any unnecessary travel, especially if they are sick.

Older adults, especially those over 65, have a greater chance of having severe complications from COVID-19. The same is true for people with weaker immune systems or those living with some types of medical conditions, including diabetes, asthma, heart disease, cancer, HIV/AIDS, kidney disease, and liver disease.

Starting two weeks before a trip, anyone planning to travel should be on the lookout for some of the following symptoms: cough, fever, chills, trouble breathing, muscle pain, sore throat, new loss of smell or taste. If you experience any of these symptoms, you should not travel at all.

And to protect yourself during travel, do your best to avoid contact with people showing symptoms. Wash your hands often with soap and water. Limit your time in public places, and, when you are out and about, wear a cloth face mask that covers your nose and mouth. Indeed, a mask may be required in some places, such as on an airplane or in a confined space like a theater, where you share the space with a lot of people.

You may wish to bring extra supplies, such as disinfecting wipes, hand sanitizer (12-ounce bottles were allowed in

Essentials

carry-on luggage at this writing), and a first-aid kit with a thermometer.

Given how abruptly travel was curtailed in March 2020, it is wise to consider protecting yourself by purchasing a travel insurance policy that will reimburse you for any costs related to COVID-19 related cancellations. Not all travel insurance policies protect against pandemic-related cancellations, so always read the fine print.

MOSQUITO-BORNE ILLNESSES

The Islands have their share of insects. Most are harmless but annoying—like cockroaches—but dengue fever, a mosquito-borne disease, has been reported in Oahu. When planning to spend time outdoors in hiking areas, wear long-sleeve clothing and pants, and use mosquito repellent containing DEET. In damp places you may encounter the dreaded local centipedes, which are brown and blue and measure up to eight inches long. Their painful sting is similar to those of bees and wasps. When camping, shake out your sleeping bag and check your shoes, as the centipedes like cozy places. When hiking in remote areas, always carry a first-aid kit.

GENERAL SAFETY PRECAUTIONS

Although Oahu is generally a safe tourist destination, it's still wise to follow the same common-sense safety precautions you would normally follow in your own hometown. Rental cars are magnets for break-ins, so don't leave any valuables in the car, not even in a locked trunk. Avoid poorly lighted areas, beach parks, and isolated areas after dark as a precaution.

■TIP➜ **Distribute your cash, credit cards, IDs, and other valuables between a deep front pocket, an inside jacket or vest pocket, and a hidden money pouch. Don't reach for the money pouch once you're in public.**

🧭 Immunizations

There are no immunization requirements for visitors traveling to the United States for tourism.

🛏 Lodging

Although Oahu is just 44 miles long and 30 miles wide—meaning you could theoretically circle the entire island before lunch—it boasts neighborhoods and lodgings with very different vibes and personalities. If you like the action and choices of big cities, consider Waikiki, a 24-hour playground with everything from surf to karaoke bars. Those who want an escape from urban life look to the island's leeward or windward sides, or to the North Shore, where the surf culture creates a laid-back atmosphere.

Most of the island's major hotels and resorts are in busy Waikiki. You don't need a car in Waikiki; everything is nearby, including major sights and parks, running and biking paths, grocery stores, and access to public transportation that can take you to places around town and around the island.

You'll find places to stay along the entire stretch of both Kalakaua and Kuhio avenues, with smaller and quieter hotels and condos at the eastern end and more business-centric accommodations on the western edge of Waikiki, near the Hawaii Convention Center, Ala Moana Center, and downtown.

The majority of tourists who come to Oahu stay in Waikiki, but choosing accommodations in downtown Honolulu affords you the opportunity to be close to shopping and restaurants at Ala Moana

Center, the largest shopping mall in the state, and easy access to the airport.

If you want to get away from the bustle of the city, consider a stay on Oahu's Leeward Coast in the Ko Olina resort area, which is about 20 minutes from the Honolulu International Airport (40 minutes from Waikiki) and has great golf courses and quiet beaches and coves that make for a relaxing getaway. But you'll need a car to get off the property if you want to explore the rest of the island; note, though, that all resorts here charge hefty fees for parking.

Other, more low-key options are on Windward Oahu or the North Shore. Both regions are rustic and charming, with quaint eateries and coffee shops, local boutiques, and some of the island's best beaches. One of Oahu's premier resorts, Turtle Bay, is located here, too.

CONDOS AND VACATION RENTALS

Vacation rentals give you the convenience of staying at a home away from home and getting to know Oahu the way the locals do. You can often save money as well, since you have a kitchen, can cook your meals, and don't pay for hotel parking. Prices, amenities, and locations of vacation homes vary considerably, meaning you should be able to find the perfect getaway on Oahu. Properties managed by individual owners can be found at online vacation-rental directories, as well as on the Oahu Visitors Bureau website. Don't be surprised to find the same homes advertised on different sites, and with different names. The major online sites such as ⊕ VRBO. com and ⊕ AirBnB.com offer a plethora of options. Compare companies, as some offer Internet specials and free nights when booking, and make sure that there will be an on-island point of contact for you should there be any issues during

your stay. Also remember to ask about the home's licensing as a vacation rental, since not all properties advertised carry the necessary license. Technically, rentals of less than 30 days are illegal on Oahu unless the property has a license for short-term vacation rentals or is a hotel with apartment units. The state does take a stand from time to time to enforce vacation rental laws, and you'll have more protection and assurance that you aren't out there on your own if something goes wrong.

FACILITIES

You can assume that all hotel rooms have private baths, phones, TVs, unless otherwise indicated, but many rentals do not have a/c, especially outside of the Waikiki high-rises. Breakfast is noted when it is included in the rate. Almost all hotels have pools, but some B&Bs and cheaper rentals do not.

PARKING

Most resorts on Oahu charge for parking, even those not in Ko Olina and Waikiki (where virtually all hotels charge for parking), so be sure to ask before you rent a car. Sometimes this is included in the hotel's resort fee, but often it is not.

PRICES

Before you book a room, try calling hotels directly. Sometimes on-property reservationists can get you the best deals, and they usually have the most accurate information about rooms, availability, and hotel amenities. Remember that many reservations centers are not on Oahu.

RESERVATIONS

Always make a reservation. Hotels often fill up, and rooms in can be particularly hard to come by in late March or early April during the Cherry Blossom Festival, and in May, when students at the many local colleges graduate.

Essentials

WHAT IT COSTS in U.S. dollars			
$	$$	$$$	$$$$
FOR TWO PEOPLE			
Under $180	$180–$260	$261–$340	Over $340

■TIP→ **Some places have a cover charge of $5–$10, but with many establishments, getting there early means you don't have to pay.**

🍸 Nightlife

Oahu is the best of all the Islands for nightlife. The locals call it *pau hana,* but you might call it happy hour (the literal translation of the Hawaiian phrase is "done with work"). On weeknights, it's likely that you'll find the working crowd, still in their business-casual attire, downing chilled beers even before the sun goes down. Those who don't have to wake up in the early morning should change into a fresh outfit and start the evening closer to 10 pm.

On the weekends, it's typical to have dinner at a restaurant before hitting the bars around 9:30. Some bar-hoppers start as early as 7, but partygoers typically don't patronize more than two establishments a night. That's because getting from one Oahu nightspot to the next usually requires transportation. Happily, cab services are plentiful, and rideshares like Uber and Lyft give Honolulu a San Francisco feel.

You can find a bar in just about any area on Oahu. Most of the clubs, however, are in Waikiki. The drinking age is 21 on Oahu and throughout Hawaii. Many bars will admit younger people but will not serve them alcohol. By law, all establishments that serve alcoholic beverages must close by 2 am. The only exceptions are a handful in Waikiki with a cabaret license, which can stay open until 4 am.

🧳 Packing

Oahu is casual: sandals, bathing suits, and comfortable, informal clothing are the norm. In summer, synthetic slacks and shirts, although easy to care for, can be uncomfortably warm.

There's a saying that when a man wears a suit during the day, he's either going for a loan or he's a lawyer trying a case. Only a few upscale restaurants require a jacket for dinner. The Aloha shirt is accepted dress on Oahu for business and most social occasions. Shorts are acceptable daytime attire, along with a T-shirt or polo shirt. There's no need to buy expensive sandals on the mainland—here you can get flip-flops (locals call them slippers) for a couple of dollars and off-brand sandals for $20. Golfers should remember that many courses have dress codes requiring a collared shirt; call courses you're interested in for details. If you're not prepared, you can pick up appropriate clothing at resort pro shops. If you're visiting in winter or planning to visit a high-altitude area, bring a sweater or light- to medium-weight jacket. A polar fleece pullover is ideal and makes a great impromptu pillow. If you're planning on doing any hiking, a good pair of boots is essential.

🌐 Passport

All visitors to the United States require a valid passport that is valid for six months beyond your expected period of stay.

Where to Stay on Oahu

NEIGHBORHOOD	LOCAL VIBE	PROS	CONS
Honolulu	Lodging options are limited in downtown Honolulu, but if you want an urban feel or to be near Chinatown, look no farther.	Access to a wide selection of art galleries, boutiques, and new restaurants as well as Chinatown.	No beaches within walking distance. If you're looking to get away from it all, this is not the place.
Waikiki	Lodgings abound in Waikiki, from youth hostels to five-star accommodations. The area is always abuzz with activity and anything you desire is within walking distance.	You can surf in front of the hotels, wander miles of beach, and explore hundreds of restaurants and bars.	This is tourist central. Prices are high, and you are not going to get the true Hawaii experience.
Windward Oahu	More in tune with the local experience, here is where you'll find most of the island's B&Bs and enjoy the lush side of Oahu.	From beautiful vistas and green jungles, this side really captures the tropical paradise most people envision when dreaming of a Hawaiian vacation.	The lushness comes at a price—it rains a lot on this side. Also, luxury is not the specialty here; if you are looking to get pampered, stay elsewhere.
The North Shore	This is true country living, with one luxurious resort exception. It's bustling in the winter (when the surf is up) but pretty slow-paced in the summer.	Amazing surf and long stretches of sand truly epitomize the beach culture in Hawaii. Historic Haleiwa has enough stores to keep shopaholics busy.	There is no middle ground for accommodations; you're either in backpacker cabanas or $300-a-night suites. There is also zero nightlife, and traffic can get heavy during winter months.
West (Leeward) Oahu	This is the resort side of the rock; there is little outside of these resorts but plenty on the grounds to keep you occupied for a week.	Ko Olina's lagoons offer the most kid-friendly swimming on the island, and the golf courses on this side are magnificent. Rare is the rainy day out here.	You are isolated from the rest of Oahu, with little in the way of shopping or jungle hikes.

2

Travel Smart ESSENTIALS

Essentials

🎭 Performing Arts

Oahu also has a thriving arts and culture scene, with community-theater productions, stand-up comedy, outdoor concerts—especially in the summer months—film festivals, and chamber-music performances. Major Broadway shows, dance companies, rock stars, and comedians come through the Islands, too. Check local newspapers such as the *Honolulu Star-Advertiser* or *Midweek* for the latest events. Websites like ⊕ *www. gohawaii.com* and ⊕ *www.hawaii.com* also have regular updated listings.

🛍 Shopping

Eastern and Western traditions meet on Oahu, where savvy shoppers find luxury goods at high-end malls and scout tiny boutiques and galleries filled with items created by local artists and artisans. Exploring downtown Honolulu, Kailua on the windward side, and the North Shore often yields the most original merchandise. Some of the small stores carry imported clothes and gifts from around the world—a reminder that, on this island halfway between Asia and the United States, shopping is a multicultural experience.

💲 Taxes

A 10.25% tax is added onto your hotel bill. A $3-per-day road tax is also assessed on each rental vehicle plus $4.50 a day if you're renting it at the airport. While Hawaii doesn't have a statewide sales tax, 4.7% will be tacked onto goods and services you purchase while on Oahu.

💵 Tipping

People who work in the service industry rely on tips, so tipping is not only common, but expected.

Tip bartenders $1–$5 per round of drinks, depending on the number of drinks; bellhops $1–$5 per bag, depending on the level of the hotel and whether you have bulky items like golf clubs and surfboards; hotel concierges $5 or more, depending on the service; hotel maids $1–$3 per day; taxi drivers 15%–20% of the fare; tour guides 15% to 20% of the cost of the tour; valet parking attendants $2–$5 each time you pick up your car; and servers 18%–20%, with 20% being the norm.

💳 Visa

Except for citizens of Canada and Bermuda, most visitors to the United States must have a visa. If you are from one of the 38 designated members of the Visa Waiver Program, then you only require an ESTA (Electronic System for Travel Authorization) as long as you are staying for 90 days or less. However, some changes were made in the Visa Waiver Program in 2015, and nationals of Visa-Waiver nations who have traveled to Iran, Iraq, Libya, Somalia, Sudan, Syria, or Yemen no longer qualify for ESTA. Also, if you have been denied a visa to visit the United States, your application for the ESTA program most likely will be denied.

📍 Visitor Information

Before you go to Hawaii, contact the Oahu Visitors Bureau (OVB) for a free vacation planner and map. The OVB website (⊕ *gohawaii.com*) has an online listing of accommodations, activities and sports, attractions, dining venues, services, transportation, travel professionals, and wedding information. The website also has a calendar of local events that will be taking place during your stay.

📅 When to Go

Low Season: The fall (from September through mid-December) is usually a slower time for tourism in Oahu. During this period, you can find better rates on just about everything: car rentals, accommodations, and tours. That beach you want to lay out at will be less crowded, too.

Shoulder Season: Later in the spring, from mid-April through June, is an in-between time. Because of Hawaii's warm weather, this in-between travel season still garners plenty of visitors to the Islands.

High Season: The busiest time in Hawaii is generally winter, from mid-December to March or mid-April, when Hawaii weather is good and temperatures moderate. Plan to make all reservations well in advance, and don't expect to find deals on accommodations.

WEATHER

In Hawaii, the thermometer generally hovers between the mid-70s to the mid-80s degrees (Fahrenheit). There are essentially just two seasons in the islands: summer and winter. Winters, from November to April, are rainier and a bit cooler than the summer months from May to October. But even if it's raining in one part of Oahu, chances are it's dry and sunny on the other coast. Oahu's Leeward or West coast is warmer and more arid, whereas the eastern, or Windward side of the island is usually cooler and wetter.

Tipping Guides for Oahu	
Bartender	$1–$5 per round of drinks, depending on the number of drinks
Bellhop	$1–$5 per bag, depending on the level of the hotel
Hotel Concierge	$5 or more, depending on the service
Hotel Doorstaff	$1–$5 for help with bags or hailing a cab
Hotel Maid	$2–$5 a day (in cash, preferably daily since cleaning staff may be different each day you stay)
Hotel Room Service Waiter	$1–$2 per delivery, even if a service charge has been added
Porter at Airport or Train Station	$1 per bag
Restroom Attendants	$1 or small change
Skycap at Airport	$1–$3 per bag checked
Spa Personnel	15%–20% of the cost of your service
Taxi Driver	15%–20%
Tour Guide	15%–20% of the cost of the tour, per person
Valet Parking Attendant	$2–$5 each time your car is brought to you
Server	20%; nothing additional if a service charge is added to the bill

Hawaiian Vocabulary

Although an understanding of Hawaiian is by no means required on a trip to the Aloha State, a *malihini,* or newcomer, will find plenty of opportunities to pick up a few of the local words and phrases. Traditional names and expressions are widely used in the Islands. You're likely to read or hear at least a few words each day of your stay.

Simplifying the learning process is the fact that the Hawaiian language contains only seven consonants—*H, K, L, M, N, P, W,* and the silent *'okina,* or glottal stop, written '—plus one or more of the five vowels. All syllables, and therefore all words, end in a vowel. Each vowel, with the exception of a few diphthongized double vowels, such as *au* (pronounced "ow") or *ai* (pronounced "eye"), is pronounced separately. Thus *'Iolani* is four syllables (ee-oh-la-nee), not three (yo-la-nee). Although some Hawaiian words have only vowels, most also contain some consonants, but consonants are never doubled.

Pronunciation is simple. Pronounce *A* "ah" as in *father; E* "ay" as in *weigh; I* "ee" as in *marine; O* "oh" as in *no; U* "oo" as in *true.*

Consonants mirror their English equivalents, with the exception of *W.* When the letter begins any syllable other than the first one in a word, it is usually pronounced as a *V. 'Awa,* the Polynesian drink, is pronounced "ava," *'ewa* is pronounced "eva."

Almost all long Hawaiian words are combinations of shorter words; they are not difficult to pronounce if you segment them. *Kalaniana'ole,* the highway running east from Honolulu, is easily understood as *Kalani ana 'ole.* Apply the standard pronunciation rules—the stress falls on the next-to-last syllable of most two- or three-syllable Hawaiian words—and Kalaniana'ole Highway is as easy to say as Main Street.

Now about that fish. Try *humu-humu nuku-nuku āpu a'a.*

The other unusual element in Hawaiian language is the *kahakō,* or macron, written as a short line (ˉ) placed over a vowel. Like the accent (´) in Spanish, the kahakō puts emphasis on a syllable that would normally not be stressed. The most familiar example is probably *Waikīkī.* With no macrons, the stress would fall on the middle syllable; with only one macron, on the last syllable, the stress would fall on the first and last syllables. Some words become plural with the addition of a macron, often on a syllable that would have been stressed anyway. No Hawaiian word becomes plural with the addition of an *S,* since that letter does not exist in the language.

The Hawaiian diacritical marks are not printed in this guide.

PIDGIN

You may hear pidgin, the unofficial language of Hawai'i. It is a Creole language, with its own grammar, evolved from the mixture of English, Hawaiian, Japanese, Portuguese, and other languages spoken in 19th-century Hawai'i, and it is heard everywhere.

GLOSSARY

What follows is a glossary of some of the most commonly used Hawaiian words. Hawaiian residents appreciate visitors who at least try to pick up the local language.

'a'ā: rough, crumbling lava, contrasting with *pāhoehoe,* which is smooth.

'ae: yes.

aikane: friend.

āina: land.

akamai: smart, clever, possessing savoir faire.

akua: god.

ala: a road, path, or trail.

ali'i: a Hawaiian chief, a member of the chiefly class.

aloha: love, affection, kindness; also a salutation meaning both greetings and farewell.

'ānuenue: rainbow.

'a'ole: no.

'apōpō: tomorrow.

'auwai: a ditch.

auwē: alas, woe is me!

'ehu: a red-haired Hawaiian.

'ewa: in the direction of 'Ewa plantation, west of Honolulu.

hala: the pandanus tree, whose leaves (*lau hala*) are used to make baskets and plaited mats.

hālau: school.

hale: a house.

hale pule: church, house of worship.

hana: to work.

haole: foreigner. Since the first foreigners were Caucasian, *haole* now means a Caucasian person.

hapa: a part, sometimes a half; often used as a short form of *hapa haole*, to mean a person who is part-Caucasian.

hau'oli: to rejoice. *Hau'oli Makahiki Hou* means Happy New Year. *Hau'oli lā hānau* means Happy Birthday.

heiau: an outdoor stone platform; an ancient Hawaiian place of worship.

he mea iki or **he mea 'ole:** you're welcome.

holo: to run.

holoholo: to go for a walk, ride, or sail.

holokū: a long Hawaiian dress, somewhat fitted, with a yoke and a train. It was worn at court, and at least one local translates the word as "expensive mu'umu'u."

holomū: a post–World War II cross between a *holokū* and a mu'umu'u, less fitted than the former but less voluminous than the latter, and having no train.

honi: to kiss; a kiss. A phrase that some tourists may find useful, quoted from a popular hula, is *Honi Ka'ua Wikiwiki:* Kiss me quick!

honu: turtle.

ho'omalimali: flattery, a deceptive "line," bunk, baloney, hooey.

huhū: angry.

hui: a group, club, or assembly. A church may refer to its congregation as a *hui* and a social club may be called a *hui*.

hukilau: a seine; a communal fishing party in which everyone helps to drive the fish into a huge net, pull it in, and divide the catch.

hula: the dance of Hawai'i.

iki: little.

ipo: sweetheart. Commonly seen as "ku'uipo," or "my sweetheart."

ka: the. This is the definite article for most singular words; for plural nouns, the definite article is usually *nā*. Since there is no *S* in Hawaiian, the article may be your only clue that a noun is plural.

Hawaiian Vocabulary

kahuna: a priest, doctor, or other trained person of old Hawai'i, endowed with special professional skills that often included prophecy or other supernatural powers.

kai: the sea, saltwater.

kalo: the taro plant from whose root *poi* (paste) is made.

kamā'aina: literally, a child of the soil; it refers to people who were born in the Islands or have lived there for a long time.

kanaka: originally a man or humanity, it is now used to denote a male Hawaiian or part-Hawaiian, but is occasionally taken as a slur when used by non-Hawaiians. *Kanaka maoli* is used by some Native Hawaiian rights activists to embrace part-Hawaiians as well.

kāne: a man, a husband. If you see this word (or kane) on a door, it's the men's room.

kapa: also called by its Tahitian name, *tapa*, a cloth made of beaten bark and usually dyed and stamped with a repeat design.

kapakahi: crooked, cockeyed, uneven. You've got your hat on *kapakahi*.

kapu: keep out, prohibited. This is the Hawaiian version of the more widely known Tongan word *tabu* (taboo).

kēia lā: today.

keiki: a child; *keikikāne* is a boy, *keikiwahine* a girl.

kōkua: to help, assist. Often seen in signs like "Please *kōkua* and throw away your trash."

kona: the leeward side of the Islands, the direction (south) from which the *kona* wind and *kona* rain come.

kula: upland.

kuleana: a homestead or small plot of ground on which a family has been installed for some generations without necessarily owning it. By extension, *kuleana* is used to denote any area or department in which one has a special interest or prerogative. You'll hear it used this way: "If you want to hire a surfboard, see Moki; that's his *kuleana*."

kupuna: grandparent; elder.

lā: sun.

lamalama: to fish with a torch.

lānai: a porch, a balcony, an outdoor living room.

lani: heaven, the sky.

lau hala: the leaf of the *hala*, or pandanus tree, widely used in handicrafts.

lei: a garland of flowers.

lōlō: feeble-minded, crazy.

luna: a plantation overseer or foreman.

mahalo: thank you.

mahina: moon.

makai: toward the ocean.

mālama: to take care of, preserve, protect

malihini: a newcomer to the Islands.

mana: the spiritual power that the Hawaiians believe inhabits all things and creatures.

manō: shark.

manuahi: free, gratis.

mauka: toward the mountains.

mauna: mountain.

mele: a Hawaiian song or chant, often of epic proportions.

Mele Kalikimaka: Merry Christmas (a transliteration from the English phrase).

Menehune: a Hawaiian pixie. The *Menehune* were a legendary race of little people who accomplished prodigious work, such as building fishponds and temples in the course of a single night.

moana: the ocean.

mu'umu'u: the voluminous dress in which the missionaries enveloped Hawaiian women. Culturally sensitive locals have embraced the Hawaiian spelling but often shorten the spoken word to "mu'u." Most English dictionaries include the spelling "muumuu."

nani: beautiful.

nui: big.

'ohana: family.

'ono: delicious.

pāhoehoe: smooth, unbroken, satiny lava.

palapala: document, printed matter.

pali: a cliff, precipice.

pānini: prickly pear cactus.

paniolo: a Hawaiian cowboy, a rough transliteration of *español,* the language of the Islands' earliest cowboys.

pau: finished, done.

pilikia: trouble. The Hawaiian word is much more widely used here than its English equivalent.

pū: large conch shell used as trumpet before start of luau and other special events.

puka: a hole.

pule: prayer, blessing. Often performed before a meal or event.

pupule: crazy, like the celebrated Princess Pupule. This word has replaced its English equivalent in local usage.

pu'u: volcanic cinder cone.

tūtū: grandmother

waha: mouth.

wahine: a female, a woman, a wife, and a sign on the ladies' room door; the plural form is *wāhine.*

wai: freshwater, as opposed to saltwater, which is *kai.*

wailele: waterfall.

wikiwiki: to hurry, hurry up (since this is a reduplication of *wiki,* quick, neither *W* is pronounced as a *V*).

Great Itineraries

Highlights of Oahu in One Week

With the capital and two thirds of the state's population, Oahu is a vibrant, ever-evolving island. Cultural, outdoor, historical, culinary, and other adventures abound. From *mauka* (mountains) to *makai* (sea), Oahu is probably the Hawaiian island most likely to please all types of travelers whether you're an outdoorsy type, a beach bum, a foodie, or a family, and a week should give you enough time to see the highlights. You can either use the bus or take taxis or rideshares while you're in Honolulu, but rent a car to get out of Waikiki and around the island for a true feel for all things Oahu in this one-week highlights itinerary.

WAIKIKI

Day 1. You'll want to get your beach legs under you after that long flight to Oahu. Given the time difference between Hawaii and the rest of the U.S. (it's 6 hours earlier than the east coast, 3 hours earlier than the west coast), you'll probably be jet-lagged. Use your earlier rising to go grab coffee and head to Waikiki, Sans Souci, or Fort DeRussy Beach. You'll see locals on their morning jogs at Kapiolani Park and catching waves at their favorite shore break. Once caffeinated, hit Kalakaua Avenue on foot, the best way to shop and sightsee. Got kiddos in tow? Try the Waikiki Aquarium or the Honolulu Zoo. Get some refreshments with tea at the Moana Surfrider, the oldest hotel in Waikiki, or mai tais and *pupu* (hors d'oeuvres) at Duke's Waikiki (a better deal at lunch). In the afternoon, it's time for a surf lesson on the beginner-friendly waves of Waikiki. Finish your day with a surfside dinner at your restaurant of choice to watch the sunset.

PEARL HARBOR

Day 2. Give yourself a whole day for Pearl Harbor, in part because the history is so rich and overwhelming and in part because you may be waiting in lines. Just be aware that tickets for the USS *Arizona* Memorial usually run out early, but you can arrive as early as 7 am. After your ferry ride out to the memorial, you can explore the USS *Bowfin* submarine or take a shuttle to Ford Island and visit the restored USS *Missouri* battleship (the "Mighty Mo") and the Pacific Aviation Museum. Only the USS *Arizona,* and the Visitor Center, which are operated by the National Park Service are free; the other sights are operated by private entities and charge admission. You won't be allowed to carry bags to any of the sights, so be sure that anything important fits in your pockets; you can pay to store your bags near the Visitor Center. Head back to Waikiki for some late-afternoon beach time and a good dinner.

DOWNTOWN HONOLULU AND CHINATOWN

Day 3. Cab or bus it to downtown Honolulu for a guided tour of the royal residence, Iolani Palace, where you'll get an excellent overview of Hawaii's monarchy era from the early 1800s through its overthrow in 1893. Next take a walk between Honolulu Hale, Kawaiahao Church, Hawaiian Mission Houses Historic Site and Archives, the Hawaii State Capitol, Washington Place, the Kamehameha I Statue, and Aliiolani Hale for historical highlights (several companies offer professionally guided walks of the area). Then, keep walking the half mile through Honolulu's business district into Chinatown for lunch at one of its eclectic eateries. For Chinese food, Little Village Noodle House is always a good bet. Browse the shops, art galleries, and cultural sites like the Maunakea

Marketplace, Chinatown Cultural Plaza, Izumo Taisha Shrine, and Kuan Yin Temple.

DIAMOND HEAD AND KAIMUKI

Day 4. Today you will go the opposite direction from downtown. Tours of Shangri La, the opulent waterfront home of heiress Doris Duke, with its Islamic art and architecture, book up well in advance, but it's well worth the effort to make an online reservation for a small surcharge. Shuttles to the Kahala home-turned-museum start and end at the Honolulu Museum of Art. After your tour, grab a to-go lunch from Diamond Head Market & Grill, and enjoy it at the picnic tables at Diamond Head State Monument and Park. Then hike the relatively easy 1½-hour trail up and down this dormant volcano. Finish the day with dinner in the foodie neighborhood of Kaimuki.

KAILUA AND SOUTH SHORE

Day 5. Head to the Windward side for a stop in Kailua, a once sleepy suburb that's become a popular visitor spot. Go for a swim at quintessential Kailua Beach, then have lunch at Kalapawai Cafe & Deli or Kono's. Next, drive along the southeastern shore via Waimanalo, and choose your afternoon adventure: 1) do the easy, stroller-friendly hike at Makapuu Lighthouse with great whale-watching views in winter and spring; 2) snorkel at Hanauma Bay State Park, the pristine nature preserve where you'll have more space to swim with the fish if you arrive after the morning-to-midday rush; or 3) stop at Halona Blowhole and the *From Here to Eternity* Halona Beach Cove nearby.

NORTH SHORE

Day 6. Explore Oahu's countryside with a drive to the North Shore. These famed beaches are home to some of the world's most famous surf breaks. Each winter, surfers from around the globe converge to catch barreling waves of 15 feet or higher. Haleiwa is the biggest town on the North Shore and is filled with surf shops, charming boutiques, and restaurants. Grab lunch from Haleiwa Joe's or Uncle Bo's Haleiwa. If you can manage to wait in the long line, enjoying a treat at Matsumoto Shave Ice is a sweet way to end the day.

On the Calendar

Local events are a fun, first-hand way to experience Oahu's diverse culture. The annual festivals, parades, concerts, tournaments, and more happening every month across the island are sure to please everyone during your trip.

January

Sony Open in Hawaii. The Sony Open in Hawaii is held annually at the Waialae Country Club in east Honolulu in early January. Part of the PGA tour, the tournament attracts many of the top players in professional golf. It's also the largest charity golf event in the Islands. ⊕ *www.sonyopeninhawaii.com* ☎ *808/523–7888*

February

Pow! Wow! Hawaii. Watch as renowned muralists and street artists transform the walls of Kakaako's businesses each year during Pow! Wow! Hawaii. The week-long event takes place around Valentine's Day and convenes dozens of local and international artists to paint murals and organize gallery shows at the nearby Lana Lane Studios. It's a fun way to explore this dynamic Honolulu neighborhood and see dynamic art installations. ⊕ *www.powwowworldwide.com/*

March

Honolulu Festival. The annual Honolulu Festival held in mid-March celebrates Hawaii's colorful blend of cultures from across the Pacific and Asia with a grand parade down Kalakaua Avenue, a craft fair, food booths, and more. It culminates with Oahu's largest fireworks display. ⊕ *www.honolulufestival.com*

April

Spam Jam. Hawaii loves its Spam, which is highlighted during this food event at the end of April. It's a Waikiki block party featuring food booths serving up unique takes on the beloved canned meat, including desserts, snacks, and more. There's also Spam merchandise and live entertainment. ⊕ *spamjamhawaii.com*

May

Lei Day. This treasured celebration is Hawaii's version of May Day. It takes place every May 1 at Kapiolani Park and includes lei-making demonstrations and contests, hula, crafts, food, and live music.

June

King Kamehameha Day. Kamehameha Day is celebrated every June 11, honoring the monarch who united the Hawaiian Kingdom. There are parades throughout the islands, and, on Oahu, the King Kamehameha Day parade is held in Waikiki and features floats and traditional *pau* riders—pau means skirt in Hawaiian—women horseback riders in ornate, colorful skirts, and draped in lei.

July

Ukulele Festival Hawaii. Learn to *kani ka pila*, or make music, at this popular annual festival, which is held in mid-July at Kapiolani Park near Waikiki. It attracts thousands with lessons, the chance to win one of 100 donated instruments, and concerts featuring talented local and visiting musicians, as well as student performers. ⊕ *www.ukulelefestivalhawaii.org*

August

Duke's Oceanfest. This weeklong festival in mid-August is the embodiment of its namesake, waterman Duke Kahanamoku. An Olympian and ambassador of Aloha, Duke loved to swim, surf, and paddle. Held along Waikiki beach, Duke's Oceanfest hosts surfing and stand-up paddling competitions, outrigger racing, and more. ⊕ *dukesoceanfest.com*

September

The Aloha Festivals. The quintessential Aloha Festivals in late September celebrates the storied, vibrant culture in the Islands. It's also one of the state's largest gatherings, drawing more than 100,000 spectators each year. The multi-event festivities features a block party, parade, music, and hula. ⊕ *www.alohafestivals.com*

October

Hawaii Food and Wine Festival. This is the can't-miss event for foodies visiting Oahu in the second half of October. Held over several days at upscale locations across the islands, the Hawaii Food and Wine Festival features notable chefs from Hawaii, the mainland, and abroad, as well as mixologists and wine producers. You'll eat some of the best foods the islands have to offer here. ⊕ *hawaiifoodandwinefestival.com*

November

Vans Triple Crown of Surfing. If you want to watch the world best surfers, just head to the North Shore in the wintertime. From November through the December, the Vans Triple Crown draws top surfers to take on these monster Oahu waves. (The holding period for the event begins in November and usually continues through December; the event officially begins when the waves are consistent.) ⊕ *www.worldsurfleague.com*

December

Honolulu City Lights. Celebrate the holidays, Oahu style, throughout December. Honolulu Hale, where the city government is located, is transformed with twinkling lights, a keiki train, and dozens of uniquely decorated Christmas trees. Don't miss Shaka Santa and Tutu Mele. ⊕ *www.honolulucitylights.org*

Contacts

✈ Air

AIRPORT Daniel K. Inouye International Airport. (*HNL*). ✉ *300 Rodgers Blvd., Airport Area* ☎ *808/836–6411* ⊕ *airports.hawaii.gov.*

GROUND TRANSPORTATION Roberts Hawaii. ☎ *808/539–9400* ⊕ *www.robertshawaii.com.* **TheBus.** ☎ *808/848–5555* ⊕ *www.thebus.org.*

MAJOR AIRLINES Alaska Airlines. ☎ *800/252–7522* ⊕ *www.alaskaair.com.* **American Airlines.** ☎ *800/433–7300* ⊕ *www.aa.com.* **Delta Airlines.** ☎ *800/221–1212 for U.S. reservations, 800/241–4141 for international reservations* ⊕ *www.delta.com.* **Hawaiian Airlines.** ☎ *800/367–5320* ⊕ *www.hawaiianairlines.com.* **Southwest.** ☎ *800/435–9792* ⊕ *www.southwest.com.* **United Airlines.** ☎ *800/864–8331 for U.S. reservations* ⊕ *www.united.com.*

LOCAL AIRLINES Mokulele Airlines. ☎ *866/260–7070* ⊕ *www.mokuleleairlines.com.*

🚌 Bus

CONTACTS Waikiki Trolley. ☎ *808/593–2822* ⊕ *waikikitrolley.com.*

🚢 Cruise

CONTACTS Norwegian Cruise Line. ☎ *866/234–7350* ⊕ *www.ncl.com.* **Un-Cruise Adventures.** ☎ *888/862–8881* ⊕ *www.uncruise.com.*

🛏 Lodging

CONTACTS Hawaiian Villa Rentals. ☎ *808/673–6800* ⊕ *www.hawaiianvillarentals.com.* **Private Homes Hawaii.** ☎ *808/896–9580* ⊕ *www.privatehomeshawaii.com.*

🚕 Taxi

CONTACTS TheCAB. ☎ *808/422–2222* ⊕ *www.thecabhawaii.com.* **Carey Honolulu.** ☎ *888/405–1792* ⊕ *www.careyhonolulu.com.* **Charley's Taxi.** ☎ *808/233–3333* ⊕ *www.charleystaxi.com.* **Elite Limousine Service.** ☎ *808/735–2431* ⊕ *www.elitelimohawaii.com.*

📍 Visitor Information

CONTACTS Hawaii Visitors & Convention Bureau. ☎ *800/464–2924 for brochures* ⊕ *www.gohawaii.com.* **Oahu Visitors Bureau.** ☎ *800/464–2924* ⊕ *www.gohawaii.com/islands/oahu.*

🌐 Websites

CONTACTS Hawaii Beach Safety. ⊕ *hawaiibeachsafety.com.* **Hawaii Department of Land and Natural Resources.** ⊕ *dlnr.hawaii.gov.* **Hawaii Tourism Authority.** ⊕ *www.gohawaii.com.* **Oahu Visitors Bureau.** ⊕ *www.gohawaii.com/islands/oahu.*

Chapter 3

HONOLULU AND PEARL HARBOR

Updated by Marla Cimini
and Anna Weaver Lopicolo

3

⊙ Sights	🚗 Restaurants	🛏 Hotels	🛍 Shopping	🍸 Nightlife
★★★★★	★★★★★	★★★★★	★★★★★	★★★★★

WELCOME TO HONOLULU AND PEARL HARBOR

TOP REASONS TO GO

★ **Variety:** The "Gathering Place" has something for everyone: beaches, shopping, restaurants, sightseeing, night-life, and hiking.

★ **History:** The island is saturated in Hawaiian his-tory, from ancient times to the modern day.

★ **Excellent food:** Oahu is a melting pot of food and drink and the center of Hawaii's farm-to-table scene.

★ **Great hotels:** The island with the highest popula-tion comes with the perks of easy access to trans-portation and lodging.

★ **The great outdoors:** The variety of Oahu's beaches and coastlines offer every oceanside activity, from lounging and swimming to snorkeling and diving.

1 **Waikiki and Diamond Head.** Most of Oahu's hotels are in Waikiki, as are shops, restaurants, and that famous beach. Beautiful Diamond Head, a great hiking spot but also a good destination for food, is just to the east.

2 **Pearl Harbor.** History is preserved and presented at multiple memorials and museums in this still-active naval base.

3 **Salt Lake.** Peaceful Moanalua Gardens is in this largely residential neighborhood.

4 **Mapunapuna.** What is mostly a warehouse and office area also has some hidden-gem restaurants and shops.

5 **Iwilei.** Stop in Iwilei for a movie and a number of good restaurants along-side the working harbor and farther inland.

6 **Downtown.** The business district is bustling during weekdays but dead in the evening. The historic district is easily walkable.

7 **Chinatown.** Chock full of history and culture, Chinatown also has some of Honolulu's trendiest bars, restaurants, and boutiques alongside long-time local shops, markets, and restaurants.

8 **Kakaako.** Completely transformed since the early 2010s, Kakaako is now a great place to shop, eat, and absorb street art.

9 **Ala Moana.** Come here for the shopping and food at the state's largest mall and enjoy the beachfront park.

10 **Makiki Heights.** Head up Tantalus for stunning views from *mauka* to *makai* (mountain to ocean).

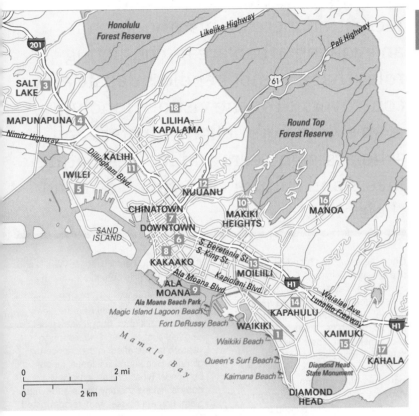

11 Kalihi. Fabulous food spots popular with locals are the hallmarks of this working-class neighborhood.

12 Nuuanu. This largely residential valley is intersected by the Pali Highway.

13 Moiliili. An excellent range of restaurants fall largely along King Street in this neighborhood overlapping with the McCully area.

14 Kapahulu. From Waikiki, head north along Kapahulu Avenue for low-key shops and restaurants.

15 Kaimuki. Kaimuki has emerged as a foodie's paradise in the last decade.

16 Manoa. Home of the largest branch of the University of Hawaii, Manoa is also known for its historic homes.

17 Kahala. This upscale residential area has a beachfront hotel to match and good-size mall.

18 Liliha-Kapalama. These neighborhoods intertwine themselves with Kalihi in locals' minds, with a similar feel and a famous bakery.

Here is Hawaii's only true metropolis, its seat of government, center of commerce and shipping, entertainment and recreation mecca, a historic site, and an evolving urban area—conflicting roles that engender endless debate and controversy. For the visitor, Honolulu is an everyman's delight: hipsters and scholars, sightseers and foodies, nature lovers and culture vultures all can find their bliss.

Once there was the broad bay of Mamala and the narrow inlet of Kou, fronting a dusty plain occupied by a few thatched houses and the great Pakaka *heiau* (shrine). Nosing into the narrow passage in 1794, British sea captain William Brown named the port Fair Haven. Later, Hawaiians would call it Honolulu, or "sheltered bay." As shipping traffic increased, the settlement grew into a Western-style town of streets and buildings, tightly clustered around the single freshwater source, Nuuanu Stream. Not until piped water became available in the early 1900s did Honolulu spread across the greening plain. Long before that, however, Honolulu gained importance when King Kamehameha I reluctantly abandoned his home on the Big Island to build a stately compound near the harbor in 1804 to better protect Hawaiian interests from the Western incursion.

Two hundred years later, the entire island is, in a sense, Honolulu—the City and County of Honolulu. The city has no official boundaries, extending across the flatlands from Pearl Harbor to Waikiki and high into the hills behind.

The main areas (Waikiki, Pearl Harbor, downtown, Chinatown) have the lion's share of the sights, but greater Honolulu also has a lot to offer. One reason to venture farther afield is the chance to glimpse Honolulu's residential neighborhoods. Types of classic Hawaiian homes include the tiny green-and-white plantation-era house, with its corrugated tin roof, two windows flanking a central door and small porch, and the breezy bungalow, with its swooping Thai-style roofline and two wings flanking screened French doors through which breezes blow into the living room. Note the tangled "Grandma-style" gardens and many *ohana* houses—small homes in the backyard of a larger home or built as apartments perched over the garage, allowing extended families to live together. Carports, which rarely house cars, are the island's version of rec rooms, where parties are held and neighbors sit to "talk story." Sometimes you see gallon jars on the flat roofs of garages or carports: these are pickled lemons fermenting in the sun. Also in the neighborhoods, you find the folksy restaurants and takeout spots favored by locals.

Planning

Getting Here and Around

AIR
Honolulu's Daniel K. Inouye International Airport (HNL) is Hawaii's busiest, with the most nonstop flights from the mainland U.S. as well as the majority of the state's international flights.

AIRPORT TRANSFERS
Some hotels have their own pickup and drop-off service, though they may charge a fee, so check when you book accommodations.

Taxi service is available on the center median just outside baggage-claim areas. Look for the yellow-shirted taxi dispatchers, who will radio for a taxi. The fare to Waikiki runs approximately $40–$45, plus 60¢ per bag and tip, with a maximum of four passengers. An oversize baggage fee may apply. Uber and Lyft also serve the airport.

Another option is to take a private shuttle service like Roberts Hawaii. The company will greet you at the arrival gate, escort you to baggage claim, and take you to your hotel. Call ahead for the service, which costs $16 per person one-way, $32 round-trip.

TheBus, the municipal bus, will take you into Waikiki for only $2.75, but all bags must fit on your lap or under your legs.

CONTACTS Roberts Hawaii. ☎ 808/539–9400 ⊕ www.robertshawaii.com. **TheBus.** ☎ 808/848–5555 ⊕ www.thebus.org.

BUS
Getting around by bus is an affordable option on Oahu, particularly in the most heavily touristed areas of Waikiki. In addition to TheBus and the Waikiki Trolley, Waikiki has brightly painted private buses, many of them free, that shuttle you to such commercial attractions as dinner cruises, garment factories, and the like.

You can travel around the island or just down Kalakaua Avenue for $2.75 on Honolulu's municipal transportation system, affectionately known as TheBus. It's one of the island's best bargains. Buses make stops in Waikiki every 10–15 minutes to take passengers to nearby shopping areas.

Free transfers have been discontinued, but you can purchase a one-day pass for $5.50. Just ask the driver as you're boarding. Exact change is required, and dollar bills are accepted. Monthly passes cost $70.

The company's website has timetables, route maps, and real-time bus tracking, or you can download the free DaBus2 app for your smartphone. You can call to speak with a representative for route advice. Or you also can find privately published booklets at most drugstores and other convenience outlets.

The Waikiki Trolley has five lines and dozens of stops that allow you to plan your own itinerary while riding on brass-trimmed, open-air buses that look like trolleys. The Historic Honolulu Tour (Red Line) travels between Waikiki and Chinatown and includes stops at the State Capitol, Iolani Palace, and the King Kamehameha statue. The Waikiki-Ala Moana Shopping Shuttle (Pink Line) runs from the T Galleria by DFS to Eggs 'n Things, stopping at various Waikiki locations and the Ala Moana Center. The Scenic Diamond Head Sightseeing Tour (Green Line) runs through Waikiki and down around Diamond Head. There's also a south shore coastline tour (Blue Line) and a line that runs to Aloha Stadium and Pearl Harbor (Purple Line). A one-day pass costs $23 to $45, four-day passes are $36.50 to $74, and seven-day passes are $41 to $79. All passes are discounted when purchased in advance.

CONTACTS Waikiki Trolley. ☎ 808/593-2822 ⊕ waikikitrolley.com.

CAR

If you plan on spending most of your time in Hawaii in Honolulu, it doesn't pay to rent a car for your entire trip, especially if you are staying in Waikiki. Hotels typically charge (a lot) for parking, and traffic can be heavy, especially during rush-hour. But having a car will make exploring the rest of Oahu easier, so consider renting only for a couple of days. Gas is expensive.

TAXI

In Honolulu, taxis cost $3.10 at the drop of the flag and each additional mile is $3.60. Taxi and limousine companies can provide a car and driver for half-day or daylong island tours, and a number of companies also offer personal guides. Remember, however, the rates are quite steep for these services, running $100 to $200 or more per day. Uber and Lyft also serve Oahu, including for airport pickups.

Hotels

The vast majority of hotels in Honolulu are in Waikiki, but there are also a few in downtown Honolulu and in the Ala Moana area between downtown and Waikiki. Away from the hopping scene of Waikiki or busy downtown, accommodations on the rest of Oahu range from quiet and romantic bed-and-breakfasts and cottages to less expensive hotels that are a great value. There are a few luxury resorts as well, where you'll truly feel like you're getting away from it all.

What It Costs In U.S. Dollars			
$	$$	$$$	$$$$
FOR TWO PEOPLE			
under 180	$180–$260	$261–$350	over $350

Hotel reviews have been shortened. For full information, visit Fodors.com.

Nightlife

Gone are the days when there was nothing to do in Honolulu at night. Any guidebook that tells you Honolulu isn't for the night owl is outdated. Most nights it's hard to pick which DJ to see at which nightclub, or which art show opening to attend. In fact, many people who arrive in Oahu expecting to find white-sand beaches and nothing else are surprised at such a vibrant nightlife. Bask in the shade of the swaying palm trees, watch the sunset over Waikiki, and dress up, because more and more clubs in Honolulu enforce a dress code.

Performing Arts

If all-night dancing isn't for you, Oahu also has a thriving arts and culture scene, with community-theater productions, stand-up comedy, outdoor concerts, film festivals, and chamber-music performances, most of it centered in Honolulu. Major Broadway shows, dance companies, rock stars, and comedians come through the Islands, too. Check local newspapers—the *Honolulu Star-Advertiser* or *Midweek*—for the latest events. Websites like ⊕ www.frolichawaii.com and ⊕ www.honolulumagazine.com also have great information.

Restaurants

There's no lack of choices when it comes to dining in Honolulu, where everything from the haute cuisine of heavy-hitting top-notch chefs to a wide variety of Asian specialties to reliable and inexpensive American favorites can be found.

Restaurant reviews have been shortened. For full information, visit Fodors. com.

What It Costs In U.S. Dollars			
$	$$	$$$	$$$$
AT DINNER			
under $17	$17–$26	$27–$35	over $35

Shopping

There are two distinct types of shopping experiences for visitors: vast malls with the customary department stores and tiny boutiques with specialty items. Three malls in Honolulu provide a combination of the standard department stores and interesting shops showcasing original paintings and woodwork from local artists and craftsmen. Shoppers who know where to look in Honolulu will find everything from designer merchandise to unusual Asian imports.

Possibilities are endless, but a bit of scouting is usually required to get past the items you'll find in your own hometown. Industrious bargain hunters can detect the perfect gift in the sale bin of a slightly hidden store at every mall.

You'll find that shops stay open fairly late in Waikiki. Stores open at around 9 am, and many don't close until 10 or even 11 pm.

Tours

Guided tours are convenient; you don't have to worry about finding a parking spot or getting admission tickets. Most of the tour guides have taken special classes in Hawaiian history and lore, and many are certified by the state of Hawaii.

On the other hand, you won't have the freedom to proceed at your own pace, nor will you have the ability to take a detour trip if something else catches your attention.

BUS AND VAN TOURS

Polynesian Adventure

BUS TOURS | This company leads tours of Pearl Harbor and other Oahu sights and also offers a circle-island tour by motor coach, van, or minicoach. ☎ *808/833–3000, 888/206–4531* ⊕ *www.polyad.com* ✉ *From $51.*

THEME TOURS

Discover Hawaii Tours

BUS TOURS | In addition to circle-island and other Oahu-based itineraries on motor- and minicoaches, this company can also get you from Waikiki to the lava flows of the Big Island or to Maui's Hana Highway and back in one day. ☎ *808/739–7911* ⊕ *www.discoverhawaiitours.com* ✉ *From $50.*

E Noa Tours

BUS TOURS | This outfitter's certified tour guides conduct circle-island, Pearl Harbor, helicopter, and shopping tours. ☎ *808/591–2561, 800/824–8804* ⊕ *www. enoa.com* ✉ *From $29.*

Waikiki and Diamond Head

Waikiki is approximately 3 miles east of downtown Honolulu.

A short drive from downtown Honolulu, Waikiki is Oahu's primary resort area. A mix of historic and modern hotels and condos front the sunny 2-mile stretch of beach, and many have clear views of Diamond Head. The area is home to much of the island's dining, nightlife, and shopping—from posh boutiques to hole-in-the-wall eateries to craft booths at the International Marketplace.

Waikiki was once a favorite retreat for Hawaiian royalty. In 1901, the Moana Hotel debuted, introducing Waikiki as an international travel destination. The region's fame continued to grow when Duke Kahanamoku helped popularize the sport of surfing, offering lessons to visitors at Waikiki. You can see Duke immortalized in a bronze statue, with a surfboard, on Kuhio Beach. Today there is a decidedly "urban resort" vibe here; streets are clean, gardens are manicured, and the sand feels softer than at beaches farther down the coast. At first glance, there isn't much of a local culture—it's mainly tourist crowds—but if you explore the neighborhood, you can still find the relaxed surf-y vibe and friendly "aloha spirit" that has drawn people here for more than a century.

Diamond Head Crater is perhaps Hawaii's most recognizable natural landmark. It got its name from sailors who thought they had found precious gems on its slopes; these later proved to be calcite crystals, a much more common mineral. Hawaiians saw a resemblance in the sharp angle of the crater's seaward slope to the oddly shaped head of the ahi fish and so called it Leahi, though later they Hawaiianized the English name to Kaimana Hila. It is commemorated in a widely known hula—*A ike i ka nani o Kaimana Hila, Kaimana Hila, kau mai i luna* ("We saw the beauty of Diamond Head, Diamond Head set high above").

The sprawling Kapiolani Park lies in the shadow of the Diamond Head Crater, which is just beyond the easternmost limits of Waikiki. King David Kalakaua established the park in 1887, named it after his queen, and dedicated it "to the use and enjoyment of the people." Kapiolani Park is a 500-acre expanse where you can go for a stroll, play all sorts of field sports, enjoy a picnic, see wild animals and tropical fish at the Honolulu Zoo and the Waikiki Aquarium, or hear live music at the Waikiki Shell or the Kapiolani Bandstand.

GETTING HERE AND AROUND

Bounded by the Ala Wai Canal on the north and west, the beach on the south, and the Honolulu Zoo to the east, Waikiki is compact and easy to walk around. TheBus runs multiple routes here from the airport and downtown Honolulu. By car, finding Waikiki from H1 can be tricky; look for the Punahou exit for the west end of Waikiki and the King Street exit for the eastern end.

For those with a Costco card, the cheapest gas on the island is at the three Costco stations. The one in Honolulu is on Arakawa Street, between Dillingham Boulevard and Nimitz Highway; the one in Waipio is at 94-1231 Ka Uka Boulevard; and the one in Kapolei is at 4589 Kapolei Parkway.

◉ Sights

Diamond Head State Monument and Park

NATURE SITE | Panoramas from this 760-foot extinct volcanic peak, once used as a military fortification, extend from Waikiki and Honolulu in one direction and out to Koko Head in the other, with surfers and windsurfers scattered like confetti on the cresting waves below. This 360-degree perspective is a great orientation for first-time visitors. On a clear day, look east past Koko Head to glimpse the outlines of the islands of Maui and Molokai.

To enter the park from Waikiki, take Kalakaua Avenue east, turn left at Monsarrat Avenue, head a mile up the hill, and look for a sign on the right. Drive through the tunnel to the inside of the crater. The ¾-mile trail to the top begins at the parking lot. Be aware that the hike to the crater is an upward ascent with numerous stairs to climb; if you aren't in the habit of getting occasional exercise, this might not be for you. At the top, you'll find a somewhat awkward scramble through a

Despite the steep climb, Diamond Head, an extinct volcanic crater on the eastern edge of Waikiki, is one of Honolulu's most popular hiking destinations.

tunnel and bunker out into the open air, but the view is worth it.

Take bottled water with you to stay hydrated under the tropical sun, as there are no water stations along the hike. ■ TIP → **To beat the heat and the crowds, rise early and make the hike before 8 am.** As you walk, note the color of the vegetation: if the mountain is brown, Honolulu has been without significant rain for a while; but if the trees and undergrowth glow green, you'll know it's the wet season (winter) without looking at a calendar. This is when rare Hawaiian marsh plants revive on the floor of the crater. Keep an eye on your watch if you're here at day's end: the gates close promptly at 6 pm. ✉ *Diamond Head Rd. at 18th Ave., Diamond Head* ☎ *808/587–0300* ⊕ *dlnr.hawaii.gov/dsp/parks/oahu/diamond-head-state-monument* ✉ *$1 per person, $5 per vehicle (cash only).*

Honolulu Zoo

ZOO | FAMILY | The world definitely has bigger and better zoos, but this one, though showing signs of age, is 42 acres covered by well-paved, walkable trails and features a lush garden with tropical flowers. To get a glimpse of the endangered *nene,* the Hawaii state bird, check out the zoo's Kipuka Nene Sanctuary. A few highlights include a Japanese Giant Salamander habitat, and an ectotherm complex, which houses a Burmese python, elongated tortoises, and a giant African snail. Though many animals prefer to remain invisible—particularly the elusive big cats—the monkeys and elephants appear to enjoy being seen and are a hoot to watch. It's best to get to the zoo right when it opens, because the animals are livelier in the cool of the morning.

Children adore the petting zoo, where they can make friends with a llama or stand in the middle of a koi pond. There's an exceptionally good gift shop. On weekends, the Art on the Zoo Fence, on Monsarrat Avenue on the Diamond Head side outside the zoo, has affordable artwork by local contemporary artists. Metered parking is available all along the

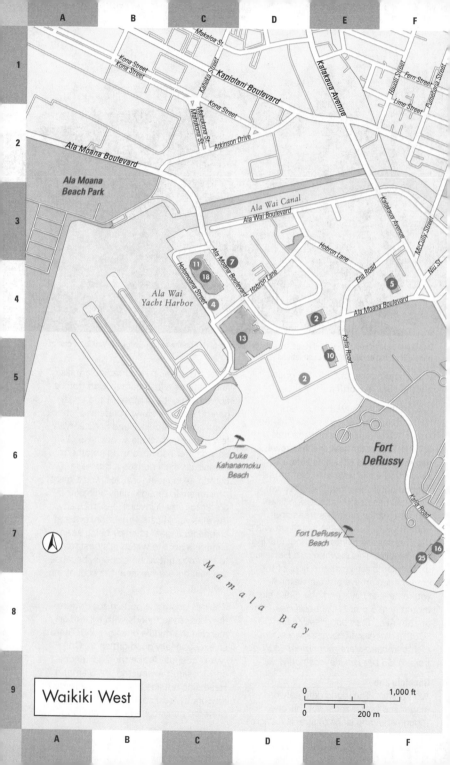

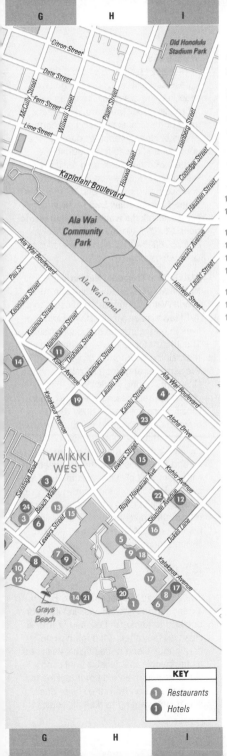

Restaurants ▼

1. Azure Restaurant **H8**
2. Bali Steak & Seafood **D5**
3. BLT Steak Waikiki **G7**
4. Chart House Waikiki **C4**
5. Doraku Sushi **H7**
6. Duke's Waikiki **I8**
7. Halekulani Bakery & Restaurant **G7**
8. Hula Grill Waikiki **I8**
9. Island Vintage Wine Bar **H7**
10. La Mer **G8**
11. 100 Sails Restaurant & Bar **C4**
12. Orchids **G8**
13. Roy's Waikiki **G7**
14. RumFire Waikiki **H8**
15. Taormina Sicilian Cuisine **G7**
16. Top of Waikiki **I7**
17. Waikiki Food Hall **I8**
18. Wolfgang's Steakhouse by Wolfgang Zwiener **H7**

Hotels ▼

1. Aqua Oasis **H6**
2. Aqua Palms Waikiki **E4**
3. The Breakers Hotel **G6**
4. Coconut Waikiki Hotel **I5**
5. DoubleTree by Hilton Alana - Waikiki Beach **F4**
6. Embassy Suites by Hilton Waikiki Beach Walk **G7**
7. The Equus **C4**
8. Halekulani Hotel **G7**
9. Halepuna Waikiki by Halekulani **G7**
10. Hilton Hawaiian Village Beach Resort **E5**
11. Holiday Inn Express Waikiki **G5**
12. Hyatt Centric Waikiki Beach **I7**
13. Ilikai Hotel & Luxury Suites **D4**
14. Luana Waikiki Hotel & Suites **G5**
15. Ohana Waikiki Malia by Outrigger **H6**
16. Outrigger Reef Waikiki Beach Resort **F7**
17. Outrigger Waikiki Beach Resort **I8**
18. Prince Waikiki **C4**
19. The Ritz-Carlton Residences, Waikiki Beach **G5**
20. The Royal Hawaiian, a Luxury Collection Resort, Waikiki **H8**
21. Sheraton Waikiki **H8**
22. Shoreline Hotel Waikiki **I7**
23. The Surfjack Hotel & Swim Club **H6**
24. Trump International Hotel Waikiki Beach Walk **G7**
25. Waikiki Shore **F7**

KEY

1 Restaurants

1 Hotels

makai (ocean) side of the park and in the lot next to the zoo—but it can fill up early. TheBus makes stops here along the way to and from Ala Moana Center and Sea Life Park (Routes 8 and 22). ⊠ *151 Kapahulu Ave., Waikiki* ☎ *808/971–7171* ⊕ *www.honoluluzoo.org* ⌇ *$19.*

Kapiolani Bandstand

ARTS VENUE | FAMILY | The Victorian-style Kapiolani Bandstand, which was originally built in the late 1890s, is Kapiolani Park's stage for community entertainment and concerts. Founded by King Kamehameha III in 1836, the Royal Hawaiian Band is the nation's only city-sponsored band, and performs free concerts at the bandstand as well as at Iolani Palace and the center stage at Ala Moana Center. Visit the band's website for concert dates, and check event-listing websites and the *Honolulu Star-Advertiser*—Oahu's local newspaper—for event information at the bandstand. ⊠ *2805 Monsarrat Ave., Waikiki* ☎ *808/922–5331* ⊕ *www. rhb-music.com.*

Waikiki Aquarium

ZOO | FAMILY | This small yet fun attraction harbors more than 3,500 organisms and 500 species of Hawaiian and South Pacific marine life, including an endangered Hawaiian monk seal and a zebra shark. The Living Reef exhibit opened in 2019 and showcases a wall of diverse corals and fascinating reef environments found along Hawaii's shorelines. Check out exhibits on the Northwestern Hawaiian Islands (which explains the formation of the island chain) and Ocean Drifters (about various types of jellyfish). A 60-foot exhibit houses sea horses, sea dragons, and pipefish. A free self-guided mobile audio tour is available via your own smartphone. The aquarium offers activities of interest to adults and children alike, including a focus on the importance of being eco-friendly and keeping our oceans clean. ⊠ *2777 Kalakaua Ave., Waikiki* ☎ *808/923–9741* ⊕ *www.waikikiaquarium.org* ⌇ *$12.*

Waikiki Shell

ARTS VENUE | Grab one of the 6,000 "grass seats" (i.e., spots on the lawn, though there are actual seats as well) for music under the stars. An eclectic array of musical acts put on concerts at this landmark venue throughout the summer and occasionally during the winter, weather permitting. Visit their website and local event-listing sites to see upcoming performers. ■ **TIP→ This venue does not allow backpacks or large purses. Check the website for other restrictions.** ⊠ *2805 Monsarrat Ave., Waikiki* ☎ *808/768–5400* ⊕ *www.blaisdellcenter. com/venues/waikiki-shell.*

Waikiki War Memorial Natatorium

MEMORIAL | This Beaux Arts–style, 1927 World War I monument, dedicated to the 101 Hawaiian servicemen who lost their lives in battle, stands proudly in Waikiki. The 100-meter saltwater swimming pool, the training spot for Olympians Johnny Weissmuller and Buster Crabbe and the U.S. Army during World War II, has been closed for decades, as the pool needs repair. Plans are under study to tear down the natatorium, though a nonprofit group continues fighting to save the facility. With both massive environmental and funding issues, the proposed refurbishment plans remain in flux. The site is closed to visitors, but you can stop by and look at it from the outside or see it from the adjacent Sans Souci/Kaimana beach. ⊠ *2777 Kalakaua Ave., Waikiki* ⊕ *natatorium.org.*

⊕ Beaches

The 2-mile strand called Waikiki Beach extends from Hilton Hawaiian Village on one end to Kapiolani Park and Diamond Head on the other. Although it's one contiguous piece of beach, it's as varied as the people that inhabit the Islands. Whether you're an old-timer looking to enjoy the action from the shade or a sports nut wanting to do it all, you can find every beach activity here without ever jumping in the rental car.

Plenty of parking exists on the west end at the Ala Wai Marina, where you can park in metered stalls around the harbor for $1 an hour. For parking on the east end, Kapiolani Park and the Honolulu Zoo also have metered parking for $1 an hour—more affordable than the $10 per hour the resorts want. ■TIP→ **If you're staying outside the area, park at either end of the beach and walk in.**

Diamond Head Beach Park

BEACH—SIGHT | You have to do a little hiking to like Diamond Head Beach. This beautiful, remote spot is at the base of Diamond Head Crater. The beach is just a small, narrow strip of sand with lots of coral in the water. This said, the views looking out from the point are breathtaking, and it's amazing to watch the windsurfers skimming along, driven by the gusts off the point. From the parking area, look for an opening in the wall where an unpaved trail leads down to the beach. Even for the unadventurous, a stop at the lookout point is well worth the time. **Amenities:** parking (no fee); showers. **Best for:** solitude; sunset; surfing; windsurfing. ⊠ *At base of Diamond Head, 3500 Diamond Head Rd., Diamond Head* ⊹ *Park at crest of Diamond Head Rd. and walk down.*

Duke Kahanamoku Beach

BEACH—SIGHT | FAMILY | Named for Hawaii's famous Olympic swimming champion, Duke Kahanamoku, this is a hard-packed beach with the only shade trees on the sand in Waikiki. It's great for families with young children because it has both shade and the calmest waters in Waikiki, thanks to a rock wall that creates a semiprotected cove. The ocean clarity here is not as brilliant as most of Waikiki because of the stillness of the surf, but it's a small price to pay for peace of mind about youngsters. The beach fronts the Hilton Hawaiian Village Beach Resort and Spa. **Amenities:** food

and drink; parking (fee); showers; toilets. **Best for:** sunset; walking. ⊠ *2005 Kalia Rd., Waikiki.*

★ Fort DeRussy Beach Park

BEACH—SIGHT | FAMILY | This is one of the finest beaches on the south side of Oahu. A wide, soft, ultrawhite beachfront with gently lapping waves makes it a family favorite for running-jumping-frolicking fun. The new, heavily shaded grass grilling area, sand volleyball courts, and aquatic rentals make this a must for the active visitor. This area includes benches as well, if you just want to take a break. The beach fronts Hale Koa Hotel as well as Fort DeRussy. **Amenities:** food and drink; lifeguards; showers; toilets; water sports. **Best for:** swimming; walking. ⊠ *2161 Kalia Rd., Waikiki.*

Gray's Beach

BEACH—SIGHT | A little guesthouse called Gray's-by-the-Sea stood here in the 1920s; now it's a very narrow strip of sand that's adjacent to the Halekulani resort and best for walking and admiring the ocean view. Beachgoers must use the elevated concrete walkway most of the time, as the tides often put sand space at a premium. If you want a look back into old Waikiki, simply have a mai tai at the open-air Reef Bar and Market Grill at the Outrigger Reef hotel a few steps away and check out a great view of Diamond Head. **Amenities:** food and drink; lifeguards; parking (fee); showers; toilets. **Best for:** walking. ⊠ *2199 Kalia Rd., Waikiki.*

Kahaloa and Ulukou Beaches

BEACH—SIGHT | The beach widens back out here, creating the "it" spot for the bikini crowd—and just about everyone else. This is where you find most of the catamaran charters for a spectacular sail out to Diamond Head, as well as surfboard and outrigger canoe rentals for a ride on the rolling waves of the Canoes surf break. Beachgoers can also rent daily chairs and umbrellas in this area. Great music and outdoor dancing beckon the

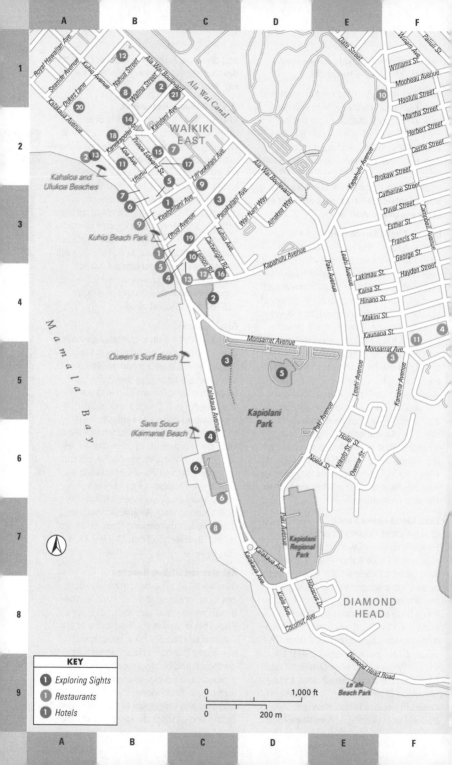

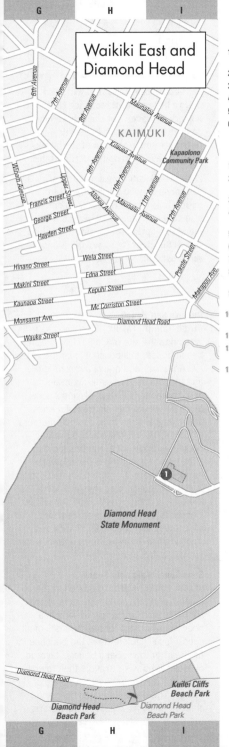

Waikiki East and Diamond Head

KAIMUKI

Kapaolono Community Park

Diamond Head State Monument

Diamond Head Road

Kuilei Cliffs Beach Park

Diamond Head Beach Park

Diamond Head Beach Park

Sights ▼

1 Diamond Head State Monument and Park **I6**
2 Honolulu Zoo **C4**
3 Kapiolani Bandstand **C5**
4 Waikiki Aquarium........**C6**
5 Waikiki Shell............. **D5**
6 Waikiki War Memorial Natatorium **C6**

Restaurants ▼

1 Arancino di Mare........**C3**
2 beachhouse at the moana................... **A2**
3 Bogart's Café.............**F5**
4 Diamond Head Market & Grill **F4**
5 d.k Steak House..........**C3**
6 Hau Tree Lanai **C7**
7 Hy's Steak House **C2**
8 Michel's at the Colony Surf **C7**
9 Morimoto Asia Waikiki **B3**
10 Side Street Inn on Da Strip...............**E1**
11 South Shore Grill.........**F5**
12 Teddy's Bigger Burgers...........**C4**
13 Tiki's Grill and Bar........**C3**

Hotels ▼

1 Alohilani Resort Waikiki Beach...........**B3**
2 Aqua Aloha Surf Waikiki..............**B1**
3 Aston at the Waikiki Banyan **C3**
4 Aston Waikiki Beach Hotel **C3**
5 Aston Waikiki Beach Tower............**B3**
6 Aston Waikiki Circle Hotel..............**B3**
7 Espacio the Jewel of Waikiki **B3**
8 Hilton Garden Inn Waikiki Beach...........**B1**
9 Hilton Waikiki Beach **C2**
10 Hotel Renew..............**C3**
11 Hyatt Regency Waikiki Resort & Spa **B2**
12 Ilima Hotel **B1**
13 Moana Surfrider, A Westin Resort & Spa, Waikiki Beach...........**A2**
14 Ohana Waikiki East by Outrigger.................**B2**
15 Pacific Monarch Hotel.....................**B2**
16 Queen Kapiolani Hotel.......................**C4**
17 Royal Grove Hotel **B2**
18 Sheraton Princess Kaiulani **B2**
19 Waikiki Beach Marriott Resort & Spa **C3**
20 Waikiki Beachcomber By Outrigger.............**A1**
21 Waikiki Sand Villa Hotel.................**C1**

Outrigger Canoes

Outrigger canoes are a simple, cheap, but often-overlooked way to have fun in Waikiki. Everyone clamors to be on the water near Waikiki, and most people go for pricey sailing trips or surf lessons.

The long, skinny, wooden boats on the beach in front of Duke's Waikiki and the Royal Hawaiian Resort allow you to get out on the water for much less money. At $25 per person for two rides, the price has changed only a little in the past decade, but the thrill hasn't changed in centuries. You will need to do a little paddling to catch these legendary waves, but the experienced captain and the beach boys will negotiate you in and out of the break as they have been doing all their lives.

If you think catching a wave on a 10-foot surfboard is a rush, wait until your whole family takes off on one in a 30-foot outrigger boat! A recommendable option for rentals is **Waikiki Beach Services** (⊕ *www.waikikibeach-services.com*).

sand-bound visitor to the lively Duke's restaurant, where shirt and shoes not only aren't required, they're discouraged. The Royal Hawaiian Hotel and the Moana Surfrider are both on this beach. **Amenities:** food and drink; lifeguards; parking (fee); showers; toilets; water sports. **Best for:** partiers; surfing. ⊠ *2259 Kalakaua Ave., Waikiki.*

Kuhio Beach Park

BEACH—SIGHT | FAMILY | Featuring a bronze statue of Duke Kahanamoku, the father of modern-day surfing, this lively beach is bordered by a landscaped walkway with a few benches and some shade. It's great for strolls and people-watching any time of day. Check out the Kuhio Beach hula mound Tuesday, Thursday, and Saturday at 6:30 (at 6 November–January) for free hula and Hawaiian-music performances and a torch-lighting ceremony at sunset. Surf lessons for beginners are available from the beach center every half hour. **Amenities:** food and drink; lifeguards; showers; toilets; water sports. **Best for:** surfing; walking. ⊠ *2461 Kalakaua Ave., Waikiki ⊹ Go past Moana Surfrider Hotel to Kapahulu Ave. pier.*

Queen's Surf Beach

BEACH—SIGHT | FAMILY | So named as it was once the site of Queen Liliuokalani's beach house, this beach is near the Waikiki Aquarium and draws a mix of locals and tourists of all ages—and it seems as if someone is always playing a steel drum. There are banyan trees for shade and volleyball nets for pros and amateurs alike. It's known as the area's premier body boarding spot at the break called "The Wall" (as surfing is not allowed here). The water fronting Queen's Surf is also an aquatic preserve, providing the best snorkeling in Waikiki. **Amenities:** lifeguards; showers; toilets. **Best for:** swimming; walking. ⊠ *2598 Kalakaua Ave., Waikiki ⊹ Across from entrance to Honolulu Zoo.*

Sans Souci (Kaimana) Beach

BEACH—SIGHT | FAMILY | Located at the eastern end of Waikiki (across from the zoo), this small rectangle of sand is a good sunning spot for beach lovers of all ages. Usually quieter than the beaches in the heart of town, Sans Souci is favored by locals who wish to avoid the crowds while still enjoying the convenience of Waikiki. There are lifeguards here and children enjoy its shallow, safe waters, which are protected (for now) by the walls of the historic natatorium, an Olympic-size saltwater swimming arena that's been closed for decades. Serious swimmers and triathletes also swim in the channel here, beyond the reef. The New Otani Kaimana Beach Hotel is next door. **Amenities:** lifeguards; parking (fee); showers; toilets. **Best for:** swimming; walking. ✉ *2776 Kalakaua Ave., Waikiki* ✥ *Across from Kapiolani Park, between New Otani Kaimana Beach Hotel and Waikiki War Memorial Natatorium.*

🍴 Restaurants

As Honolulu's tourist hub, Waikiki is dense with restaurants, from upscale dining rooms with a view to budget-friendly Japanese noodle shops. Over the years, it has become a great destination for food-lovers, as a new generation of innovative chefs is creating inventive menus. There's also been a renewed focus on using local ingredients, indigenous produce, and farm- and ocean-to-table cuisine. Although there are a number of familiar "chain" restaurants here (as well as traditional steak houses), you can also find some solid choices for a variety of meals at all price points.

Arancino di Mare

$$ | ITALIAN | Three locations in town offer fresh seafood, hand-trimmed beef, pastas cooked to order, handmade pizza dough and bread, house-made desserts, and meats and cheeses imported from Italy. Locals as well as tourists come here to enjoy dishes that use only fresh, authentic ingredients. **Known for:** excellent spaghetti pescatore with shrimp, calamari, mussels, and clams; local favorite; small and casual in Waikiki, elegant date-night setting in Kahala. [$] *Average main: $26* ✉ *Waikiki Beach Marriott Resort, 2552 Kalakaua Ave., Waikiki* ☎ *808/931–6273* 🌐 *www.arancino.com.*

Azure Restaurant

$$$$ | MODERN HAWAIIAN | With tables practically on the sand, the Royal Hawaiian Resort's restaurant offers beautiful ocean and Diamond Head views along with world-class cuisine. This legendary indoor-outdoor restaurant has an expansive terrace on the same level as the beach, so you'll feel calm, island vibes as soon as you arrive. **Known for:** oceanfront views and price tag to match; excellent service; beautifully presented dishes. [$] *Average main: $45* ✉ *Royal Hawaiian Resort , 2259 Kalakaua Ave., Waikiki* ☎ *808/931–7440* 🌐 *www.azurewaikiki.com.*

Bali Steak & Seafood

$$$$ | STEAKHOUSE | Spacious and sprawling with lovely ocean views, this many-windowed, multilevel room takes delightful advantage of the restaurant's perch above the beach, facing Diamond Head. The chef serves up an extensive contemporary menu that includes a variety of seafood, steaks, salads, and chops accented with East–West fusion flavors. **Known for:** partnerships with local farmers for farm-to-table offerings; attentive staff; splurge prices. [$] *Average main: $40* ✉ *Hilton Hawaiian Village, 2005 Kalia Rd., Waikiki* ☎ *808/941–2254* 🌐 *www.hiltonhawaiianvillage.com/dining/bali-steak-and-seafood* 🕒 *Closed Sun. and Mon. No lunch.*

beachhouse at the moana

$$$$ | MODERN HAWAIIAN | A truly lovely spot for elegant oceanfront dining, beachhouse serves upscale seafood and modern Hawaiian dishes in a picturesque setting on the veranda of the historical Moana Surfrider Resort, the oldest hotel in Waikiki. Avid fans say the views and romantic location are worth the price. **Known for:** oceanfront dining; gourmet dinners and afternoon tea; romantic setting. [$] *Average main: $44* ✉ *Moana Surfrider Hotel, 2365 Kalakaua Ave., Waikiki* ☎ *808/921–4600* 🌐 *www.beachhousewaikiki.com.*

BLT Steak Waikiki

$$$$ | **STEAKHOUSE** | BLT Steak remains one of the swankiest rooms in town, offering a blend of global fare with local ingredients, but heavy on the meat. From the polished wood tables and local artwork to the dark leather booths, this is a place for an intimate tête-à tête over a karma cherry margarita, while you decide to go surf or turf. **Known for:** bar menu with excellent burgers, swanky cocktails, and raw oysters; creative sides like jalapeño mashed potatoes and spicy barbecue Kahuku corn; lofty prices deserving of a soothing cocktail. [$] *Average main: $48* ✉ *Trump International Hotel Waikiki Beach Walk, 223 Saratoga Rd., Waikiki* ☎ *808/683–7440* 🌐 *www.bltrestaurants.com/blt-steak/waikiki* 🕒 *No lunch.*

★ **Bogart's Café**

$$ | **AMERICAN** | With more than 20 years as a local favorite, Bogart's is an unassuming spot that's situated in a strip mall near Diamond Head and away from the bustle of Waikiki. Serving breakfast, lunch, and a newly introduced dinner service, it's an equally great spot for a bagel or açai bowl in the morning as for a sophisticated dinner after sunset. **Known for:** a local favorite for breakfast and lunch; great pasta dishes for dinner; a neighborhood staple. [$] *Average main: $22* ✉ *3045 Monsarrat Ave., Waikiki* ☎ *808/739–0999* 🌐 *www.bogartscafe.com.*

Chart House Waikiki

$$$$ | **AMERICAN** | Enjoy the sunset views over the yacht harbor as you take in live music nightly while sipping a signature "Guy-Tai" cocktail at this Waikiki landmark. The restaurant opened in 1969 by surfing legend Joey Cabell, and the massive menu retains the mid-century notion of "fine dining"—oysters Rockefeller, shrimp cocktail, and steaks (from a garlicky tenderloin to a Wagyu New York strip), along with island nods such as ahi wontons, poke, and macadamia-nut-crusted mahimahi. **Known for:** sought-after tables on the lanai; old-time steak house atmosphere with dim lighting and strong cocktails; generations of regulars. [$] *Average main: $48* ✉ *1765 Ala Moana Blvd., Waikiki* ☎ *808/941–6669* 🌐 *www.charthousehonolulu.com* 🕒 *No lunch.*

Diamond Head Market & Grill

$ | **AMERICAN** | Just five minutes from Waikiki hotels is award-winning chef Kelvin Ro's one-stop food shop—indispensable if you have accommodations with a kitchen or if you want a quick grab-and-go meal. Join surfers, beachgoers, and Diamond Head hikers at the take-out window to order gourmet sandwiches and plates such as hand-shape burgers, portobello mushroom sandwiches, Korean kalbi ribs, and grilled ahi with wasabi-ginger sauce, rice, and salad. Grab-and-go selections include sandwiches, bentos, and salads. **Known for:** excellent desserts and scones; picnic fare for the beach; well-priced grab-and-go dinners. [$] *Average main: $12* ✉ *3158 Monsarrat Ave., Diamond Head* ☎ *808/732–0077* 🌐 *www.diamondheadmarket.com.*

d.k Steakhouse

$$$$ | **STEAKHOUSE** | Honolulu has its share of national-chain steak houses, but D.K. Kodama's local steak house serves steaks free from hormones, antibiotics, and steroids straight from Oahu's first dry-aging room. **Known for:** addictive potatoes au gratin topped with Maui onions and Parmesan; local flavors, local ownership, and locally sourced produce and select meats; sunset views from outdoor tables. [$] *Average main: $55* ✉ *Waikiki Beach Marriott Resort & Spa, 2552 Kalakaua Ave., Waikiki* ☎ *808/931–6280* 🌐 *www.dksteakhouse.com* 🕒 *No lunch.*

Doraku Sushi

$$ | **JAPANESE** | From entrepreneur Kevin Aoki, son of Benihana founder Rocky Aoki, comes this low-lit, bells-and-whistles, sushi-roll chain (Miami and Atlanta have other branches), a bustling destination with indoor-outdoor seating. The

menu is extensive and features sushi, a variety of rolls, sashimi, and more. **Known for:** a happening bar scene, with both early and late happy hours; tempura everything, including brownies; creative rolls like the Emperor seafood roll. [$] *Average main: $25* ✉ *Royal Hawaiian Center, 2233 Kalakaua Ave., Waikiki* ☎ *808/922–3323* 🌐 *www.dorakusushi.com.*

Duke's Waikiki

$$$ | **AMERICAN** | **FAMILY** | Locals often take visiting friends and family from the mainland to this popular open-air hotel restaurant for the beachfront setting—it's right in front of the famed Canoes surf break in Waikiki—and bar scene and *pupu* (hors d'oeuvres) more than the food. Named for the father of modern surfing and filled with Duke Kahanamoku memorabilia, it offers a large salad bar and a crowd-pleasing menu that includes fish, prime rib, and *huli huli* (rotisserie). **Known for:** iconic local spot with great views, fun bar scene, and perfect location in Waikiki; Duke's on Sunday is so popular that musician Henry Kapono wrote a song about it (Duke's on Sunday); bar seating offers better service. [$] *Average main: $28* ✉ *Outrigger Waikiki Beach Resort , 2335 Kalakaua Ave., Waikiki* ☎ *808/922–2268* 🌐 *www.dukeswaikiki.com.*

★ **Halekulani Bakery & Restaurant**

$$ | **CONTEMPORARY** | If you're craving fresh-baked French pastries and quality coffee, this is place to go when you're in Waikiki. Located adjacent to the Halepuna hotel lobby, this bakery and restaurant combo offers a wide range of freshly baked breads and gourmet pastries, including fluffy chocolate croissants and fruit tarts. **Known for:** delicious French pastries; innovative restaurant menu; all-day dining. [$] *Average main: $26* ✉ *Halepuna Waikiki by Halekulani, 2233 Helumoa Rd., Waikiki* ☎ *808/921–7272* 🌐 *www.halepuna.com/bakery.*

Hau Tree Lanai

$$$$ | **AMERICAN** | Countless anniversaries, birthdays, and family milestones have been celebrated under this spectacular *hau* tree, where it's said that even Robert Louis Stevenson found shade as he mused and wrote about Hawaii. Still today, diners are captivated by the shade, the beach views, the romantic setting, and a menu that delivers everything from eggs Benedict to a sizzling steak. **Known for:** the romantic beach dining spot folks dream about; spectacular views of the beach and water by day and by night; a solid menu, big portions, and attentive service. [$] *Average main: $48* ✉ *The New Otani Kaimana Beach Hotel, 2863 Kalakaua Ave., Waikiki* ☎ *808/921–7066* 🌐 *www.kaimana.com.*

Hula Grill Waikiki

$$$ | **HAWAIIAN** | The placid younger sister of boisterous Duke's, downstairs, this restaurant and bar resemble an open-air plantation-period summer home with kitschy decor, stone-flagged floors, warm wood, and floral prints. The food is carefully prepared and familiar with a few island-inspired dishes, such as the loco moco and tropical pancakes. **Known for:** spectacular views from the window tables; reliable local dining experience with the kitsch to know you're in Waikiki; nice bar scene for drinks and snacks. [$] *Average main: $28* ✉ *Outrigger Waikiki Beach Resort, 2335 Kalakaua Ave., Waikiki* ☎ *808/923–4852* 🌐 *www.hulagrillwaikiki.com.*

Hy's Steak House

$$$$ | **STEAKHOUSE** | If the Rat Pack reconvened for big steaks and a bigger red, they'd feel right at home at Hy's, which hasn't changed much since it opened in 1976. The formula: prime-grade beef cooked over an open kiawe-wood fire (aka mesquite), old-style service, a clubby atmosphere, and a wine list recognized for excellence by *Wine Spectator.* Aside from the signature steaks, specialties include beef Wellington, miso-marinated

sea bass, and a relatively "new" addition of ahi sashimi fresh from the auction. **Known for:** dark woods, club chairs, banquettes, and that fabulous 1970s feel; a wine list fit for the most persnickety palate; desserts flambéed tableside. [$] *Average main: $60* ✉ *Waikiki Park Heights Hotel, 2440 Kuhio Ave., Waikiki* ☎ *808/922–5555* 🌐 *www.hyshawaii.com* ⏲ *No lunch.*

★ Island Vintage Wine Bar

$$ | WINE BAR | Tucked away on the second floor of the Royal Hawaiian Center is a newly opened Island Vintage Wine Bar (a sister restaurant of the nearby bustling Island Vintage café). Stylish and sleek, this fun, cozy spot offers a selection of over 40 different wines by the glass from across the world. **Known for:** vending-machine style wines by the glass; a subdued happy hour; massive Wagyu burgers. [$] *Average main: $25* ✉ *Royal Hawaiian Center , 2301 Kalakaua Ave., Bldg. C, Level 2, Waikiki* ☎ *808/799–9463* 🌐 *www.islandvintagewinebar.com.*

La Mer

$$$$ | FRENCH | Well-regarded La Mer is one of the most romantic dining spots on Oahu, with spectacular views of Diamond Head. Featuring neoclassical French cuisine, the restaurant remains a popular "special occasion" restaurant, offering three prix-fixe options (with three-, four-, or seven courses). **Known for:** it doesn't get more romantic than this; an impressive wine list and a sommelier to match; a classy bar scene that includes the romance at a less staggering price. [$] *Average main: $160* ✉ *Halekulani Hotel, 2199 Kalia Rd., Waikiki* ☎ *808/923–2311* 🌐 *www.halekulani.com/la-mer-restaurant* ⏲ *No lunch* 👔 *Jacket required.*

Michel's at the Colony Surf

$$$$ | FRENCH | Often called Waikiki's most romantic spot, Michel's is an old-school French favorite on Waikiki's tranquil Gold Coast, where you are paying for the spectacular beachside sunset views in addition to the delicious, classic French fare. It opened in 1962, so the ambience seems somewhat dated, with lots of wood and stone and bow-tied servers preparing things like lobster bisque and steak tartare tableside. **Known for:** the sound of the surf and live music most nights; classic French cuisine with some local twists; a pricy experience and a vibe that steps back in time. [$] *Average main: $55* ✉ *Colony Surf, 2895 Kalakaua Ave., Waikiki* ☎ *808/923–6552* 🌐 *www.michelshawaii.com* ⏲ *No lunch.*

Morimoto Asia Waikiki

$$$$ | JAPANESE FUSION | Locals were surprised when chef Masahara Morimoto vacated the Modern for new digs at the renovated and rebranded Alohilani Resort (formerly the Pacific Beach Hotel), but loyalists have not been disappointed. The sleek space includes an open-air lanai and gorgeous bar, as well as a dining room designed for entertaining clients or celebrating with friends. **Known for:** attentive service and great food; casual elegance in a lovely spot in Waikiki; Asian fusion menu with enough classics to draw loyalists. [$] *Average main: $41* ✉ *Alohilani Resort, 2490 Kalakaua Ave., Waikiki* ☎ *808/922–0022* 🌐 *www.morimotoasiawaikiki.com.*

100 Sails Restaurant & Bar

$$$$ | ECLECTIC | FAMILY | After the top-to-bottom renovations of the Prince Hotel in 2017, the former Prince Court (known for its buffet and views) has become the 100 Sails, featuring a new take with the same commitment to great food and great views. Slightly more casual than its predecessor, the spacious and airy 100 Sails continues the everything-you-can-imagine buffet tradition (with crab legs and prime rib, of course) along with plenty of à la carte "small bites." But the chef never loses focus on locally sourced ingredients and knock-out presentation. **Known for:** international buffet for every meal; views and sunsets to rival any other Waikiki location; high-quality food and a huge selection. [$] *Average main:*

$58 ✉ Hawaii Prince Hotel Waikiki, 100 Holomoana St., Waikiki ☎ 808/944–4494 🌐 www.princewaikiki.com/dining/honolulu-american-restaurant/.

Orchids

$$$$ | SEAFOOD | Perched along the seawall at historic Gray's Beach, Orchids in the luxe Halekulani resort is open all day—it's a locus of power breakfasters, ladies who lunch, celebrating families at the over-the-top Sunday brunch, and the gamut at dinner. The louvered walls are open to the breezes, sprays of orchids add color, the food is perfectly prepared, and the wine list is intriguing. **Known for:** island breezes, ocean sounds, and five-star service and food; lovely ocean views and live music at sunset; a menu with something for just about everyone. *[$] Average main: $42 ✉ Halekulani Hotel, 2199 Kalia Rd., Waikiki ☎ 808/923–2311 🌐 www.halekulani.com/dining/orchids-restaurant.*

Roy's Waikiki

$$$ | HAWAIIAN | FAMILY | Enjoy a taste of modern Hawaiian cuisine from the chef who started it all, Roy Yamaguchi. Situated in the center of Waikiki, the sprawling, stylish restaurant has been serving innovative pan-Asian dishes since 2007 and remains a fan favorite. **Known for:** iconic status among Waikiki restaurants; nightly happy hour on the lanai; lunch served only on the lanai. *[$] Average main: $29 ✉ 226 Lewers St., Waikiki ☎ 808/923–7697 🌐 www.royyamaguchi.com.*

RumFire Waikiki

$$ | ASIAN FUSION | If the perfect sunset happy hour means cocktails, bite-size shareable plates, tropical breezes, ocean sounds, and flaming oversized torches, then "Meet me at Rumfire" should be your calling card. The restaurant launched a new menu in 2020, featuring items such as fresh grilled mahimahi, mole chicken tacos, and "local style" sesame-ahi poke. **Known for:** beachside nightlife scene with great food and cocktails; fabulous location right on the beach; gathering spot for young professionals. *[$] Average main: $25 ✉ Sheraton Waikiki, 2255 Kalakaua Ave., Waikiki ☎ 808/922–4422 🌐 www.rumfirewaikiki.com.*

Pupu 🍴

Entertaining Hawaii-style means having a lot of *pupu*—the local term for appetizers or hors d'oeuvres. Locals eat these small portions of food mostly as they wind down from their workday, relax, and enjoy a couple of drinks. This island-style happy hour is referred to as *pau hana*. Popular pupu include sushi, tempura, teriyaki chicken or beef skewers, barbecued meat, and the favorite: *poke* (pronounced "po-keh"), or raw fish, seasoned with seaweed, shoyu, and other flavorings.

Side Street Inn on Da Strip

$$ | ECLECTIC | FAMILY | The original Hopaka Street pub is famous as the place where celebrity chefs gather after hours; this second location is also popular and situated on bustling Kapahulu Avenue, closer to Waikiki. Local-style bar food—salty panfried pork chops with a plastic tub of ketchup, lup cheong fried rice, and passion fruit–glazed ribs—are served in huge, shareable portions. **Known for:** portions that can seemingly feed you for a week; popular local spot with a crowd of regulars; sports-bar feel with lots of fried food. *[$] Average main: $20 ✉ 614 Kapahulu Ave., Waikiki ☎ 808/739–3939 🌐 www.sidestreetinn.com ⏲ No lunch.*

South Shore Grill

$ | AMERICAN | Just a couple of minutes out of Waikiki on trendy Monsarrat Avenue near the base of Diamond Head, South Shore Grill is an affordable counter-service spot coveted by locals. This place has something for everyone, including fish tacos, Cajun shrimp tacos, salads, and generously sized plate lunches. **Known for:** casual surfer vibe; takeout for the beach; peanut butter temptation for dessert. [$] *Average main: $12* ✉ *3114 Monsarrat Ave., Diamond Head* ☎ *808/734–0229* 🌐 *www.southshoregrill.com.*

Taormina Sicilian Cuisine

$$$$ | **ITALIAN** | Honolulu has its share of Italian restaurants, and Taormina, taking its culinary cues from Sicily, is considered one of the best by foodies, locals, and visitors alike. In a sleek, elegant room (there is outdoor seating, but this is one place it's best to dine indoors), the menu includes clean, well-executed classics, from porcini risotto with sautéed foie gras to a breaded veal chop "*alla Taormina*" (the restaurant's take on veal Parmesan). **Known for:** intimate quiet respite in bustling Waikiki; authentic Sicilian cuisine; extensive wine list. [$] *Average main: $36* ✉ *Waikiki Beach Walk, 227 Lewers St., Waikiki* ☎ *808/926–5050* 🌐 *www.taorminarestaurant.com.*

Teddy's Bigger Burgers

$ | **BURGER** | Modeled after 1950s diners, this local franchise serves classic moist and messy burgers, along with turkey and veggie burgers, as well as salads, and chicken breast and fish sandwiches. The fries are crisply perfect, and the shakes rich and sweet. **Known for:** messy burgers, great fries, and rich milk shakes; diner-style service, with food to go; dependable quick lunch across the island. [$] *Average main: $11* ✉ *Waikiki Grand Hotel, 134 Kapahulu Ave., Waikiki* ☎ *808/926–3444* 🌐 *www.teddysbb.com.*

★ **Tiki's Grill and Bar**

$$$ | **MODERN HAWAIIAN** | Tiki's is the kind of fun place people come to Waikiki for: a retro–South Pacific spot with a back-of-the-bar faux volcano, open-air lounge with live local music, indoor-outdoor dining, and a fantastic view of the beach across the street. Chef Ronnie Nasuti, who for years helmed the Roy's flagship restaurant, a stronghold of Hawaiian regional cuisine, turns out beautifully composed plates and manages to put fresh twists on the super familiar—like lilikoi wasabi-grilled wings, watermelon and feta salad, and Thai-style shrimp puttanesca. **Known for:** surprisingly good food in a made-for-TV setting; Pacific Rim menu inspired by a noted island chef; can get pricey, but a fun experience worthy of a hana hou (encore). [$] *Average main: $27* ✉ *Aston Waikiki Beach Hotel, 2570 Kalakaua Ave., Waikiki* ☎ *808/923–8454* 🌐 *www.tikisgrill.com.*

Top of Waikiki

$$$$ | **MODERN AMERICAN** | Top of Waikiki, which opened in 1965, remains one of the best spots in town to take in Honolulu's stunning panorama. Lance Kosaka, who was executive chef at Alan Wong's Pineapple Room, turns out contemporary American dishes with island flavor, and his menu includes seafood dishes such as garlic shrimp, scallops, and poke—as well as beet, avocado, and goat cheese salad, and a selection of steaks that bring guests back again and again. **Known for:** rotating restaurant views; creative cuisine for varied tastes; nice remodel, but still feels like a mid-century rotating restaurant. [$] *Average main: $40* ✉ *Waikiki Business Plaza, 2270 Kalakaua Ave., Waikiki* ☎ *808/923–3877* 🌐 *www.topofwaikiki.com* 🕒 *No lunch.*

★ **Waikiki Food Hall**

$ | **HAWAIIAN** | **FAMILY** | Opened in early 2020 on the third floor of the Royal Hawaiian Center, the new Waikiki Food Hall is a bright, lively, upscale food court. You can choose from a variety of local and Japanese options here—from massive, juicy burgers to spicy shrimp tacos and exquisitely beautiful smoothies topped with colorful, edible designs. **Known for:** new and modern; a wide selection of upscale options; lots of seating. [$] *Average main: $12* ✉ *Royal Hawaiian Center, 2201 Kalakaua Ave., Bldg. C, 3rd fl., Waikiki* ✥ *Above the Cheesecake Factory* ☎ *808/922–2299 for*

Malasadas 🍴

Malasadas are a contribution of the Portuguese, who came to the Hawaiian Islands to work on the plantations. Roughly translated, the name means "half-cooked," which refers to the origin of these deep-fried, heavily sugared treats said to have been created as a way to use up scraps of rich, buttery egg dough. They are similar to fluffy donuts, and are offered in a multitude of flavors; some are fruit or cream-filled. A handful of bakeries specialize in them: Leonard's (933 Kapahulu Avenue); Kamehameha Bakery (1284 Kalani Street, unit D-106); and Pipeline Bakery (3632 Waialae Avenue). Honolulu restaurants sometimes serve an upscale version stuffed with fruit puree, and they can usually be found at farmers markets, fairs, and carnivals. Eat them fresh and hot or not at all.

Royal Hawaiian Center 🌐 www.waikiki-foodhall.com.

Wolfgang's Steakhouse by Wolfgang Zwiener

$$$$ | **STEAKHOUSE** | Sequestered in the Royal Hawaiian Shopping Center, this open-air New York–style steak house brings loyalists back for beautifully aged steaks, attentive service, and its unique gruff New Yorker attitude. This Honolulu outpost of the NY-based original serves good steaks that have been dry-aged on-site, with classics like shrimp cocktail, slabs of Canadian bacon, crab cakes, creamed spinach, jumbo broiled lobster, and the token grilled fish selection. **Known for:** classic NY steak house vibe, food, and service; great location in the heart of Waikiki; surprisingly varied brunch menu (with a killer Bloody Mary, of course). [$] *Average main: $55 ✉ Royal Hawaiian Center, 2201 Kalakaua Ave., Waikiki ☎ 808/922–3600 🌐 www.wolf-gangssteakhouse.net.*

🛏 Hotels

Hotels in Waikiki range from superluxe resorts to no-frills lodging, the kind of small, beachy places where shirtless surfers hang out in the lobby. It's where the heart of the visitor action is on Oahu. Those traveling with families might want to take into consideration easy access to the beach, restaurants, and other activities, as parking in the area can sometimes be difficult and pricey. Room sizes, styles, and configurations can vary tremendously even in the same hotel, so it's important to ask questions if you have a specific requirement or prefer an ocean view. Some hotels—even if they are not located on the sand—provide beach towels, chairs, and sometimes sunblock for guests, so be sure to inquire about their offerings. For those looking to be slightly removed from the scene, choose accommodations on the *ewa* (western) end of Waikiki.

★ **Alohilani Resort Waikiki Beach**

$$$ | **HOTEL** | Opened in 2018 in the center of Waikiki, the modern, stylish high-rise is across the street from the beach. **Pros:** new and modern; several restaurants in the hotel; great kid's club. **Cons:** resort fee is $45 per day; large hotel and can feel impersonal; you must cross the street for the beach. [$] *Rooms from: $275 ✉ 2490 Kalakaua Ave., Waikiki ☎ 808/922–1233 🌐 www.alohilaniresort.com 🛏 839 rooms 🍴 No meals.*

Aqua Aloha Surf Waikiki

$ | **HOTEL** | This affordable property just two blocks from Waikiki Beach offers

Waikiki and Honolulu, looking west to Diamond Head, as seen from above

surfer-chic accommodations at a decent value. **Pros:** refrigerators in all rooms; pool with sundeck and cabanas; on-site coin-operated laundry. **Cons:** no view; amenity fee of $25 per day; 10-minute walk to beach. [$] *Rooms from: $169* ✉ *444 Kanekapolei St., Waikiki* ☎ *866/970–4160, 808/954–7410* 🌐 *www.aquaaston.com* 🛏 *202 rooms* 🍴 *Free Breakfast.*

Aqua Oasis

$ | **HOTEL** | A trellised open-air lobby of Italian marble, a koi pond, hanging egg chairs, and a guava smoothie greet you on arrival at this Lewers Street hideaway, about a five-minute stroll from Kalakaua Avenue and through one of the many public-access ways to the beach. **Pros:** all rooms have lanai; on-site coin-operated laundry; karaoke lounge adjacent to lobby. **Cons:** rooms are slightly dated; valet parking only; $25 per night resort fee. [$] *Rooms from: $129* ✉ *320 Lewers St., Waikiki* ☎ *808/923–2300, 866/767–4528, 808/441–7781* 🌐 *www.aquaaston.com* 🛏 *96 rooms* 🍴 *Free Breakfast.*

Aqua Palms Waikiki

$ | **HOTEL** | Across from the Hilton Hawaiian Village on Ala Moana Boulevard, just as it curves toward Waikiki's Kalakaua Avenue, the 12-story Aqua Palms offers studio and one-bedroom-suite accommodations. **Pros:** full kitchens in suites; location is easily walkable to park, beach, convention center, and activities; hotel shuttle to shopping and throughout Waikiki. **Cons:** closest beach access is through the Hilton Hawaiian Village, across the street; resort fee is $25 per day; not all rooms have lanai. [$] *Rooms from: $129* ✉ *1850 Ala Moana Blvd., Waikiki* ☎ *808/954–7424 reservations local number, 866/970–4165 reservations toll-free, 808/947–7256 direct to hotel's front desk* 🌐 *www.aquaaston.com/hotels/aqua-palms-waikiki* 🛏 *263 rooms* 🍴 *No meals.*

Aston at the Waikiki Banyan

$$ | **RENTAL** | **FAMILY** | Families and active travelers love the convenience and action of this hotel, just a block from Waikiki Beach, the aquarium, the zoo, and

bustling Kalakaua Avenue. **Pros:** many rooms have great views with kitchens; walking distance to shops, beach, restaurants, and activities; fabulous and massive recreation deck for the entire family. **Cons:** rooms are individually owned so conditions can vary greatly; resort fee is $25 per day; sharing hotel with residents. [$] *Rooms from: $200* ✉ *201 Ohua Ave., Waikiki* ☎ *808/922–0555, 877/997–6667 toll-free for reservations* 🌐 *www.astonwaikikibanyan.com* 🛏 *876 suites* 🍴 *No meals.*

Aston Waikiki Beach Hotel

$$ | HOTEL | FAMILY | A good choice for families, this large high-rise hotel is directly across the street from a protected stretch of Kuhio Beach and near Kapiolani Park. **Pros:** fun for families; great beach access; new "coconut club" lounge access for certain rooms/packages. **Cons:** active lobby area and crowded elevators; resort fee of $35 per day; no longer offers free breakfast to all guests. [$] *Rooms from: $249* ✉ *2570 Kalakaua Ave., Waikiki* ☎ *808/922–2511 direct to hotel, 877/997–6667 reservations toll-free, 800/877–7666 reservations toll-free* 🌐 *www.astonwaikikibeach.com* 🛏 *645 rooms* 🍴 *No meals.*

Aston Waikiki Beach Tower

$$$$ | RENTAL | FAMILY | You'll find the elegance of a luxury all-suites condominium combined with the intimacy and service of a boutique hotel in the center of Waikiki. **Pros:** roomy suites with quality amenities; great private lanai and views; a recreation deck with something for everyone. **Cons:** no on-site restaurants; you must cross a busy street to the beach; space, amenities, and location don't come cheap. [$] *Rooms from: $699* ✉ *2470 Kalakaua Ave., Waikiki* ☎ *808/926–6400, 855/776–1766 toll-free* 🌐 *www.astonwaikikibeachtower.com* 🛏 *140 suites* 🍴 *No meals.*

Aston Waikiki Circle Hotel

$$ | HOTEL | This unusual, 14-story, circular hotel—built to resemble a Chinese lantern—is a Waikiki landmark, though the rooms are small, with tiny bathrooms that have only showers. **Pros:** unbeatable location and views; on-site surfboard lockers and complimentary beach gear; Eggs 'N Things, a local icon, is right downstairs. **Cons:** small rooms; showers only; interior design, though charming to some, may feel dated to others; resort fee is $25 per day. [$] *Rooms from: $200* ✉ *2464 Kalakaua Ave., Waikiki* ☎ *808/923–1571, 877/997–6667 toll-free for reservations* 🌐 *www.astonwaikikicircle.com* 🛏 *104 rooms* 🍴 *No meals.*

The Breakers Hotel

$ | RENTAL | Despite an explosion of high-rise construction all around it, the Breakers continues to transport guests back to 1960s-era Hawaii in this small, low-rise complex about two blocks from the beach. **Pros:** intimate atmosphere with fabulous poolside courtyard; great location; a throwback to a different era. **Cons:** a bit worn down and dated; parking space is extremely limited (but free); showers only. [$] *Rooms from: $170* ✉ *250 Beach Walk, Waikiki* ☎ *808/923–3181, 800/923–7174 toll-free* 🌐 *www.breakers-hawaii.com* 🛏 *63 rooms* 🍴 *No meals.*

Coconut Waikiki Hotel

$ | HOTEL | FAMILY | Overlooking the Ala Wai Canal, this reasonably priced boutique hotel has a more residential feel than a typical resort, with a cobblestone driveway, a lobby with rattan living room–style furnishings, a small fitness center, and a tiny swimming pool tucked in a backyard. **Pros:** no resort fee; free Wi-Fi throughout hotel; on-site coin-operated laundry. **Cons:** three blocks to the beach on a busy street can be tiring; only valet parking available; area is more residential and can be a long way from the action, particularly at night. [$] *Rooms from: $149* ✉ *450 Lewers St., Waikiki* ☎ *866/974–2626 toll-free, 808/923–8828* 🌐 *www.coconutwaikikihotel.com* 🛏 *81 rooms* 🍴 *Free Breakfast.*

Doubletree by Hilton Alana - Waikiki Beach

$$ | HOTEL | A convenient location—10 minutes' walk from the Hawaii Convention Center—a professional staff, pleasant public spaces, and a 24-hour business center and small gym draw a global business clientele to this reliable chain hotel. **Pros:** walkable to the beach and Ala Moana mall; walk-in glass showers with oversize rain showerheads; heated outdoor pool and 24-hour fitness center. **Cons:** a 10-minute walk to the beach; little local flavor; resort fee is $30 per day. $ *Rooms from: $230* ⊠ *1956 Ala Moana Blvd., Waikiki* ☎ *808/941–7275* ⊕ *www.hilton.com* ↷ *317 rooms* ⦿ *No meals.*

Embassy Suites by Hilton Waikiki Beach Walk

$$$ | RESORT | FAMILY | In a place where space is at a premium, this all-suites resort offers families and groups traveling together a bit more room to move about, with two 21-story towers housing one- and two-bedroom suites. **Pros:** no resort fee; spacious and modern rooms; complimentary hot breakfast and evening reception daily. **Cons:** no direct beach access; lobby feels more like a business hotel; property can seem busy and noisy. $ *Rooms from: $319* ⊠ *201 Beachwalk St., Waikiki* ☎ *800/362–2779 toll-free, 808/921–2345 direct to hotel* ⊕ *www.embassysuiteswaikiki.com* ↷ *369 suites* ⦿ *Free Breakfast.*

The Equus

$ | HOTEL | FAMILY | This small, boutique hotel has been completely renovated with a Hawaiian country theme that pays tribute to Hawaii's polo-playing history. **Pros:** casual and fun atmosphere; attentive staff; nicely furnished rooms. **Cons:** busy, hectic area; must cross a major road to get to the beach; resort fee is $25 a day. $ *Rooms from: $160* ⊠ *1696 Ala Moana Blvd., Waikiki* ☎ *808/949–0061* ⊕ *www.equushotel.com* ↷ *67 rooms* ⦿ *No meals.*

Espacio the Jewel of Waikiki

$$$$ | HOTEL | With the tag-line "The Jewel of Waikiki," the hotel, which opened in 2019, is perhaps the most luxurious hotel experience in Hawaii, best compared to a private, posh beachfront retreat with customizable offerings. **Pros:** incredible ocean views; height of opulence and luxury; highest level of service. **Cons:** swimming pool is shared and on small side; pricey; across the street from the beach. $ *Rooms from: $3000* ⊠ *2452 Kalakaua Ave., Waikiki* ☎ *855/945–4089 toll-free, 808/377–2246 direct to hotel* ⊕ *www.espaciowaikiki.com* ↷ *9 rooms* ⦿ *Free Breakfast.*

★ Halekulani Hotel

$$$$ | RESORT | The luxurious Halekulani exemplifies the translation of its name— the "house befitting heaven"—and from the moment you step into the lobby, the attention to detail and impeccable service wrap you in privilege at this prime beachfront location away from Waikiki's bustle. **Pros:** heavenly interior and exterior spaces; wonderful dining opportunities in-house; no resort fee. **Cons:** might feel a bit formal for Waikiki; pricey; beachfront here is narrow, with little room for sunbathing. $ *Rooms from: $500* ⊠ *2199 Kalia Rd., Waikiki* ☎ *808/923–2311 direct to hotel, 800/367–2343 reservations toll-free* ⊕ *www.halekulani.com* ↷ *453 rooms* ⦿ *No meals.*

★ Halepuna Waikiki by Halekulani

$$$$ | HOTEL | Completely renovated and given a new name in late 2019, the former Waikiki Parc makes a contemporary statement, offering the same attention to detail in service and architectural design as its elegant sister hotel, the Halekulani, but without the beachfront location and higher prices. **Pros:** modern, new, and well-appointed; great access to Waikiki Beach and Beach Walk shopping and dining; no resort fee. **Cons:** no direct beach access; rooms can be small; swimming pool can get busy during prime time. $ *Rooms from: $366* ⊠ *2233 Helumoa*

Rd., Waikiki ☎ 808/921–7272 direct to hotel, 800/422–0450 reservations toll-free ⊕ www.halepuna.com ⤴ 297 rooms ⍟ No meals.

Hilton Garden Inn Waikiki Beach

$$ | HOTEL | FAMILY | Opened in 2016 in the heart of Waikiki, this midrange chain hotel was one of the first resorts to enhance a formerly gritty stretch of Kuhio Avenue. **Pros:** newer hotel; central location near International Market Place, shopping, and dining; moderately priced and no resort fee. **Cons:** the large resort can feel impersonal; valet-only parking; two-block walk to the beach. $ *Rooms from: $189* ✉ *2330 Kuhio Ave., Waikiki* ☎ *808/892–1820* ⊕ *www.hiltongarden-inn.com* ⤴ *623 rooms* ⍟ *No meals.*

Hilton Hawaiian Village Beach Resort

$$$ | RESORT | FAMILY | Location, location, location: this mega resort and convention destination sprawls over 22 acres on Waikiki's widest stretch of beach, with the green lawns of neighboring Fort DeRussy creating a buffer zone to the high-rise lineup of central Waikiki. **Pros:** activities and amenities can keep you and the kids busy for weeks; stellar spa; Friday-night fireworks. **Cons:** size of property can be overwhelming; resort fee is $50 per day; parking is expensive ($43 per day for self-parking). $ *Rooms from: $310* ✉ *2005 Kalia Rd., Waikiki* ☎ *808/949–4321, 800/774–1500 toll-free* ⊕ *www.hiltonhawaiianvillage.com* ⤴ *4499 rooms* ⍟ *No meals.*

Hilton Waikiki Beach

$$ | HOTEL | Two blocks from Kuhio Beach, this 37-story high-rise, located on the Diamond Head end of Waikiki, is great for travelers who want to be near the action, but not right in it. **Pros:** central location; helpful staff; pleasant, comfortable public spaces. **Cons:** resort fee is $30 per day; very few rooms have views; older property that shows some wear. $ *Rooms from: $219* ✉ *2500 Kuhio Ave., Waikiki* ☎ *808/922–0811 direct to*

hotel, 888/370–0980 toll-free ⊕ www.hiltonwaikikibeach.com ⤴ 609 rooms ⍟ No meals.

★ Holiday Inn Express Waikiki

$ | HOTEL | Budget-friendly with a number of unexpected perks, this 44-story chain hotel opened in 2017 after a major renovation. **Pros:** free breakfast with large selection; modern conveniences abound; select rooms have great views. **Cons:** resort fee is $25 per day; busy hotel and lobby can feel crowded; three-block walk to beach. $ *Rooms from: $179* ✉ *2058 Kuhio Ave., Waikiki* ☎ *877/859–5095 toll-free for reservations, 808/947–2828 direct to hotel* ⊕ *www.ihg.com* ⤴ *596 rooms* ⍟ *Free Breakfast.*

Hotel Renew

$ | HOTEL | Located a block from world-famous Waikiki Beach, this stylish boutique hotel is fresh from a 2019 redesign and is focused on wellness and renewal, a chic change from the big resorts that dominate the oceanfront here. **Pros:** free beach supplies, including towels, chairs, umbrellas, and snorkel gear; personalized, upscale service; close to zoo, aquarium, and beach. **Cons:** no pool; daily amenity fee of $25; rooms are on the small side. $ *Rooms from: $159* ✉ *129 Paoakalani Ave., Waikiki* ☎ *808/687–7700, 877/997–6667 toll-free* ⊕ *www.hotelrenew.com* ⤴ *72 rooms* ⍟ *No meals.*

Hyatt Centric Waikiki Beach

$$ | HOTEL | Modern and stylish, the Hyatt Centric is one of the newer hotels in Waikiki, with a friendly staff and seven different room sizes and configurations that might remind guests of a "mini" Andaz. **Pros:** new and modern; spacious rooms and bathrooms; lovely pool deck. **Cons:** resort fee is $33 per day; rooms don't have lanai; not on the beach. $ *Rooms from: $199* ✉ *349 Seaside Ave., Waikiki* ☎ *808/237–1234* ⊕ *www.hyatt.com* ⤴ *230 rooms* ⍟ *No meals.*

Hyatt Regency Waikiki Resort & Spa
$$$ | **RESORT** | **FAMILY** | This large high-rise hotel, where the lively atrium-style lobby is the focal point, is across the street from Kuhio Beach, but there's no resort between it and the Pacific Ocean. **Pros:** public spaces are open; elegant and very professional spa; kid-friendly and close to the beach. **Cons:** in a very busy and crowded part of Waikiki; on-site pool is quite small; resort fee is $45 per day. [$] *Rooms from: $300* ✉ *2424 Kalakaua Ave., Waikiki* ☎ *808/923–1234 direct to hotel, 800/633–7313 toll-free for reservations* 🌐 *www.hyattregencywaikiki.com* 🛏 *1230 rooms* 🍴 *No meals.*

Ilikai Hotel & Luxury Suites
$$$ | **RESORT** | **FAMILY** | At the *ewa* (western) edge of Waikiki overlooking the Ala Wai Small Boat Harbor, this iconic high-rise resort stands at the entrance to Waikiki and is a Honolulu landmark. **Pros:** views of sunset from most rooms on the ewa side; western edge of Waikiki keeps you out of the chaos while still close to everything; Wi-Fi throughout the property. **Cons:** resort fee is $25 per day; five-minute walk to the beach; despite renovations, it still shows its age. [$] *Rooms from: $300* ✉ *1777 Ala Moana Blvd., Waikiki* ☎ *808/954–7417, 866/536–7973 toll-free* 🌐 *www.ilikaihotel.com* 🛏 *779 rooms* 🍴 *No meals.*

Ilima Hotel
$ | **RENTAL** | Tucked away on a residential side street near Waikiki's Ala Wai Canal, this locally owned, 17-story, condominium-style hotel is a throwback to old Waikiki, offering large units that are ideal for families. **Pros:** free parking in Waikiki is a rarity; great value; free Wi-Fi. **Cons:** furnishings are dated; resort fee is $20 per day; no ocean views. [$] *Rooms from: $160* ✉ *445 Nohonani St., Waikiki* ☎ *808/923–1877, 800/801–9366* 🌐 *www.ilima.com* 🛏 *98 units* 🍴 *No meals.*

Luana Waikiki Hotel & Suites
$$ | **HOTEL** | **FAMILY** | At the entrance to Waikiki near Fort DeRussy is this welcoming hotel offering both rooms and condominium units, all with private lanai. **Pros:** coin-operated laundry facilities on-site; sundeck with barbecue grills; free yoga and folding bicycles. **Cons:** no direct beach access; resort fee is $25 per day; pool is small. [$] *Rooms from: $199* ✉ *2045 Kalakaua Ave., Waikiki* ☎ *808/955–6000 direct to hotel, 855/747-0755 toll-free* 🌐 *www.aquaaston.com* 🛏 *225 units* 🍴 *No meals.*

Moana Surfrider, A Westin Resort & Spa, Waikiki Beach
$$$$ | **RESORT** | This historic beauty—the oldest hotel in Waikiki—is still a wedding and honeymoon favorite, with a sweeping main staircase and Victorian furnishings in its historic (and expensive) Moana Wing; rooms in the 1950s-era Diamond Head Tower and Surfrider tower are more contemporary. **Pros:** elegant, historic property; best place on Waikiki Beach to watch hula and have a drink; can't beat the location. **Cons:** you'll likely dodge bridal parties in the lobby; resort fee is $37 per day; expensive parking ($35/day for self-parking across the street). [$] *Rooms from: $479* ✉ *2365 Kalakaua Ave., Waikiki* ☎ *808/922–3111, 866/716–8112 toll-free* 🌐 *www.moana-surfrider.com* 🛏 *791 rooms* 🍴 *No meals.*

Ohana Waikiki East by Outrigger
$$ | **HOTEL** | If you want to be in central Waikiki and don't want to pay beachfront lodging prices, consider the Ohana Waikiki East. **Pros:** close to the beach and reasonable rates; decent on-site eateries, including a piano bar; in the middle of the Waikiki action. **Cons:** some rooms with no lanai and very basic public spaces; an older property with signs of wear and tear; resort fee is $22 per day. [$] *Rooms from: $229* ✉ *150 Kaiulani Ave., Waikiki* ☎ *808/922–5353 direct to hotel, 866/956–4262 toll-free* 🌐 *www.ohanahotelsoahu.com* 🛏 *441 rooms* 🍴 *No meals.*

Ohana Waikiki Malia by Outrigger

$$ | HOTEL | Close to the *ewa* (western) end of Waikiki, this older hotel comprises a pair of buildings, one with standard rooms, the other with one-bedroom suites that have kitchenettes. **Pros:** central to shopping and dining in Waikiki; on-site coin-operated laundry facilities; good value for the basics. **Cons:** no views and small pool; dated property that shows; resort fee of $22 per day. [$] *Rooms from: $205* ⊠ *2211 Kuhio Ave., Waikiki* ☎ *808/923–7621 direct to hotel, 866/956–4262 toll-free* ⊕ *www. ohanahotelsoahu.com* ⤳ *332 rooms* |◎| *No meals.*

Outrigger Reef Waikiki Beach Resort

$$$ | HOTEL | FAMILY | With a prime oceanfront location, the Outrigger Reef offers an updated experience with an abundance of island flavor. **Pros:** on the beach; direct access to Waikiki Beach Walk; attentive staff. **Cons:** room decor is dated; views from nonoceanfront rooms are uninspiring; resort fee is $35 per day. [$] *Rooms from: $340* ⊠ *2169 Kalia Rd., Waikiki* ☎ *808/923–3111 direct to hotel, 866/956–4262 toll-free, 800/688–7444* ⊕ *www.outriggerreef-onthebeach.com* ⤳ *669 rooms* |◎| *No meals.*

Outrigger Waikiki Beach Resort

$$$$ | RESORT | FAMILY | Outrigger's star property sits on one of the finest sections of Waikiki Beach and is a visitor favorite for its array of cultural activities, live music, dining options, and bar scene. **Pros:** the best beach bar in Waikiki; shopping, activities, and services abound on the property; on-site coin-operated laundry. **Cons:** a busy property—many people use it as a throughway to the beach; resort fee is $35 per day; rooms are dated. [$] *Rooms from: $450* ⊠ *2335 Kalakaua Ave., Waikiki* ☎ *808/923–0711, 808/956–4262, 800/442–7304 toll-free* ⊕ *www.outriggerwaikikihotel.com* ⤳ *525 rooms* |◎| *No meals.*

Hotel Cultural Programs 🛏

Hotels, especially in Waikiki, are fueling a resurgence in Hawaiian culture, thanks to repeat visitors who want a more authentic island experience. In addition to lei-making and hula-dancing lessons, you can learn how to strum a ukulele, listen to Grammy Award–winning Hawaiian musicians, watch a revered master *kumu* (teacher) share the art of ancient hula and chant, chat with a marine biologist about Hawaii's endangered species, learn about the island's sustainability efforts, or get a lesson in the art of canoe making.

Pacific Monarch Hotel

$$ | RENTAL | FAMILY | One block from the western end of Waikiki Beach, this 34-story high-rise condominium resort has a rooftop deck—with a freshwater pool, hot tub, and sauna—with sweeping views of Waikiki and the Pacific Ocean. **Pros:** fantastic view from rooftop pool; hospitality lounge; all rooms have lanai and views. **Cons:** stairs to the pool deck are fairly steep, dark, and may be difficult for some; resort fee is $25 per day; older property with the wear to show for it. [$] *Rooms from: $183* ⊠ *2427 Kuhio Ave., Waikiki* ☎ *808/923–9805* ⊕ *www. pacificmonarch.com* ⤳ *216 rooms* |◎| *No meals.*

Prince Waikiki

$$$$ | HOTEL | This slim, renovated high-rise offers luxury oceanfront rooms and suites overlooking the Ala Wai Yacht Harbor at the *ewa* (western) edge of Waikiki. **Pros:** fantastic views from all rooms; no resort fee; parking included. **Cons:** busy property; no beach access; rooms don't have lanai. [$] *Rooms from: $400* ⊠ *100 Holomoana St., Waikiki* ☎ *888/977–4623*

toll-free for reservations, 808/956–1111 direct to hotel ⊕ www.princewaikiki.com ⌐ 563 rooms ⏐◯⏐ No meals.

Queen Kapiolani Hotel

$$$ | HOTEL | After a multimillion-dollar renovation in 2018, the Queen Kapiolani Hotel reopened with a contemporary look combined with a retro nod the 1970s. **Pros:** incredible Diamond Head views; renovated in 2018; beach gear available at valet desk. **Cons:** resort fee is $40 per day; bathrooms are small and dated despite renovation; noise from pool bar can be bothersome. $ Rooms from: $280 ⊠ 150 Kapahulu Ave., Waikiki ☎ 808/650–7841 ⊕ www.queenkapiolani. com ⌐ 315 rooms ⏐◯⏐ No meals.

The Ritz-Carlton Residences, Waikiki Beach

$$$$ | HOTEL | Ritz-Carlton Residences, Waikiki Beach (the only Ritz-Carlton on Oahu) welcomes well-heeled guests from across the globe with its signature elegance and impeccable service. **Pros:** very private; luxuriously appointed apartments; pampering service. **Cons:** not close to the beach; pricey, particularly given distance from beach; families can sometimes overrun the facilities. $ Rooms from: $669 ⊠ 383 Kalaimoku St., Waikiki ☎ 808/922–8111 ⊕ www. ritzcarlton.com ⌐ 552 units ⏐◯⏐ No meals.

Royal Grove Hotel

$ | HOTEL | Two generations of the Fong family have put their heart and soul into the operation of this tiny (by Waikiki standards), pink, six-story, hotel that feels like a throwback to the days of boarding houses—an era in which rooms were outfitted for function, not style, and served up with a wealth of simple hospitality at a price that didn't break the bank. **Pros:** very economical Waikiki option; no resort fee; a throwback to another era. **Cons:** no air-conditioning in some rooms; rooms and property are very dated; no on-site parking. $ Rooms from: $150 ⊠ 151 Uluniu Ave., Waikiki ☎ 808/923–7691 ⊕ www.royalgrovehotel. com ⌐ 87 rooms ⏐◯⏐ No meals.

Looking for a Private Beach? 🛎

Oahu's oldest hotels—the Royal Hawaiian Hotel and Moana Surfrider—are also the only hotels in Waikiki with property lines that extend into the sand. They have created private roped-off beach areas with lounge chairs and umbrellas that can be accessed only by hotel guests. The areas are adjacent to the hotel properties at the top of the beach.

★ The Royal Hawaiian, a Luxury Collection Resort, Waikiki

$$$$ | RESORT | There's nothing like the iconic "Pink Palace of the Pacific," which is on 14 acres of prime Waikiki Beach and which has held fast to the luxury and grandeur that first defined it in the 1930s, when it became a favorite of the rich and famous. **Pros:** can't beat it for history; mai tais and sunsets are amazing; luxury in a prime location. **Cons:** resort fee is $38 per day; you'd better like pink; be prepared to share the luxury with brides and galas. $ Rooms from: $500 ⊠ 2259 Kalakaua Ave., Waikiki ☎ 808/923–7311, 866/716–8110 toll-free ⊕ www.royal-hawaiian.com ⌐ 528 rooms ⏐◯⏐ No meals.

Sheraton Princess Kaiulani

$$$ | HOTEL | FAMILY | The Princess Kaiulani sits across the street from the regal Moana Surfrider, without some of the more elaborate amenities (such as a spa or a kid's club), but with rates that are considerably kinder to the wallet. **Pros:** in the heart of everything in Waikiki, with the beach right across the street; beach service with chairs, towels, fruit, and water available; great value for the location. **Cons:** lobby area can feel like Grand Central Station; pool closes at 7 pm; resort fee $33 per day. $ Rooms from: $289 ⊠ 120 Kaiulani Ave., Waikiki

☎ 808/922–5811, 866/716–8109 toll-free ⊕ www.princess-kaiulani.com ➷ 1040 rooms ⦿ No meals.

Sheraton Waikiki

$$$$ | HOTEL | FAMILY | If you don't mind crowds, this enormous hotel that towers over its neighbors on Waikiki could be the place for you. **Pros:** location in the heart of everything; variety of on-site activities and dining options; swimming pools often ranked among the Islands' best. **Cons:** busy atmosphere clashes with laid-back Hawaiian style; resort fee is $35 per day; room sizes and views vary. Ⓢ *Rooms from: $409 ✉ 2255 Kalakaua Ave., Waikiki ☎ 808/922–4422, 866/716–8109 toll-free for reservations ⊕ www.sheraton-waikiki. com ➷ 1636 rooms* ⦿ No meals.

Shoreline Hotel Waikiki

$$ | HOTEL | Situated right on the bustling Seaside Avenue in Waikiki, this 14-story, 1970s-era, modernist boutique hotel is another old dame that's been brought back to life as an urban-chic property. **Pros:** great location in the middle of bustling Waikiki; no resort fee; hipster decor a refreshing break from old-style Hawaiiana. **Cons:** if splashy colors everywhere aren't your thing, skip it; rooms are small and inconsistent, so ask about the details; pool very small. Ⓢ *Rooms from: $250 ✉ 342 Seaside Ave., Waikiki ☎ 808/931–2444, 855/931–2444 toll-free ⊕ www.shorelinehotelwaikiki.com ➷ 135 rooms* ⦿ No meals.

The Surfjack Hotel & Swim Club

$$$ | HOTEL | Numerous Waikiki properties have transformed their mid-century digs into hip, 21st-century style, but none has done it as well as this 1960s-inspired boutique hotel with a surfing vibe. **Pros:** hipster, urban-chic vibe that works; retro, locally designed decor; Ed Kenney restaurant on-site. **Cons:** resort fee is $25 per day; far from the beach; rooms can be inconsistent. Ⓢ *Rooms from: $290 ✉ 412 Lewers St., Waikiki ☎ 808/923–8882 ⊕ www.surfjack.com ➷ 112 rooms* ⦿ No meals.

Trump International Hotel Waikiki Beach Walk

$$$$ | HOTEL | FAMILY | An upscale high-rise property, the Trump hotel has been drawing visitors since it opened in late 2009; the style of over-the-top luxury offered here may not be to all tastes, but based on the reviews of enthusiastic returning guests, the hotel delivers. **Pros:** no resort fee; on the edge of Waikiki so a bit quieter; great views of Friday fireworks and nightly sunsets. **Cons:** must cross street to reach the beach; you may encounter political protestors outside at times; small pool often filled with kids. Ⓢ *Rooms from: $550 ✉ 223 Saratoga Rd., Waikiki ☎ 808/683–7777, 877/683–7401 toll-free ⊕ www.trumphotelcollection.com ➷ 462 rooms* ⦿ No meals.

Waikiki Beach Marriott Resort & Spa

$$$$ | RESORT | FAMILY | On the eastern edge of Waikiki, this flagship Marriott sits on about five acres across from Kuhio Beach and close to Kapiolani Park, the Honolulu Zoo, and the Waikiki Aquarium. **Pros:** stunning views of Waikiki; airy, tropical public spaces; unbeatable location. **Cons:** large impersonal hotel, sometimes confusing to navigate; Kalakaua Avenue can be noisy; resort fee is $37 per day. Ⓢ *Rooms from: $350 ✉ 2552 Kalakaua Ave., Waikiki ☎ 808/922–6611, 800/367–5370 toll-free ⊕ www.marriottwaikiki. com ➷ 1310 rooms* ⦿ No meals.

Waikiki Beachcomber by Outrigger

$$ | HOTEL | FAMILY | Located almost directly across from the Royal Hawaiian Center and next door to the new and revamped International Market Place, the Beachcomber is a well-situated high-rise hotel for families as well as those looking for a boutique feel in the heart of the action. **Pros:** great beach views from some rooms; renovated and stylish; lovely pool area. **Cons:** very busy area in the thick of Waikiki action; not beachfront; resort fee is $30 per day. Ⓢ *Rooms from: $260 ✉ 2300 Kalakaua Ave., Waikiki ☎ 808/922–4646, 877/418–0711 ⊕ www.*

waikikibeachcomber.com ⤳ 496 rooms ⫶◯⫶ No meals.

Waikiki Sand Villa Hotel

$ | HOTEL | FAMILY | Families and those looking for an economical rate without sacrificing proximity to Waikiki's beaches, dining, and shopping return to the Waikiki Sand Villa year after year. **Pros:** fun bar; pool and foot spa great for lounging; no resort fee. **Cons:** the noise from the bar might annoy some; 10-minute walk to the beach; street noise from Ala Wai can get loud. $ Rooms from: $165 ⊠ 2375 Ala Wai Blvd., Waikiki ☎ 808/922–4744, 800/247–1903 toll-free ⊕ www.sandvilla-hotel.com ⤳ 214 rooms ⫶◯⫶ No meals.

Waikiki Shore

$$ | RENTAL | FAMILY | Nestled between Fort DeRussy Beach Park and the Outrigger Reef Resort, this is the only condo hotel directly on Waikiki Beach. **Pros:** right on the beach; great views from spacious private lanai; units available in different sizes. **Cons:** units can vary and some are dated; extra cleaning fee can be expensive; two management companies rent here, so ask questions when booking. $ Rooms from: $230 ⊠ 2161 Kalia Rd., Waikiki ☎ 808/952–4500 Castle reservations, 808/922–3871 Outrigger reservations local, 800/688–7444 Outrigger reservations toll-free ⊕ www.castleresorts.com ⤳ 168 suites ⫶◯⫶ No meals.

🍸 Nightlife

BARS

★ Duke's Waikiki

BARS/PUBS | Making the most of its spot on Waikiki Beach, Duke's is a bustling destination featuring live music everyday. This laid-back bar-and-grill's surf theme pays homage to Duke Kahanamoku, who popularized the sport in the early 1900s. Contemporary Hawaiian musicians like Henry Kapono and Maunalua have performed here, as have nationally known musicians like Jimmy Buffett. It's not unusual for surfers to leave their boards

🛏 Condo Comforts

The local **Foodland** grocery-store chain has two locations near Waikiki, one in Market City in Kaimuki (⊠ 2939 Harding Ave., near intersection with Kapahulu Ave. and highway overpass, ☎ 808/734–6303, and the other in the Ala Moana Center (⊠ 1450 Ala Moana Blvd., ☎ 808/949–5044). A number of smaller convenience stores are in the middle of Waikiki, including **Coco Cove** (⊠ 2284 Kalakaua Ave., ☎ 808/924-6677) also has fresh poke, apparel, beach stuff, and tourist-oriented items.

outside to step in for a casual drink after a long day on the waves. The cocktail menu is filled with island-style drinks: try a sunset sour or coconut mojito while watching the Waikiki waves. ⊠ Outrigger Waikiki, 2335 Kalakaua Ave., Suite 116, Waikiki ☎ 808/922–2268 ⊕ www.dukeswaikiki.com.

Genius Lounge Sake Bar & Grill

BARS/PUBS | Removed from the tourist traps along Kalakaua Avenue, the Genius Lounge is tucked away on the third floor of a former apartment building on Lewers Street. The extensive drink menu offers beer and wine, cocktails, house-made sangria, and, of course, sake. Locally inspired dishes are also available. Though small, the space is open to the outdoors and furnished with dark woods and lit by candles, making for an intimate setting for small gatherings and Friday-night dates. The crowd is mostly Asian visitors and transplants, but a daily happy hour (6–8 pm) lures office workers and pre-club prowlers. ⊠ 346 Lewers St., 3rd fl., Waikiki ☎ 808/626–5362 ⊕ www.geniusloungehawaii.com.

Hideout

BARS/PUBS | The Hideout is a mini-oasis on the outdoor lobby level of the Laylow Hotel, one of Waikiki's newer hotels. Technically, it's not a rooftop bar, but with a fire pit (surrounded by sand), tiki torches, comfy couches, and palm trees swaying overhead, it certainly exudes rooftop vibes. The Hideout has a full menu, but it's best to come here for some pre- or postdinner drinks and pupu (a few favorites are poke tacos and pork belly Brussels sprouts). And with a daily happy hour from 4:30 to 6:30 pm, it's easier on your wallet, too. Get the Lime in the Coconut, made with Old Lahaina rum, lime, coconut, and mango boba at the bottom of the martini glass. ⊠ *Laylow Hotel, 2299 Kuhio Ave., Waikiki* ☎ *808/628–3060* ⊕ *www.hideoutwaikiki. com.*

★ Lewers Lounge

BARS/PUBS | A great spot for predinner drinks or postsunset cocktails, Lewers Lounge offers a relaxed but chic atmosphere in the middle of Waikiki. The menu features a selection of classic and contemporary cocktails. Some standouts include Chocolate Dreams (made with Van Gogh Dutch Chocolate Vodka) and the Lost Passion (featuring a rich blend of tequila, Cointreau, and fresh juices topped with champagne). Enjoy your libation with great nightly live jazz and tempting desserts, such as the hotel's famous coconut cake. Or just sit back and relax in the grand setting of the luxurious lounge, which is decked in dramatic drapes and cozy banquettes. ⊠ *Halekulani Hotel, 2199 Kalia Rd., Waikiki* ☎ *808/923–2311* ⊕ *www.halekulani.com.*

Lulu's Waikiki

BARS/PUBS | Even if you're not a surfer, you'll love this place's retro vibe and the unobstructed second-floor view of Waikiki Beach. The open-air setting, casual dining menu, and tropical drinks are all you need to help you settle into your vacation. The venue transforms from a nice spot for breakfast, lunch, or dinner (happy hour is 3 to 5 pm) to a bustling, high-energy club with live music lasting into the wee hours. ⊠ *Park Shore Waikiki Hotel, 2586 Kalakaua Ave., Waikiki* ☎ *808/926–5222* ⊕ *www.luluswaikiki.com.*

★ Mai Tai Bar at the Royal Hawaiian

BARS/PUBS | The bartenders here sure know how to mix up a killer mai tai. This is, after all, *the* establishment that first made the famous drink in the Islands. The pink umbrella-shaded tables at the outdoor bar are front-row seating for sunsets and also have an unobstructed view of Diamond Head. It's an ideal spot to soak in the island vibes just steps from the sand. Contemporary Hawaiian musicians hold jam sessions onstage nightly. ⊠ *Royal Hawaiian Hotel, 2259 Kalakaua Ave., Waikiki* ☎ *808/923–7311* ⊕ *www.royal-hawaiian.com.*

★ Maui Brewing Co

BREWPUBS/BEER GARDENS | Maui Brewing Co. has been a longtime Hawaii craft beer favorite. And while you can get the Lahaina-made beer in local grocery stores and restaurants, it's best to head straight to the source. Thankfully, you don't have to island-hop since the brewery opened a brewpub in Waikiki. (Even better—Maui Brewing now has a second Oahu location in Kailua.) Ask the staff about Maui Brewing's limited-release drafts, to imbibe the brand's hidden gems, or order a flight to taste a few freshly brewed beers. Maui Brewing strives to source local ingredients for its beer and food, so it's likely what you order was grown and harvested here. There's a big food selection here, too: the poke bowl with locally caught tuna, kale salad with Waianae-based Naked Cow Dairy feta, and a Brewmaster pizza made with Honolulu-based Kukui sausage. ⊠ *Waikiki Beachcomber by Outrigger, 2300 Kalakaua Ave., 2nd fl., Waikiki* ☎ *808/843–2739* ⊕ *www.maui-brewingco.com/waikiki.*

Moana Terrace

BARS/PUBS | FAMILY | Three floors up from busy Waikiki, this casual, open-air terrace by the Waikiki Beach Marriott Resort & Spa pool is where some of Hawaii's finest musicians play every evening. Check out the daily happy hour specials. Order a drink served in a fresh pineapple (and perhaps a light snack), and watch the sun dip into the Pacific. ⊠ *Waikiki Beach Marriott Resort & Spa, 2552 Kalakaua Ave., Waikiki* ☎ *808/922–6611* ⊕ *www.marriotthawaii.com.*

RumFire

BARS/PUBS | Locals and visitors head here for the convivial atmosphere, trendy decor, and the million-dollar view of Waikiki Beach and Diamond Head. Come early to get a seat for happy hour (3–5 pm daily). If you're feeling peckish, there's a menu of tasty, Asian-influenced small-plates. RumFire also features original cocktails, signature shots, and daily live music. On Friday and Saturday night, the bar gets even livelier once local DJs start spinning at 9:30. ⊠ *Sheraton Waikiki, 2255 Kalakaua Ave., Waikiki* ☎ *808/922–4422* ⊕ *www.rumfirewaikiki.com.*

The Study

BARS/PUBS | It's tricky to find the Study at the Modern Honolulu—it's behind a huge, revolving bookcase in the lobby across from the registration desk. It's an uberchic space, with intimate alcoves and oversize sofas that are both hip and inviting. The bar features literary-theme cocktails with premium spirits, like the Great Gatsby, the Huckleberry Finn, and the War and Peace. This bar attracts a hip crowd, features live music every night, and has a great weeknight happy hour. ⊠ *The Modern Honolulu, 1775 Ala Moana Blvd., Waikiki* ☎ *808/450–3396 main/ hotel number* ⊕ *www.themodernhonolulu.com/the-study.*

Tiki's Grill & Bar

BARS/PUBS | Tiki torches light the way to this fun restaurant and bar overlooking Kuhio Beach. A mix of locals and visitors

Mai Tais

Hard to believe, but the cocktail known around the world as the mai tai has been around for more than 50 years. Although the recipe has changed slightly over the years, the original formula, created by bar owner Victor J. "Trader Vic" Bergeron, included 2 ounces of 17-year-old J. Wray & Nephew rum over shaved ice, ½ ounce Dekuyper orange curaçao, ¼ ounce Trader Vic's rock candy syrup, ½ ounce orgeat syrup, and the juice of one fresh lime. Done the right way, this tropical drink still lives up to the name "mai tai!," meaning "out of this world!"

heads here for happy hour and, later, to enjoy its kitschy cool, casual vibe. There's great nightly entertainment featuring contemporary Hawaiian musicians playing lively and popular cover tunes. The drinks menu is extensive and (not surprisingly) tiki-focused. Don't leave without sipping on the Lava Flow (rum, coconut milk, pineapple juice, strawberry puree) or noshing on the famous coconut shrimp, ahi poke, and macadamia-crusted fish of the day. And if you love the tiki vibe, you can purchase an array of whimsical merchandise, including the colorful tiki mugs. ⊠ *Aston Waikiki Beach Hotel, 2570 Kalakaua Ave., Waikiki* ☎ *808/923–8454* ⊕ *www.tikisgrill.com.*

Waiolu Ocean View Lounge

MUSIC CLUBS | Hawaiian bars should have two things: stellar views of the sunset over the ocean and equally awesome mai tais. Both are on offer at the Waiolu Ocean View Lounge at the posh Trump International Hotel. And on Friday, take in the Waikiki evening fireworks show from here. There's live music, ranging from contemporary to Hawaiian, Thursday through Sunday night, with an attractive crowd showing up around 8 pm. It's busy but not suffocating, and seats are scarce once the music starts at 6:30 pm, so reserve a table in advance. Go for sunset or the late-night happy hour daily. ⊠ *Trump International Hotel, 223 Saratoga Rd., Waikiki* ☎ *808/683–7456* ⊕ *www.trumpwaikikihotel.com.*

Wang Chung's Karaoke Bar

BARS/PUBS | Dubbed the "Friendliest Bar in Waikiki," this charming karaoke bar is a must-see on any trip to the island. The positive vibe comes from owner Dan Chang, who personally welcomes his guests. (He might even hug you.) The bar is located in the lobby of the Stay Hotel and has a full kitchen cranking out Asian- and Latin-inspired dishes. It's known for a lively late-night crowd and innovative cocktails. The list of karaoke songs is extensive, but it gets jammed, so arrive early if you really want to add your name to the list and sing a song. Don't be surprised if the entire bar starts singing along. ⊠ *Stay Hotel Waikiki, 2424 Koa Ave., Waikiki* ☎ *808/201–6369* ⊕ *www.wangchungs.com.*

CLUBS

Hula's Bar and Lei Stand

DANCE CLUBS | Hawaii's oldest and best-known gay-friendly nightspot offers panoramic views of Diamond Head by day and high-energy club music by night. Check out the all-day happy hour, which starts at 10 am. There's an abundance of drink specials on weekends and discounted pitchers of beer and cocktails on Sunday. There are plenty of great food options, too, including nachos, tacos, pork sliders, and more. Celebrity patrons have included Elton John, Adam Lambert, and Dolly Parton. ⊠ *Waikiki Grand Hotel, 134 Kapahulu Ave., 2nd fl., Waikiki* ☎ *808/923–0669* ⊕ *www.hulas.com.*

Sky Waikiki

MUSIC CLUBS | Offering a bird's eye view of the city and coastline, Sky Waikiki's rooftop bar sits 19 stories above the city, just below Top of Waikiki, the strip's iconic revolving restaurant (and is managed by the same company). From the couches on the welcoming open-air lanai, you are treated to nearly 360-degree scenic views of Diamond Head, the Waikiki beaches, and the classic coral Royal Hawaiian hotel. It's one of the best spots to take in a Waikiki sunset. The bar offers happy hour drink specials daily, and the club inside exudes contemporary-LA chic every night. Resident DJs spin on Friday and Saturday night. Be sure to order the popular SkyTai cocktail as you enjoy the views. ⊠ *Waikiki Trade Center, 2270 Kalakaua Ave., Waikiki* ☎ *808/979–7590* ⊕ *www.skywaikiki.com.*

🎭 Performing Arts

DINNER CRUISES AND SHOWS

Magic of Polynesia

MAGIC | FAMILY | Hawaii's top illusionist, John Hirokawa, displays mystifying sleight of hand in this highly entertaining show, which incorporates contemporary hula and Islands music into its acts. It's held in the Waikiki Beachcomber by Outrigger's $7½-million showroom. Reservations are required for dinner (nightly at 5:45) and the show (at 7). Menu choices range from ginger sesame glazed chicken to a deluxe steak-and-lobster combo. Walk-ins are permitted if you just want the entertainment. The box office is open daily from noon to 9 pm. ⊠ *Waikiki Beachcomber by Outrigger, 2300 Kalakaua Ave., Waikiki* ☎ *808/971–4321* ⊕ *www.robertshawaii.com/oahu-tours/magic-of-polynesia* 🎟 *Show from $35 per person.*

FILM

Sunset on the Beach

FILM | FAMILY | It's like watching a movie at the drive-in, minus the car and the speaker box. Bring a blanket and find a spot on the sand to enjoy live entertainment, food from top local restaurants, and a movie on a 30-foot screen. Held three to four times each year on Queen's Surf Beach across from the Honolulu Zoo,

Sunset on the Beach is a favorite event for both locals and visitors. Additionally, season premieres of the TV show *Hawaii Five-0* were celebrated at Sunset on the Beach until the show ended in 2020; get there early if you want a good spot to view the film. If the weather is blustery, beware of flying sand. ⊠ *Queen's Surf Beach, Kalakaua Ave., Waikiki* ⊕ *www.sunsetonthebeach.net* 🎟 *Free.*

LUAU

The luau is an experience that everyone, both local and tourist, should have. It's an exciting way to experience the "aloha spirit" and learn a bit about island culture. Today's luau still offer traditional foods and entertainment, but there's often a fun, contemporary flair. With many, you can watch the roasted pig being carried out of its *imu*, a hole in the ground used for cooking food with heated stones.

Luau prices average around $100 per person—some are cheaper, others twice that amount—and are held around the island, not just in Waikiki. Reservations—and a camera—are a must.

Royal Hawaiian Luau: Aha'aina

ARTS-ENTERTAINMENT OVERVIEW | With traditional island dancing and cultural demonstrations in a beachfront location, the Royal Hawaiian's Aha'aina luau is an entertaining show with hula, fire dancing, great music, and more. The buffet-style dinner includes Hawaiian-inspired specialties and luau favorites. A professional and upscale event, it takes place on the hotel's sprawling oceanfront lawn, a prime location. Luau options range from "cocktail and show" (1½-hour event) to "premium dinner and show" (three-hour event). This luau is scheduled for two nights a week (Monday and Thursday), so be sure to reserve in advance during the high season. ⊠ *The Royal Hawaiian, a Luxury Collection Resort, 2259 Kalakaua Ave., Waikiki* 🕾 *808/921–4600* ⊕ *www.royal-hawaiianluau.com* 🎟 *From $85.*

Waikiki Starlight Luau

THEMED ENTERTAINMENT | FAMILY | This Waikiki luau is done spectacularly on the rooftop of the Hilton Hawaiian Village. There isn't an imu ceremony, but the live entertainment is top-notch, and the views are unparalleled. Prices vary depending on your age and where you want to sit. The event also includes dinner with traditional specialties, games, and cultural activities, such as hula lessons and conch blowing. It's held Sunday–Thursday at 5. ⊠ *Hilton Hawaiian Village, 2005 Kalia Rd., Waikiki* 🕾 *808/941–5828* ⊕ *www.hiltonhawaiian-village.com* 🎟 *From $117.*

MUSIC

★ Blue Note Hawaii

MUSIC | Music lovers adore this intimate venue, which draws local and national acts throughout the year. Acoustics are fantastic, and seating is at tables, all with excellent views. The ambience is sophisticated, and the food here is excellent, too, with small and large plates offered. It's worthwhile to find out who's performing while you're in town so you can purchase tickets in advance, since the more popular acts sell out quickly. This 300-seat room is centrally located (in the Outrigger Hotel), so you can go for a drink at Duke's before or after the show. ⊠ *Outrigger Waikiki Beach Resort, 2335 Kalakaua Ave., Waikiki* 🕾 *808/777–4890* ⊕ *www.bluenotehawaii.com* 🎟 *From $35.*

Honolulu Zoo Concerts

CONCERTS | FAMILY | Since the early 1980s, the Honolulu Zoo Society has sponsored hour-long evening concerts branded the "Wildest Show in Town." They're held at 6 pm on Wednesday, June–August. Listen to local legends play everything from Hawaiian to jazz to Latin music. Take a brisk walk through the zoo, or join in the family activities. This is an alcohol-free event, and there's food for those who haven't brought their own picnic supplies. Gates open at 4:35. ■ **TIP**→ **This is one of**

the best deals in town. ✉ *Honolulu Zoo, 151 Kapahulu Ave., Waikiki* ☎ *808/971–7171* ⊕ *www.honoluluzoo.org* ✉ *From $5.*

Ke Kani O Ke Kai

CONCERTS | Every other Thursday evening June–August, the Waikiki Aquarium holds an ocean-side concert series called Ke Kani O Ke Kai. You can listen to top performers while enjoying food from local restaurants. The aquarium stays open throughout the night, so you can see the marine life in a new light. Bring your own beach chairs or blankets. Proceeds support the aquarium, the third-oldest in the United States. Doors open at 5:30 pm; concerts start at 7 pm. ✉ *Waikiki Aquarium, 2777 Kalakaua Ave., Waikiki* ☎ *808/923–9741* ⊕ *www.waikikiaquarium.org* ✉ *From $50.*

THEATER

Hawaii can be an expensive gig for touring shows and music artists that depend on major theatrical sets. Not many manage to stop here, and those that do sell out fast. Oahu has developed several excellent local theater companies, which present first-rate entertainment all year long. Anyone who attends is always surprised to learn that the Honolulu Theatre for Youth is the only professional troupe in the state. Community support for these groups is strong.

Diamond Head Theatre

THEATER | The repertoire of the third-oldest community theater in the United States includes a little of everything: musicals, dramas, and experimental productions. ✉ *520 Makapuu Ave., Diamond Head* ☎ *808/733–0274* ⊕ *www.diamondheadtheatre.com* ✉ *From $15.*

🛍 Shopping

Throughout Waikiki, there are notable shops located in hotels, malls, and other shopping centers. The abundance of name-brand as well as specialty stores can be convenient or overwhelming, depending on your sensibilities. Clothing, jewelry, and handbags from Europe's top designers sit next to Hawaii's ABC Stores, a chain of convenience stores that sells groceries as well as tourist items and souvenirs. Now more than ever, it's possible to find interesting, locally produced items at reasonable prices in Waikiki, but shoppers have to be willing to search beyond the $4,000 purses and the tacky wooden tikis to find innovation and quality.

CLOTHING

Blue Ginger

CLOTHING | **FAMILY** | Look inside this little shop across from The Yardhouse for brightly colored, beach-casual clothing, bags, jewelry, and accessories in soft cotton and rayon aloha prints. It offers a decent selection of Hawaii-made items for adults and children. ✉ *227 Lewers St., Waikiki* ☎ *808/924–7900* ⊕ *www.blueginger.com.*

Newt at the Royal

CLOTHING | Newt is known for high-quality, handwoven Panama hats and tropical sportswear for men and women. ✉ *The Royal Hawaiian Hotel, 2259 Kalakaua Ave., Waikiki* ☎ *808/923–4332* ⊕ *www.newtattheroyal.com.*

GALLERIES

Na Hoku Gallery

JEWELRY/ACCESSORIES | This is a smaller version of the designer and island-lifestyle jewelry store whose original is located in the Ala Moana Shopping Center. It offers a selection of Tahitian pearls as well as other ocean- and marine-theme jewelry. ✉ *Outrigger Waikiki, 2335 Kalakaua Ave., Waikiki* ☎ *808/922–0556* ⊕ *www.nahoku.com.*

FOOD

★ Honolulu Cookie Company

FOOD/CANDY | Did someone say "free samples"? To really impress those back home, pick up a box of locally baked, gourmet cookies. Choose from dozens of delicious flavors of premium shortbread delights with a wide variety of sizes, all designed for travel. In addition to the location in the Royal Hawaiian Center, there are a number of these stores in Waikiki, so you probably won't be able to avoid them—even if you try. ⊠ *Royal Hawaiian Center, 2233 Kalakaua Ave., Waikiki* ☎ *808/931–8937.*

GIFTS

★ House of Mana Up

GIFTS/SOUVENIRS | It's fun to browse around this innovative shop selling an array of locally made Hawaiian items. Mana Up is a ground-breaking organization that promotes Hawaii-based entrepreneurs and shares their unique products with consumers. The new, 2,600-square-foot retail store is in the Royal Hawaiian Center. It's an experiential shop that showcases these inventive products while sharing stories of the nearly 40 makers behind them. You can find a wide range of great items on the shelves here, including gourmet chocolate, edible coffee bars, cool locally made art, sustainable food wraps, surf-inspired clothing, extra-comfy flip-flops (called slippers in Hawaii), children's books, and much more. You're certain to enjoy the interesting experience of shopping here, and all of the profits are used to support these small businesses. ⊠ *Royal Hawaiian Center, 2201 Kalakaua Ave., Space A108 (1st fl.), Waikiki* ☎ *808/425–4028* ⊕ *www.manauphawaii.com.*

Sand People

GIFTS/SOUVENIRS | This cute shop stocks beach-inspired, easy-to-carry gifts, such as fish-shaped Christmas ornaments, Hawaiian-style notepads, frames, charms in the shape of flip-flops (known locally as "slippahs"), soaps, kitchen accessories, ceramic clocks, and other fun island-themed items. There's another branch in the International Marketplace, one in Kailua, as well as three each on Kauai and Maui. ⊠ *Moana Surfrider, 2369 Kalakaua, Waikiki* ☎ *808/924–6773.*

JEWELRY

Philip Rickard

JEWELRY/ACCESSORIES | The heirloom design collection of this famed jeweler highlights custom Hawaiian jewelry, particularly its Wedding Collection, which is often sought by celebrities. Made in many different gold colors and platinum, the jewelry features traditional Hawaiian scrolling patterns, enameled names, and inlays. ⊠ *International Market Place, 2330 Kalakaua Ave., Level 1, Banyan Court, #105, Waikiki* ☎ *808/924–7972* ⊕ *www.philiprickard.com.*

SHOPPING CENTERS

Royal Hawaiian Center

SHOPPING CENTERS/MALLS | An open and inviting facade has made this three-block-long center a garden of Hawaiian shops. There are more than 110 stores and restaurants, including the Apple Store and ABC stores, as well as local gems such as Oiwi Ocean Gear, Fighting Eel, Honolulu Cookie Company, and Koi Honolulu, a cool clothing boutique. Check out tropical Panama hats at Hawaiian Island Arts or offerings at Island Soap & Candleworks, while Royal Hawaiian Quilt offers handmade Hawaiian quilts, pillow covers, kitchen accessories, and more. A number of restaurants at all price points round out the dining options, along with the newly-opened Waikiki Food Hall, complimentary cultural classes, plus a theater and nightly outdoor entertainment. ⊠ *2201 Kalakaua Ave., Waikiki* ☎ *808/922–0588* ⊕ *www.royalhawaiiancenter.com.*

T Galleria by DFS, Hawaii

SHOPPING CENTERS/MALLS | It's all about designer brands here: Hermès, Cartier, Michael Kors, Dior, and Marc Jacobs are among the shops on the Waikiki Luxury Walk in this enclosed mall, as well as Hawaii's largest beauty and cosmetic store. The third floor caters to duty-free shoppers only and features an exclusive Watch Shop. ⊠ *330 Royal Hawaiian Ave.,*

Waikiki ☎ *808/931–2700* ⊕ *www.dfs.com/en/tgalleria-hawaii.*

2100 Kalakaua

SHOPPING CENTERS/MALLS | The ultimate destination for designer shopping in Hawaii is in an elegant town house–style center known as Luxury Row. Shops include Chanel, Coach, Tiffany & Co., Yves Saint Laurent, Bottega Veneta, Gucci, Hugo Boss, Miu Miu, and Montcler. ✉ *2100 Kalakaua Ave., Waikiki* ☎ *808/922–2246* ⊕ *www.luxuryrow.com.*

Waikiki Beach Walk

SHOPPING CENTERS/MALLS | This open-air shopping center greets visitors at the west end of Waikiki's Kalakaua Avenue with 70 locally owned stores and restaurants. Get reasonably priced, fashionable resort wear for yourself at Mahina; find unique pieces by local artists at Under the Koa Tree; or buy local delicacies from the Poke Bar. Of course, you can pick up T-shirts, bathing suits, and casual beach attire here as well. And you can also browse Koa and sandalwood gifts at Martin & MacArthur in the nearby Outrigger Reef and Sheraton Waikiki hotels, as well as other locations. The mall also features free local entertainment on the outdoor-fountain stage at least once a week. ✉ *226 Lewers St., Waikiki* ☎ *808/931–3591* ⊕ *www.waikikibeachwalk.com.*

🏃 Activities

SPAS

Excellent day and resort spas can be found throughout Oahu, primarily in the resorts of Waikiki. Individual treatments and day packages offer a wide choice of rejuvenating therapies, some of which are unique to the Islands. Try the popular *lomilomi* massage with kukui-nut oil (*lomi* meaning to rub, knead, and massage using palms, forearms, fingers, knuckles, elbows, knees, feet, even sticks). Add heated *pohaku* (stones) placed on the back to relieve sore muscles, or choose a facial using natural ingredients such as coconut, mango, papaya, ti leaf, Hawaiian honey, or ginger. Many full-service spas offer private couples' treatment rooms, fitness suites, yoga, and hydrotherapy pools.

Abhasa Spa

SPA/BEAUTY | Natural organic skin and body treatments are the highlights at this spa tucked away in the Royal Hawaiian Hotel's coconut grove. Vegetarian-lifestyle spa therapies, color-light therapy, a facial fusing invigorating lomilomi technique with pohaku are all available. You can choose to have your treatment in any of Abhasa's eight indoor rooms or in one of its three garden cabanas. ✉ *Royal Hawaiian Hotel, 2259 Kalakaua Ave., Waikiki* ☎ *808/922–8200* ⊕ *www.abhasa.com.*

LaaKea Spa Hawaii

SPA/BEAUTY | Only steps off the beach, this renovated Aveda Concept spa provides aromatherapy treatments, massages, and facials. Each room is extra spacious not just to give therapists area to move, but also to accommodate guests with mobility impairments. Signature massages include a stress-fix body massage that relieves jet lag and stiffness from traveling and a massage using lomi techniques and pohaku. ■ **TIP→ Book the last appointment of the day—usually 4, 5, or 6 pm—so you can watch the sunset as you're finishing your massage treatment.** ✉ *Outrigger Reef on the Beach, 2169 Kalia Rd., Waikiki* ☎ *808/926–2882, 866/926–2882* ⊕ *www.outriggerreef-onthebeach.com.*

Mandara Spa at the Hilton Hawaiian Village Beach Resort & Spa

SPA/BEAUTY | From its perch in the Kalia Tower, Mandara Spa, an outpost of the chain that originated in Bali, overlooks the mountains, ocean, and downtown Honolulu. Fresh Hawaiian ingredients and traditional techniques headline an array of treatments. Try an exotic upgrade, such as reflexology or a Balinese body polish. Or relieve achy muscles with a traditional

Thai poultice massage. The delicately scented, candlelit foyer can fill up quickly with robe-clad conventioneers, so be sure to make a reservation. There are spa suites for couples, a private infinity pool, and a boutique. ✉ *Hilton Hawaiian Village Beach Resort & Spa, 2005 Kalia Rd., 3rd and 4th fl., Kalia Tower, Waikiki* ☎ *808/945–7721* ⊕ *www.mandaraspa. com.*

Na Hoola Spa at the Hyatt Regency Waikiki Resort & Spa

SPA/BEAUTY | Na Hoola is the premier resort spa in Waikiki, with 16 treatment rooms sprawling across 10,000 square feet and two floors of the Hyatt on Kalakaua Avenue. Arrive early for your treatment to enjoy the postcard views of Waikiki Beach. Four packages identified by Hawaii's native healing plants—noni, kukui, awa, and kalo—combine various body, face, and hair treatments; the spa also has luxurious packages that last three to six hours. The Kele Kele body wrap employs a self-heating mud wrap to release tension and stress. The small exercise room is for use by hotel guests only. ✉ *Hyatt Regency Waikiki Resort & Spa, 2424 Kalakaua Ave., Waikiki* ☎ *808/923–1234, 808/237–6330 for reservations* ⊕ *www.nahoolaspawaikiki. com.*

Royal Kaila Spa

SPA/BEAUTY | The Marriott's spa, which faces Waikiki Beach, uses nature-based Aveda products in all its therapies. Linger with a cup of tea between treatments and gaze through 75-foot-high windows at the activity outside. Lush Hawaiian foliage, sleek Balinese teak furnishings, and a mist of ylang-ylang and nutmeg in the air inspire relaxation. Treatments incorporate natural minerals and sea salts as well as the healing power of plant essences. ✉ *Waikiki Beach Marriott Resort & Spa, 2552 Kalakaua Ave., Waikiki* ☎ *808/369–8088* ⊕ *www.royalkaila-spa.com.*

The Spa at Trump Waikiki

SPA/BEAUTY | The Spa at Trump offers private changing and showering areas for each room, creating an environment of uninterrupted relaxation. No matter what treatment you choose, it is inspired by "personal intention," such as purify, balance, heal, revitalize, or calm, to elevate the senses throughout your time there. Don't miss the signature gemstone treatments, which feature products by Shiffa; or treat yourself to a Naturally Yours facial to emerge with younger-looking skin. The Healing Hawaiian Ocean Ritual is one of the most popular massages to begin—or end—your day. ✉ *Trump International Hotel Waikiki, 223 Saratoga Rd., Waikiki* ☎ *808/683–7466* ⊕ *www.trumpwaikiki-hotel.com.*

★ SpaHalekulani

SPA/BEAUTY | SpaHalekulani mines the traditions and cultures of the Pacific Islands with massages and body and facial therapies. Try the Samoan Nonu, which uses warm stones and healing nonu gel to relieve muscle tension. The exclusive line of bath and body products is scented by maile, lavender orchid, or coconut passion. Facilities are specific to treatment but may include Japanese furo bath or steam shower. ✉ *Halekulani Hotel, 2199 Kalia Rd., Waikiki* ☎ *808/931–5322* ⊕ *www.halekulani.com/living/ spahalekulani.*

Pearl Harbor

Pearl Harbor is approximately 9 miles west of downtown Honolulu, beyond Honolulu International Airport.

December 7, 1941. Every American then alive recalls exactly what he or she was doing when the news broke that the Japanese had bombed Pearl Harbor, the catalyst that brought the United States into World War II. Those who are younger have learned about the events of the fateful day, when more than 2,000 people died, and a dozen ships were sunk. Here, in what is still a key Pacific naval base, the attack is remembered every day by thousands of visitors. In recent years, the memorial has been the site of reconciliation ceremonies involving Pearl Harbor veterans from both sides. There are five distinct sights in Pearl Harbor, but only two are part of Pearl Harbor National Memorial. The others are privately operated. It's possible to make reservations for the national park sites at ⊕ *www.recreation.gov.*

★ Battleship *Missouri* Memorial

MILITARY SITE | Together with the *Arizona* Memorial, the USS *Missouri*'s presence in Pearl Harbor perfectly bookends America's World War II experience, which began December 7, 1941, and ended on the "Mighty Mo's" starboard deck with the signing of the Terms of Surrender. In 2017, the battleship underwent a $3.5-million renovation (now complete) to replace rusted steel and repaint its upper decks. It's the biggest preservation effort to the *Missouri* since it was dry-docked in 2009 for a $15.5-million top-to-bottom paint job. To begin your visit, pick up tickets online or at the Pearl Harbor Visitor Center. Then board a shuttle bus for the eight-minute ride to Ford Island and the teak decks and towering superstructure of the last battleship ever built. Join a guided tour to learn more about the *Missouri*'s long and dramatic history. For history buffs, the Heart of the *Missouri* tour (for an additional $25) provides an up-close look into the battleship's engineering spaces, including access to its engine rooms, gun turret, damage control station, and aft battery plot room.

The *Missouri* is 887 feet long, 209 feet tall, with nine 116-ton guns capable of firing up to 23 miles. Absorb these numbers during the tour, then stop to take advantage of the view from the decks. Near the entrance is a gift shop, as well as a lunch wagon and shave ice stand that serve hamburgers, hot dogs, pizza, and other treats. ⊠ *Ford Island, 63 Cowpens St., Pearl Harbor* ✛ *You cannot drive directly to the USS Missouri; you must take a shuttle bus from Pearl Harbor Visitor Center* ☎ *808/455–1600* ⊕ *ussmissouri.org* ⊠ *From $30* ⊗ *No bags allowed. Storage lockers available at main Pearl Harbor Visitor Center.*

Pearl Harbor Aviation Museum

MUSEUM | This museum opened on December 7, 2006, as a tribute to aviation in the Pacific. Located on Ford Island in Hangars 37 and 79, actual seaplane hangars that survived the Pearl Harbor attack, the museum is made up of a theater where a short film on Pearl Harbor kicks off the tour, an education center, a restoration shop, a gift store, and a restaurant. Exhibits—many of which are interactive and involve sound effects—include an authentic Japanese Zero in a diorama setting, vintage aircraft, and the chance to play the role of a World War II pilot using flight simulators. Various aircraft are employed to narrate the great battles: the Doolittle Raid on Japan, the Battle of Midway, Guadalcanal, and so on. The actual Stearman N2S-3 in which President George H.W. Bush soloed is housed in Hangar 79. Ride in Fighter Ace 360 Flight Simulators, and take a docent-led tour for additional fees. Purchase tickets online, at the Pearl Harbor Visitor Center, or at the museum itself after you get off the shuttle bus. ⊠ *Ford Island, 319 Lexington Blvd., Pearl Harbor* ✛ *You cannot drive directly to the museum; you must take a shuttle bus to Ford Island from the Pearl Harbor Visitor Center* ☎ *808/441–1000* ⊕ *pearlharboraviationmuseum.org* ⊠ *$25* ⊗ *No bags allowed. Storage lockers available at main Pearl Harbor Visitor Center.*

Pearl Harbor National Memorial

NATIONAL/STATE PARK | Two Hawaii sights associated with the devastating Japanese attack on Pearl Harbor on December 7, 1941, are part of this national monument, which has been given a much less cumbersome name, and also tells the story of the internment of Japanese Americans, battles in the Aleutian Islands, and the occupation of Japan after World War II. The location, Pearl Harbor, is still a working military base as well as the most-visited sight in Oahu. Five distinct destinations are on the base: the visitor center and the USS *Arizona* Memorial, which are part of the national monument, as well as the USS *Bowfin,* the USS *Missouri,* and the Pacific Aviation Museum, all of which are privately operated. You can walk to the visitor center or the USS *Bowfin* from the parking lot, but the USS *Arizona* Memorial requires a ferry ride, and access to the USS *Missouri* and Pearl Harbor Aviation Museum (and USS *Oklahoma* submarine memorial) require a shuttle bus. If you have not reserved tickets in advance (⊕ *www.recreation.gov*), all members of your party must be present; regardless, you'll need proper government-issued ID to gain access to the base. A large number of timed-entry tickets for the USS *Arizona* Memorial are available on a first-come-first-served basis starting at 7 am daily. No bags of any kind are allowed at any of the sights (except for the visitor center)—not even small purses—but cameras, cell phones, and wallets can be hand-carried. A bag check is available for $5 at the visitor center. Children under four can visit the larger USS *Bowfin* site but are not allowed on the submarine itself. ⊠ *Pearl Harbor Visitor Center, 1 Arizona Memorial Pl., Pearl Harbor* ☎ *808/422–3399, 877/444–6777 timed ticket reservations* ⊕ *www.nps.gov/valr* 🎟 *Visitor center and USS Arizona Memorial free; advance ticket convenience fee $1; fees for other sites.*

★ **Pearl Harbor Visitor Center**

INFO CENTER | The Pearl Harbor Visitor Center reopened after a $58-million renovation and is now the gateway to the Pearl Harbor National Memorial and the starting point for visitors to this historic site. At the visitor center are interpretive

exhibits in two separate galleries (*Road to War* and *Attack*) that feature photographs and personal memorabilia from World War II veterans. But there are other exhibits, a bookstore, and a Remembrance Circle, where you can learn about the people who lost their lives on December 7, 1941. Survivors are sometimes on hand to give their personal accounts and answer questions. The visitor center is also where you start your tour of the USS *Arizona* Memorial if you have secured a walk-in or reserved a timed ticket (reserve at ⊕ *www. recreation.gov*). ⊠ *Pearl Harbor National Memorial, 1 Arizona Memorial Pl., Pearl Harbor* ☎ *808/954–8759, 866/332–1941 toll-free* ⊕ *pearlharborvisitorcenter.org* 🎟 *Free (timed-entry ticket fee $1)* ☞ *Advanced tickets can be reserved 60 days prior, 1 day prior, and on the day of your desired tour.*

★ **USS *Arizona* Memorial**

MEMORIAL | Lined up tight in a row of seven battleships off Ford Island, the USS *Arizona* took a direct hit on December 7, 1941, exploded, and rests still on the shallow bottom where she settled. A visit to the Pearl Harbor National Memorial begins prosaically—a line, your wait filled with shopping, visiting the museum, and strolling the grounds (though you can reserve timed tickets online 60 days or 1 day prior at ⊕ *www.recreation. gov* and skip the wait). When your tour starts, you watch a short documentary film, then board the ferry to the memorial. The swooping, stark-white memorial, which straddles the wreck of the USS *Arizona,* was designed by Honolulu architect Alfred Preis to represent both the depths of the low-spirited, early days of the war, and the uplift of victory. A somber, contemplative mood descends upon visitors during the ferry ride; this is a place where 1,777 people died. Gaze at the names of the dead carved into the wall of white marble. Look at oil on

Continued on page 119

USS *West Virginia* (BB48), 7 December 1941

PEARL HARBOR

December 7, 1941. Every American then alive recalls exactly what he or she was doing when the news broke that the Japanese had bombed Pearl Harbor, the catalyst that brought the United States into World War II.

Although it was clear by late 1941 that war with Japan was inevitable, no one in authority seems to have expected the attack to come in just this way, at just this time. So when the Japanese bombers swept through a gap in Oahu's Koolau Mountains in the hazy light of morning, they found the bulk of America's Pacific fleet right where they hoped it would be: docked like giant stepping stones across the calm waters of the bay named for the pearl oysters that once prospered there. More than 2,000 people died that day, including 49 civilians. A dozen ships were sunk.

And on the nearby air bases, virtually every American military aircraft was destroyed or damaged. The attack was a stunning success, but it lit a fire under America, which went to war with "Remember Pearl Harbor" as its battle cry. Here, in what is still a key Pacific naval base, the attack is remembered every day by thousands of visitors, including many curious Japanese, who for years heard little World War II history in their own country. In recent years, the memorial has been the site of reconciliation ceremonies involving Pearl Harbor veterans from both sides.

GETTING AROUND

Pearl Harbor is both a working military base and the most-visited Oahu attraction. Four distinct destinations share a parking lot and are linked by footpath, shuttle, and ferry.

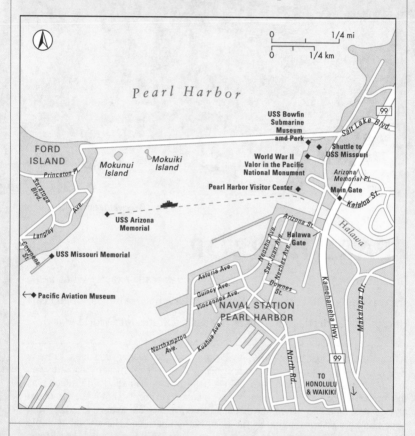

The visitor center is accessible from the parking lot. The *USS Arizona* Memorial itself is in the middle of the harbor; get tickets for the ferry ride at the visitor center. The USS *Bowfin* is also reachable from the parking lot. The USS *Missouri* is docked at Ford Island, a restricted area of the naval base. Vehicular access is prohibited. To get there, take a shuttle bus from the station near the *Bowfin*.

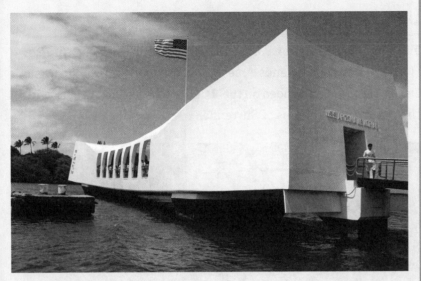

ARIZONA MEMORIAL

Snugged up tight in a row of seven battleships off Ford Island, the USS Arizona took a direct hit that December morning, exploded, and rests still on the shallow bottom where she settled.

The swooping, stark-white memorial, which straddles the wreck of the USS *Arizona*, was designed to represent both the depths of the low-spirited, early days of the war, and the uplift of victory.

A visit here begins at the Pearl Harbor Visitor Center, which recently underwent a $58 million renovation. High definition projectors and interactive exhibits were installed, and the building was modernized. From the visitor center, a ferry takes you to the memorial itself, and a new shuttle hub now gives access to sites that were previously inaccessible, like the USS *Utah* and USS Oklahoma.

A somber, contemplative mood descends upon visitors during the ferry ride to the *Arizona*; this is a place where 1,177 crewmen lost their lives.

Gaze at the names of the dead carved into the wall of white marble. Scatter flowers (but no lei—the string is bad for the fish). Salute the flag. Remember Pearl Harbor.

☎ *808/422–0561*
⊕ *www.nps.gov/valr*

USS *MISSOURI* (BB63)

Together with the Arizona Memorial, the Missouri's presence in Pearl Harbor perfectly bookends America's WWII experience that began December 7, 1941, and ended on the "Mighty Mo's" starboard deck with the signing of the Terms of Surrender.

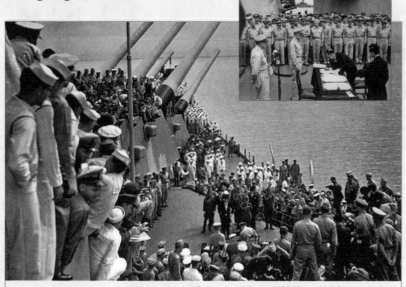

Surrender of Japan, USS Missouri, 2 September 1945

In the parking area behind the USS *Bowfin* Museum, board a shuttle for an eight-minute ride to Ford Island and the teak decks and towering superstructure of the *Missouri*. The last battleship ever built, the *Missouri* famously hosted the final act of WWII, the signing of the Terms of Surrender. The commission that governs this floating museum has surrounded her with buildings tricked out in WWII style with quonset huts serving as shaded eating areas for the nearby lunch wagon and a Victory Store housing a souvenir shop and covered with period mottos ("Don't be a blabateur").

■TIP→ **Definitely hook up with a tour guide (no additional charge) or audio tour—these add a great deal to the experience.**

The *Missouri* is all about numbers: 209 feet tall, six 239,000-pound guns, capable of firing up to 23 miles away. Absorb these during the tour, then stop to take advantage of the view from the decks. The Mo is a work in progress, with only a handful of her hundreds of spaces open to view.

☎ *808/455-1600* or ☎ *877/644-4896*
⊕ *www.ussmissouri.org*

USS *BOWFIN* (SS287)

SUBMARINE MUSEUM & PARK

Launched one year to the day after the Pearl Harbor attack, the USS Bowfin sank 44 enemy ships during WWII and now serves as the centerpiece of a museum honoring all submariners.

Although the *Bowfin* no less than the *Arizona* Memorial commemorates the lost, the mood here is lighter. Perhaps it's the childlike scale of the boat, a metal tube just 16 feet in diameter, packed with ladders, hatches, and other obstacles, like the naval version of a jungle gym. Perhaps it's the World War II-era music that plays in the covered patio. Or it might be the museum's touching displays—the penciled sailor's journal, the Vargas girlie posters. Aboard the boat nicknamed "Pearl Harbor Avenger," compartments are fitted out as though "Sparky" was away from the radio room just for a moment, and "Cooky" might be right back to his pots and pans. The museum includes many artifacts to spark family conversations, among them a vintage dive suit that looks too big for Shaquille O'Neal.

A caution: The Bowfin could be hazardous for very young children; no one under four allowed.

☎ *808/423–1341*
⊕ *www.bowfin.org*

PACIFIC AVIATION MUSEUM PEARL HARBOR

This museum opened on December 7, 2006, as as a tribute to aviation in the Pacific. Located on Ford Island in Hangars 37 and 79, actual seaplane hangars that survived the Pearl Harbor attack, the museum is made up of a theater where a short film on Pearl Harbor kicks off the tour, an education center, a shop, and a restaurant. Exhibits—many of which are interactive and involve sound effects—include an authentic Japanese Zero in a diorama setting, vintage aircraft, and the chance to play the role of a World War II pilot using one of six flight simulators. Various aircrafts are employed to narrate the great battles: the Doolittle Raid on Japan, the Battle of Midway, Guadalcanal, and so on. The actual Stearman N2S-3 in which President George H. W. Bush soloed is housed in Hangar 79. ☎ *808/441–1000* ⊕ *www.pacificaviationmuseum.org* ✉ *$25, $35 with the one-hour Legends of Pearl Harbor add-on, $10.50 extra for flight simulator*

PLAN YOUR PEARL HARBOR DAY LIKE A MILITARY CAMPAIGN

DIRECTIONS

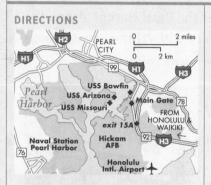

Take H–1 west from Waikiki to Exit 15A and follow signs. Or take TheBus route 20 or 47 from Waikiki. Beware high-priced private shuttles. It's a 30-minute drive from Waikiki.

WHAT TO BRING

Picture ID is required during periods of high alert; bring it just in case.

You'll be standing, walking, and climbing all day. Wear something with lots of pockets and a pair of good walking shoes. Carry a light jacket, sunglasses, hat, and sunscreen.

No purses, packs, or bags are allowed. Take only what fits in your pockets. Cameras are okay but without the bags. A private bag storage booth is located in the parking lot near the visitors' center ($5). Leave nothing in your car; theft is a problem despite bicycle security patrols.

HOURS

Hours are 7 am to 5 pm for the visitor center, though the attractions open at 8 am. The *Arizona* Memorial starts giving out tickets on a first-come, first-served basis at 7 am; the last tickets are given out at 3 pm. Spring break, summer, and holidays are busiest, and tickets sometimes run out by noon or earlier.

TICKETS

Arizona: Free. Add $7.50 for museum audio tours, and $1 if you reserve your ticket in advance online.

Aviation: From $25 adults, from $12 children. Add $10 for aviator's guided tour.

Missouri: $25 adults, $13 children. Add $25 for in-depth, behind-the-scenes tours.

Bowfin: $15 adults, $7 children. Children under 4 may go into the museum but not aboard the *Bowfin*.

A 1-day Passport to Pearl Harbor ticket includes all ships and exhibits, including the USS Arizona audio tour for $72 per adult, $35 per child; plus $1 per ticket for the reservation fee (buy at ⊕ www.recreation.gov).

KIDS

This might be the day to enroll younger kids in the hotel children's program. Preschoolers chafe at long waits, and attractions involve some hazards for toddlers. Older kids enjoy the *Bowfin* and *Missouri*, especially.

MAKING THE MOST OF YOUR TIME

Expect to spend at least half a day; a whole day is better if you're a military history buff.

At the *Arizona* Memorial, you'll get a ticket, be given a tour time, and then have to wait anywhere from 15 minutes to 3 hours. You must pick up your own ticket so you can't hold places. If the wait is long, skip over to the *Bowfin* to fill the time.

SUGGESTED READING

Pearl Harbor and the USS Arizona Memorial, by Richard Wisniewski. $5.95. 64-page magazine-size quick history.

Bowfin, by Edwin P. Hoyt. $14.95. Dramatic story of undersea adventure.

The Last Battleship, by Scott C. S. Stone. $11.95. Story of the Mighty Mo.

the water's surface, still slowly escaping from the sunken ship. Scatter flowers (but no lei—the string is bad for the fish). Salute the flag. Remember Pearl Harbor. ⊠ *Pearl Harbor National Memorial, Pearl Harbor* ☎ *808/422–3399* ⊕ *www.nps. gov/valr* ✉ *Free (advanced reservation timed-entry tickets $1); museum audio tours $8; "deluxe" tour with extra smartphone and virtual reality center access $13; "passport" tour that also includes visiting the Bowfin, Missouri, and Pearl Harbor Aviation Museum $72. Arrive early for limited same-day tickets.*

USS *Bowfin* Submarine Museum and Park
MILITARY SITE | Launched one year to the day after the Pearl Harbor attack, the USS *Bowfin* claimed to have sunk 44 enemy ships during World War II and now serves as the centerpiece of a museum honoring all submariners. Although the *Bowfin* no less than the *Arizona* Memorial commemorates the lost, the mood here is lighter. Perhaps it's the childlike scale of the boat, a metal tube just 16 feet in diameter, packed with ladders, hatches, and other obstacles, like the naval version of a jungle gym. Aboard the boat nicknamed "Pearl Harbor Avenger," compartments are fitted out as though "Sparky" was away from the radio room just for a moment, and "Cooky" might be right back to his pots and pans. The museum includes many artifacts to spark family conversations, among them a vintage dive suit known as JAKE that looks too big for Shaquille O'Neal and is now in the gift shop window. A guided audio tour is included with admission. A snack bar is also on-site. The *Bowfin* could be hazardous for very young children; no one under four is allowed on the submarine, though children can visit the museum. You can also purchase shuttle tickets to access the USS *Oklahoma* submarine memorial at the *Bowfin*'s ticket counter, though you'll probably want to include that stop along with a visit to the USS *Missouri* or Pearl Harbor Aviation Museum, both of which are on Ford Island

along with the sunken *Oklahoma*. The *Bowfin* site remains partially open during a $20-million renovation and expansion set to be completed in mid-2020; in the end it will be renamed The Pacific Fleet Submarine Museum at Pearl Harbor. ⊠ *11 Arizona Memorial Pl., Pearl Harbor* ☎ *808/423–1341* ⊕ *www.bowfin.org* ✉ *$15* ☞ *Tickets available in advance or on arrival.*

Salt Lake

There's no longer a lake, salty or not, in this suburb of Honolulu. Instead you'll find a largely residential neighborhood with a commercial core at Salt Lake Shopping Center plus the oasis of Moanalua Gardens.

⊙ Sights

Moanalua Gardens
GARDEN | This lovely and peaceful 24-acre park is a great place to spread out a blanket, have a picnic, take a snooze, fly a kite, or simply idle an afternoon away. You'll often see Japanese visitors taking pictures by a sprawling monkeypod tree nicknamed the Hitachi Tree and famous for advertising the Hitachi brand in Japan. There's a koi pond, a summer cottage once belonging to King Kamehameha V, a Chinese Hall, a taro patch, and a small gift shop. To reach Moanalua Gardens, take the Moanalua Freeway (78) westbound. Take the Tripler exit, then take a right on Jarrett White Road. Turn left at the first cross street onto Mahiole Street. The gardens are on the left, a serene pocket of green surrounded by busy roads. ⊠ *2850 Moanalua Rd., Salt Lake* ☎ *808/834–8612* ⊕ *www.moanaluagardens.com* ✉ *$5.*

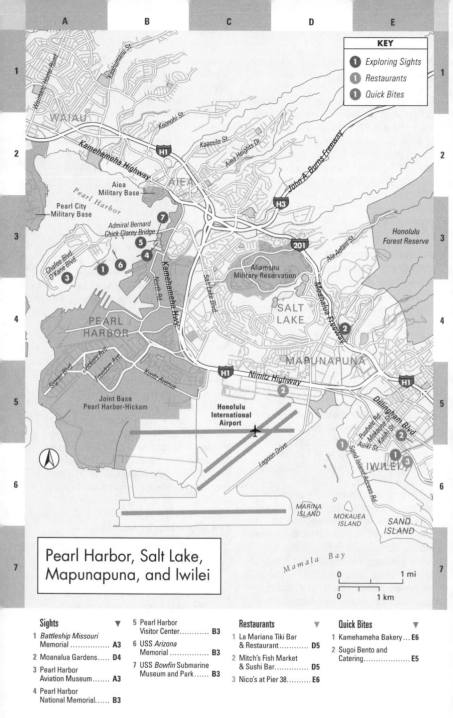

KEY

- ① Exploring Sights
- ① Restaurants
- ① Quick Bites

Pearl Harbor, Salt Lake, Mapunapuna, and Iwilei

0 —— 1 mi
0 —— 1 km

Sights ▼

1 *Battleship Missouri* Memorial **A3**
2 Moanalua Gardens **D4**
3 Pearl Harbor Aviation Museum **A3**
4 Pearl Harbor National Memorial **B3**
5 Pearl Harbor Visitor Center **B3**
6 USS *Arizona* Memorial **B3**
7 USS *Bowfin* Submarine Museum and Park **B3**

Restaurants ▼

1 La Mariana Tiki Bar & Restaurant **D5**
2 Mitch's Fish Market & Sushi Bar **D5**
3 Nico's at Pier 38 .... **E6**

Quick Bites ▼

1 Kamehameha Bakery ... **E6**
2 Sugoi Bento and Catering **E5**

Mapunapuna

Mapunapuna is an area filled with factories and offices surrounding the airport. Tucked amid car dealerships, a Kaiser Permanente medical center, and warehouses are fast-food joints, a Chinese restaurant, local plate-lunch places and Mitch's, a somewhat undiscovered gem of a sushi spot.

🍴 Restaurants

Mitch's Fish Marker & Sushi Bar

$$$$ | SUSHI | This microscopic sushi bar is an adjunct of a wholesale seafood market operated by gregarious South African expatriate Douglas Mitchell, who oversees the sushi chefs and keeps customers chatting. The fish, air-freighted from around the world, is ultrafresh, well cut (into huge pieces—to the regret of those who follow the one-bite rule), and prepared for the serious sushi lover. **Known for:** hole-in-the-wall atmosphere; BYOB; otoro (fattiest part of tuna). $ *Average main: $60 ⊠ 524 Ohohia St., near Honolulu International Airport, Mapunapuna ☎ 808/837–7774 ⊕ mitchssushi.com.*

Iwilei

Before the arrival of Captain Cook, Iwilei was a network of fishponds. After his arrival, it became home to a prison, railway depot, and houses of ill repute. (When the red-light district was shut down in 1916, one prostitute hopped a ship to Pago Pago. Also on the ship was Somerset Maugham, who immortalized her as Sadie Thompson in his short story "Rain.") Today, it is an industrial zone offering a few reasons to visit—the Dole Cannery shopping complex with a multiplex (home to the Hawaii International Film Festival each fall) being the primary one. The shopping center really was a pineapple cannery before its conversion;

almost any local of a certain age has tales of summer jobs there.

🍴 Restaurants

La Mariana Tiki Bar & Restaurant

$$ | AMERICAN | FAMILY | The last of Honolulu's old-school tiki bars is tucked away in the industrial area of Sand Island next to its working marina. Come for stiff mai tais (cocktails are all made with bottled mixers—no handcrafted anything here) and the throwback decor of hanging puffer-fish lamps, glass floats, rattan, and bamboo, and tikis galore. **Known for:** ahi spring rolls and poke, fried calamari; live singalong piano music; parking can be difficult and service slow so leave yourself plenty of time. $ *Average main: $20 ⊠ 50 Sand Island Access Rd., Iwilei ☎ 808/848–2800 ⊕ www.lamarianasailingclub.com.*

★ Nico's at Pier 38

$$ | SEAFOOD | FAMILY | Lyonnaise chef Nico Chaiz's harborside restaurant is steps from the Honolulu Fish Auction, which explains his "line to plate" concept—superfresh fish dishes at a reasonable price. But he lets his French flag fly in dishes like steak frites and bouillabaisse, too. **Known for:** pan-seared ahi steak crusted in toasted seaweed and sesame seeds; excellent double cheeseburger; lunch at the bar with a cold beer. $ *Average main: $21 ⊠ 1129 N. Nimitz Hwy., Pier 38, Iwilei ☎ 808/540–1377 ⊕ www.nicospier38.com.*

☕ Coffee and Quick Bites

Kamehameha Bakery

$ | BAKERY | Long-established Kamehameha Bakery may have moved in 2015 from its old North School Street location, but it keeps turning out old-school classics along with some newer treats that have become cult favorites. You'll salivate as you stare at the bakery cases filled with inexpensive pastries, donuts, cookies, and breads. **Known for:** variety of mala-sadas; friendly service; early opening (before dawn) and selling out of many things by midmorning. $ *Average main: $1* ⊠ *City Square Shopping Center, 1284 Kalani St., Unit D106, Iwilei* ☎ *808/845–5831* ⊕ *kamehamehabakeryhi.com.*

Sugoi Bento and Catering
$ | MODERN HAWAIIAN | This breakfast-and-lunch spot was among the first of a new wave of plate-lunch places to take particular care with quality and nutrition, offering brown rice and green salad as options instead of the usual white rice and mayo-loaded mac salad. Sweet-and-spicy garlic chicken and *mochiko* (rice-batter-dipped and fried) chicken, adapted from traditional Japanese dishes, are specialties that bring locals back again and again. **Known for:** local favorites; grab-and-go for the beach; ample parking. $ *Average main: $11* ⊠ *City Square Shopping Center, 1286 Kalani St., Suite B-106, Iwilei* ☎ *808/841–7984* ⊕ *sugoihawaii.com* ⊗ *No dinner.*

🎭 Performing Arts

FILM
Hawaii International Film Festival
FILM | One of the biggest film events in the state, the annual fall festival showcases top films from all over the world, as well as some by local filmmakers (many are Hawaii premieres; a few are world premieres) screened day and night to packed crowds—it's a must-see for film adventurers. A majority of films are screened at the Regal Dole Cannery Theaters, but festival organizers have recently branched out to other venues as well. There's also a smaller spring showcase of films. Check the official HIFF website for updated locations and dates. ⊠ *Regal Dole Cannery Theaters, 735 B Iwilei Rd., Iwilei* ☎ *808/792–1577* ⊕ *hiff.org.*

🛍 Shopping

GIFTS
Indich Collection
HOUSEHOLD ITEMS/FURNITURE | Bring home some aloha you can sink your bare feet into. Designs from this exclusive Hawaiian rug collection depict Hawaiian petroglyphs, banana leaves, heliconia, and other tropical plants or scenery. There's an additional Oahu location off Nimitz Highway. ⊠ *550 Ward Ave., Kakaako* ☎ *808/596–7333* ⊕ *indichcollection.com.*

Downtown

Honolulu's past and present play a delightful counterpoint throughout the downtown area, which is approximately 6 miles east of Honolulu International Airport. Postmodern glass-and-steel office buildings look down on the Aloha Tower, built in 1926 and, until the early 1960s, the tallest structure in Honolulu. Hawaii's history is told in the architecture of these few blocks: the cut-stone turn-of-the-20th-century storefronts of Merchant Street, the gracious white-columned American-Georgian manor that was the home of the Islands' last queen, the jewel-box palace occupied by the monarchy before it was overthrown, the Spanish-inspired stucco and tile-roofed Territorial Era government buildings, and the 21st-century glass pyramid of the First Hawaiian Bank Building.

GETTING HERE AND AROUND
To reach downtown Honolulu from Waikiki by car, take Ala Moana Boulevard to Alakea Street and turn right; three blocks up on the right, between South King and Hotel streets, there's a municipal parking lot in Alii Place. There are also public parking lots in buildings along Alakea, Smith, Beretania, and Bethel streets (Chinatown Gateway on Bethel Street is a good choice). The best parking downtown, however, is metered street

parking along Punchbowl Street—when you can find it.

Another option is to take the highly popular and convenient TheBus to the Aloha Tower Marketplace, or take a trolley from Waikiki.

◉ Sights

Aloha Tower Marketplace

VIEWPOINT | In fall 2015, the marketplace surrounding the circa-1926 Aloha Tower welcomed Hawaii Pacific University students with learning facilities, as well as housing in the Waterfront Loft residences on the second and third floors. Most marketplace businesses are now geared toward the university crowd. But you can still get a bird's-eye view of this working harbor by taking a free ride up to the observation deck of Aloha Tower daily from 9 to 5. In its day, the tower lighthouse could be seen from 15 miles at sea. Visitors with young kids in tow might want to stop at The Old Spaghetti Factory before or after going to the top of the tower. Cruise ships usually dock at Piers 10 and 11 alongside the marketplace, and Atlantis Cruises and the Star of Honolulu leave from here, too. ⊠ 1 Aloha Tower Dr., Downtown ⊹ At Piers 10 and 11 ⊕ www.alohatower.com ☒ Free.

Hawaiian Mission Houses Historic Site and Archives

MUSEUM | The determined Hawaii missionaries arrived in 1820, gaining royal favor and influencing a wide array of island life. Their descendants became leaders in government, business, and education. At Hawaiian Mission Houses Historic Site and Archives (previously Mission Houses Museum), you can learn about their influence and walk through their original dwellings, including Hawaii's oldest Western-style wooden structure, a white-frame house that was prefabricated in New England and shipped around the Horn. A new *hale pili* (traditional Hawaiian dwelling) sits nearby. Certain

areas of the museum may be seen only on one of the hourly guided tours. Docents paint an excellent picture of what mission life was like. Special Hawaiian, architectural, and history tours are offered on certain days. Rotating displays showcase such arts as Hawaiian quilting, portraits, and even toys, and a rich archival library is also open to the public. ⊠ 553 S. King St., Downtown ☎ 808/447–3910 ⊕ www.missionhouses. org ☒ $12 ⊘ Closed Sun. and Mon.

Hawaii State Art Museum

MUSEUM | Hawaii was the first state in the nation to legislate that a portion of the taxes paid on commercial building projects be set aside for the purchase of artwork. The state bought an ornate period-style building (that once was the Armed Services YMCA Building), and. in 2002, opened a 12,000-square-foot museum on the second floor dedicated to the art of Hawaii in all its ethnic diversity. HiSAM, as it's nicknamed, has a **Diamond Head Gallery** featuring new acquisitions and thematic shows from the state art collection and the Hawaii Foundation on Culture and the Arts. The **Ewa Gallery** houses more than 150 works documenting Hawaii's visual-arts history since becoming a state in 1959. Also included are an outdoor sculpture gallery, a gift shop, the excellent Artizen by MW café, and educational meeting rooms. All galleries and programs at the museum are free. Check for free monthly events, including live entertainment on First Fridays, and family-friendly Super Saturdays. ⊠ 250 S. Hotel St., 2nd fl., Downtown ☎ 808/586–0300 ⊕ hisam.hawaii.gov ☒ Free ⊘ Closed Sun.

Hawaii State Capitol

GOVERNMENT BUILDING | The capitol's architecture is richly symbolic: the columns resemble palm trees, the legislative chambers are shaped like volcanic cinder cones, and the central court is open to the sky, representing Hawaii's open society. Replicas of the Hawaii state

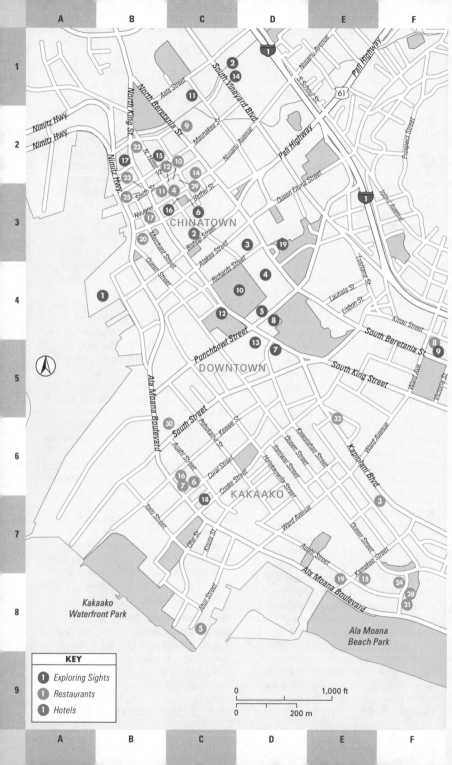

Downtown, Chinatown, Kakaako, and Ala Moana

seal, each weighing 7,500 pounds, hang above both its entrances. The building, which in 1969 replaced Iolani Palace as the seat of government, is surrounded by reflecting pools, just as the Islands are embraced by water. A pair of statues, often draped in lei, flank the building: one of the beloved Queen Liliuokalani and the other of the sainted Father Damien de Veuster, famous for helping Molokai's Hansen's disease (leprosy) patients. Free guided tours are now offered only through district legislators' offices, but you can take a self-guided tour by downloading or picking up a brochure in Room 415. ☒ 415 S. Beretania St., Downtown ☎ 808/586–0221 ⊕ governor.hawaii.gov/hawaii-state-capitol-tours ☒ Free ⊘ Closed weekends.

Hawaii State Library

LIBRARY | This beautifully renovated main library was built in 1913. Its Samuel Manaiakalani Kamakau Room, on the first floor in the *mauka* (Hawaiian for "mountain") courtyard, houses an extensive Hawaii and Pacific book collection and pays tribute to Kamakau, a missionary student whose 19th-century writings in English offer rare and vital insight into traditional Hawaiian culture. ☒ 478 S. King St., Downtown ☎ 808/586–3500 ⊕ librarieshawaii.org ☒ Free ⊘ Closed Sun.

Honolulu Hale

GOVERNMENT BUILDING | This Mediterranean Renaissance–style building was constructed in 1929 and serves as the center of government for the City and County of Honolulu. Stroll through the shady, open-ceiling lobby with exhibits of local artists. During the winter holiday season, the Hale becomes the focal point for the annual Honolulu City Lights, a display of lighting and playful holiday scenes spread around the campus, including the famous, gigantic Shaka Santa and Tute Mele. The mayor's office keeps a calendar of upcoming events. ☒ 530 S. King St., Downtown ☎ 808/768–4385 for

general city info ⊕ www.honolulu.gov/visitors ☒ Free ⊘ Closed weekends.

★ Honolulu Museum of Art

MUSEUM | Originally built around the collection of a Honolulu matron who donated much of her estate to the museum, the academy is housed in a maze of courtyards, cloistered walkways, and quiet, low-ceiling spaces. There's an impressive permanent collection that includes the third-largest collection of Hiroshige's *ukiyo-e* Japanese prints in the country (donated by James Michener); Italian Renaissance paintings; and American and European art by Monet, van Gogh, and Whistler, among many others. The newer Luce Pavilion complex, nicely incorporated into the more traditional architecture of the place, has a traveling-exhibit gallery, a Hawaiian gallery, an excellent café, and a gift shop. The Doris Duke Theatre screens art films. This is also the jumping-off point for tours of Doris Duke's striking estate, which is now the Shangri La Museum of Islamic Art, Culture, and Design. If you wish to visit, you should reserve tickets well in advance. ☒ 900 S. Beretania St., Downtown ☎ 808/532–8700 ⊕ www.honolulumuseum.org ☒ $20 (free 1st Wed. and 3rd Sun. of month) ⊘ Closed Mon.

★ Iolani Palace

CASTLE/PALACE | America's only official royal residence was built in 1882 on the site of an earlier palace. It contains the thrones of King Kalakaua and his successor (and sister) Queen Liliuokalani. Bucking the stereotype of simple island life, the palace had electric lights even before the White House. Downstairs galleries showcase the royal jewelry, and a kitchen and offices restored to the glory of the monarchy. The palace is open for guided tours or self-guided audio tours, and reservations are recommended. ■ TIP→ **If you're set on taking a guided tour, call or book online for reservations a few days in advance.** Tours are available only in the mornings and are limited. The palace

Shangri La

The marriage of heiress Doris Duke to a much older man when she was 23 didn't last. But their around-the-world honeymoon did leave her with two lasting loves: Islamic art and architecture, which she first encountered on that journey; and Hawaii, where the honeymooners made an extended stay while Doris learned to surf and befriended islanders unimpressed by her wealth.

Today, visitors to her beloved Oahu home—where she spent most winters—can share both loves by touring her estate. The sought-after tours are coordinated by and begin at the Honolulu Museum of Art in downtown Honolulu. A short van ride then takes small groups on to the house itself, on the far side of Diamond Head. *For more information, see the listing in Southeast Oahu.*

gift shop and ticket office was formerly the Iolani Barracks, built to house the Royal Guard. ☒ *364 S. King St., Downtown* ☎ *808/522–0832* ⊕ *www.iolanipalace.org* ✉ *$27 guided tour, $20 audio tour* ⊘ *Closed Sun. (except for monthly Kamaaina Sun.).*

Kamehameha I Statue

PUBLIC ART | Paying tribute to the Big Island chieftain who united all the warring Hawaiian Islands into one kingdom at the turn of the 18th century, this statue, which stands with one arm outstretched in welcome, is one of three originally cast in Paris by American sculptor T. R. Gould. The original statue, lost at sea and replaced by this one, was eventually salvaged and is now in Kapaau, on the Big Island, near the king's birthplace. Each year on the king's birthday (June 11), the more famous copy is draped in fresh lei that reach lengths of 18 feet and longer. A parade proceeds past the statue, and Hawaiian civic clubs, women in hats and impressive long *holoku* dresses, and men in sashes and cummerbunds honor the leader whose name means "The One Set Apart." ☒ *417 S. King St., outside Aliiolani Hale, Downtown.*

Kawaiahao Church

RELIGIOUS SITE | Fancifully called Hawaii's Westminster Abbey, this historic house of worship witnessed the coronations, weddings, and funerals of generations of Hawaiian royalty. Each of the building's 14,000 coral blocks was quarried from reefs offshore at depths of more than 20 feet and transported to this site. Interior woodwork was created from the forests of the Koolau Mountains. The upper gallery displays paintings of the royal families. The graves of missionaries and of King Lunalilo are adjacent. Services in English, with songs and prayers in Hawaiian, are held each Sunday. An all-Hawaiian service is held at 5 pm on the second and fourth Sunday of the month (Kawaiahao's affiliation is United Church of Christ). Although there are no guided tours, you can look around the church at no cost. ☒ *957 Punchbowl St., at King St., Downtown* ☎ *808/469–3000* ⊕ *www.kawaiahao.org* ✉ *Free.*

Washington Place Foundation

HOUSE | This white-column mansion was built by sea captain John Dominis, whose son married Liliuokalani, the woman who became the Islands' last queen. Deposed by American-backed forces, the queen returned to the home—which is in sight of the royal palace—and lived there until

Take a guided tour of Iolani Palace, America's only royal residence, built in 1882.

her death. It was then home to Hawaii's sitting governors from 1922 to 2002. The nonprofit Washington Place Foundation now operates the gracious estate. In 2013, it underwent a major renovation to repair the building's roof and its lanai. It is open for one public tour on Thursday only (required reservations can be made by phone or online and should be made well in advance due to the limited tour spots). ✉ *320 S. Beretania St., Downtown* ☎ *808/586–0248 for tour reservations* 🌐 *www.washingtonplacefoundation.org* 🎟 *Donations accepted* 🕒 *Closed Fri.–Wed.*

🍴 Restaurants

Honolulu Museum of Art Café

$$ | AMERICAN | The Honolulu Museum of Art's cool courtyards and galleries filled with works by masters from Monet to Hokusai are well worth a visit and, afterward, so is this popular lunch restaurant. The open-air café is flanked by a burbling water feature and 8-foot-tall ceramic "dumplings" by artist Jun Kaneko—a tranquil setting in the shade of a 75-year-old monkeypod tree in which to eat your salad or sandwich. **Known for:** piadina pesto-caprese flatbread sandwich; limited but beautifully prepared menu of soups, salads, sandwiches, and mains; nice spot for Sunday brunch. [$] *Average main: $18* ✉ *Honolulu Museum of Art, 900 S. Beretania St., Downtown* ☎ *808/532–8734* 🌐 *www.honolulumuseum.org/394-museum_cafe* 🕒 *Closed Mon. No dinner.*

Murphy's Bar & Grill

$ | AMERICAN | FAMILY | Located on the edge between the financial district and Chinatown, Honolulu's go-to Irish bar serves Guinness on tap and an Irish-American menu of pubby favorites such as spicy chicken wings, jalapeño poppers, fish 'n' chips, corned beef and cabbage, and grilled New York steak—without that Waikiki price tag. But probably the most popular menu item is the Blarney Burger, gooey with Guinness-infused cheddar cheese. **Known for:** stick-to-your-ribs Irish fare; creative salads that add diversity (and heart relief) to an otherwise heavy menu; fun setting that has you smiling on the way out the door. $ *Average main: $16 ⊠ 2 Merchant St., Downtown* ☎ *808/531–0422* ⊕ *www. murphyshawaii.com.*

PAI Honolulu

$$$ | MODERN AMERICAN | Michelin-star restaurant chef Kevin Lee and his general manager wife Justine are at the helm of the innovative, upscale Pai (short for *ho'opai* meaning "to encourage" in Hawaiian). The tantalizing and surprising fusion cuisine is served in a modern, arched dining room and patio tucked into the atrium of the Harbor Court condo building. **Known for:** house-made breads; superb cocktails and wine pairings; attention to detail in each dish. $ *Average main: $30 ⊠ Harbor Court, 55 Merchant St., Suite 110, Downtown* ☎ *808/744–2531* ⊕ *paihonolulu.com* ⊗ *Closed Sun. and Mon. No lunch Tues. or Sat.*

Vino Italian Tapas & Wine Bar

$$ | WINE BAR | Vino has a lock on local oenophiles and pau hana time groups, who make a beeline for this wine bar and restaurant. Chef Keith Endo creates his take on contemporary Mediterranean-inspired cuisine, including house-made pastas, sausage and cheese, all paired with wines selected by the nationally recognized sommelier Chuck Furuya. **Known for:** regular wine-food pairing dinners; jumbo shrimp in a resonant cioppino sauce; great happy hour spot. $ *Average main: $25 ⊠ Waterfront Plaza, 500 Ala Moana Blvd., Suite 6F, Kakaako* ☎ *808/524–8466* ⊕ *www.vinohawaii.com* ⊗ *Closed Mon. No lunch.*

Yanagi Sushi

$$$ | JAPANESE | One of relatively few restaurants to serve the complete menu until 2 am (until 10 pm on Sunday), Yanagi is a full-service Japanese restaurant offering not only sushi and sashimi around a small bar, but also *teishoku* (combination menus), tempura, stews, and grill-it-yourself shabu-shabu. The fish can be depended on for freshness and variety.

Known for: late-night happy hour; baked crabmeat volcano roll, spicy shrimp tempura roll, or live abalone sashimi; local favorite. $ *Average main: $28 ⊠ 762 Kapiolani Blvd., Downtown* ☎ *808/597–1525* ⊕ *www.yanagisushi-hawaii.com.*

🛏 Hotels

Aston at the Executive Centre Hotel

$$ | HOTEL | Downtown Honolulu's only hotel is an all-suites high-rise in the center of the business district, within walking distance of the historic Capitol District, museums, and Honolulu's Chinatown, and a 10-minute drive from Honolulu International Airport. **Pros:** discounted passes to nearby 24 Hour Fitness; great restaurant (Hukilau) in the lobby; good spot for overnighting before or after a cruise. **Cons:** no beach within walking distance; suites are individually owned, so quality of room can vary; parking is very expensive. $ *Rooms from: $260 ⊠ 1088 Bishop St., Downtown* ☎ *808/539–3000, 855/945-4090 toll-free reservations* ⊕ *www.astonhotels.com/resort/overview/aston-at-the-executive-centre-hotel* ⌦ *90 suites* ⦿ *No meals.*

◐ Nightlife

BARS

★ Bar Leather Apron

BARS/PUBS | This James Beard Award–nominated bar at this intimate cocktail spot, oddly situated in the mezzanine of a downtown Honolulu office building, seats only six at the bar along with a few other tables. So you'll want to make reservations to enjoy bespoke cocktails that utilize only the finest liquors and ingredients. Owners Tom Park and Justin Park (no relation) have cultivated a reputation for their E Ho'o Pau Mai Tai made with a 5-year-old, raisin-infused El Dorado rum and another, 12-year-old El Dorado rum, as well as coconut water syrup, spiced orgeat, ohia blossom honey, lime, vanilla, and absinthe, and served up with a kiawe wood smoke presentation. The bar is closed on Sunday and Monday. ⊠ *Topa Financial Center, 745 Fort St., Mezzanine Level, Suite 127A, Downtown* ☎ *808/524–0808* ⊕ *www.barleatherapron.com.*

Murphy's Bar & Grill

BARS/PUBS | On the edge of Chinatown and the financial district, this bar has served drinks to such locals and visitors as King Kalakaua and Robert Louis Stevenson since the late 1800s. The kind of Irish pub you would find in Boston, Murphy's offers a break from all the tropical, fruit-garnished drinks found in Waikiki, and it's definitely the place to be on St. Patrick's Day. Friendly bartenders and waitstaff serve Guinness on tap, pub food favorites, and Irish specialties like corned beef and cabbage and shepherd's pie. If you time it right, you can try their incredible homemade pies, which are served only on Fridays and quickly sell out. ⊠ *2 Merchant St., Downtown* ☎ *808/531–0422* ⊕ *www.murphyshawaii.com.*

🎭 Performing Arts

DINNER CRUISES AND SHOWS

Most dinner cruises depart either from the piers adjacent to the Aloha Tower Marketplace in downtown Honolulu or from Kewalo Basin, near Ala Moana Beach Park, and head along the coast toward Diamond Head. There's usually a buffet-style dinner with local flavor, dancing, drinks, a sensational sunset, and even potential whale spotting between December to April. Some cruises offer discounts for online reservations. Most major credit cards are accepted. In all cases, reservations are essential.

Atlantis Cruises

ENTERTAINMENT CRUISE | The sleekly high-tech *Majestic,* designed to sail smoothly in rough waters, powers farther along Waikiki's coastline than its competitors. Enjoy seasonal whale-watching trips between January and March during the day or year-round sunset cocktail and dinner cruises aboard the 400-passenger boat. (Atlantis is also known for its submarine tours off Waikiki.) The boat's dining room is elegantly laid out, and the standard Hawaii buffet fare will fill you up while you enjoy a tropical cocktail, champagne, beer, or guava juice. Honeymooners and those celebrating anniversaries and birthdays—and even the occasional proposal—are the majority of passengers, and add to the festive atmosphere along with the live Hawaiian music accompaniment. Make sure to head up to the top deck for the best view of Waikiki and the sunset. ■TIP→ **For the sunset cruise, if you plan on having two or more alcoholic beverages plus coffee, tea, or soda, it's worth it to purchase the $25 drink package.** ⊠ *1 Aloha Tower Rd., Pier 6, Downtown* ☎ *808/973–9800, 800/381–0237* ⊕ *majestichawaii.com* 🚢 *From $66.*

Star of Honolulu Cruises

ENTERTAINMENT CRUISE | The award-winning, 1,500-passenger *Star of Honolulu* boasts four sunset dinner-cruise packages, from a roast beef buffet and Polynesian show to a romantic seven-course fine-dining excursion with live jazz. The company also runs whale-watching and special holiday cruises. ⊠ *Aloha Tower Marketplace, 1 Aloha Tower Dr., Pier 8, Downtown* ☎ *808/983–7730* ⊕ *www.starofhonolulu.com* 🚢 *From $99.*

FILM

Doris Duke Theatre–Honolulu Museum of Arts

FILM | Art, international, classic, and silent films are screened at the intimate, 280-seat Doris Duke Theatre, which doubles as a concert venue. Many short film festivals are scheduled throughout the year on regional and global themes. Although small, the theater is still classy and comfortable. It is known for its great sound system. ⊠ *Doris Duke Theatre, 900 S. Beretania St., Downtown* ☎ *808/532–6097* ⊕ *honolulumuseum.org.*

MUSIC

Chamber Music Hawaii

MUSIC | This group, consisting of four ensembles, has been around for decades and performs 20 to 25 concerts a year at the **Honolulu Museum of Arts' Doris Duke Theatre** (✉ *901 S. Beretania St., Honolulu*), the **Paliku Theatre at Windward Community College** (✉ *45-720 Keaahala Rd., Kaneohe*), the **UH West Oahu library** (✉ *1001 Farrington Hwy., Kapolei*), and other locations around the island. Seasons run from fall through spring. ✉ *Downtown* ☎ *808/722–0172* ⊕ *www. chambermusichawaii.org.*

First Friday

MUSIC | Rain or shine, on the first Friday of every month, the downtown Honolulu and Chinatown districts come alive. The more family-friendly early evening art tours evolve into an adults-only club atmosphere. Art galleries and restaurants usually stay open late, and local musicians and DJs provide the sound track for the evening. ✉ *Chinatown* ⊕ *www. firstfridayhawaii.com* 💳 *Free entrance to galleries; cover charge for some nightclubs.*

Hawaii Opera Theatre

OPERA | Locals refer to it as "HOT," probably because the Hawaii Opera Theatre has been turning the opera-challenged into opera lovers since 1960. All operas are sung in their original language with a projected English translation. ✉ *Neal S. Blaisdell Center Concert Hall, 777 Ward Ave., Honolulu* ☎ *808/596–7372 main office, 800/836–7372 toll-free* ⊕ *www. hawaiiopera.org.*

THEATER

Hawaii can be an expensive gig for touring shows and music artists that depend on major theatrical sets. Not many manage to stop here, and those that do sell out fast. Oahu has developed several excellent local theater companies, which present first-rate entertainment all year long. Anyone who attends is always surprised to learn that the Honolulu

Theatre for Youth is the only professional troupe in the state. Community support for these groups is strong.

Hawaii Theatre Center

THEATER | This beautifully restored theater, built in the 1920s in a Beaux Arts style, hosts a wide variety of events, including international theatrical productions and touring acts, festivals, and films. It's easily the loveliest theater in Hawaii. Tours cost $10 and are offered every first Tuesday of the month at 11 am (same-day tickets only). Admission for performances varies. ✉ *1130 Bethel St., Downtown* ☎ *808/528–0506 for questions about docent tours* ⊕ *www.hawaiitheatre.com.*

★ Honolulu Theatre for Youth

THEATER | FAMILY | This group stages delightful productions August–May with creative props and engaging stories. Founded in 1955, it's one of the oldest children's theaters in the country (it's the only professional theater in Hawaii), serving more than 5 million people through school and family performances and drama-education programs. ✉ *Tenney Theatre, 229 Queen Emma Sq., Downtown* ☎ *808/839–9885* ⊕ *www.htyweb.org.*

Kumu Kahua Theatre

THEATER | This troupe sticks to producing only plays written by local playwrights about island life and Hawaiian experiences. It stages five or six productions a year in a 100-seat auditorium that's perfect for getting up close and personal with the cast. ✉ *46 Merchant St., Downtown* ☎ *808/536–4441* ⊕ *www.kumukahua.org* 💳 *$25 ($20 on Thurs.).*

🛍 Shopping

Downtown/Chinatown shopping is an entirely different, constantly changing experience from what you'll find elsewhere in Honolulu. Focus on the small galleries—which are earning the area a strong reputation for its arts and culture renaissance—and the burgeoning array of hip, home-decor stores tucked between ethnic restaurants. ■ TIP→ **Don't miss the festive atmosphere on the first Friday of every month, when stores, restaurants, and galleries stay open 5–9 pm for the Downtown Gallery Walk.**

Chinatown

Chinatown's original business district was made up of dry-goods and produce merchants, tailors and dressmakers, barbers, herbalists, and dozens of restaurants. The meat, fish, and produce stalls remain, but the mix is heavier now on gift and curio stores, lei stands, jewelry shops, and bakeries, with a smattering of noodle makers, travel agents, and dozens of restaurants.

The name "Chinatown" here has always been a misnomer. Though three-quarters of Oahu's Chinese lived closely packed in these 25 acres in the late 1800s, even then the neighborhood was half Japanese. Today you hear Vietnamese and Tagalog as often as Mandarin and Cantonese, and there are voices of Japan, Singapore, Malaysia, Korea, Thailand, Samoa, and the Marshall Islands, as well.

Perhaps a more accurate name is the one used by early Chinese: *Wah Fau* (Chinese port), signifying a landing and jumping-off place. Chinese laborers, as soon as they completed their plantation contracts, hurried into the city to start businesses here. It's a launching point for today's immigrants, too: Southeast Asian shops almost outnumber Chinese; stalls carry Filipino specialties like winged beans and goat meat; and you'll find Japanese, Cambodian, Laotian, Thai, and Korean cuisine and goods for sale.

In the half century after the first Chinese laborers arrived in Hawaii in 1851, Chinatown was a link to home for the all-male cadre of workers who planned to return to China rich and respected. Merchants not only sold supplies, they held mail, loaned money, wrote letters, translated

Buying Flowers and Fruit 💼

You can bring home fresh pineapple, papaya, or coconut to share with friends and family. Orchids will also brighten your home and remind you of your trip to the Islands. By law, all fresh fruit and plant products must be inspected by the Department of Agriculture before export. Ask at the shop about Department of Agriculture rules so a surprise confiscation doesn't spoil your departure. Shipping to your home usually is best.

documents, sent remittances to families, served meals, offered rough bunkhouse accommodations, and were the center for news, gossip, and socializing.

Although much happened to Chinatown in the 20th century—beginning in January 1900, when almost the entire neighborhood was burned to the ground to halt the spread of bubonic plague—it remains a bustling, crowded, noisy, and odiferous place bent primarily on buying and selling and sublimely oblivious to its status as a National Historic District or the encroaching gentrification on nearby Nuuanu Avenue.

GETTING HERE AND AROUND
Chinatown occupies 15 blocks immediately north of downtown Honolulu—it's flat, compact, and very walkable. ■ TIP→ **Bring cash to use at the ethnic markets, eateries, stores, and vendor stalls that don't accept credit cards or have a minimum spending amount to use one.**

◉ Sights

Foster Botanical Garden
GARDEN | Some of the trees in this botanical garden, which opened in 1931, date

from 1853, when Queen Kalama allowed a young German doctor to lease a portion of her land. More than 150 years later, you can see these trees and countless others along with bromeliads, orchids, and other tropical plants, some of which are rare or endangered. Look out in particular for the cannonball tree and the redwood-size Quipo tree. A docent-led tour is available every day at 10:30 am (call for reservations). ⊠ *180 N. Vineyard Blvd., Chinatown* ☎ *808/768–7135, 808/768–7135 for daily guided tours reservations* ⊕ *www.honolulu.gov/parks/ hbg/honolulu-botanical-gardens* ⊠ *$5.*

Hawaii Theatre
ARTS VENUE | Opened in 1922, this theater earned rave reviews for its neoclassical design, with Corinthian columns, marble statues, and plush carpeting and drapery. Nicknamed the "Pride of the Pacific," the facility was rescued from demolition in the early 1980s and underwent a $30-million renovation. Listed on both the State and National Register of Historic Places, it has become the centerpiece of revitalization efforts of Honolulu's downtown area. The 1,400-seat venue hosts concerts, theatrical productions, dance performances, and film screenings. Guided tours of the theater end with a mini-concert on the historic orchestral pipe organ and can be booked through the box office. If interested one of the weekly tours on Tuesdays at 11 am, call a few days ahead to reserve. ⊠ *1130 Bethel St., Chinatown* ☎ *808/528–0506* ⊕ *www.hawaiitheatre.com* ⊠ *$10* ⊙ *Closed Wed.–Mon.*

Izumo Taishakyo Mission of Hawaii
RELIGIOUS SITE | From Chinatown Cultural Plaza, cross a stone bridge to the Izumo Taishakyo Mission of Hawaii to visit the shrine established in 1906. It honors Okuninushi-no-Mikoto, a *kami* (god) who is believed in Shinto tradition to bring good fortune if properly courted (and thanked afterward). ⊠ *215 N. Kukui St., Chinatown* ⊕ *At the canal*

☎ *808/538–7778* ⊕ *izumotaishahawaii. com.*

Kuan Yin Temple
RELIGIOUS SITE | A couple of blocks *mauka* (toward the mountains) from Chinatown is the oldest Buddhist temple in the Islands. Mistakenly called a goddess by some, Kuan Yin, also known as Kannon, is a *bodhisattva*—one who chose to remain on Earth doing good even after achieving enlightenment. Transformed from a male into a female figure centuries ago, she is credited with a particular sympathy for women. You will see representations of her all over the Islands: holding a lotus flower (beauty from the mud of human frailty), as at the temple; pouring out a pitcher of oil (like mercy flowing); or as a sort of Madonna with a child. Visitors are permitted but be aware this is a practicing place of worship. ⊠ *170 N. Vineyard Blvd., Chinatown* ⊕ *Park at Foster Botanical Gardens.*

Maunakea Marketplace
MARKET | On the corner of Maunakea and Hotel streets is this busy plaza surrounded by shops and an air-conditioned indoor market and food court where you can buy fresh seafood and local produce in season or chow down on banana lumpia and fresh fruit smoothies and bubble tea (juices and flavored teas with tapioca balls inside). It gets packed every year for the annual Chinese Lunar New Year. ⊠ *1120 Maunakea St., Chinatown* ⊕ *geyserholdings.com/maunakea.*

Nuuanu Avenue
NEIGHBORHOOD | Here on Chinatown's main *mauka–makai* drag and on Bethel Street, which runs parallel, are clustered art galleries, restaurants, a few tattoo parlors, bars and pubs, an antiques auctioneer, several dress shops, one small theater/exhibition space (the Arts at Mark's Garage), and one historic stage (the Hawaii Theatre). You can also take in the unique early 1900s architecture of the buildings. **First Friday** art nights, when galleries stay open until 9 pm,

draw crowds. Many stay later and crowd Chinatown's bars. If you like art and people-watching and are fortunate enough to be on Oahu the first Friday of the month, this event shouldn't be missed. ✉ *Nuuanu Ave., Chinatown.*

Oahu Market

MARKET | In this tenant-owned market founded in 1904, you'll find a taste of old-style Chinatown, where you might spot a whole butchered pig, head intact, on display and where glassy-eyed fish of every size and hue lie forlornly on ice. Bizarre magenta dragonfruit, ready-to-eat char siu and pork belly, and binsbrimming with produce add to Oahu Market's color. You'll find some of the cheapest Oahu prices on fruits and vegetables in this and other Chinatown markets. ✉ *N. King St., Chinatown* ✥ *At Kekaulike St.*

🍴 Restaurants

Fete

$$ | **HAWAIIAN** | Fete slipped into its cozy brick-walled space amid the Chinatown culinary boom in 2016, and it's been packing in regulars ever since. Folks come for the burgers and specials at lunch; for dinner, try one of the pastas, locally sourced seafood, or to-die-for twice-fried Kauai chicken with grits and collard greens. **Known for:** Brooklyn-meets-Hawaii menu; great pau hana/happy hour menu; craft cocktails and extensive drink menu. [$] *Average main: $25* ✉ *2 N. Hotel St., Chinatown* ☎ *808/369–1390* 🌐 *fetehawaii.com.*

Legend Seafood Restaurant

$ | **CHINESE** | At this large Chinatown institution, the dim sum cart ladies stop at your table and show you their Hong Kong–style fare. This is a great place to try dim sum for the first time before going exploring. **Known for:** still-warm custard tarts; dim sum, reasonably priced by the dish; easy parking in the cultural plaza parking lot. [$] *Average main: $13* ✉ *Chinese Cultural Plaza, 100 N. Beretania St., Suite 108, Chinatown* ☎ *808/532–1868* 🌐 *www.legendseafoodhonolulu.com.*

Little Village Noodle House

$$ | **CHINESE** | Unassuming and budget-friendly, Little Village is so popular with locals that it expanded to the space next door. Considered some of the best Chinese food on Oahu, the extensive Pan-Asian menu is filled with crowd-pleasers like honey-walnut shrimp and crispy orange chicken. **Known for:** something for everyone on the menu; fun interior design with village decor; BYOB. [$] *Average main: $18* ✉ *1113 Smith St., Chinatown* ☎ *808/545–3008* 🌐 *www.littlevillagehawaii.com.*

★ **Livestock Tavern**

$$ | **MODERN AMERICAN** | Livestock Tavern scores big with its seasonal offerings of comfort foods, craft cocktails, and cowboy-minimalist decor. Although meat commands the menu, offerings like burrata, creative salads, sandwiches, and fish round out the possibilities. **Known for:** lively bar scene; go-to lunch spot; fresh-cut fries. [$] *Average main: $20* ✉ *49 N. Hotel St., Chinatown* ☎ *808/537–2577* 🌐 *www.livestocktavern.com* ⏲ *Closed Sun. No lunch Sat.*

Lucky Belly

$$ | **ASIAN** | A hip local crowd sips cocktails and slurps huge bowls of familiar noodle dishes with a modern twist at this popular fusion ramen bar. The service here is unpretentious and attentive if you eat in, but you can also order your food to go. **Known for:** steaming hot pot dishes; small but unique cocktail menu; "Belly Bowl" with smoked bacon, sausage, and pork belly. [$] *Average main: $17* ✉ *50 N. Hotel St., Chinatown* ☎ *808/531–1888* ⏲ *Closed Sun.*

Mei Sum Chinese Dim Sum Restaurant

$ | **CHINESE** | In contrast to the sprawling, noisy halls in which dim sum is generally served, Mei Sum is compact and shiny bright, not to mention a favorite of locals who work in the area. Be ready to guess and point at the color photos of dim sum favorites or the items on the carts as they come by, or ask fellow diners for suggestions. **Known for:** deep-fried garlic eggplant; house special garlic rice; dim sum made fresh daily. $ *Average main: $11* ✉ *1170 Nuuanu Ave., Suite 102, Chinatown* ✛ *Next to post office* ☎ *808/531–3268* ⊕ *meisumdimsum.com.*

Pho To Chau Restaurant

$ | **VIETNAMESE** | Those people lined up on River Street know where to get bowls of steaming *pho* (Vietnamese beef noodle soup) with all the best trimmings. This hole-in-the-wall storefront was the go-to pho spot long before hipsters and foodies found Chinatown. **Known for:** no-frills service and sometimes a wait for food once seated; old school 1970s decor; large pho can be easily shared. $ *Average main: $10* ✉ *1007 River St., Chinatown* ☎ *808/533–4549* ▭ *No credit cards* ⊘ *No dinner* ⚲ *Cash only.*

⭐ The Pig and the Lady

$$ | **MODERN ASIAN** | Chef Andrew Le's casual noodle house attracts downtown office workers by day and becomes a creative contemporary restaurant at night, pulling in serious chowhounds. Drawing on both his Vietnamese heritage and multicultural island flavors, the talented, playful Le is a wizard with spice and acid, turning out dishes of layered flavor. **Known for:** bahn mi sandwiches at lunch and pho all day; house-made soft-serve custards and sorbets, including unexpected flavors; Hanoi-style egg coffee. $ *Average main: $20* ✉ *83 N. King St., Chinatown* ☎ *808/585–8255* ⊕ *www. thepigandthelady.com* ⊘ *Closed Sun. and Mon.*

⭐ Senia

$$$ | **MODERN AMERICAN** | Since opening in 2016, this small, sophisticated restaurant and its chefs have been nominated several times over for James Beard Awards. It's no wonder, as every item on the modern American menu is carefully concocted and artfully plated. **Known for:**

Senia cookie made with peanut butter, toffee, and Valrhona chocolate; sophisticated cocktails and an encyclopedic wine menu; charred cabbage that looks like a mossy rock but mesmerizes the tastebuds. $ *Average main: $30* ✉ *75 N. King St., Chinatown* ✛ *Between The Pig & The Lady and Smith & Kings* ☎ *808/200–5412* ⊕ *restaurantsenia.com* ⊘ *Closed Sun. No lunch Mon. or Sat.*

Terry's Place

$$ | **BISTRO** | This country-style European bistro (formerly known as HASR Bistro) is in a quiet courtyard next to its sister wine shop. Owner Terry Kakazu brings her wine expertise to the menu of classic, elevated comfort food. **Known for:** small plates to share; extensive wine list; great place for groups and celebrations. $ *Average main: $25* ✉ *31 N. Pauahi St., Chinatown* ☎ *808/533–4277* ⊕ *terrysplace808.com* ⊘ *Closed Sun. and Mon. No lunch.*

🍸 Nightlife

BARS

Encore Saloon

BARS/PUBS | Hawaii isn't a hotbed for quality Mexican cuisine, so when Encore opened in 2016, it was a welcome addition to Chinatown's already buzzing bar and restaurant scene. The mezcal-focused bar also serves good Mexican-inspired food, but its drinks menu is most impressive, offering more than 50 varieties of tequila and mezcal, both of which are distilled from agave. You can also get a traditional margarita here, as well as wine and canned beer. If you're hungry, order the pork carnitas burrito. The bar is closed on Sunday. ✉ *10 N. Hotel St., Chinatown* ☎ *808/367–1656* ⊕ *encoresaloon.com.*

J. Dolan's

BARS/PUBS | This place bills itself as an Irish pub that serves New York–style pizza. The drinks and rotating beers on tap are just as popular as the pizza since they're reasonably priced by Honolulu standards. The classics are always on the menu in this "Cheers"-like bar, but J.J. Dolan's daily specials are toothsome and inventive. From downtown professionals to local families, these pies are crowd-pleasers. ⊠ *1147 Bethel St., Chinatown* ☎ *808/537–4992* ⊕ *www.jdolans.com.*

Manifest

BARS/PUBS | With exposed red brick, big skylights, and rotating exhibitions from local photographers and painters, Manifest Hawaii has an artist's loft feel to it. Café by day, and bar/club/music venue by night, Manifest has both a good cup of Joe and quality cocktails. It's closed on Sunday. ⊠ *32 N. Hotel St., Chinatown* ⊕ *www.manifesthawaii.com.*

The Tchin Tchin! Bar

BARS/PUBS | This chill Chinatown bar gets its name from the Chinese expression "qing, qing" (which means "please please"), often used as a toast; soldiers returning from the Chinese Opium Wars introduced it in France and throughout Europe. With an extensive wine menu—by the glass and the bottle—plus a selection of single malt bourbon, whiskey, and scotch, it's an ideal spot for a drink or tapas-style food. The bar's open-air rooftop lanai is the best place to sit, romantically lit with string lights and featuring a large living wall flourishing with ferns. The bar is closed on Sunday and Monday. ⊠ *39 N. Hotel St., Chinatown* ☎ *808/528–1888* ⊕ *www.thetchintchinbar.com.*

CLUBS

The Dragon Upstairs

MUSIC CLUBS | Though it was once more cool and jazz-centric, The Dragon Upstairs remains a hole-in-the-wall bar to stop at for an eclectic mix of bands, open mikes, live karaoke, and comedy acts (there's usually a small cover charge for live bands). Tucked above Hank's Cafe Honolulu, this small venue is painted a

deep red and decorated with dragons and Chinese theater masks. The bar menu is basic but adequate. It's closed Sunday. ⊠ *1038 Nuuanu Ave., Chinatown* ☎ *808/526–1411.*

● Shopping

Chinatown offers the typical mix of the tacky and unique, depending on individual taste, but it is an experience not to be missed. The vital, bright colors of fresh fruits and vegetables blend with the distinct scent of recently killed pigs and poultry. Tucked in between are authentic shops with Asian silk clothing at reasonable prices. The bustling, ethnic atmosphere adds to the excitement. If you're hungry for a local experience, you should at least walk through the area, even if you don't plan to purchase the mysterious herbs in the glass jars lining the shelves.

Curio shops sell everything from porcelain statues to woks, ginseng to Mao shoes. Visit the New Hong Kong Market for fresh fruit, crack seed (Chinese dried fruit popular for snacking), and row upon row of boxed, tinned delicacies with indecipherable names.

Chinatown Cultural Plaza offers fine-quality jade. Chinatown is also Honolulu's lei center, with shops strung along Beretania and Maunakea; the locals have favorite shops where they're greeted by name. In spring, look for gardenia nosegays wrapped in ti leaves.

GALLERIES

Louis Pohl Gallery

ART GALLERIES | Stop in this gallery to browse modern works from some of Hawaii's finest artists. In addition to pieces by resident artists, there are monthly exhibitions by local and visiting artists. ⊠ *1142 Bethel St., Suite A, Chinatown* ☎ *808/521–1812* ⊕ *www.louispohlgallery.com.*

HOME DECOR

★ Place

HOUSEHOLD ITEMS/FURNITURE | This design studio/workshop is known for its sophisticated assemblage of carefully chosen home items in all price ranges. You'll find a global collection of fine lighting, furniture, and textiles, as well as art by local artists and artisans curated by owner and interior designer Mary Philpotts McGrath, who creates a Hawaiian sense of place. ✉ *54 S. School St., #100, Chinatown* ☎ *808/275–3075* 🌐 *www.placehawaii.com.*

Kakaako

This 600-acre section of Honolulu between Ala Moana Center and downtown is in the middle of a decade-long redevelopment plan that began in 2012; it remains a neighborhood in transition. Now home to everything from ramshackle mechanic shops to the University of Hawaii's medical school, Kakaako's old warehouses and mom-and-pop storefronts are being replaced by gleaming luxury condos, shops, and restaurants. Many new condo buildings in the Ward/Kaakao area have already been finished, and others grow taller by the day or are about to break ground. It's also home to new big-box stores including T.J. Maxx, as well as smaller local boutiques. Every month seems to bring new happenings such as the Honolulu Night Market, a pop-up shopping event.

👁 Sights

POW! WOW! Hawaii Murals

PUBLIC ART | The POW! WOW! Worldwide art collective was founded in Hawaii in 2010 and has now spread to nearly 20 cities around the world. Its most visible form on Oahu are several blocks colorful, eclectic, and innovative murals on the sides of once-derelict looking warehouses and other buildings. Every year around Valentine's Day, artists from all over come to refresh and add new murals to the collection, and the event wraps up with a big food, art, and entertainment festival centered at the SALT at Kakaako complex. Grab a bite to eat, and wander around any time of the year to take in this unique street art. ✉ *Kakaako* ✣ *Murals are centered on Cooke, Auahi, and Pohukaina Sts.* ☎ *808/223–7462* 🌐 *powwowhawaii.com.*

🍴 Restaurants

53 by the Sea

$$$$ | **CONTEMPORARY** | Housed in a McVilla aimed at attracting a Japanese wedding clientele, this restaurant serves contemporary Continental food that focuses primarily on beautifully plated, well-prepared standards—albeit with a million-dollar view of Honolulu. Perched at water's edge, with famed surf break Point Panic offshore, 53 by the Sea uses its setting to great advantage—the crescent-shape dining room faces the sea, so even if you're not at a table nestled against the floor-to-ceiling windows, you have a fine view. **Known for:** odd villa decor that somehow works; free valet parking; wedding chapel on-site in case the mood strikes. [$] *Average main: $50* ✉ *53 Ahui St., Kakaako* ☎ *808/536–5353* 🌐 *53bythesea.com.*

Hank's Haute Dogs

$ | **HOT DOG** | **FAMILY** | Owner Hank Adaniya's idea of a hot dog involves things like a duck and foie gras sausage with truffle mustard and stone fruit compote. Originally a true hole-in-the-wall, the gentrified Hank's is still a tiny spot where you can go classic with the Chicago Dog, made with the traditional fixings (including neon-green relish), or gourmet with the butter-seared lobster sausage topped with garlic-relish aioli. **Known for:** 11 varieties of dogs daily, plus another five or so daily specials; fries, truffle fries, and onion rings to die for; part of Kakaako's SALT area. [$] *Average main: $9* ✉ *324*

You won't soon forget the eye-popping murals the Pow! Wow! collective has painted on the buildings in the redeveloping Kakaako neighborhood.

Coral St., Kakaako ☎ *808/532–4265* 🌐 *www.hankshautedogs.com* ☞ *Remember to get parking validated.*

Highway Inn Kakaako

$ | **MODERN HAWAIIAN** | **FAMILY** | Highway Inn serves up what it does best: local favorites like Kalbi ribs, *kalua* (roasted in an underground oven) pork sliders, beef stew, and old-fashioned hamburger steaks. For those looking to try *poi* (the puddinglike dish made of pounded taro), this is a good spot. **Known for:** Kakaako location is in SALT complex; relatively close to the cruise terminal; signature combo plates. [$] *Average main: $16* ✉ *680 Ala Moana Blvd., Kakaako* ☎ *808/954–4955* 🌐 *myhighwayinn.com.*

Merriman's Honolulu

$$$ | **BISTRO** | Oahu residents were excited when a full-fledged Merriman's finally landed on Oahu in 2018 after previously being on neighbor islands only. This is fine dining without the fussiness, where your cordial and well-trained servers will present your "Bag O' Biscuits" or smoking oysters on the half shelf with equal aplomb and know all the details of each menu item. **Known for:** lobster pot pie; tableside poke; Waialua chocolate purse (a take on molten lava cake). [$] *Average main: $35* ✉ *1108 Auahi St., Suite 170, Kakaako* ☎ *808/215–0022* 🌐 *merrimanshawaii.com.*

Moku Kitchen

$$ | **HAWAIIAN** | **FAMILY** | In the hip SALT complex, Moku's draws locals, including both foodies and families, as well as visitors looking for authentic farm-to-table cuisine in a laid-back, urban setting. One of legendary chef Peter Merriman's restaurants, Moku focuses on upcountry farm fare cooked in the on-site rotisserie; locally sourced pizzas, salads, and sandwiches; and an impressive list of craft cocktails and beers. **Known for:** twice-daily happy hour (3–5:30 pm and 9–11 pm); impressive list of craft cocktails, wine, and beer, including the signature monkeypod mai tai; live music almost nightly. [$] *Average main: $20* ✉ *SALT at Our Kakaako, 660 Ala Moana*

Blvd., Kakaako ☎ *808/591–6658* 🌐 *www.mokukitchen.com.*

Nobu Honolulu

$$$$ | **JAPANESE FUSION** | Always a local favorite, Nobu's move from Waikiki to a chic Ward high-rise has only made it better. Still anchored in its award-winning "New Style" Japanese cuisine, the restaurant serves up signature Nobu dishes found at all the restaurants along with original Hawaii options like Kurobuta pork belly and ahi poke. **Known for:** casual elegance at serious prices; black cod lacquered with sweet den miso and yellowtail sashimi with jalapeño; a bar scene that rarely disappoints. [$] *Average main: $38* ✉ *Waiea at Ward Village, 1118 Ala Moana Blvd., Kakaako* ☎ *808/237–6999* 🌐 *www.noburestaurants.com* 🕒 *No lunch.*

Panya

$$ | **ECLECTIC** | This easy-breezy café run by Hong Kong–born sisters Alice and Annie Yeung offers a crowd-pleasing menu of contemporary American (salads, sandwiches, pastas) and Asian (Thai-style steak salad, Japanese-style fried chicken, Singaporean seafood *laksa*), served in a disco-tinged space (there's also a full bar). They're also known for their pastries, dessert, and happy hour. **Known for:** French-style pastries and cakes; eclectic and extensive menu; Japanese cheesecake. [$] *Average main: $18* ✉ *1288 Ala Moana Blvd., Kakaako* ☎ *808/946–6388* 🌐 *panyabistro.com.*

Scratch Kitchen & Meatery

$$ | **MODERN AMERICAN** | Tucked into the chic South Shore Market in Kakaako's Ward Village, this former Chinatown spot has moved uptown with its hipster decor, open kitchen, and creative comfort food. It's popular for breakfast and brunch and has both small plates and generous entrées on its dinner menu. **Known for:** milk 'n' cereal pancakes; spicy (and good) chicken and waffles; large portions. [$] *Average main: $18* ✉ *South Shore Market at Ward Village, 1170 Auahi St., Kakaako* ✥ *Enter on side of building, along Queen St.* ☎ *808/589–1669* 🌐 *scratch-hawaii.com.*

Tangö Contemporary Cafe

$$ | **ECLECTIC** | On the ground floor of a glass-sheathed condominium, Tangö's spare contemporary setting stays humming at breakfast, lunch, and dinner. Finnish chef Göran Streng honors his heritage a bit with unfussy dishes such as gravlax with crispy skin, but the menu is, by and large, "general bistro," running from bouillabaisse to herb-crusted rack of lamb with some Asian nods. **Known for:** Hamakua mushroom risotto; loco moco (unlike any you'll have elsewhere); attentive staff. [$] *Average main: $25* ✉ *Hokua Bldg., 1288 Ala Moana Blvd., Kakaako* ☎ *808/593–7288* 🌐 *tangocafehawaii.com* 🕒 *No dinner Sun.*

🍸 Nightlife

BARS

Aloha Beer Co.

BREWPUBS/BEER GARDENS | At this cool brewpub, you order everything at the counter and then pick a spot to sit in either the industrial indoor taproom or the casual outdoor area. (The HI Brau Room upstairs, which has its own speakeasy-style entrance, is definitely worth checking out for unique cocktails, too.) With 12 beers on draft, including the Hop Lei IPA, Waimanalo Farmhouse, Froot Loops, and Portlock Porter, you can find something to your taste. If you're hungry, there's also pretty good food—snacking boards, hearty sandwiches, small plates, and steak frites—to nosh on. ✉ *700 Queen St., Kakaako* ☎ *808/544–1605* 🌐 *www.alohabeer.com.*

★ **Bevy**

BARS/PUBS | Tucked at the end of a row of new boutiques in Kakaako, Bevy is urban, modern, and furnished with up-cycled materials (its benches are upholstered in denim jeans, and its table tops feature flattened wine boxes). Locals in the know go for artisan cocktails created by owner and award-winning mixologist Christian Self, who deftly concocts libations with obscure ingredients and complex flavors. One happy hour (4–7 pm) bright spot is the $1.50 oyster shooters. There's a live DJ on Friday and Saturday night, but the bar is closed on Sunday. (Next door is Taco-ako, Self's street taco lunch spot.) ⊠ *675 Auahi St., Kakaako* ☎ *808/594–7445* ⊕ *www.bevyhawaii.com.*

★ **Honolulu Beerworks**

BREWPUBS/BEER GARDENS | Oahu's brewing scene has erupted in Kakaako's industrial neighborhood, and one brewpub in particular has led the charge: Honolulu Beerworks. In a converted warehouse, this is a beer connoisseur's paradise. Owner Geoff Seideman and his crew brew nine beers—in addition to limited releases—such as the Pia Mahiai Saison (made with local oranges, other citrus, and Big Island honey) or the rich South Shore Stout. When you need some *ono* grinds (delicious food) to go along with your local brew, order the bar's ahi dip. It's a regular spot for many locals, particularly on the weekends. You might just make new friends sitting at one of the bar's long picnic tables, made from reclaimed wood. It's closed Sunday. ⊠ *328 Cooke St., Kakaako* ☎ *808/589–2337* ⊕ *www.honolulubeerworks.com.*

★ **Waikiki Brewing Company**

BREWPUBS/BEER GARDENS | This company not only brews its own quality craft beer but also serves delicious food. Although the original is still operational in Waikiki at 1945 Kalakaua Avenue, this second location opened in 2017. The brewery always offers nine beers on tap, including the Skinny Jeans IPA and the Hana Hou Hefe, to which orange peel and strawberry puree are added before fermentation. You can also buy six-packs at the bar to go. What makes this location unique is that the chef smokes meat in-house using local kiawe wood, resulting in tender and flavorful beef brisket, pulled pork, chicken, and bratwurst. Accompanying barbecue sauces are made with Waikiki Brewing beer. ⊠ *831 Queen St., Kakaako* ☎ *808/591–0387* ⊕ *waikikibrewing.com.*

⊕ Performing Arts

DANCE

Ballet Hawaii

DANCE | Established in 1975, Ballet Hawaii is a local company active throughout the year. Its annual, Hawaii-theme *The Nutcracker* is usually held at the nearby **Blaisdell Concert Hall** (777 Ward Avenue) at Christmastime and is a local holiday tradition. Other performances can be seen at the **Hawaii Theatre** (1130 Bethel Street) in Chinatown and other local theaters. ⊠ *777 S. Hotel St., Kakaako* ☎ *808/521–8600* ⊕ *ballethawaii.org* ⊠ *From $40.*

MUSIC

Hawaii Symphony Orchestra

MUSIC | The Hawaii Symphony Orchestra is the latest incarnation of the now-defunct, century-old Honolulu Symphony, with the mission to bring international talent to a Hawaiian audience of any age. The orchestra performs at the Neil Blaisdell Concert Hall under the advisement of the internationally acclaimed conductor, JoAnn Falletta, and features guest conductors and soloists. Ticket prices vary. ⊠ *Honolulu* ☎ *808/380–7784* ⊕ *hawaiisymphonyorchestra.org.*

⬤ Shopping

CLOTHING

Anne Namba Designs

CLOTHING | This designer combines the beauty of classic kimonos with contemporary styles to make unique pieces for career and evening. In addition to women's apparel, she designs a men's line. ⊠ *324 Kamani St., Kakaako* ☎ *808/589–1135* ⊕ *annenamba.com.*

HOME DECOR

fishcake

HOUSEHOLD ITEMS/FURNITURE | A place to find unusual art, fishcake is a gallery for designers that hosts changing exhibitions and events by favorite artists near and far. Plus, you'll find a unique collection of small and large home items you won't find anywhere else in Honolulu. The gallery also offers interior design services. A weekday café has a rotation of pop-up coffee and tea spots. ✉ *307 Kamani St., Suite C, Kakaako* ☎ *808/593–1231* 🌐 *fishcake.us.*

SPORTING GOODS

Boca Hawaii

SPORTING GOODS | This triathlon shop near the Bike Factory offers training gear and bike rentals ($40–$50 a day depending on rental length, $200 per week), aerial yoga and capoeira classes, and nutritional products. **TIP→ Inquire directly about the latest schedule of classes at the store, which is owned and operated by top athletes.** ✉ *330 Cooke St., Kakaako* ☎ *808/591–9839* 🌐 *bocahawaii.com.*

Ala Moana

Ala Moana abuts Waikiki to the east (stopping at the Ala Wai Canal) and King Street to the north. Kakaako, Kewalo Basin Harbor, and the Blaisdell Center complex roughly mark its western edge. Probably its most notable attraction is the sprawling Ala Moana Center, jam-packed with almost any store you could wish for.

Beaches

Honolulu proper only has one beach: Ala Moana. Popular with locals, it hosts everything from Dragon Boat competitions to the Lantern Floating Ceremony.

Ala Moana Regional Park (*Ala Moana Beach Park*)

BEACH—SIGHT | **FAMILY** | A protective reef makes Ala Moana essentially a ½-mile-wide saltwater swimming pool. Very smooth sand and no waves create a haven for families and stand-up paddle surfers. After Waikiki, this is the most popular beach among visitors, and the free parking area can fill up quickly on sunny weekend days. On the Waikiki side is a peninsula called Magic Island, with shady trees and paved sidewalks ideal for jogging. Ala Moana Beach Park (officially know as Ala Moana Regional Park) also has playing fields, tennis courts, and a couple of small ponds for sailing toy boats. The beach is for everyone, but only in the daytime; after dark it's a high-crime area, with lots of homeless people. **Amenities:** food and drink; lifeguards; parking (free); showers; toilets. **Best for:** swimming; walking. ✉ *1201 Ala Moana Blvd., Ala Moana.*

Restaurants

Akasaka

$$ | **JAPANESE** | Step inside this tiny sushi bar tucked between the strip clubs behind the Ala Moana Hotel, and you'll swear you're in an out-of-the-way Edo neighborhood in some indeterminate time. Don't be deterred by its dodgy neighbors or its reputation for inconsistent service. **Known for:** popular spot for late-night food; spicy tuna roll; no pretense, nothing fancy. [$] *Average main: $21* ✉ *1646 B Kona St., Suite B, Ala Moana* ☎ *808/942–4466.*

Bac Nam

$ | **VIETNAMESE** | Tam and Kimmy Huynh's menu is much more extensive than most, ranging far beyond the usual pho and *bun* (cold noodle dishes) found at many Vietnamese restaurants. The no-frills, hole-in-the-wall atmosphere is welcoming and relaxed at this go-to spot for locals, who swear it's the best in town. **Known for:** spring and summer rolls; limited free parking behind the restaurant; excellent crabmeat curry soup. [$] *Average main: $12* ✉ *1117 S. King St.,*

Ala Moana ☎ 808/597–8201 ⏲ Closed Sun.

Chef Chai

$$$ | **FUSION** | This contemporary dining room in a condo building on the edge of Kakaako offers an eclectic, global fusion of seafood, meats, and creative starters and salads, with a focus on healthier options. Situated right across from Blaisdell Arena and Concert Hall, Chef Chai's is the go-to spot before and after the theater and concerts. **Known for:** early-bird and prix-fixe menu options that will leave you stuffed; ahi tartare with avocado mousse in miniwaffle cones; excellent desserts. [$] *Average main: $30 ✉ Pacifica Honolulu, 1009 Kapiolani Blvd., Ala Moana ☎ 808/585–0011 🌐 www.chefchai.com ⏲ Closed Mon.*

Mariposa

$$$ | **ASIAN** | Yes, the popovers and the wee cups of bouillon are there at lunch, but in every other regard, the menu at this Neiman Marcus restaurant departs from the classic model, incorporating a clear sense of Pacific place. The breezy, open-air veranda, with a view of Ala Moana Beach Park, twirling ceiling fans, and life-size hula-girl murals say Hawaii. **Known for:** extensive cocktail menu; corn chowder; lovely interiors reminiscent of Hawaii plantation days. [$] *Average main: $35 ✉ Neiman Marcus, Ala Moana Center, 1450 Ala Moana Blvd., Ala Moana ☎ 808/951–3420 🌐 neimanmarcushawaii.com/Restaurants/Mariposa.htm.*

★ MW Restaurant

$$$ | **HAWAIIAN** | The "M" and "W" team of husband-and-wife chefs Michelle Karr-Ueko and Wade Ueko bring together their collective experience (20 years alongside chef Alan Wong, a side step to the famed French Laundry, and some serious kitchen time at comfort food icon Zippy's) to create a uniquely local menu with a decidedly upscale twist. But don't overlook dessert. **Known for:** scrumptious desserts (save room); small bar that turns out nice craft cocktails; excellent fish dishes. [$] *Average main: $35 ✉ 1538 Kapiolani Blvd., Suite 107, Ala Moana ✣ Behind strip shopping center; walk down side to lights in back ☎ 808/955–6505 🌐 www.mwrestaurant.com.*

Shokudo Japanese Restaurant & Bar

$$ | **JAPANESE** | With a soaring ceiling, crazy red mobile sculpture, contemporary Japanese grazing plates, fruity vodka "sodas," and hungry young people, Shokudo is a culinary house of fun ranging from new-wave fusion dishes to more traditional noodle bowls and sushi. Do get the signature honey toast for dessert—a hollowed-out loaf of Japanese sandwich bread stuffed with cubes of its toasted innards and vanilla ice cream that's drizzled with honey. **Known for:** honey toast for dessert; sushi pizza; popular, but losing charm for old-timers with hit-or-miss service. [$] *Average main: $21 ✉ Ala Moana Pacific Center, 1585 Kapiolani Blvd., Ala Moana ☎ 808/941–3701 🌐 www.shokudojapanese.com.*

Sorabol Korean Restaurant

$$ | **KOREAN** | Open 24 hours a day on weekends and until 1 am on weeknights, with a tiny parking lot and a maze of booths and private rooms, Sorabol offers a vast menu encompassing the entirety of day-to-day Korean cuisine, plus sushi. It's great for wee hour "grinds" (local slang for food): *bibimbap* (veggies, meats, and eggs on steamed rice), *kalbi* and *bulgogi* (barbecued meats), meat or fish *jun* (thin fillets battered with egg then fried), and kimchi pancakes. **Known for:** late-night dining; simple but good Korean food; inconsistent service. [$] *Average main: $24 ✉ 805 Keeaumoku St., Ala Moana ☎ 808/947–3113 🌐 www.sorabolhawaii.com.*

★ Vintage Cave Honolulu

$$$$ | **CONTEMPORARY** | Vintage Cave is a luxurious, pricey, art-filled reinvention of what was once the brick-lined basement of Shirokyua department store.

The restaurant now offers two options: the more casual, Italian-focused Vintage Cave Café (for mere mortals) and the ultraluxe French-Japanese fusion Vintage Cave Club for those seeking an over-the-top experience. **Known for:** an elaborate dining experience with attentive service; dress-to-impress, though a jacket is no longer mandatory for men; Wagyu beef. *[$] Average main: $300 ✉ Ala Moana Shopping Center, 1450 Ala Moana Blvd., Suite 2250, Level B, Row D, Ala Moana ☎ 808/441–1744 🌐 vintagecave.com.*

Hotels

Ala Moana Hotel

$$$ | **HOTEL** | A decent value in a pricey hotel market, this well-located hotel is connected to Oahu's largest mall, the Ala Moana Center, by a pedestrian ramp and is a 10-minute walk to Waikiki. **Pros:** great value (and no resort fee); refreshed pool deck, lobby, and a new Starbucks; quick walk to the beach, convention center, and shopping. **Cons:** outside the heartbeat of Waikiki; smaller and older rooms in Kona Tower; expensive parking. *[$] Rooms from: $269 ✉ 410 Atkinson Dr., Ala Moana ☎ 808/955–4811, 866/488–1396 🌐 www.alamoanahotelhonolulu.com 🛏 1100 rooms 🍴 No meals.*

Nightlife

BARS

Makai Bar

BARS/PUBS | After a long day of shopping at Ala Moana Center, the fourth-floor Makai Bar (formerly known as the Mai Tai Bar) is a perfect spot to relax. There's live entertainment and happy hour specials for both food and drink. There's never a cover charge and no dress code. To avoid waiting in line, get here before 9 pm. *✉ Ala Moana Center, 1450 Ala Moana Blvd., Ala Moana 🌐 instagram.com/themakaibar.*

Shopping

Getting to the Ala Moana shopping centers from Waikiki is quick and inexpensive thanks to TheBus and the Waikiki Trolley.

BOOKS

★ Na Mea Hawaii

BOOKS/STATIONERY | In addition to Island-style clothing for adults and children, Hawaiian cultural items, and unusual artwork such as Niihau-shell necklaces, this boutique's book selection covers Hawaiian history and language and includes children's books set in the Islands. Na Mea also has daily classes on Hawaiian language, culture, and history. *✉ Ward Village, 1200 Ala Moana Blvd., Suite 270, Ala Moana ☎ 808/596–8885 🌐 nameahawaii.com.*

CLOTHING

Reyn Spooner

CLOTHING | This is a good place to buy the aloha-print fashions residents wear. Look for the limited-edition Christmas shirt, a collector's item manufactured each holiday season. Reyn Spooner has seven locations statewide and offers styles for men and children and, sometimes, limited-edition women's wear. *✉ Ala Moana Shopping Center, 1450 Ala Moana Blvd., Shop 2247, Ala Moana ☎ 808/949–5929 🌐 reynspooner.com.*

CRAFTS

'Auana Quilts (Hawaiian Quilt Collection)

CRAFTS | Traditional island comforters, wall hangings, pillows, bags, and other Hawaiian-print quilt accessories are the specialty here. There is also a store in the Royal Hawaiian Hotel and one on Waikiki Beach Walk. *✉ Ala Moana Shopping Center, 1450 Ala Moana Blvd., Shop 1106, Ala Moana ☎ 808/955–9550 🌐 hawaiian-quilts.com.*

Na Hoku

JEWELRY/ACCESSORIES | If you look at the wrists of *kamaaina* (local) women, you might see Hawaiian heirloom bracelets

Inexpensive Local Souvenirs

Hawaii can be an expensive place. If you are looking to bring someone a gift, consider the following, which can be found all over the island:

Locally published, Hawaii-theme books for children and adults can be found at places like **Na Mea Hawaii/ Native Books** and **Bookends Kailua.**

Try the coconut peanut butter from **North Shore Goodies.** Just when you thought peanut butter couldn't get any better, someone added coconut to it and made it even more delicious.

If you are a fan of plate lunches, **Rainbow Drive-In** has T-shirts with regular orders—"All rice," "Gravy all over," "Boneless"—printed on them. They come packed in an iconic plate lunch box.

Relive your memories of tea on the Veranda by purchasing Island Essence Tea, created by the **Moana Surfrider.**

Harvested from a salt farm on Molokai, **Hawaii Traditional Gourmet Sea Salts** come in a variety of flavors, including black lava, red alaea clay, and classic. They're colored to match their flavor, so they are beautiful as well as tasty.

Foodland makes insulated cooler bags that are decorated with uniquely local designs that go beyond tropical flowers and coconuts. Look for the pidgin or poke designs. **Whole Foods** Hawaii-theme reuseable totes are also very popular.

Made with all-natural, local ingredients, like kukui-nut oil, local flowers, herbs, even seaweed, indigenous bar soap is available online or in stores, like **Blue Hawaii Lifestyle.**

fashioned in either gold or silver and engraved in a number of Islands-inspired designs. Na Hoku sells these and other traditional Hawaiian jewelry along with an array of modern Island influenced styles in designs that capture the heart of the Hawaiian lifestyle in all its elegant diversity. There are a number of other Na Hoku locations on Oahu and the other islands (as well as in the continental United States). ✉ *Ala Moana Center, 1450 Ala Moana Blvd., Shop 2006, Ala Moana* ☎ *808/946–2100* ⊕ *nahoku.com.*

FOOD

Honolulu Cookie Co.

FOOD/CANDY | Hugely popular with Islands residents and visitors, these pineapple-shape shortbread cookies half-dipped in milk or dark chocolate come in an assortment of flavors from macadamia nut to mango and lilikoi. Made locally in Kalihi, these gourmet cookies come in boxes and tins of varying sizes at a number of locations in Ala Moana and Waikiki. ✉ *Ala Moana Shopping Center, 1450 Ala Moana Blvd., Ala Moana* ☎ *808/945– 0787* ⊕ *honolulucookie.com.*

Longs Drugs

FOOD/CANDY | For gift items in bulk, try one of the many outposts of Longs, the perfect place to stock up on chocolate-covered macadamia nuts, candies, cookies, island tea, and 100% Kona coffee—at reasonable prices—to carry home. ✉ *Ala Moana Shopping Center, 1450 Ala Moana Blvd., 2nd level, Ala Moana* ☎ *808/941–4010* ⊕ *alamoana-center.com/en/directory/longs-drugs-789. html.*

GIFTS

Blue Hawaii Lifestyle

GIFTS/SOUVENIRS | The Ala Moana store carries a large selection of locally made products, including soaps, honey, tea, salt, chocolates, art, and CDs. Every item, in fact, is carefully selected from various Hawaiian companies, artisans, and farms, from the salt fields of Molokai to the lavender farms on Maui to the single-estate chocolate on Oahu's North Shore. A café in the store serves healthy smoothies, panini, tea, and espresso. ✉ *Ala Moana Shopping Center, 1450 Ala Moana Blvd., Shop 2312, Ala Moana* ☎ *808/949–0808* ⊕ *bluehawaiilifestyle. com.*

SHOPPING CENTERS

Ala Moana Shopping Center

SHOPPING CENTERS/MALLS | The world's largest open-air shopping mall is five minutes from Waikiki by bus. More than 350 stores and 160 dining options (including multiple food courts) make up this 50-acre complex, which is a unique mix of national and international chains as well as smaller, locally owned shops and eateries—and everything in between. Shirokiya Japan Village Walk and the newer Lanai@Ala Moana are worth stopping at for a range of casual dining options in one spot. Thirty-five luxury boutiques in residence include Gucci, Louis Vuitton, and Christian Dior. All of Hawaii's major department stores are here, including the state's only Neiman Marcus and Nordstrom, plus Macy's, Target, and Bloomingdale's. ✉ *1450 Ala Moana Blvd., Ala Moana* ☎ *808/955–9517* ⊕ *alamoana-center.com.*

Ward Village

SHOPPING CENTERS/MALLS | Heading west from Waikiki toward downtown Honolulu, you'll run into a section of town with five distinct shopping-complex areas; there are more than 135 specialty shops and 40 eateries here. The Ward Entertainment Center features 16 movie screens, including a state-of-the-art, 3-D, big-screen auditorium, and all theaters having reclining chairs and access to an extended food menu and alcoholic beverages for those of age. The South Shore Market is a contemporary collection of local shops and restaurants, plus T.J. Maxx and Nordstrom Rack. For distinctive Hawaiian gifts, such as locally made muumuu, koa-wood products, and Niihau shell necklaces, visit Martin & MacArthur and Na Mea Hawaii. Over at the Ward Gateway Center, the Ohana Hale Marketplace is worth a stop to visit 140 local small businesses including food stalls, apparel and accessories shops, and gift and craft stands. You can hop on TheBus or take a trolley from Waikiki. There's also free parking around the entire Ward Village, though sometimes you have to circle for awhile to find a spot. Valet-park is also available. ✉ *1050-1200 Ala Moana Blvd., Ala Moana* ☎ *808/591–8411* ⊕ *www.wardvillageshops.com.*

🏃 Activities

SPAS

Hoala Salon and Spa

SPA/BEAUTY | This Aveda concept spa has everything from Vichy showers to hydrotherapy rooms to customized aromatherapy. Ladies, they'll even touch up your makeup for free before you leave. ✉ *Ala Moana Shopping Center, 3rd fl., 1450 Ala Moana Blvd., Ala Moana* ☎ *808/947–6141* ⊕ *www.hoalasalonspa.com.*

Makiki Heights

Makiki includes the more unassuming neighborhood where President Barack Obama grew up. Other highlights include the exclusive Punahou School he attended and the notable Central Union Church, as well as the Tantalus area overlook.

Oahu's Best Shave Ice 🍴

Islands-style shave ice (never *shaved* ice—it's a pidgin thing) is said to have been born when neighborhood kids hung around the icehouse, waiting to pounce on the shavings from large blocks of ice, carved with ultrasharp Japanese planes that created an exceptionally fine-textured granita.

In the 1920s, according to the historian for syrup manufacturer Malolo Beverages & Supplies, Ltd., Chinese vendors developed sweet fruit concentrates to pour over the ice.

The evolution continued with mom-and-pop shops adding their own touches, such as hiding a nugget of Japanese sweet bean paste in the center; placing a small scoop of ice cream at the bottom; and adding *li hing* powder (a Chinese seasoning used on preserved fruits).

There's nothing better on a sticky hot day. Not all of Oahu's best shave ice is in Honolulu, but these two are.

Waiola. Waiola Shave Ice, off Kapahulu Avenue, is known for its finely shaved ice, wide variety of flavors, and, more recently, its regular appearances in the reboot of *Hawaii Five-0*. In real life, the service is a bit surly, and the prices are slightly higher than for most other shave ice, but it's close to Waikiki. ✉ *525 Kapahulu Ave., Kapahulu.*

Uncle Clay's House of Pure Aloha. Located in a strip mall in the residential neighborhood of Aina Haina, Uncle Clay's (HOPA) is a happy place. They specialize in all-natural syrups house-made from cane sugar and locally sourced fruits. They've even got a flavor called "kalespin"—a combination of kale and spinach. A second location at Ala Moana Shopping Center is by the Lanai@Ala Moana food court on the mall's second level. ✉ *Aina Haina Shopping Center, 820 W. Hind Dr., Aina Haina (right off Kalanianaole Hwy.)*

👁 Sights

Tantalus and Round Top Scenic Drive
SCENIC DRIVE | A few minutes and a world away from Waikiki and Honolulu, this scenic drive shaded by vine-draped trees has frequent pullouts with views of Diamond Head and the *ewa* side of Honolulu. It's a nice change of pace from urban life below. At Puu Ualakaa Park, stop to see the sweeping view from Manoa Valley to Honolulu. To start the drive, go to Punchbowl Memorial Cemetery, and follow Tantalus Drive as it climbs uphill. ✉ *3200 Round Top Dr., Makiki Heights.*

🍴 Restaurants

★ **Honolulu Burger Co.**
$ | **BURGER** | **FAMILY** | Owner Ken Takahashi retired as a nightclub impresario on the Big Island to become a real-life burger king. This modest storefront is the home of the locavore burger, made with range-fed beef, Manoa lettuce, tomatoes, and a wide range of toppings, all island-grown—and you can taste the difference. **Known for:** miso kutie burger topped with red miso glaze and Japanese cucumber slices; blue Hawaii burger with blue cheese and bacon; showing up at local farmers markets or its own food truck. [$] *Average main: $12* ✉ *1295 S. Beretania St., Makiki Heights* ☎ *808/626–5202* 🌐 *honoluluburgerco.com.*

The Bishop Museum is Hawaii's state historical museum and the repository for the royal artifacts of the last surviving direct descendant of King Kamehameha the Great.

Kalihi-Liliha-Palama

North of downtown Honolulu, just off H1, is the tightly packed neighborhood of Kalihi. It's home to large industrial pockets but also the stellar Bishop Museum, Lion Coffee headquarters, and great local eateries like Mitsu-Ken. Liliha-Kapalama is a sliver of land that runs from ocean to mountain (known as an *ahupuaa* in Hawaiian) and is presided over by famed Kamehameha Schools—which from its hillside perch looks down on this warren of modest homes and shops—and the Bishop Museum. There are also some great food establishments here including Helena's Hawaiian Food and Liliha Bakery (not to be missed for its *ono coco* puffs).

◉ Sights

★ Bishop Museum

MUSEUM | Founded in 1889 by Charles R. Bishop as a memorial to his wife, Princess Bernice Pauahi Bishop, the museum began as a repository for the royal possessions of this last direct descendant of King Kamehameha the Great. Today, it's the state's designated history and culture museum. Its five exhibit halls house almost 25 million items that tell the history of the Hawaiian Islands and their Pacific neighbors. The complex also features a 16,500-square-foot science adventure wing with a three-story simulated volcano at its center, where regular "lava melts" take place, much to the enjoyment of younger patrons. The renovated Pacific Hall (formerly Polynesian Hall) now focuses on the history of the entire Pacific region.

The Hawaiian Hall, with state-of-the art and often interactive displays, teaches about the Hawaiian culture. Spectacular Hawaiian artifacts—lustrous feather capes, bone fishhooks, the skeleton of a giant sperm whale, photography and crafts displays, and an authentic, well-preserved grass house—are displayed inside a three-story, 19th-century, Victorian-style gallery. The building

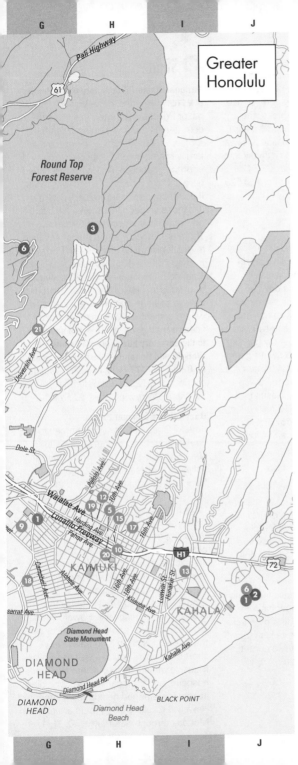

Greater
Honolulu

Sights ▼

1 Bishop Museum **B3**
2 Dolphin Quest at
  The Kahala Hotel & Resort **J8**
3 Lyon Arboretum.................... **H3**
4 National Memorial
  Cemetery of the Pacific **D5**
5 Queen Emma Summer Palace **E3**
6 Tantalus and Round Top
  Scenic Drive....................... **G3**

Restaurants ▼

1 Alan Wong's
  Restaurant Honolulu **E6**
2 Chef Mavro **F6**
3 Chiang Mai Thai Cuisine **F6**
4 Fukuya Delicatessen **F6**
5 Himalayan Kitchen **H7**
6 Hoku's **J8**
7 Honolulu Burger Co................. **E6**
8 Imanas Tei **F6**
9 Izakaya Nonbei **G7**
10 Koko Head Cafe.................... **H7**
11 Mitsu-Ken **B3**
12 Mud Hen Water.................... **H7**
13 Olive Tree Cafe..................... **I7**
14 Peace Café **F6**
15 The Surfing Pig Hawaii............ **H7**
16 Sushi Sasabune.................... **E6**
17 3660 On the Rise **H7**
18 Tokkuri Tei **G7**
19 Town **H7**
20 12th Avenue Grill.................. **H7**
21 Waioli Kitchen & Bake Shop **G4**

Quick Bites ▼

1 Leonard's Bakery **G7**
2 Waiola Shave Ice.................. **F6**

Hotels ▼

1 The Kahala Hotel & Resort **J8**

alone, with its huge Victorian turrets and immense stone walls, is worth seeing. Also check out the planetarium, daily tours, *lauhala*-weaving and science demonstrations, special exhibits, the Shop Pacifica, and the Bishop Museum Café, which serves *ono* (delicious) Hawaiian food by local restaurant Highway Inn. ✉ *1525 Bernice St., Kalihi* ☎ *808/847–3511* 🌐 *www.bishopmuseum.org* 🎟 *$25 (parking $5).*

🍴 Restaurants

Mitsu-Ken

$ | **HAWAIIAN** | Mitsu-Ken's garlic chicken may haunt your dreams, which makes it worth the trek to a downscale neighborhood to find the joint. Line up and order the plate lunch with rice and salad (or just the chicken), and sink your teeth into this crispy, profoundly garlicky masterpiece drizzled with a sweet glaze. **Known for:** delicious breakfast bentos; cash only; good stop before the Swap Meet (it opens at 5 am and closes by 1 pm). [$] *Average main: $8* ✉ *2300 N. King St., Kapalama* ☎ *808/848–5573* 💳 *No credit cards* 🕒 *Closed Sun. and Mon. No dinner.*

Nuuanu

Immediately *mauka* of Kalihi, off Pali Highway, are a renowned resting place and a carefully preserved home where royal families retreated during the doldrums of summer. Nuuanu Pali was the sight of a famous battle that was key to King Kamehameha I's success in uniting all the Hawaiian Islands under his rule and becoming the Islands' first monarch. Nuuanu Valley is known for its lush, quiet beauty and has several notable cemeteries, churches, and embassies.

👁 Sights

National Memorial Cemetery of the Pacific

CEMETERY | Nestled in the bowl of Puowaina, or Punchbowl Crater, this 112-acre cemetery is the final resting place for more than 50,000 U.S. war veterans and family members and is a solemn reminder of their sacrifice. Among those buried here is Ernie Pyle, the famed World War II correspondent who was killed by a Japanese sniper on Ie Shima, an island off the northwest coast of Okinawa. There are intricate stone maps providing a visual military-history lesson. Puowaina, formed 75,000–100,000 years ago during a period of secondary volcanic activity, translates as "Hill of Sacrifice." Historians believe this site once served as an altar where ancient Hawaiians offered sacrifices to their gods. ■ **TIP→ The entrance to the cemetery has unfettered views of Waikiki and Honolulu—perhaps the finest on Oahu.** ✉ *2177 Puowaina Dr., Nuuanu* ☎ *808/532–3720* 🌐 *www.cem.va.gov/cem/cems/nchp/nmcp.asp* 🎟 *Free.*

Queen Emma Summer Palace

HOUSE | Queen Emma, King Kamehameha IV's wife, used this small but stately New England–style home in Nuuanu Valley as a retreat from the rigors of court life in hot and dusty Honolulu during the mid- to late-1800s. Hourlong guided tours highlight the residence's royal history and its eclectic mix of European, Victorian, and Hawaiian furnishings, most of which are original to the home. There are excellent examples of feathered-covered kahilis, umeke bowls, and koa-wood furniture. Visitors also learn how Queen Emma established what is today the largest private hospital in Hawaii, opened a school for girls, and ran as a widow for the throne, losing to King Kalakaua. A short drive away, you can visit the Royal Mausoleum in Nuuanu, where she, her husband, and their son, Albert, who died at age 4, are buried beside many other Hawaiian royals. Guided tours are offered Monday through Saturday at 10, 11, 1,

and 2, and on Sunday at 11 and 1. ✉ *2913 Pali Hwy., Nuuanu* ☎ *808/595–3167* 🌐 *www.daughtersofhawaii.org* 🎟 *$10.*

Moiliili

Packed into the neighborhood of Moiliili are flower and lei shops, restaurants, and little stores selling Hawaiian and Asian goodies.. Most places of interest are along King Street, between Isenberg and Waialae avenues.

🍴 Restaurants

★ Alan Wong's Restaurant Honolulu

$$$$ | MODERN HAWAIIAN | James Beard Award–winning Alan Wong is the undisputed king of Hawaiian regional cuisine, earning love and respect for his humble demeanor and practice as much as for his food. The "Wong Way," as it's not-so-jokingly called by his staff, includes an ingrained understanding of the aloha spirit, evident in the skilled but unstarched service and creative and playful interpretations of Islands cuisine. **Known for:** well-deserved awards and accolades, which line the walls; ginger-crusted onaga (red snapper); "The Coconut" haubia sorbet in chocolate shell. [$] *Average main: $43* ✉ *McCully Court, 1857 S. King St., 3rd fl., Moiliili* ☎ *808/949–2526* 🌐 *alanwongs.com* 🕒 *No lunch.*

★ Chef Mavro

$$$$ | MODERN EUROPEAN | Marseilles transplant George Mavrothalassitis, who took two hotel restaurants to the top of the ranks before opening this well-regarded restaurant in 1998, is passionate about the care he takes to draw out the truest and most concentrated flavors, to track down the freshest fish, to create one-of-a-kind wine pairings, and marry French technique with global flavors and local ingredients. The menu changes quarterly, every dish (including dessert) matched with a select wine. **Known for:** exquisite prix-fixe cuisine; a focus on innovative uses for the freshest produce; wine pairings unmatched on Oahu. [$] *Average main: $195* ✉ *1969 S. King St., Moiliili* ☎ *808/944–4714* 🌐 *chefmavro.com* 🕒 *No lunch.*

Chiang Mai Thai Cuisine

$$ | THAI | Long beloved for its northern Thai classics based on family recipes, such as spicy curries and stir-fries and sticky rice in woven-grass baskets, Chiang Mai is a short cab ride from Waikiki. Some dishes, like the signature barbecue Cornish game hen with lemongrass and spices, show how acculturation can create interesting pairings. **Known for:** spring rolls and Chiang Mai wings; limited parking in a small lot in back; local business-lunch favorite. [$] *Average main: $25* ✉ *2239 S. King St., Moiliili* ☎ *808/941–1151* 🕒 *No lunch weekends.*

Fukuya Delicatessen

$ | JAPANESE | Get a taste of local Japanese culture at this family operation on the main thoroughfare in local-style Moiliili, a mile or so *mauka* out of Waikiki. Open since 1939, the delicatessen offers takeout breakfasts and lunches, Japanese snacks, noodle dishes, and confections—and it's a local favorite for catering, from parties to funeral gatherings. **Known for:** nori-wrapped chicken; mochi tray, offering samples of everything; kid-friendly menu. [$] *Average main: $8* ✉ *2710 S. King St., Moiliili* ☎ *808/946–2073* 🌐 *fukuyadeli.com* 🕒 *Closed Mon. and Tues. No dinner.*

Imanas Tei

$$$ | JAPANESE | Nihonjin (Japanese nationals) and locals flock to this tucked-away, bamboo-ceilinged restaurant for its tasteful, simple decor and equally tasteful—and perfect—sushi, sashimi, *nabe* (hot pots prepared at the table), and grilled dishes. You assemble your meal dish by dish, and the cost can add up if you aren't careful. **Known for:** simple food that some feel is better than in Japan; long waits; traditional izakaya experience.

The Punch Bowl, yet another extinct volcanic crater, is home to the National Memorial Cemetery of the Pacific, the largest military cemetery in Hawaii.

$ Average main: $30 ✉ 2626 S. King St., Moiliili ☎ 808/941–2626, 808/934–2727 ⊘ Closed Sun. No lunch.

Peace Café

$ | VEGETARIAN | This tranquil little storefront with a rustic country communal table is a nurturing sanctuary on a fast-food-loving island. Place your order at the counter, serve yourself fruit-infused water from a large glass beverage jar, and wait for your vegan plates, salads, and sandwiches. **Known for:** tempeh katsu; yogini plate (a mountain of brown rice, beans, greens, and seaweed); mellow and calming setting. $ Average main: $10 ✉ 2239 S. King St., Moiliili ☎ 808/951–7555 ⊕ peacecafehawaii.com ⊘ No dinner Sun.

Sushi Sasabune

$$$$ | JAPANESE | Try to get a coveted seat at the counter, and prepare for an unforgettable sushi experience—if you behave. This is the home of Seiji Kumagawa—Honolulu's Sushi Nazi, who prefers that diners eat omakase-style, letting the chef send out his favorite choices, each priced individually (prices add up quickly). **Known for:** one of Honolulu's top sushi spots; fast service; no phone calls allowed in the restaurant. $ Average main: $150 ✉ 1417 S. King St., Moiliili ☎ 808/947–3800 ⊘ Closed Sun. and Mon. No lunch Sat.

🛍 Shopping

This neighborhood, although considered separate from the University of Hawaii's Manoa campus, has a distinct college-town feel. About 3 miles from Waikiki, the area needs updating in some sections. Nevertheless, a look past the tired exteriors reveals a haven for excellent family-owned restaurants, health food stores, and shops that have a loyal following in the residential community.

JEWELRY

Maui Divers Design Center

JEWELRY/ACCESSORIES | For a look into the harvesting and design of coral and black pearl jewelry, visit this shop and take a free tour at its adjacent factory near the Ala Moana Shopping Center. ■ **TIP→ Avoid the "Pick a Pearl" option unless you're prepared to be upsold on a jewelry setting or two for the pearls "found" in your shells.** ✉ *1520 Liona St., Moiliili* ☎ *808/943–8350* 🌐 *mauidivers.com.*

Kapahulu

Walk just a few minutes from the eastern end of Waikiki, and you'll find yourself in this very local main drag of restaurants, bars, and shops (**Bailey's Antiques and Aloha Shirts** (✉ *517 Kapahulu Ave.*) is the place for rare, wearable collectibles). The original **Leonard's Bakery** (✉ *933 Kapahulu Ave.*) is where malasadas (Portuguese deep-fried doughnuts rolled in sugar) were first popularized.

🍴 Restaurants

Izakaya Nonbei

$$$ | **JAPANESE** | Teruaki Mori designed this pub, one of the most traditional of Honolulu's izakayas, to make you feel that you're in a northern inn during winter in his native Japan. Dishes not to miss include *aji tataki* (seared, vinegar-marinated jack mackerel topped with ginger); *karei karaage* (delicate deep-fried flounder); fried *gobo* (burdock) chips; and crab, avocado, and bacon salad. **Known for:** great happy hour and late-night spot; tiny spot with a huge menu; long waits (reservations strongly recommended). [$] *Average main: $30* ✉ *3108 Olu St., Kapahulu* ☎ *808/734–5573* 🌐 *izakayanonbei.com.*

Tokkuri Tei

$$$$ | **JAPANESE** | The playful atmosphere at this local favorite belies the quality of the food created by chef Hideaki "Santa" Miyoshi. Best to just say *Omakase, kudasai* ("Chef's choice, please"), and he'll order for you. **Known for:** Japanese food that delivers time and again; salmon skin salad; ahi tartare poke, which is everything locals dream about. [$] *Average main: $40* ✉ *449 Kapahulu Ave., #201, Kapahulu* ☎ *808/732–6480* 🌐 *www.tokkuritei-hawaii.com* 🕒 *No lunch Sun.*

☕ Coffee and Quick Bites

Leonard's Bakery

$ | **BAKERY** | Whether you spell it *malasada* or *malassada,* when you're in Hawaii, you must try these deep-fried, holeless Portuguese doughnuts. Leonard's Bakery is the most famous of all the island establishments making malasadas and was the first island bakery to commercialize their production. **Known for:** original and various filled malasadas; pao doce (Portuguese sweet bread); small parking lot and long lines. [$] *Average main: $2* ✉ *933 Kaphalulu Ave., Kapahulu* ☎ *808/737–5591* 🌐 *leonardshawaii.com.*

Waiola Shave Ice

$ | **CAFÉ** | **FAMILY** | Off Kapahulu Avenue, longtime local favorite Waiola Shave Ice, known for its powdery shave ice (or snow cone) and wide variety of flavors, has become nationally known through its regular appearance on the reboot of *Hawaii Five-0*. It's a fast-moving line, so know your order when you get to the window. **Known for:** a large menu allowing for lots of customization; excellent example of a Hawaii classic; slightly brusk service. [$] *Average main: $4* ✉ *3113 Mokihana St., Kapahulu* ☎ *808/735–8886* 🌐 *www.waiolashaveice.com.*

🛍 Shopping

Kapahulu, like many older neighborhoods, should not be judged at first glance. It begins at the Diamond Head end of Waikiki and continues up to the H1 freeway and is full of variety; shops and restaurants are located primarily on Kapahulu Avenue.

SPORTING GOODS

Island Paddler

SPORTING GOODS | Fashionable beach clothing, bathing suits, hats, beach bags, and rash guards supplement a huge selection of canoe paddles and paddling accessories. ■ **TIP→ Check out the wooden decorative paddles: they become works of art when mounted on the wall at home.** ✉ *716 Kapahulu Ave., Kapahulu* ☎ *808/737–4854* 🌐 *www.islandpaddler-hawaii.com.*

Snorkel Bob's

SPORTING GOODS | The chain, popular throughout the Islands, sells or rents necessary gear—including fins, snorkels, wet suits, and beach chairs—and schedules ocean activities with other suppliers. This is a good place to seek advice about the best snorkeling beaches and conditions, which vary considerably with the season. ✉ *702 Kapahulu Ave., Kapahulu* ☎ *808/735–7944* 🌐 *snorkelbob.com.*

Kaimuki

Ten minutes beyond Kapahulu, this commercial thoroughfare runs through an old neighborhood filled with cool old Craftsman bungalows (which are, alas, slowly being knocked down to make room for ticky-tacky boxes). Kaimuki has steadily been developing into a food mecca (challenged only by Chinatown), with a slew of award-winning restaurants and bars in a range of culinary styles. If you want to know what trends are happening in Hawaii food today, this is a neighborhood to visit. It may have the highest and most diverse concentration of eateries on the island, from an elevated barbecue spot and a shabu-shabu house to a chic, contemporary bistro and a nougat manufacturer.

🍴 Restaurants

Himalayan Kitchen

$$ | ASIAN | Owned by a Nepalese chef, Himalayan Kitchen aims to serve all the cuisines of that high-altitude region, and the menu tries to stretch a bit beyond Indian standards—curries, biriyanis, tandoori grills. Hawaii is not an epicenter of Indian cuisine, so this joint does what it can to introduce new flavors while staying true to the standbys. **Known for:** buffet-only lunch; cozy neighborhood atmosphere; challenging parking. [$] *Average main: $17* ✉ *1137 11th Ave., Kaimuki* ☎ *808/735–1122* 🌐 *himalayankitchenhawaii.com* 🕒 *No lunch Mon.*

★ Koko Head Cafe

$ | MODERN HAWAIIAN | When Lee Anne Wong, best known as a competitor on the first season of Bravo's "Top Chef," moved to the Islands, foodies waited with bated breath for her first brick-and-mortar restaurant. And this is it: a lively and laid-back café in Kaimuki, where she took the concept of breakfast and flipped it, creating innovative dishes like Elvis's Revenge, a peanut butter-and-banana tempura sandwich with candied "billionaire's bacon." Try her signature dumplings, which change daily. **Known for:** cornflake french toast; creative cocktail menu; crazy busy weekends. [$] *Average main: $13* ✉ *1145c 12th Ave., Kaimuki* ☎ *808/732–8920* 🌐 *kokoheadcafe.com* 🕒 *No dinner.*

Mud Hen Water

$$ | HAWAIIAN | The name of this restaurant perched on busy Waialae Avenue is the English translation of *Waialae* (meaning a gathering spot around a watering hole). Chef Ed Kenney (of Town, Kaimuki Superette, and Mahina & Sun's fame) explores modern interpretations of the Hawaiian foods he remembers from his childhood with an ever-changing locavore menu. **Known for:** small plates and snacks; beet poke; sorbetto and gelato. [$] *Average main: $17* ✉ *3452 Waialae*

Ave., Kaimuki ☎ 808/737–6000 🌐 mudhenwater.com ⏲ Closed Mon.

The Surfing Pig Hawaii

$$$ | **BARBECUE** | This fancier sibling of the island's three Kono's barbecue spots focuses on Americana-tinged-with-Hawaiian food and drinks served in a small, lofted eatery with a surfer-industrial vibe. Heaping portions of juicy smoked and grilled meats are the specialty, but The Surfing Pig also has several great fish appetizers and entrées. **Known for:** old-fashioned with bacon-infused bourbon, bacon garnish, and "smoking" cloche presentation; pork, beef, and porchetta slider trio; a strong brunch alternative in the neighborhood. [$] *Average main: $30 ✉ 3605 Waialae Ave., Kaimuki ☎ 808/744–1992 🌐 thesurfingpighawaii.com.*

3660 on the Rise

$$$$ | **MODERN HAWAIIAN** | Named for its address on Honolulu's premier Waialae Avenue, this restaurant brought fresh dining to Kaimuki when it opened in 1992, inspiring a neighborhood dining renaissance. Loyalists swear by the steaks, crab cakes, and the signature dish, ahi katsu wrapped in *nori* (seaweed) and deep-fried with a wasabi-ginger butter sauce. **Known for:** special-occasion restaurant; good desserts; somewhat dated interior. [$] *Average main: $38 ✉ 3660 Waialae Ave., Kaimuki ☎ 808/737–1177 🌐 3660ontherise.com ⏲ Closed Mon. No lunch.*

★ Town

$$ | **AMERICAN** | Town remains a hot spot for Honolulu's creative class and farm-to-table diners, where chef-owner Ed Kenney and his partner Dave Caldiero offer an eclectic menu that embraces Hawaii ingredients in unique ways, ranging from hand-cut pastas and refreshing, composed salads to clean preparations of fish and meat. The menu is constantly changing, reflecting what's fresh and available. **Known for:** eclectic menu that suits both meat eaters and vegetarians; trendy atmosphere; lunch option. [$] *Average main: $25 ✉ 3435 Waialae Ave., Kaimuki ☎ 808/735–5900 🌐 www.townkaimuki.com.*

12th Avenue Grill

$$$ | **MODERN AMERICAN** | A local favorite since the doors opened, this award-winning American brasserie from chef-owner Kevin Hanney keeps surprising loyalists with an expanding menu and lively bar scene. The longtime favorite grilled pork chop is joined on the menu by other excellent meat and fish dishes and beautifully prepared soups, salads, and small plates. **Known for:** passion-fruit mochi cake with vanilla-ginger syrup; commitment to locally sourced ingredients; smoked ahi bruschetta. [$] *Average main: $28 ✉ 1120 12th Ave., Kaimuki ☎ 808/732–9469 🌐 www.12thavegrill.com ⏲ No lunch.*

Nightlife

BARS

BREW'd Craft Pub

BREWPUBS/BEER GARDENS | The Kaimuki night scene got a bit livelier when BREW'd Craft Pub opened in 2014. After all, this local pub stays open until 2 am. It's a small place—you have to squeeze between nearby dining companions to get in and out of your table—but the wait staff is friendly and knowledgeable about the pub's 150-plus beer menu. BREW'd also offers better versions of the standard pub fare than you'll find at some places in town, including a good braised beef poutine. It's closed Sunday. *✉ 3441 Waialae Ave., Suite A, Kaimuki ✥ Corner of 9th and Waialae Aves. ☎ 808/732–2337 🌐 brewdcraftpub.com.*

Shopping

FLOWERS AND PLANTS

Kawamoto Orchid Nursery

FLOWERS | Kawamoto grows all flowers on its 3½-acre orchid farm near downtown Honolulu. Their specialty is the Cattleya, a favorite for Mother's Day, but they also grow hundreds of hybrids. The nursery now does the bulk of its business online, and they have decades of experience shipping temperamental orchids to the mainland. It's closed on Sunday. ✉ *Kawamoto Orchid Nursery, 2630 Waiomao Rd., Kaimuki* ☎ *808/732–5808* 🌐 *kawamotoorchids.com.*

SPORTING GOODS

Downing Hawaii

SPORTING GOODS | Look for old-style Birdwell surf trunks here, along with popular labels such as Quiksilver, Roxy, DaKine, and Billabong, which supplement Downing's own line of surf wear and surfboards. ✉ *3021 Waialae Ave., Kaimuki* ☎ *808/737–9696* 🌐 *downingsurf.com.*

Manoa

Manoa is probably best known as the home of the University of Hawaii's main campus. The surrounding area is chock-full of interesting coffee shops, restaurants, and stores fed by the collegiate and professorial crowd. History and beauty linger around verdant Manoa Valley at places like the Manoa Chinese Cemetery, Manoa Falls, and Lyon Arboretum. Manoa Valley Theatre puts on top-notch community theater productions year-round.

👁 Sights

Lyon Arboretum

GARDEN | Tucked all the way back in Manoa Valley, this is a gem of an arboretum operated by the University of Hawaii. Hike to a waterfall, or sit and enjoy beautiful views of the valley while having a picnic. You'll also see an ethnobotanical garden, a Hawaiian hale and garden, and one of the largest palm collections anywhere—all within a parklike setting. Its educational mission means there are regular talks and walks plus classes on lei-making, lauhala weaving, Hawaiian medicinal arts, and more, which you can take for an additional fee. Docents give 60-minute tours weekdays at 10 am (you must call ahead to reserve a spot). There are also self-guided tours. ✉ *3860 Manoa Rd., Manoa* ☎ *808/988–0456* 🌐 *manoa.hawaii.edu/lyon* 🎟 *From $5 (suggested donation); guided tour $10* 🕒 *Closed Sun.*

🍴 Restaurants

★ Waioli Kitchen & Bake Shop

$ | **AMERICAN** | Dating from 1922, this historic café is surrounded by the verdant Manoa Valley landscape, part of the Hawaii Salvation Army headquarters and independently operated by Ross and Stefanie Anderson since late 2018. A short menu of simple, delicious breakfast and lunch items are ordered at the counter and delivered to your chosen table, either inside the cozy, multiroom bungalow or on the covered lanai. **Known for:** braised short rib loco moco; assorted housemade pastries, scones, muffins, breads, jams, and jellies; honey and salt produced on the property and a burgeoning garden. [$] *Average main: $10* ✉ *Salvation Army Headquarters, 2950 Manoa Rd., Manoa* ☎ *808/744–1619* 🌐 *waiolikitchen.com* 🕒 *Closed Mon.*

🎟 Performing Arts

THEATER

Kennedy Theatre

THEATER | Eclectic programs—everything from Hawaiian language to musical theater to Bollywood—are offered at this space at the Manoa campus of the University of Hawaii. The theater, which opened in 1963, was designed by internationally renowned architect I. M. Pei. ✉ *1770 East-West Rd., Manoa* ☎ *808/956–7655* 🌐 *manoa.hawaii.edu/liveonstage.*

Manoa Valley Theatre

THEATER | From September through July, wonderful performances grace this intimate community theater in lush Manoa

Valley. ✉ *2833 E. Manoa Rd., Manoa* ☎ *808/988–6131* 🌐 *www.manoavalleytheatre.com.*

Kahala

Oahu's wealthiest neighborhood has streets lined with multimillion-dollar homes. At intervals along tree-lined Kahala Avenue are narrow lanes that provide public access to Kahala's quiet, narrow coastal beaches offering views of Koko Head. Kahala Mall includes restaurants, a movie theater, and a Whole Foods grocery store. Kahala is also the home of the private Waialae Country Club and golf course, site of the annual Sony Open PGA golf tournament in January.

Sights

Dolphin Quest at The Kahala Hotel & Resort

ZOO | This worldwide dolphin-encounter group has an Oahu location in the Kahala Hotel & Resort, where trained Atlantic bottlenose dolphins hold court in their outdoor lagoon adjacent to the pool area. Activities with the creatures go on throughout the day and can be watched from lanai, walkways, and even some rooms. Programs include the Kid's Aquatic Adventure, a 90-minute session of feeding and interacting with dolphins, fish, and other aquatic animals, as well as various interactive programs for teens and adults. ✉ *The Kahala Hotel & Resort, 5000 Kahala Ave., Kahala* ☎ *808/739–8918* 🌐 *dolphinquest.com/oahu-hawaii/* 🎟 *From $155 for a 15-min encounter for young children.*

Restaurants

Hoku's

$$$$ | **ASIAN FUSION** | Everything about this room speaks of quality and sophistication: the wall of windows with their beach views, the avant-garde cutlery and dinnerware, the solicitous staff, and the carefully constructed Euro-Pacific cuisine. The menu constantly changes, and new executive chef Jonathan Mizukami—along with chef du cuisine Eric Oto—is focusing even more on seasonal cuisine along with Hoku's standard for fresh, local ingredients (including herbs from the hotel's on-site herb garden). **Known for:** relaxed elegance in the grande dame of Hawaii's social scene; panoramic views from every table; setting and service that can outshine the food. [$] *Average main: $55* ✉ *The Kahala Hotel & Resort, 5000 Kahala Ave., Kahala* ☎ *808/739–8760* 🌐 *hokuskahala.com* ⏲ *No lunch.*

Olive Tree Cafe

$ | **GREEK** | An Iranian Hellenophile owns this bustling, self-serve café that dishes up the best taramasalata, falafel, and souvlaki in town. Stand in line at the counter to order while your companion tries to finagle one of the outdoor tables. **Known for:** no-frills Greek food; cash only, and BYOB with no corkage fee; small portions for the price. [$] *Average main: $14* ✉ *4614 Kilauea Ave., Suite 107, Kahala* ☎ *808/737–0303* 💳 *No credit cards* ⏲ *No lunch.*

Hotels

★ **The Kahala Hotel & Resort**

$$$$ | **RESORT** | **FAMILY** | Hidden away in the upscale residential neighborhood of Kahala (on the other side of Diamond Head from Waikiki), this elegant oceanfront hotel, one of Hawaii's very first luxury resorts, has played host to celebrities, princesses, the Dalai Lama, and nearly every president since Lyndon Johnson. **Pros:** away from hectic Waikiki; top-notch Hoku's restaurant; heavenly spa. **Cons:** far from Waikiki; in a residential neighborhood, so not much to do within walking distance of hotel; small pool. [$] *Rooms from: $395* ✉ *5000 Kahala Ave., Kahala* ☎ *808/739–8888, 800/367–2525 toll-free* 🌐 *kahalaresort.com* 🛏 *338 rooms* 🍴 *No meals.*

🛍 Shopping

The upscale residential neighborhood of Kahala, near the slopes of Diamond Head, is 10 minutes by car from Waikiki and has a shopping mall and some gift stores.

ART GALLERIES

Nohea Gallery

ART GALLERIES | This shop is really a gallery representing hundreds of artisans who specialize in koa furniture, bowls, and boxes, as well as art glass and ceramics. Original paintings and prints—all with an island theme—add to the selection. The store also carries unique handmade Hawaiian jewelry starting under $20 with ti leaf, maile, and coconut-weave designs. Home items like locally made kitchen towels and "Tutu Nene" hand-sewn native Hawaiian ducks make for great souvenirs. (A second Nohea Gallery location is in the Hyatt Regency Waikiki.) ✉ *Kahala Mall, 4211 Waialae Ave., Kahala* ☎ *808/762–7407* ⊕ *noheagallery.com.*

SHOPPING CENTERS

Kahala Mall

SHOPPING CENTERS/MALLS | This indoor mall has more than 100 stores and restaurants with a mix of both local and national retailers including Macy's, Reyn Spooner, an Apple store, Island Sole footwear, and T&C Surf. Don't miss homegrown boutiques, clothing stores, and galleries like Magnolia, Fighting Eel, Mahina, and SOHA Living. You can also browse local foods and products at Whole Foods. The recently renovated Kahala Theaters now has a full kitchen and bar and provides post-shopping entertainment. ✉ *4211 Waialae Ave., Kahala* ☎ *808/732–7736* ⊕ *www.kahalamallcenter.com.*

🏃 Activities

SPAS

The Kahala Spa

SPA/BEAUTY | Escape the hustle and bustle of metro Honolulu at the elegant yet homey Kahala property favored by celebrities and U.S. presidents. The two-story spa suites feature wooden floors, handmade Hawaiian quilts, Kohler infinity-edged whirlpool tubs, private vanity areas, and private gardens where clients can relax with a green tea extract infused with various fruits. Custom treatments merge Hawaiian, Asian, and traditional therapies. "Romance packages" are also available. ✉ *The Kahala Hotel & Resort, 5000 Kahala Ave., Kahala* ☎ *808/739–8938* ⊕ *www.kahalaresort.com.*

Liliha-Kapalama

This sliver of land that runs from ocean to mountain (known as an *ahupuaa* in Hawaiian) is presided over by famed Kamehameha Schools, which from its hillside perch looks down on this warren of modest homes and shops—and the Bishop Museum. There are also some great food establishments here including Helena's Hawaiian Food and Liliha Bakery (not to be missed for its *ono coco* puffs).

Chapter 4

WEST (LEEWARD) AND CENTRAL OAHU

4

Updated by
Cheryl Crabtree

◉ Sights	🍴 Restaurants	🛏 Hotels	🛍 Shopping	🍸 Nightlife
★★★☆☆	★★★☆☆	★★★★★	★★★☆☆	★★★☆☆

WELCOME TO WEST (LEEWARD) AND CENTRAL OAHU

TOP REASONS TO GO

★ **Gorgeous beaches:** From Pokai Bay and surf mecca Makaha to Yokohama Bay, the leeward side of the island affords excellent opportunities to ditch tourist troves and connect with real Hawaiians who live and play along a mostly undeveloped shoreline.

★ **Ko Olina:** A privately owned development on the southwest corner of Oahu, Ko Olina offers the region's best options for dining, nightlife, and golf, and one of the island's best luaus.

★ **Shopping:** Head to Central Oahu to shop for discounted traditional island souvenirs at the region's premium outlets and big box stores—where you're more likely to find easier parking.

★ **Blast to the past:** Visit Hawaii's Plantation Village and Dole Pineapple Plantation to learn about Oahu's commercial farming roots.

★ **Oahu's best sunsets:** The west-facing leeward side of the island is an ideal place to watch the sun dip into the Pacific at the end of the day.

Leeward and Central Oahu generally refer to the regions west and north of Pearl Harbor. Heading west from Honolulu, the H1 freeway leads to Oahu's "second city," Kapolei. From there, Farrington Highway continues west and north to the Ko Olina resorts and the Hawaiian communities of Nanakuli and Waianae, to the beach and end of the road at Keaweula, aka Yokohama Bay. Central Oahu occupies the fertile central valley, home of plantations, farms, military installations, working-class towns like Wahiawa, as well as predominately residential communities, which include Ewa Beach, Mililani, and Waipio. Oahu's commercial and residential future is expected to center here in the coming decades, and this area will expand and evolve more than any other region on the island. The central plateau in particular is meant to be a sustainable farming hub to ensure abundant fresh food supplies no matter what happens in the rest of the world. The new HART (Honolulu Authority for Rapid Transportation) trains will begin to run along the 10-mile stretch between Aloha Stadium and Kapolei in late 2020, giving everyone an easier way to reach West Oahu attractions.

1 Kapolei. Hawaii's "second city" is a newish development meant to ease the burden of the congested Honolulu area and boost the future of the state.

2 Ko Olina. Protected lagoons and myriad lodging, dining, and activity options attract thousands of visitors to this privately owned community.

3 Waianae. Many native Hawaiians live in and around Waianae, a modest town that anchors the leeward side of the island.

4 Wahiawa. A small but busy town in the heart of Central Oahu, Wahiawa serves as an important center for military personnel and workers at nearby farms and the Dole Pineapple Plantation.

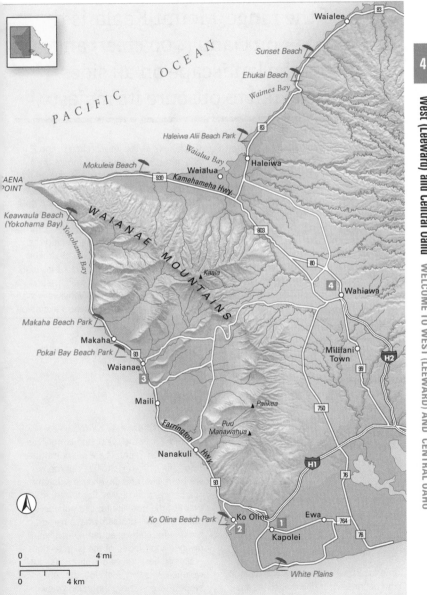

The rugged Waianae and Kaala mountain ranges bisect the leeward side of the island from the central plateau. The queen of the range, Mount Kaala, is the highest peak on Oahu (4,003 feet) and dominates the landscape on all sides when clouds fail to obscure its majesty.

The tall mountains shield the western slopes from trade winds and heavy rain that falls to the north and east. The western side thus appears drier, and beaches are known for their pristine white sands and crystal-clear waters, excellent settings for snorkeling and diving. This geography (combined with flows from the western slopes of the parallel eastern Koolau range) also results in abundant water flows to the fertile central valley plains—where much of Oahu's delectable bounty originates.

The region's eastern portion edges Pearl Harbor and includes Aloha Stadium, Hawaii's Plantation Village, the Wet 'n Wild water park, and the Waikele Premium Outlets near Waipio. Kapolei, Oahu's burgeoning "second city," lies due west of Pearl Harbor. It was a planned community, where, for years, the government has been trying to attract enough jobs to lighten inbound traffic to downtown Honolulu. A major mall and community center, Ka Makana Alii, opened here in 2017 to serve an expected influx of shoppers in the ensuing decades. Ko Olina—a lively, privately owned community centered on a golf course, several major resorts, and four man-made lagoons—occupies the southwestern tip of the island.

Some locals avoid Leeward and Central Oahu because of traffic that tends to bottleneck at the intersection of the H1, H2, and H3 freeways. But those who time their travels to avoid the traffic find great rewards throughout the region, especially the chance to explore the gorgeous and remote west coast beaches, including such far-flung Hawaiian communities of Nanakuli and Waianae and the end of the road at Keawaula, aka Yokohama Bay. A rest stop and a walk through the 3-acre maze at the Dole Plantation (the world's largest) near Wahiawa is well worth including in any Leeward excursion itinerary.

Planning

Beaches

The North Shore may be known as "country," but the west side is truly the rural area on Oahu. There are commuters from this side to Honolulu, but many are born, live, and die on this side with scarcely a trip to town. For the most part, there's little hostility toward outsiders, but occasional problems have flared up, mostly due to drug abuse, which has ravaged the fringes of the island—generally on the order of car break-ins, not violence. In short, lock your car when you stop to take in the breathtaking views, don't bring valuables, and enjoy the amazing beaches.

The beaches on the west side are expansive and empty. Most Oahu residents and tourists don't make it to this side simply because of the drive; in traffic it can take almost 90 minutes to make it to Kaena Point from downtown Honolulu. But you'll be hard-pressed to find a better sunset anywhere.

Getting Here and Around

AIRPORT TRANSFERS
Roberts Hawaii
Roberts Hawaii runs shuttle services from Daniel K. Inouye International Airport to Ko Olina. Fares are $16 each way. ☎ 808/539–9400 ⊕ *www.robertshawaii. com.*

BUS
It might be possible to rely on public transportation if you are staying at one of the Ko Olina hotels. TheBus routes C and 40 run up and down the westside. Route 52 travels from Ala Moana Center in Honolulu to Wahiawa and Haleiwa on the North Shore; the trip takes about 1¼ hours from Honolulu to Wahiawa and about 1½ hours to Haleiwa. Ko Olina runs its own private transportation vans that stop at resorts and the marketplace every half-hour or so.

CAR
It's relatively easy to get to West Oahu, which begins at folksy Waipahu and continues past Makakilo and Kapolei on H1 and Highway 93, Farrington Highway. It takes about a half-hour to get to Ko Olina from Waikiki, but rush hour traffic can create delays. A couple of cautions as you head to the leeward side: Highway 93 is a narrow, winding, two-lane road, notorious for accidents. There's an abrupt transition from an expansive freeway to a two-lane highway at Kapolei, and by the time you reach Nanakuli, it's a country road, so *slow down.* Also be aware

of congestion between Ko Olina and Waianae during commuter hours.

TAXI
If you don't rent a car, ride shares like Uber or Lyft are the most popular option in the region between Honolulu and Ko Olina. Roberts Hawaii also offers transportation to the Premium Outlets at Waikele and to Ko Olina.

Hotels

The full-service Ko Olina resorts and vacation rentals are your best options in this area, which doesn't have many short-term accommodations at all apart from basic motels. But be sure to factor in the hefty parking and resort fees when comparing with other lodgings elsewhere on the island.

PRICES
Hotel reviews have been shortened. For full information, visit Fodors.com.

What It Costs In U.S. Dollars			
$	$$	$$$	$$$$
FOR TWO PEOPLE			
under 180	$180–$260	$261–$350	over $350

Restaurants

Dining opportunities abound at the Four Seasons Oahu, Aulani, and Marriott's Beach Vacation Club within the Ko Olina community. The fear of traffic congestion on the freeways prevents some locals and visitors from driving here for dinner, but many come for lunch and happy hours, as well as to mark special occasions with a fancy meal and west-side sunset experience.

PRICES
Restaurant reviews have been shortened. For full information, visit Fodors.com.

What It Costs In U.S. Dollars			
$	$$	$$$	$$$$
AT DINNER			
under $17	$17–$26	$27–$35	over $35

Safety

Car break-ins and beach thefts are common on the leeward side, so keep all your belongings in sight, and never leave anything in your car.

Kapolei

Kapolei is approximately 20 miles (30 minutes by car) west of downtown Honolulu and 12 miles (20 minutes by car) from Mililani; traffic can double or triple the driving time.

The planned community of Kapolei, where, for years, the government has been trying to attract enough jobs to lighten inbound traffic to downtown Honolulu, is often called Oahu's "Second City." It occupies much of 1800s business mogul James Campbell's 4,100-acre Ewa Plain estate, which once cultivated vast tracts of sugarcane and pineapple. Its first phases broke ground starting in the 1980s. Today, it is a thriving community with government centers, industrial parks, big box malls, businesses small and large, and the University of Hawaii West Oahu Campus. The Ko Olina complex to the west is officially part of the district and has a Kapolei zip code. The new elevated Honolulu Rail Transit line, scheduled to open in late 2020, will connect east Kapolei to Aloha Stadium in Honolulu.

GETTING HERE AND AROUND

You can get to Kapolei in 30 minutes by car from downtown Honolulu if the traffic isn't too heavy.

⊙ Sights

Hawaii's Plantation Village

MUSEUM | Starting in the 1800s, immigrants seeking work on the sugar plantations came to these Islands like so many waves against the shore. At this living museum 30 minutes from downtown Honolulu (without traffic), visit authentically furnished buildings, original and replicated, that re-create and pay tribute to the plantation era. See a Chinese social hall; a Japanese shrine, sumo ring, and saimin stand; a dental office; and historic homes. The village is open for guided tours only. ⊠ *Waipahu Cultural Gardens Park, 94-695 Waipahu St., Waipahu* ☎ *808/677–0110* ⊕ *www.hawaiiplantationvillage.org* ⊠ *$15* ⊗ *Closed Sun.*

Beaches

White Plains Beach Park

BEACH—SIGHT | **FAMILY** | Concealed from the public eye for many years as part of the former Barbers Point Naval Air Station, this beach is reminiscent of Waikiki but without the condos and the crowds. It is a long, sloping beach with numerous surf breaks, but it is also mild enough at the shore for older children to play freely. It has views of Pearl Harbor and, over that, Diamond Head. Although the sand lives up to its name, the real joy of this beach comes from its history as part of a military property for the better part of a century. Expansive parking, great restroom facilities, and numerous tree-covered barbecue areas make it a great day-trip spot. As a bonus, a Hawaiian monk seal takes up residence here several months out of the year (seals are rare in the Islands). **Amenities:** lifeguards; parking (no fee); showers; toilets. **Best for:** surfing; swimming. ⊠ *Essex Rd. and Tripoli Rd., Kapolei* ⊹ *Take Makakilo Exit off H1 West, then turn left. Follow it into base gates, make left. Blue signs lead to beach.*

🛍 Shopping

SHOPPING CENTERS

Aloha Stadium Swap Meet & Marketplace

SHOPPING CENTERS/MALLS | This thrice-weekly outdoor bazaar attracts hundreds of vendors and even more bargain hunters. Every Hawaiian souvenir imaginable can be found here, from coral shell necklaces to bikinis, as well as a variety of ethnic wares, from Chinese brocaded dresses to Japanese pottery. There are also ethnic foods, silk flowers, and luggage in aloha floral prints. Shoppers must wade through the typical sprinkling of used and counterfeit goods to find value. Wear comfortable shoes, use sunscreen, and bring bottled water. The flea market takes place in the Aloha Stadium parking lot Wednesday and Saturday 8–3, Sunday 6:30–3. Admission is $1 per person ages 12 and up.

You can take either Uber or Lyft from your hotel. The Waikiki Trolley Purple Line also stops at the Swap Meet. For a cheaper but slower ride, take The Bus (⊕ *www.thebus.org*). You might also ask your hotel concierge about shared shuttle services. The new Hawaiian Rail trains will connect Aloha Stadium with Kapolei when they start running (scheduled for sometime in 2020). So you could shop at the swap meet and hop on the train to Ka Makana Alii to treasure-hunt even longer—all without a car! ✉ *Aloha Stadium, 99-500 Salt Lake Blvd., Aiea* ☎ *808/486–6704* ⊕ *www.alohastadiumswapmeet.net.*

Waikele Premium Outlets

SHOPPING CENTERS/MALLS | Armani Exchange, Calvin Klein, Coach, and Saks Fifth Avenue outlets anchor this discount destination of around 50 stores. You can take a shuttle from Waikiki for the 30-minute ride to the outlets for $18 round-trip, but the companies do change frequently. Reservations are recommended. ✉ *94-790 Lumiaina St., Waipahu* ☎ *808/676–5656* ⊕ *www.premiumoutlets.com/outlet/waikele.*

Ko Olina

24 miles west of downtown Honolulu.

For centuries, Hawaiian nobility rejuvenated at this pristine enclave on the island's southwestern. Today, Ko Olina is a major visitor hub, part of a decades-long master plan to attract jobs to the leeward side. The privately owned, 642-acre complex is a community unto itself, with one guarded public entrance/exit off Farrington Highway. It includes a golf course, three natural lagoons, a series of four man-made lagoons, three major resorts (each with a range of restaurants, shops, and activities), 4½ miles of walking paths, and a shopping area with additional restaurants and cafés. It's also home to the famed Paradise Cove Luau.

The Lanikuhonua Nature Preserve, with its pristine beach, edges the north end of the complex. The shoreline is public, but most of the 11-acre site belongs to the Lanikuhonua Cultural Institute, a private nonprofit that preserves and promotes Hawaiian culture.

The lagoons are open to the public, but public parking is limited (first-come, first-served, sunrise to sunset). Come early (before 10 am) to nab one of the prized spots. If you do manage to find a space, plan to walk at least a short bit to the lagoons along public access paths. Even resort guests pay hefty fees to park on-site. If you park far away from your ultimate destination, you can hop aboard the free Ko Olina shuttle vans that circle the community every half-hour.

GETTING HERE AND AROUND

You can get to Ko Olina in 45 minutes from downtown Honolulu by car unless traffic is heavy, and then it might take well over an hour.

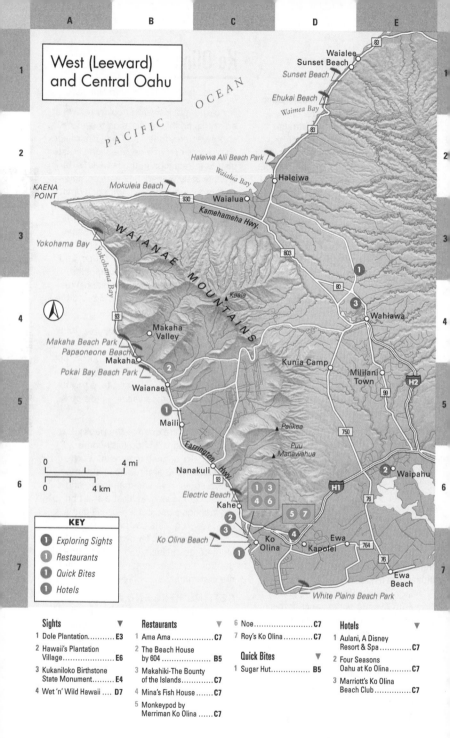

West (Leeward) and Central Oahu

PACIFIC OCEAN

KAENA POINT

Yokohama Bay

WAIANAE MOUNTAINS

Yokohama Bay

Makaha Beach Park
Papaoneone Beach
Pokai Bay Beach Park

Makaha Valley

Keala

Palikea

Puu Manawahua

Waialee
Sunset Beach
Sunset Beach

Ehukai Beach
Waimea Bay

Haleiwa Alii Beach Park
Waialua Bay

Mokuleia Beach

Haleiwa

Waialua

Kamehameha Hwy.

Wahiawa

Kunia Camp

Mililani Town

Makaha

Waianae

Maili

Farrington Hwy.

Nanakuli

Electric Beach

Kahe

Ko Olina Beach

Ko Olina

Kapolei

Ewa

Ewa Beach

Waipahu

White Plains Beach Park

0   4 mi
0   4 km

KEY
- ① Exploring Sights
- ① Restaurants
- ① Quick Bites
- ① Hotels

Sights

Wet'n'Wild Hawaii
AMUSEMENT PARK/WATER PARK | FAMILY | This 29-acre family attraction has water-slides, water cannons, and waterfalls. ✉ *400 Farrington Hwy., Ko Olina* ✣ *Off H1 at Exit 1* ☎ *808/674–9283* 🌐 *www.wetnwildhawaii.com* 🎟 *$50, parking $8 per car.*

Beaches

Electric Beach
BEACH—SIGHT | Directly across from the electricity plant—hence the name—Electric Beach (also known as Kahe Point) is a haven for tropical fish, making it a great snorkeling spot. The expulsion of hot water from the plant raises the temperature of the ocean, attracting Hawaiian green sea turtles, spotted moray eels, and spinner dolphins. Although the visibility is not always the best, the crowds are often small, but growing, and the fish are guaranteed. It's best to wear reef shoes here because of the sharp rocks. Unfortunately, there can be a strong current here, so it's not very kid-friendly. This is also a great place to stop for a picnic and admire the views. **Amenities:** parking (no fee); showers; toilets. **Best for:** snorkeling; sunset. ✉ *Farrington Hwy., Ko Olina* ✣ *1 mile west of Ko Olina Resort.*

Ko Olina Beach
BEACH—SIGHT | FAMILY | This is the best spot on the island if you have small kids. The resort area commissioned a series of four man-made lagoons, but, as it has to provide public beach access, you are the winner. Huge rock walls protect the lagoons, making them into perfect spots for the kids to get their first taste of the ocean without getting bowled over. The large expanses of seashore grass and hala trees that surround the semicircle beaches are made-to-order for nap time. A 1½-mile jogging track connects the lagoons. Due to its appeal for *keiki* (children), Ko Olina is popular, and the parking lot fills up quickly when school is out and on weekends, so try to get here before 10 am. The biggest parking lot is at the farthest lagoon from the entrance. There are actually three resorts here: Aulani (the Disney resort), Four Seasons Resort Oahu, and the Ko Olina Beach Villas Resort (which has a time-share section as well). **Amenities:** food and drink; parking (no fee); showers; toilets. **Best for:** sunset; swimming; walking. ✉ *92 Aliinui Dr., 23 miles west of Honolulu, Ko Olina* ✣ *Take Ko Olina exit off H1 West and proceed to guard shack.*

Restaurants

Ama Ama
$$$$ | MODERN HAWAIIAN | There's nothing "Mickey Mouse" about the food at the fine-dining restaurant of this Disney resort. Add to that the views of the Ko Olina lagoons and Pacific Ocean—and live music by top local performers Thursday–Sunday nights—and you have an evening worth the pretty penny. **Known for:** outstanding views and setting; consistently good food; hit-or-miss service. [$] *Average main: $44* ✉ *Aulani, a Disney Resort & Spa, 92-1185 Aliinui Dr., Ko Olina* ☎ *808/674–6200* 🌐 *www.disneyaulani.com/dining.*

Makahiki—The Bounty of the Islands
$$$$ | HAWAIIAN | FAMILY | The buffet restaurant at Disney's Aulani resort offers a wide variety of locally produced items, as well as familiar dishes from stateside and the rest of the world. You'll find sustainable Hawaiian seafood, Asian selections, familiar grilled meats and vegetables, and a kids' menu; an à la carte menu is also available. **Known for:** true reflection of Hawaii; wide array of food to please every member of the family; popular character breakfasts (which book up weeks in advance). [$] *Average main: $57* ✉ *Aulani, a Disney Resort & Spa, 92-1185 Aliinui Dr., Ko Olina* ☎ *808/674–6200* 🌐 *www.disneyaulani.com/dining* 🕓 *No lunch.*

Ko Olina, a planned resort community on the island's southwestern shore, the is the biggest tourist area on Leeward Oahu.

★ Mina's Fish House

$$$$ | **SEAFOOD** | Michael Mina, a James Beard Award winner, designed an exceptional line-to-table menu that celebrates the local catch to match the panoramic views spilling from indoor and lanai oceanfront tables. This might be the only restaurant in Hawaii (or the world) to have an on-site "fish sommelier," who guides you through the mind-boggling menu that includes a wide variety of cooking techniques, flavorings, and portions—from fillet to whole fish—and helps you choose the best matches for your particular palate. **Known for:** char-broiled Hawaiian seafood tower; Kona lobster dishes; daily happy hour. [$] *Average main: $51* ✉ *Four Seasons Oahu Ko Olina Resort, 92-1001 Olani St., Ko Olina* ☎ *808/679–0079* 🌐 *www.michaelmina.net* 🕑 *No lunch weekdays.*

Monkeypod by Merriman Ko Olina

$$ | **HAWAIIAN** | Local farm-to-table guru Peter Merriman is known throughout Hawaii for his inventive and popular restaurants. Monkeypod at Ko Olina captures his creativity and locally inspired food mantra perfectly. **Known for:** lobster deviled eggs and fresh fish tacos; indoor/outdoor setting; life-changing strawberry cream pie. [$] *Average main: $26* ✉ *Ko Olina Resort, 92-1048 Olani St., Ko Olina* ☎ *808/380–4086* 🌐 *www.monkeypod-kitchen.com.*

Noe

$$$$ | **ITALIAN** | Classic dishes from southern Italy's Amalfi Coast dominate the menu at this sleek Four Seasons restaurant, with seating indoors in various intimate and more social spaces, and outdoors overlooking a nature preserve. Locals come to celebrate special occasions, while guests from throughout the Ko Olina community come to feast on house-made pastas—especially the signature tagliatelle with truffle pesto and mushrooms—and multiple dishes that showcase Kona lobster. **Known for:** four-course tasting menu; extensive Italian wine list; weekend brunch. [$] *Average main: $49* ✉ *Four Seasons Oahu at Ko Olina, 92-1001 Olani St., Ko Olina*

☎ *808/679–0079* 🌐 *www.noeitalian.com*
🕒 *No lunch weekdays.*

Roy's Ko Olina
$$$$ | **HAWAIIAN** | The Ko Olina outpost of Roy's famed restaurant chain overlooks the 18th hole of the Ko Olina Golf Club course and reflects a distinct westside vibe, as most of the friendly staff come from this side of the island and exude an authentic "aloha" spirit. Dine on Roy's Hawaii-Asian-Europe fusion signature dishes and the chef's westside-influenced creations out on the patio or in Roy's iconic wood-beam-and-concrete interior. **Known for:** braised short ribs and other Roy's signature dishes; great getaway from Ko Olina resort crowds; scenic golf course views. [$] *Average main: $42* ✉ *Ko Olina Golf Club, 92-1220 Aliinui Dr., Kapolei* ☎ *808/676–7697* 🌐 *www.royyamaguchi.com.*

Hotels

★ **Aulani, A Disney Resort & Spa**
$$$$ | **RESORT** | **FAMILY** | Disney's first property in Hawaii melds the Disney magic with breathtaking vistas, white sandy beaches, and sunsets that even Mickey stops to watch. **Pros:** tons to do on-site; family-friendly done right; Painted Sky: HI Style Studio. **Cons:** a long way from Waikiki; character breakfasts require advance reservation (book far in advance); areas and events can get really busy. [$] *Rooms from: $524* ✉ *92-1185 Aliinui Dr., Kapolei* ☎ *714/520–7001, 808/674–6200, 866/443–4763* 🌐 *www.disneyaulani.com* 🛏 *832 rooms* 🍴 *No meals.*

★ **Four Seasons Oahu at Ko Olina**
$$$$ | **RESORT** | Oahu welcomed this luxurious new property to Ko Olina with great excitement—the first Four Seasons on the island, with nearly every room and suite in the 17-story hotel offering floor-to-ceiling windows and a private lanai, all with an ocean view. **Pros:** luxurious and exclusive; secluded, even in the Ko Olina complex; amenities and options abound. **Cons:** an hour from Waikiki; luxury doesn't come cheap; it doesn't always measure up to other Four Seasons. [$] *Rooms from: $675* ✉ *92-1001 Olani St., in the Ko Olina complex, Ko Olina* ☎ *808/679–0079, 844/387–0308* 🌐 *www.fourseasons.com/oahu* 🛏 *371 rooms* 🍴 *No meals.*

Marriott's Ko Olina Beach Club
$$$$ | **RENTAL** | **FAMILY** | Though primarily a time-share property, Marriott Ko Olina also offers nightly rentals, which range from hotel-style standard guest rooms to expansive and elegantly appointed one- or two-bedroom guest villa apartments, all located within a 642-acre gated community. **Pros:** suites are beautifully decorated and have ample space for families; nice views; resort area offers entertainment, shopping, and dining options beyond the property. **Cons:** an hour to Honolulu and Waikiki; rooms and suites vary, so ask when booking; the coast beyond Ko Olina is rural without a lot for visitors to do. [$] *Rooms from: $500* ✉ *92-161 Waipahe Pl., Ko Olina* ☎ *808/679–4700, 800/845–5279* 🌐 *www.marriott.com* 🛏 *544 units* 🍴 *No meals.*

Performing Arts

Paradise Cove Luau
THEMED ENTERTAINMENT | One of the largest shows on Oahu, the lively Paradise Cove Luau is held in the Ko Olina resort area, about 45 minutes from Waikiki (if there's light traffic). Drink in hand, you can stroll through the authentic village, learn traditional arts and crafts, and play local games. The stage show includes a fire-knife dancer, singing emcee, and both traditional and contemporary hula and other Polynesian dances. A finale dance features participation from the audience. Admission includes the buffet, activities, and the show. You pay extra for table service, box seating, and shuttle transport to and from Waikiki—the stunning sunsets are free. It starts daily at 5. ✉ *92-1089 Alii Nui Dr., Ko Olina*

☎ *808/842–5911* ⊕ *www.paradisecove. com* ☒ *From $107; round-trip transportation from Waikiki $18.*

Waianae

9 miles north of Ko Olina.

Waianae refers to both the town and the western (leeward) shores of Oahu, from Ko Olina up to Yokohama Bay and the end of the road near Kaena Point. It's mostly rural, without tourist traps and few restaurants apart from fast food outlets, tiny cafés, and hole-in-the-wall poke shacks. Still, the Waianae coast is well worth a day trip, mostly to experience an area where "real" Hawaiians, descendants of natives who populated the coast centuries before the *haoles* arrived, live and play. The beaches boast crystal-clear water. Turtles and dolphins swim near the shores, and when surf's up, Oahu's finest shredders show up to have fun and wow the watchers on the sand.

GETTING HERE AND AROUND

Waianae is about 15 or 20 minutes north of Ko Olina by car along Highway 93.

🏖 Beaches

Makaha Beach Park

BEACH—SIGHT | This beach provides a slice of local life most visitors don't see. Families string up tarps for the day, fire up hibachis, set up lawn chairs, get out the fishing gear, and strum ukulele while they "talk story" (chat). Legendary waterman Buffalo Keaulana can be found in the shade of the palms playing with his grandkids and spinning yarns of yesteryear. In these waters, Buffalo not only invented some of the most outrageous methods of surfing, but also raised his world-champion son Rusty. He also made Makaha the home of the world's first international surf meet in 1954, and it still hosts his Big Board Surfing Classic. With its long, slow-building waves, it's a great

spot to try out longboarding. The swimming is generally decent in summer, but avoid the big winter waves. The only parking is along the highway, but it's free. **Amenities:** lifeguards; showers; toilets. **Best for:** surfing; swimming. ☒ *84-450 Farrington Hwy., Waianae* ✛ *Go 32 miles west of Honolulu on the H1, then exit onto Farrington Hwy. The beach will be on your left.*

Pokai Bay Beach Park

BEACH—SIGHT | This gorgeous swimming and snorkeling beach is protected by a long breakwater left over from a now-defunct boat harbor. The beach's entire length is sand, and a reef creates smallish waves perfect for novice surfers. **Amenities:** parking (no fee); showers; toilets. **Best for:** snorkeling; swimming. ☒ *85-027 Waianae Valley Rd., Waianae* ✛ *Off Farrington Hwy.*

Yokohama Bay

BEACH—SIGHT | You'll be one of the few outsiders at this Waianae Coast beach at the very end of the road. If it weren't for the little strip of paved road, it would feel like a deserted isle: no stores, no houses, just a huge sloping stretch of beach and some of the darkest-blue water off the island. Locals come here to fish and swim in waters calm enough for children in summer. Early morning brings with it spinner dolphins by the dozens just offshore. Although Makua Beach up the road is the best spot to see these animals, it's not nearly as beautiful or sandy as "Yokes." **Amenities:** lifeguards; parking (no fee); showers; toilets. **Best for:** solitude; sunset; swimming. ☒ *81-780 Farrington Hwy., Waianae* ✛ *About 7 miles north of Makaha.*

🍴 Restaurants

The Beach House by 604

$$ | HAWAIIAN | Housed in a former officer's dining hall right on the west-facing beach at Pokai Bay, the hip, casual younger sibling of Pearl Harbor's

In the summer, when the surf is calm, Makaha is a great snorkeling destination; in the winter, it's a popular surfing spot, especially for locals.

Restaurant 604 is a great place to stop for a bite before or after a surf session at Makaha or a day-trip up the westside to Yokohama Bay. The island-inspired menu focuses on comfort foods and includes everything from poke, burgers and fries, and pizzas to traditional island plates with fish and rice; during happy hour and sunset time, locals congregate to watch sports on large-screen TVs and watch the golden orb dip into the crystal-clear seas. **Known for:** excellent sunset-viewing spot; lively happy hour; live music Thursday–Sunday. $ *Average main: $17* ⊠ *85-010 Army St., Waianae* ☎ *808/725-2589* ⊕ *www.beachhouse604.com.*

☕ Coffee and Quick Bites

Sugar Hut
$ | **BAKERY** | The only bakery and dessert shop in Waianae, this tiny little storefront whips up a couple dozen flavors of French macarons, truffles, cupcakes, pies, parfaits, and cream puffs daily. You can also find standard desserts like cookies, brownies, and Rice Krispies treats.

Known for: macarons and other excellent baked goods and desserts; lots of sweet tooth in a tiny package; bargain-priced "ugly ducklings". $ *Average main: $5* ⊠ *87-070 Farrington Hwy., Waianae* ⊹ *Look for Crab Shack restaurant and park in tiny lot out front* ☎ *808/722-7539* ⊕ *www.sugarhuthawaii.com.*

Wahiawa

Wahiawa is approximately 20 miles (30–35 minutes by car) north of downtown Honolulu, 20 miles (30 minutes by car) northeast of Ko Olina.

Oahu's central plain is a patchwork of old towns and new residential developments, military bases, farms, ranches, and shopping malls, with a few visit-worthy attractions and historic sites scattered about. Central Oahu encompasses the Moanalua Valley, residential Pearl City and Mililani, and the old plantation town of Wahiawa, on the uplands halfway to the North Shore.

James Dole first planted pineapples in the central plateau in the early 1900s, and the Dole Pineapple Plantation fields still border the northern limits of Wahiawa, a small town with a heavy military and working-class vibe. Lake Wilson (Wahiawa Reservoir) surrounds three sides of the town, and Highway 99 crosses two bridges (and several stoplights) to pass through. Wahiawa is the commercial hub for several military bases, including Schofield Barracks, Wheeler Army Airfield, and the U.S. Naval Computer and Telecommunications Area Master Station Pacific. The main drag—a five-block stretch of Highway 99 where traffic often slows to a snail's pace—was once a fast-food mecca but in recent years has given birth to a handful of decent cafés, restaurants, and an outpost of Black Sheep Cream Co., a popular Oahu ice creamery.

GETTING HERE AND AROUND
For Central Oahu, all sights are most easily reached by either the H1 or H2 freeway. Highway 99 goes through Schofield Barracks. Highway 80 goes through Wahiawa town.

 Sights

Dole Plantation
COLLEGE | FAMILY | Pineapple plantation days are nearly defunct in Hawaii, but you can still celebrate Hawaii's famous golden fruit at this promotional center with exhibits, a huge gift shop, a snack concession, educational displays, and the world's second-largest maze. Take the self-guided Garden Tour, or hop aboard the Pineapple Express for a 20-minute train tour to learn a bit about life on a pineapple plantation. Kids love the more than 3-acre Pineapple Garden Maze, made up of 14,000 tropical plants and trees. If you do nothing else, stop by the cafeteria in the back for a delicious pineapple soft-serve Dole Whip. This is about a 40-minute drive from Waikiki, a suitable stop on the way to or from the North Shore. ✉ *64-1550 Kamehameha Hwy., Wahiawa* ☎ *808/621–8408* ⊕ *www.doleplantation.com* ⌨ *Plantation free, Pineapple Express $12, maze $9, garden tour $8.*

Kukaniloko Birthstone State Monument
MEMORIAL | In the cool uplands of Wahiawa is haunting Kukaniloko, where noble chieftesses went to give birth to high-ranking children. One of the most significant cultural sites on the island, the lava-rock stones here were believed to possess the power to ease the labor pains of childbirth. The site is marked by approximately 180 stones covering about a half acre. It's a 40- to 45-minute drive from Waikiki. ✉ *Kamehameha Hwy. and Whitmore Ave., Wahiawa* ✛ *The north side of Wahiawa town.*

Chapter 5

NORTH SHORE

Updated by
Cheryl Crabtree

◉ Sights	🍴 Restaurants	🛏 Hotels	🛍 Shopping	🍸 Nightlife
★★★★★	★★★☆☆	★★★★☆	★★★☆☆	★☆☆☆☆

WELCOME TO NORTH SHORE

TOP REASONS TO GO

★ **Scenes of old Hawaii:** The wild, relatively undeveloped North Shore looks and feels more like the Oahu that existed centuries ago. Walk along blufftop and valley trails to discover ancient sites, and swim and fish in the crystal-clear waters that sustained ancient communities.

★ **Farm-fresh bounty:** Oahu natives refer to the North Shore as the "country"—the source of much of the island's produce and seafood.

★ **World-famous beaches and waves:** Banzai Pipeline, Sunset Beach, Waimea Bay—in winter they are the hallowed waters of surfing's greatest breaks. In summer, the glorious beaches provide the perfect setting for snorkeling and marine wildlife spotting.

★ **Laid-back vibe:** The North Shore is the antithesis of Waikiki. You won't find any high-rises or freeways here; outside of touristy Haleiwa, it's just miles of scenic coastline and country roads.

The main North Shore towns include Haleiwa (the hub), neighboring Waialua, Pupukea (just north of Waimea Bay), and the Kahuku district, which stretches from Kawela Bay and Kuilima/Turtle Bay to Kahuku town.

1 Waialua. Life here once revolved around a sugar mill, but now it's a tranquil, mostly residential community that anchors the remote, uncrowded northwestern stretches of Oahu.

2 Haleiwa. The North Shore's touristy commercial hub reflects an early 1900s plantation-era vibe.

3 Pupukea. This is world surf culture's center of the universe, in the heart of a 7-mile stretch of the world's best breaks.

4 Kahuku. The easternmost North Shore district is home to the legendary Turtle Bay Resort, famed shrimp shacks, and family-owned farms.

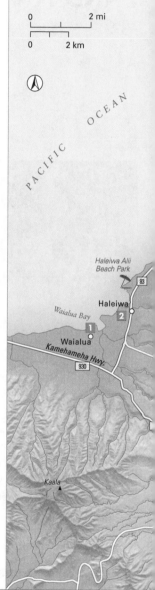

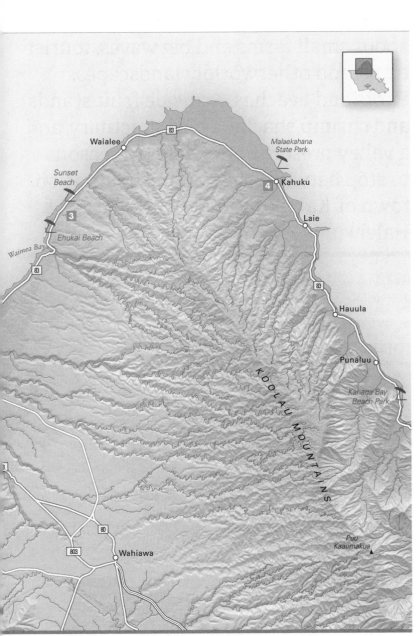

Malaekahana
State Park

Waialee

Sunset
Beach

3

Ehukai Beach

Waimea Bay

83

83

4 Kahuku

Laie

83

Hauula

Punaluu

Kahana Bay
Beach Park

KOOLAU MOUNTAINS

3

80

803

Wahiawa

Puu
Kaaumakua

An hour from town and a world away in atmosphere, Oahu's North Shore, roughly from Kahuku Point to Kaena Point, is about small farms and big waves, tourist traps, and otherworldly landscapes. Parks and beaches, roadside fruit stands and shrimp shacks, a bird sanctuary, and a valley preserve offer a dozen reasons to stop between the onetime plantation town of Kahuku and the surf mecca of Haleiwa.

Haleiwa has had many lives, from resort getaway in the 1900s to plantation town through the 20th century to its life today as a surf and tourist magnet. Beyond Haleiwa is the tiny village of Waialua; a string of beach parks; an airfield where gliders, hang gliders, and parachutists play; and, at the end of the road, Kaena Point State Recreation Area, which offers a brisk hike, striking views, and whale-watching in season.

Pack wisely for a day's North Shore excursion: swim and snorkel gear, light jacket and hat (the weather is mercurial, especially in winter), sunscreen and sunglasses, bottled water and snacks, towels and a picnic blanket, and both sandals and closed-toe shoes for hiking. A small cooler is nice; you may want to pick up some fruit or fresh corn. As always, leave valuables in the hotel safe, and lock the car whenever you park.

Planning

Beaches

"North Shore, where the waves are mean, just like a washing machine," sing the Kaau Crater Boys about this legendary side of the island. And in winter, they are absolutely right. At times, the waves overtake the road, stranding tourists and locals alike. When the surf is up, there are signs on the beach telling you how far to stay back so that you aren't swept out to sea. The most prestigious big-wave contest in the world, the Eddie Aikau, is held at Waimea Bay on waves the size of a five- or six-story building. The Triple Crown of Surfing roams across three North Shore beaches in the winter months.

All this changes come summer when this tiger turns into a kitten, with water smooth enough to water-ski on and ideal for snorkeling. The fierce Banzai

Pipeline surf break becomes a great dive area, allowing you to explore the coral heads that, in winter, have claimed so many lives on the ultrashallow but big, hollow tubes created here. Even with the monster surf subsided, this is still a time for caution: lifeguards are scarce, and currents don't subside just because the waves do.

That said, it's a place like no other on Earth, and must be explored. From the turtles at Mokuleia to the tunnels at Shark's Cove, you could spend your whole trip on this side and not be disappointed. A drive to the North Shore takes about one hour from Waikiki, but allot a full day to explore the beaches and Haleiwa, a burgeoning destination that has managed to retain its surf-town charm.

Getting Here and Around

AIR
Daniel K. Inouye International Airport in Honolulu is the island's only airport, so it's also the gateway to the North Shore, despite the 45-minute drive (more with traffic).

AIRPORT TRANSFERS
North Shore Transport provides shuttle transportation to and from Honolulu International Airport, transfers to other hotels and resorts, and shuttles to nearby towns and activities. Airport transfers start at $166 per person.

Roberts Hawaii Airport Shuttles take passengers from Daniel K. Inouye International Airport to Turtle Bay. Prices start at $90 per person (based on two-person minimum, otherwise individual passengers are $180).

CONTACTS North Shore Transport.
☎ 808/225–0522. **Roberts Hawaii.**
☎ 808/539–9400 ⊕ www.robertshawaii. com/airport-shuttle/oahu.

BUS
TheBus provides frequent daily service to the North Shore and is a practical way to get around, as parking is limited and fills quickly, especially in Haleiwa and at popular surf breaks. However, bags must fit under your seat or on your lap, so TheBus is not an option if you have checked bags and want to travel from the airport. (Surfboards aren't allowed either.) Route 60 travels from Honolulu to Kaneohe and up the windward side to Turtle Bay, Pupukea, and Haleiwa and back. Route 52 transports riders from Ala Moana Center to Haleiwa, traversing Central Oahu.

CAR
From Waikiki, the quickest route to the North Shore is H1 east to H2 north, and then the Kamehameha Highway past Wahiawa. You'll hit Haleiwa in just under an hour. The windward route (H1 east, H3, Likelike or Pali Highway, through the mountains, or Kamehameha Highway north) takes at least 90 minutes to Haleiwa, but the drive is far prettier.

TAXI
Taxis are very expensive and hard to find, but Uber and Lyft have become popular options in recent years, especially for rides to and within the Haleiwa area. Most visitors who come up from Honolulu for day trips without a car sign up with a tour company.

Hotels

North Shore accommodation options are extremely limited compared to Honolulu and the southern shores of Oahu. Turtle Bay resort is the only major hotel in the area, and the adjacent Kuilima condos provide legal short-term rentals. County of Honolulu law requires a 30-day minimum for most other vacation rental properties on the North Shore; currently, short-term rentals are legal only at condo complexes within 3,000 feet of a resort.

PRICES

Hotel reviews have been shortened. For full information, visit Fodors.com.

What It Costs In U.S. Dollars			
$	$$	$$$	$$$$
FOR TWO PEOPLE			
under 180	$180–$260	$261–$350	over $350

Restaurants

Most North Shore eateries cluster in Haleiwa town and at the Turtle Bay resort, which has several options ranging from casual poolside bars to upscale dining at Alaia, the resort's signature restaurant. The iconic shrimp shacks and other food trucks park mostly on the south side of Haleiwa and the famed hub in Kahuku, at North Shore's eastern limits; some travel to North Shore beaches and surf breaks during busy seasons. No North Shore trek is complete without a stop at a shrimp truck and a slice of pie at Ted's Bakery.

PRICES

Restaurant reviews have been shortened. For full information, visit Fodors.com.

What It Costs In U.S. Dollars			
$	$$	$$$	$$$$
AT DINNER			
under $17	$17–$26	$27–$35	over $35

Waialua

30 miles northwest of Honolulu.

A tranquil, multicultural burg with sleepy residential areas, uncrowded beach parks, and small mom-and-pop businesses, Wailua provides refuge from neighboring (and often tourist-choked) Haleiwa. In the 1900s, Waialua Sugar Company attracted workers from around the world, and their descendants continue to live and work here. The former sugar operation buildings now hold a General Store and eclectic, trendy shops, art studios, maker spaces for surfboard shapers and other craftspeople, and a coffee mill. Waialua is also the gateway to a wild and scenic coastline that includes Mokuleia Beach Park, Kaena Point State Recreation Area, and Dillingham Airport, where gliders and parachutists launch and land.

GETTING HERE AND AROUND

Waialua, a tiny town just west of Haleiwa, is about a 45-minute drive from Honolulu via the H2 and Highway 99 or Highway 803 through Central Oahu. TheBus Route 52 transports passengers between Honolulu and Haleiwa, and Route 76 connects Haleiwa and Waialua, but the trip takes considerably longer.

⊙ Sights

Kaena Point State Park

NATIONAL/STATE PARK | FAMILY | The name means "the heat" and, indeed, this windy barren coast lacks both shade and freshwater (or any man-made amenities). Pack water, wear sturdy closed-toe shoes, don sunscreen and a hat, and lock the car. The hike is along a rutted dirt road, mostly flat and nearly 3 miles long, (one-way) ending in a rocky, sandy headland. It is here that Hawaiians believed the souls of the dead met with their family gods, and, if judged worthy to enter the afterlife, leapt off into eternal darkness at Leinaakauane, just south of the point. In summer and at low tide, the small coves offer bountiful shelling; in winter, don't venture near the water. Rare native plants dot the landscape, and seabirds like the Laysan albatross nest here. If you're lucky, you might spot seals sunbathing on the rocks. From November through March, watch for humpbacks spouting and breaching. Binoculars

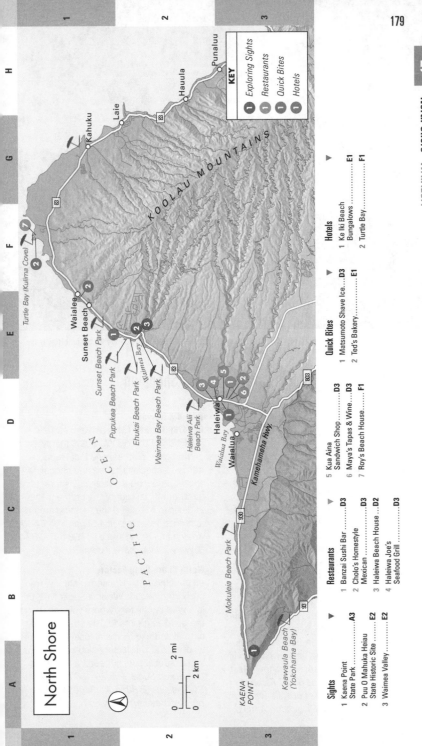

North Shore

KOOLAU MOUNTAINS

KAENA POINT

Turtle Bay (Kulima Cove)

Waialee

Sunset Beach

Sunset Beach Park

Pupukea Beach Park

Ehukai Beach Park

Waimea Bay

Waimea Bay Beach Park

Haleiwa Alii Beach Park

Haleiwa

Waialua Bay

Waialua

Kamehameha Hwy.

Mokuleia Beach Park

Keawaula Beach (Yokohama Bay)

Kahuku

Laie

Hauula

Punaluu

KEY

1 Exploring Sights
1 Restaurants
1 Quick Bites
1 Hotels

0 2 mi
0 2 km

Sights ▶

1 Kaena Point
   State Park **A3**
2 Puu O Mahuka Heiau
   State Historic Site **E2**
3 Waimea Valley **E2**

Restaurants ▶

1 Banzai Sushi Bar **D3**
2 Cholo's Homestyle
   Mexican **D3**
3 Haleiwa Beach House ..**D2**
4 Haleiwa Joe's
   Seafood Grill **D3**
5 Kua Aina
   Sandwich Shop..........**D3**
6 Maya's Tapas & Wine ..**D3**
7 Roy's Beach House.......**F1**

Quick Bites ▶

1 Matsumoto Shave Ice...**D3**
2 Ted's Bakery..............**E1**

Hotels ▶

1 Ke Iki Beach
   Bungalows **E1**
2 Turtle Bay.................**F1**

Kaena Point is remote and barren, but it's a beautiful place of religious significance for ancient Hawaiians, who believed it was where the souls of the dead departed for the afterlife.

and a camera are highly recommended. ⊠ *69-385 Farrington Hwy., Waialua* ⊕ *dlnr.hawaii.gov/dsp/parks/oahu/ kaena-point-state-park.*

🏖 Beaches

Mokuleia Beach Park

BEACH—SIGHT | There is a reason why the producers of the TV show *Lost* chose this beach for their set. On the remote northwest point of the island, it is about 10 miles from the closest store or public restroom. Its beauty is in its lack of facilities and isolation—all the joy of being stranded on a deserted island without the trauma of the plane crash. The beach is wide and white, the waters bright blue (but a little choppy) and full of sea turtles and other marine life. Mokuleia is a great secret find; just remember to pack supplies and use caution, as there are no lifeguards. **Amenities:** parking (no fee). **Best for:** sunset, walking. ⊠ *68-67 Farrington Hwy., Haleiwa* ✛ *West of Haleiwa town center, across from Dillingham Airfield.*

🛍 Shopping

GIFTS

Island X Hawaii

GIFTS/SOUVENIRS | This eclectic store in a section of the old Waialua Sugar Mill carries gifts, clothes, and local food items—especially coffee and chocolate that is produced in Waialua. Visitors get a short unofficial tour of the coffee plants and cacao trees and the roasting area just outside. ⊠ *Waialua Sugar Mill, 67-106 Kealohanui St., Waialua* ☎ *808/637–2624* ⊕ *www.islandxhawaii.com.*

North Shore Soap Factory

GIFTS/SOUVENIRS | Housed in a converted silo in the historic Waialua Sugar Mill, this is a working factory where you can watch the soap as it's made. The soaps are all natural and use as many local ingredients as possible. The factory also sells lotions and essential oils, gift sets, and T-shirts. ⊠ *Waialua Sugar Mill, 67-106 Kealohanui St., Waialua* ☎ *808/637–8400* ⊕ *www. northshoresoapfactory.com.*

Haleiwa

30 miles northwest of Honolulu, 3 miles northeast of Waialua.

North Shore's shopping, dining, and surf culture hub, Haleiwa has preserved and melded its historic plantation-era roots with a laid-back 1960s era vibe. During the 1920s this seaside hamlet boasted a posh hotel at the end of a railroad line (both long gone), while the '60s saw hippies gathered here, followed by surfers from around the world. The town sits amid a picture-perfect setting on Waialua Bay, where the Anahulu River empties into the harbor. Haleiwa Alii Beach Park and Haleiwa Beach border the bay and provide endless opportunities for water sports and other activities.

Today, the streets of Historic Haleiwa Town reflect a fun mix of old and new, with charming general stores and contemporary boutiques, galleries, and eateries. Be sure to stop in at Liliuokalani Protestant Church, founded by missionaries in the 1830s. It's fronted by a large, stone archway built in 1910 and covered with night-blooming cereus. Also check out the historic Rainbow Bridge, whose iconic double arches appear on many local works of art.

GETTING HERE AND AROUND

Haleiwa is about a 45-minute drive from Honolulu via the H2 and Highway 99 through Central Oahu. TheBus Route 52 transports passengers between Honolulu and Haleiwa via Central Oahu, and Route 60 travels around the windward side of the island, from Haleiwa to Kahuku and south to Kaneohe and Honolulu.

Beaches

Haleiwa Alii Beach Park

BEACH—SIGHT | **FAMILY** | The winter waves are impressive here, but in summer, the ocean is like a lake, ideal for family swimming. The beach itself is big and often full of locals. Its broad lawn off the highway invites volleyball and Frisbee games and groups of barbecuers. This is also the opening break for the Triple Crown of Surfing, and the grass is often filled with art festivals or carnivals. **Amenities:** lifeguards; parking (no fee); showers; toilets. **Best for:** surfing; swimming. ✉ *66-167 Haleiwa Rd., Haleiwa* ✥ *North of Haleiwa town center and past harbor.*

Restaurants

Banzai Sushi Bar

$$ | **JAPANESE FUSION** | An array of authentic Japanese dishes made with Hawaiian seafood and fresh, seasonal, mostly organic North Shore veggies and fruits attract locals and visitors alike to this hip yet family-friendly sushi house. The extensive menu includes everything from classic sashimi and tempura to off-the-wall sushi rolls, Wagyu beef and broiled fish entrées, and various vegetarian and gluten-free options are all on the menu. **Known for:** full bar with good selection of Japanese whiskeys and sakes; unusual rolls using macadamia nuts and island spices; some traditional Japanese seating. [$] *Average main: $26* ✉ *North Shore Marketplace, 66-246 Kamehameha Hwy., Suite B, Haleiwa* ☎ *808/637–4404* 🌐 *banzaisushibarhawaii.com.*

Cholo's Homestyle Mexican

$ | **MEXICAN** | There are a few institutions on the North Shore that are the area's great gathering places. Foodland (the great grocery store) is one, and the other is Cholo's. **Known for:** excellent ahi tacos; lively happy hour; fresh mango margaritas. [$] *Average main: $16* ✉ *North Shore Marketplace, 66-250 Kamehameha Hwy., Haleiwa* ☎ *808/637–3059* 🌐 *www.cholos.mx.*

Haleiwa Beach House

$$ | **AMERICAN** | One of the newer restaurants on the North Shore takes full advantage of its epic views of the water and the glorious building it calls home (it

was formerly occupied by longtime local icon Jameson's by the Sea). The menu is chock full of surf-and-turf options, from juicy burgers to grilled steaks, blackened fish to lobster and shrimp red Thai curry. **Known for:** view and setting that can't be beat; solid, reliable beef, seafood, salads, and kids options; craft beers on draft and a nice wine list. [$] *Average main: $25* ✉ *62-540 Kamehameha Hwy, Haleiwa* ☎ *808/637–3435* 🌐 *www.haleiwabeachhouse.com.*

Haleiwa Joe's Seafood Grill
$$$ | **AMERICAN** | After the long drive to the North Shore, watching the boats and surfers come and go from the harbor while you enjoy a mai tai on Haleiwa Joe's open-air lanai may be just what you need.This casual little joint, just past the Anahulu Stream Bridge, rarely changes (and to some, that might feel dated), but regulars appreciate the familiarity. A more upscale Kaneohe location overlooks the lush Haiku Gardens. **Known for:** reliable food with a nice harbor setting; crunchy coconut shrimp; good daily fish specials. [$] *Average main: $27* ✉ *66-011 Kamehameha Hwy., Haleiwa* ☎ *808/637–8005* 🌐 *haleiwajoes.com.*

Kua Aina Sandwich Shop
$ | **BURGER** | This North Shore spot has gone from funky burger shack (it first opened in 1975) to institution, with crowds of tourists and locals standing in line to order the large, hand-formed burgers heaped with bacon, cheese, and pineapples. Frankly, there are better burgers to be had around the island, but this place commands a truly loyal following. **Known for:** a pilgrimage stop on the North Shore surf circuit; tourists by the busload; decent burgers and fries. [$] *Average main: $11* ✉ *66-160 Kamehameha Hwy., Haleiwa* ☎ *808/637–6067* 🌐 *kua-ainahawaii.com.*

Maya's Tapas & Wine
$$ | **TAPAS** | A cozy space with a slightly sophisticated (for North Shore) vibe, Maya's serves up classic Spanish and Mediterranean dishes with Island twists. Here, seafood paella is made with local line-caught fish and shrimp, a burger combines Molokai venison and Kunoa beef, and hand-tossed flatbreads come with roasted local veggies and macadamia nut pesto. **Known for:** craft cocktails and sangria; savory paella and other specials; popular happy hour and Sunday brunch. [$] *Average main: $22* ✉ *66-250 Kamehameha Hwy., Unit D-101, Haleiwa* ☎ *808/200–2964* 🌐 *www.mayastapasandwine.com* ⏲ *No dinner Sun.*

☕ Coffee and Quick Bites

Matsumoto Shave Ice
$ | **CAFÉ** | For a real slice of Haleiwa life, stop at Matsumoto Shave Ice, a family-run business in a building dating from 1910, for cool treats that are available in every flavor imaginable. For something different, order a shave ice with adzuki beans—the red beans are boiled until soft, mixed with sugar, and then placed in the cone with the ice on top. **Known for:** one of the most popular shave ice spots on Oahu; the Masumoto with lemon, pineapple, and coconut syrup; house-made adzuki beans. [$] *Average main: $4* ✉ *66-111 Kamehameha Hwy., Suite 605, Haleiwa* ☎ *808/637–4827* 🌐 *www.matsumotoshaveice.com.*

🛏 Hotels

Ke Iki Beach Bungalows
$$ | **RENTAL** | At this 1½-acre, sloped, beachfront lot with six duplex bungalows, you can choose from studios and one- or two-bedroom units—outfitted with breezy beach-house furnishings, individual grills, hammocks, and picnic tables—and enjoy access to a 200-foot strand of sugary white-sand beach running between the North Shore's famous Waimea Bay and Ehukai Beach (Banzai Pipeline). **Pros:** outdoor showers, meditation area, and beachfront seating for nightly stargazing; popular with families

for reunions and weddings; steps to the beach and bike path to Sunset Beach and Waimea Bay. **Cons:** a bit far from restaurants and shopping; high surf in winter months; some bungalows close to highway noise. [$] *Rooms from: $185* ✉ *59-579 Ke Iki Rd., Haleiwa* ☎ *808/638–8829, 866/638–8229* 🌐 *www.keikibeach.com* 🛏 *11 units* 🍴 *No meals.*

Shopping

The North Shore has no major malls, but it does have a couple open-air shopping complexes and numerous shops and makeshift stands—some on the side of the road, others a bit more hidden—where you'll find one-of-a-kind treasures. Eclectic shops are the best place to find skin-care products made on the North Shore, Hawaiian music CDs, sea glass and shell mobiles, coffee grown in the Islands, and clothing items unavailable anywhere else. Be sure to chat with the owners in each shop. North Shore residents are an animated, friendly bunch with multiple talents. Stop in for coffee and the shop's owner might reveal a little about his or her passion for creating distinguished pieces of artwork.

SHOPPING CENTERS

Haleiwa Store Lots

SHOPPING CENTERS/MALLS | In 2015, the North Shore town debuted a shiny new complex, the Haleiwa Store Lots. Its most notable tenant is the legendary Matsumoto Shave Ice. (You'll know it by the long line of people.) The open-air shopping center has several locally owned stores such as Haleiwa Fruit Stand and the casual beach-chic boutique Guava Shop, and it's also home to surf photographer Clark Little's art gallery. ✉ *66-111 Kamehameha Hwy., Haleiwa* 🌐 *www.haleiwastorelots.com.*

North Shore Marketplace

SHOPPING CENTERS/MALLS | While playing on the North Shore, check out this open-air plaza that includes art galleries, clothing, gelato, and jewelry stores. And don't miss the Silver Moon Emporium for eclectic Islands fashions. People drive out of their way for the Coffee Gallery or for happy hour at Cholo's Homestyle Mexican Restaurant or Maya's Tapas and Wine. ✉ *66-250 Kamehameha Hwy., Haleiwa* ☎ *808/637–4416* 🌐 *www.northshoremarketplacehawaii.com.*

CLOTHING

The Growing Keiki

CLOTHING | Frequent visitors return to this store year after year for a fresh supply of unique, locally made, Hawaiian-style clothing for youngsters. ✉ *66-051 Kamehameha Hwy., Haleiwa* ☎ *808/637–4544* 🌐 *www.thegrowingkeiki.com.*

★ **Silver Moon Emporium**

CLOTHING | The small boutique carries everything from Brighton jewelry and European designer wear to fashionable T-shirts, shoes, and handbags. Expect attentive and personalized yet casual service. The stock changes frequently, and there's always something wonderful on sale. No matter what your taste, you'll find something for everyday wear or special occasions. ✉ *North Shore Marketplace, 66-250 Kamehameha Hwy., Haleiwa* ☎ *808/637–7710.*

FOOD

Tropical Fruits Distributors of Hawaii

FOOD/CANDY | Avoid the hassle of airport inspections. This company specializes in packing inspected pineapple and papaya; they will deliver to your hotel and to the airport check-in counter, or ship to the mainland United States and Canada. Think about ordering online. ✉ *Dole Plantation, 64-1550 Kamehameha Hwy., Haleiwa* ☎ *808/621–8408* 🌐 *www.dolefruithawaii.com.*

SPORTING GOODS

Surf 'N Sea

SPORTING GOODS | This North Shore water-sports store has everything you need for an active vacation under one roof. Purchase rash guards, swimwear,

T-shirts, footwear, hats, and shorts. Book scuba-diving tours and lessons and rent kayaks, snorkeling or scuba gear, spears for free diving, surfboards, stand-up paddleboards, and body boards. Experienced surfing instructors will take beginners to the small breaks on the notoriously huge (winter) or flat (summer) North Shore beaches. Warning to fishing enthusiasts: a fishing pole is the one ocean apparatus this shop doesn't carry. ⊠ 62-595 Kamehameha Hwy., Haleiwa ☎ 800/899–7873 ⊕ www.surfnsea.com.

Pupukea

6 miles northeast of Haleiwa.

Pupukea is a tiny village that anchors the Seven Mile Miracle—the legendary stretch of North Shore coast that faithfully serves up some of the world's best barrels and perfectly shaped waves every winter. It's also home to Foodland, the only grocery store between Kahuku/Laie and Haleiwa, which means you're likely to rub elbows with seasoned professional surfers and visiting celebrities, along with slipper-clad locals, in the checkout line. Across the street are Shark's Cove and Three Tables, both excellent snorkeling and scuba sites when the winter swells abate. Banzai Pipeline and Sunset Beach are just a mile up the road. Drive up the hill behind Foodland to explore the sacred Puu o Mahuka Heiau, the largest shrine on the island.

◉ Sights

Puu o Mahuka Heiau State Historic Site
ARCHAEOLOGICAL SITE | Worth a stop for its spectacular views from a bluff high above the ocean overlooking Waimea Bay, this sacred spot is the largest heiau on the island and spans nearly 2 acres. At one time it was used as a *heiau luakini,* or a temple for human sacrifices. It's now on the National Register of Historic Places. Turn up the road at the Pupukea Foodland

and follow the road up to the heiau. ⊠ Pupukea Rd., ½ mile north of Waimea Bay, Haleiwa ✛ From Rte. 83, turn right on Pupukea Rd. and drive 1 mile uphill ⊕ dlnr.hawaii.gov/dsp/parks/oahu/puu-o-mahuka-heiau-state-historic-site.

★ Waimea Valley
NATURE PRESERVE | FAMILY | Waimea may get lots of press for the giant winter waves in the bay, but the valley itself is a newsmaker and an ecological treasure in its own right. The local nonprofit is working to conserve and restore the natural habitat. Follow the Kamananui Stream up the valley through the 1,875 acres of gardens. The botanical collections here have more than 5,000 species of tropical flora, including a superb gathering of Polynesian plants. It's the best place on the island to see native species, such as the endangered Hawaiian moorhen. You can also see the restored Hale o Lono *heiau* (shrine) along with other ancient archaeological sites; evidence suggests that the area was an important spiritual center. Daily activities include botanical walking tours and cultural tours. At the back of the valley, Waihi Falls plunges 45 feet into a swimming pond. ∎**TIP**➔ **Bring your board shorts—a swim is the perfect way to end your hike, although the pond can get crowded. Be sure to bring mosquito repellent, too; it can get buggy.** ⊠ 59-864 Kamehameha Hwy., Haleiwa ☎ 808/638–7766 ⊕ www.waimeavalley.net ⊠ $18.

⛱ Beaches

Ehukai Beach Park
BEACH—SIGHT | What sets Ehukai apart is the view of the famous Banzai Pipeline. Here the winter waves curl into magnificent tubes, making it an experienced wave-rider's dream. It's also an inexperienced swimmer's nightmare. Spring and summer waves, on the other hand, are more accommodating to the average person, and there's good snorkeling. Except when the surf contests are going on, there's no reason to stay on the central

While Waimea Bay is known for its big winter waves and surf culture, the Waimea Valley is an area of great historical significance. It's also known for its botanical specimens, including big tropical trees.

strip. Travel in either direction from the center, and the conditions remain the same but the population thins out, leaving you with a magnificent stretch of sand all to yourself. **Amenities:** lifeguards; parking (no fee); showers; toilets. **Best for:** snorkeling; surfing. ⊠ *59-337 Ke Nui Rd., Haleiwa* ⊹ *1 mile north of Foodland at Pupukea.*

★ **Pupukea Beach Park** (*Shark's Cove*)
BEACH—SIGHT | Surrounded by shady trees, Pupukea Beach Park is pounded by surf in the winter months but offers great diving and snorkeling in summer (March through October). The cavernous lava tubes and tunnels are great for both novice and experienced snorkelers and divers. It's imperative that you wear reef shoes at all times since there are a lot of sharp rocks. Sharp rocks also mean that this beach isn't the best for little ones. Some dive-tour companies offer round-trip transportation from Waikiki. Equipment rentals and dining options are nearby. **Amenities:** parking (no fee); showers; toilets. **Best for:** diving; snorkeling;

swimming. ⊠ *Haleiwa* ⊹ *3½ miles north of Haleiwa, across street from Foodland.*

Sunset Beach Park
BEACH—SIGHT | The beach is broad, the sand is soft, the summer waves are gentle—making for good snorkeling—and the winter surf is crashing. Many love searching this shore for the puka shells that adorn the necklaces you see everywhere. **Amenities:** lifeguards; parking (no fee); showers; toilets. **Best for:** snorkeling; sunset; surfing. ⊠ *59-144 Kamehameha Hwy., Haleiwa* ⊹ *1 mile north of Ehukai Beach Park.*

★ **Waimea Bay Beach Park**
BEACH—SIGHT | Made popular in that old Beach Boys song "Surfin' U.S.A.," Waimea Bay Beach Park is a slice of big-wave heaven, home to king-size 25- to 30-foot winter waves. Summer is the time to swim and snorkel in the calm waters. The shore break is great for novice bodysurfers. Due to its popularity, the postage-stamp parking lot is quickly filled, but it's also possible to park along

Shrimp Shacks 🍴

No drive to the North Shore is complete without a shrimp stop. Shrimp stands dot Kamehameha Highway from Kahaluu to Kahuku. For about $12, you can get a shrimp plate lunch or a snack of chilled shrimp with cocktail sauce, served from a rough hut or converted van (many permanently parked) with picnic-table seating.

The shrimp-shack phenomenon began with a lost lease and a determined restaurateur. In 1994, when Giovanni and Connie Aragona couldn't renew the lease on their Haleiwa deli, they began hawking their best-selling dish—an Italian-style scampi preparation involving lemon, butter, and lots of garlic—from a truck alongside the road. About the same time, aquaculture was gaining a foothold in nearby Kahuku, with farmers raising sweet, white shrimp and huge, orange-whiskered prawns in shallow freshwater ponds. The ready supply and the success of the first shrimp truck led to many imitators.

Although it's changed hands, that first business lives on as **Giovanni's Original Shrimp Truck**, parked in Kahuku town. Signature dishes include the garlic shrimp and a spicy shrimp sauté, both worth a stop.

But there's plenty of competition: at least a dozen stands, trucks, or stalls are operating at any given time, with varying menus (and quality).

Not all of that shrimp comes fresh from the ponds; much of it is imported. The only way you can be sure you're buying local, farm-raised shrimp is if the shrimp is still kicking. **Romy's Kahuku Prawns and Shrimp Hut** (Kamehameha Highway, near Kahuku) is an arm of one of the longest-running aquaculture farms in the area; it sells live shrimp and prawns and farm-raised fish along with excellent plate lunches.

the side of the road and walk in. **Amenities:** lifeguards; parking (no fee); showers; toilets. **Best for:** snorkeling; surfing; swimming. ✉ *61-31 Kamehameha Hwy., Haleiwa* ✥ *Across from Waimea Valley, 3 miles north of Haleiwa.*

☕ Coffee and Quick Bites

Ted's Bakery

$ | **AMERICAN** | Sunburned tourists and salty surfers rub shoulders in their quest for Ted's famous chocolate *haupia* pie (layered coconut and dark chocolate puddings topped with whipped cream) and hearty plates—like garlic shrimp, gravy-drenched hamburger steak, and mahimahi. Parking spots and the umbrella-shaded tables are a premium, so be prepared to grab and go; if you can't get enough of that haupia goodness, Foodland and other grocery chains typically stock a selection of the famous pies as well. **Known for:** Ted's pies, which seem to show up at every Oahu pot luck; reliable all-day dining; plate lunches. [$] *Average main: $12* ✉ *59-024 Kamehameha Hwy., Haleiwa* ☎ *808/638–8207* 🌐 *www.tedsbakery.com.*

Kahuku

Kawela Bay is 5½ miles northeast of Pupukea, Kahuku is about 9 miles northeast of Pupukea.

The Kahuku district, which stretches from Kahuku town to Kawela Bay, includes Kahuku Point, the northernmost

Did You Know?

Beach Boys fans flock to Waimea Bay, the beach with winter waves reaching 30 feet, made popular in "Surfin' U.S.A."

point on Oahu. It's best known for fresh fruits and veggies from local farms (watch for farm stands along the highway), shrimp shacks, and exceptional high school football stars who go on to play at top-tier colleges and the NFL. Kahuku town is a collection of brand-name stores and tiny mom-and-pop shops amid modest residential neighborhoods filled with longtime island residents. Multimillion-dollar homes line the shores of the gated Kawela Bay community, but the public can access the beach off Kamehameha Highway at Kawela Camp. Park on the side of the road and walk about a quarter mile along a trail to get there.

Beaches

Turtle Bay (*Kuilima Cove*)

BEACH—SIGHT | **FAMILY** | Now known more for its resort (the Turtle Bay resort) than its magnificent beach at Kuilima Cove, Turtle Bay is mostly passed over on the way to the better-known beaches of Sunset and Waimea. But for the average visitor with average swimming capabilities, this is a good place to be on the North Shore. The crescent-shape beach is protected by a huge sea wall. You can see and hear the fury of the northern swell while blissfully floating in cool, calm waters. The convenience of this spot is also hard to pass up—there is a concession selling sandwiches and sunblock right on the beach. The resort has free parking for beach guests. **Amenities:** food and drink; parking (no fee); showers; toilets. **Best for:** sunset; swimming. ✉ *57-20 Kuilima Dr., 4 miles north of Kahuku, Kahuku* ✣ *Turn into Turtle Bay Resort and follow signs to public parking lot and beach access spots.*

Restaurants

Roy's Beach House

$$$$ | **MODERN HAWAIIAN** | Loyalists of Roy Yamaguchi's iconic spots in Hawaii Kai and Waikiki are thrilled that he's also represented on the North Shore, in this rustic-beam-and-concrete-floor pavilion literally on the sand at Turtle Bay. All the favorites are served at this more beach-casual spot, from the miso butterfish to the beef short ribs, along with a more casual lunch menu. **Known for:** casual, romantic setting right on the beach; Roy's signature dishes; special-occasion celebrations. [$] *Average main: $42* ✉ *Turtle Bay, 57-091 Kamehameha Hwy., Kahuku* ☎ *808/293–0801* 🌐 *www.roysbeachhouse.com.*

Hotels

★ **Turtle Bay**

$$$$ | **RESORT** | Sprawling over nearly 1,300 acres of natural landscape on the edge of Kuilima Point in Kahuku, the Turtle Bay resort boasts spacious guest rooms averaging nearly 500 square feet and with lanai that showcase stunning peninsula views. **Pros:** fabulous open public spaces in a secluded area of Oahu; beautiful two-level spa; excellent location for exploring the North Shore. **Cons:** very remote—even Haleiwa is a 20-minute drive; hefty resort fee; 24/7 resort living isn't for everyone. [$] *Rooms from: $360* ✉ *57-091 Kamehameha Hwy., Kahuku* ☎ *808/293–6000, 800/203–3650, 866/827–5321 for reservations* 🌐 *www.turtlebayresort.com* 🛏 *535 rooms* 🍴 *No meals.*

Chapter 6

WINDWARD OAHU

WITH HAWAII KAI

Updated by
Trina Kudlacek

◉ Sights	🍴 Restaurants	🛏 Hotels	🛍 Shopping	🍸 Nightlife
★★★★☆	★★☆☆☆	★☆☆☆☆	★★☆☆☆	★☆☆☆☆

WELCOME TO WINDWARD OAHU

TOP REASONS TO GO

★ **Beautiful beaches:** Although Oahu's windward side is known more for windsurfing than swimming, there are still some gorgeous beaches with magnificent views.

★ **Stunning emerald green cliffs:** These are the kinds of dramatic backdrops that you see in movies.

★ **Fewer crowds:** Windward Oahu is primarily residential, so it just doesn't get the crowds of more touristy areas like Waikiki (or even Haleiwa).

★ **Local life:** If you want to see how Oahu locals really live, then make for the windward side, including some of the small villages that are still around.

★ **Polynesian Cultural Center:** The best Polynesian cultural experience on the island is here.

Locals refer to the east side of Oahu as the windward side because of the east-to-west trade winds, which once carried sailing ships to the islands in years gone by and which still keep Hawaii cooler and lower in humidity than other Polynesian islands in the South Pacific. Because this side of the island sees much more frequent—usually daily—showers, it is cooler and much greener than the leeward side, where most hotels are found. A day trip to the windward side feels like a visit to another island with its slower pace, fewer crowds, and drop dead gorgeous scenery.

1 Hawaii Kai. This strip mall–filled suburb on the southeast shore is a great place to stop for picnic supplies or lunch before heading to Hanauma Bay or beginning your cliff-hugging drive to the Windward side.

2 Waimanalo. Nestled between the Koolau mountains and a spectacular beach with turquoise blue waters, this small village is where many native Hawaiian families live.

3 Kailua. With two of Oahu's top beaches and filled with upscale boutiques and great restaurants, Kailua is popular with locals and visitors alike.

4 Kaneohe. The sprawling suburb is the largest of Oahu's windward villages. It's next to the stunning Koolaus, which means restaurants and sights that include a backdrop of incredible scenery.

5 Kaaawa. So small you may well pass right through it before realizing you're there, Kaaawa's claim to fame is as the next door neighbor to popular Kualoa Ranch.

6 Laie. Most folks make the trek up to the most northern village on the windward side to spend a day and evening at the Polynesian Cultural Center. If making a day trip of the Windward side, consider stopping here for picnic provisions.

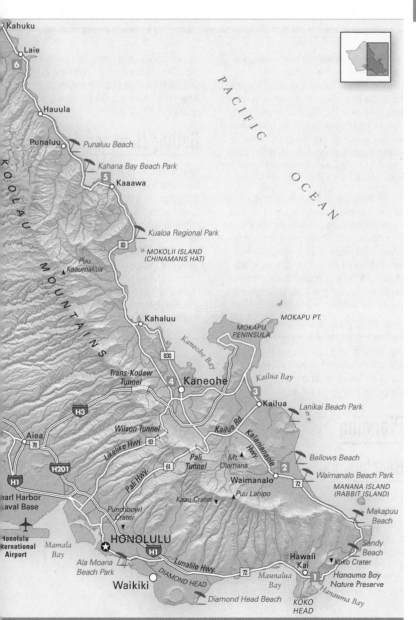

Kahuku

Laie

6

Hauula

Punaluu

Punaluu Beach

Kahana Bay Beach Park

5 Kaaawa

Kualoa Regional Park

83

MOKOLII ISLAND
(CHINAMANS HAT)

KOOLAU MOUNTAINS

Puu
Kaaumakua

PACIFIC

OCEAN

Kahaluu

Kaneohe Bay

830

MOKAPU
PENINSULA

MOKAPU PT.

Trans-Kodaw
Tunnel

4 Kaneohe

Kailua Bay

H3

3 Kailua

Lanikai Beach Park

Wilson Tunnel

Likelike Hwy.

63

Kailua Rd.

Kalanianaole Hwy.

Aiea

78

Pali
Tunnel

61

Mt.
Olomana

Bellows Beach

H201

Pali Hwy.

2

Waimanalo

72

Waimanalo Beach Park

MANANA ISLAND
(RABBIT ISLAND)

H1

Kaau Crater

Puu Lanipo

earl Harbor
aval Base

Punchbowl
Crater

Makapuu
Beach

Honolulu
ternational
Airport

Mamala
Bay

HONOLULU

H1

Hawaii
Kai

Sandy
Beach

Koko Crater

Ala Moana
Beach Park

Lunalilo Hwy.

72

Maunalua
Bay

1

Hanauma Bay
Nature Preserve

Waikiki

DIAMOND HEAD

Diamond Head Beach

KOKO
HEAD

Hanauma Bay

Looking at Honolulu's topsy-turvy urban sprawl, you would never suspect the windward side existed.

It's a secret Oahuans like to keep, so they can watch the awe on the faces of their guests when the car emerges from the tunnels through the mountains and they gaze for the first time on the panorama of turquoise bays and emerald valleys watched over by the knife-edged Koolau ridges. Jaws literally drop. Every time. And this just a 15-minute drive from downtown.

It's on this side of the island where many native Hawaiians live. Evidence of traditional lifestyles is abundant in crumbling fishponds, rock platforms that once were altars, taro patches still being worked, and throw-net fishermen posed stock-still above the water (though today, they're invariably wearing polarized sunglasses, the better to spot the fish).

Here the pace is slower, more oriented toward nature. Beachgoing, hiking, diving, surfing, and boating are the draws, along with a visit to the Polynesian Cultural Center and poking through little shops and wayside stores.

Planning

Beaches

The windward side lives up to its name, with ideal spots for windsurfing and kiteboarding, or for the more intrepid, hang gliding. For the most part, the waves are mellow, and the bottoms are all sand—making for nice spots to visit with younger kids. The only drawback is that this side of Oahu does tend to get more rain. But the vistas are so beautiful that a little sprinkling of "pineapple juice" shouldn't dampen your experience; plus, it benefits the waterfalls that cascade down the Koolaus.

Getting Here and Around

Keeping in mind there is really only one road that follows the windward coastline from Waikiki, you do have several options to get to this side. You can spend a day hugging the coast as you drive east and then turn north until you arrive at the home of the Polynesian Cultural Center, Laie. For this partial "circle island tour" first head east on the H1 interstate past Diamond Head until it becomes Kalanianaole Highway. Look for Kamehameha Highway once you get to Kaneohe and continue following this two-lane road all the way to the North Shore. Just as spectacular but a much more direct route is by taking the H1 Highway to either the Pali, Like Like, or H3 interstate across the mountains and through the tunnels to Kaneohe and beyond. While the Pali Highway gives you the option of stopping to take in the view at the Pali Lookout, the H3 offers the most breathtakingly beautiful arrival to this side of the island.

CAR

Though TheBus serves the entire island, you'll need a car to fully explore the windward side.

Hotels

Regulations severely limiting bed-and-breakfast and short-term vacation rentals on Oahu were adopted in 2019, largely driven by residents of the windward side. This translates into a scarcity of lodging options, but those you'll find are embedded within windward communities rather than the tourist enclaves of Waikiki and Ko Olina.

PRICES

Hotel reviews have been shortened. For full information, visit Fodors.com.

What It Costs in U.S. Dollars			
$	$$	$$$	$$$$
FOR TWO PEOPLE			
under $180	$180–$260	$261–$350	over $350

Restaurants

Many folks on the windward side never travel to "Town" (Honolulu) in search of great dining options. Join the locals for fine dining in Hawaii Kai, locally brewed beer, mac nut pancakes worth waiting in line for, shave ice, or Mediterranean-inspired pupu.

PRICES

Restaurant reviews have been shortened. For full information, visit Fodors.com.

What It Costs in U.S. Dollars			
$	$$	$$$	$$$$
AT DINNER			
under $17	$17–$26	$27–$35	over $35

Hawaii Kai

Approximately 10 miles southeast of Waikiki.

Driving southeast from Waikiki on busy, four-lane Kalanianaole Highway, you'll pass a dozen bedroom communities tucked into the valleys at the foot of the Koolau Range, with fleeting glimpses of the ocean from a couple of pocket parks. Suddenly, civilization falls away, the road narrows to two lanes, and you enter the rugged coastline of Koko Head and Ka Iwi.

This is a cruel coastline: dry, windswept, and with rocky shores and untamed waves that are notoriously treacherous. While walking its beaches, do not turn your back on the ocean, don't venture close to wet areas where high waves occasionally reach, and be sure to heed warning signs.

At this point, you're passing through Koko Head Regional Park. On your right is the bulging remnant of a pair of volcanic craters that the Hawaiians called Kawaihoa, known today as Koko Head. To the left is Koko Crater and an area of the park that includes a hiking trail, a dryland botanical garden, a firing range, and a riding stable. Ahead is a sinuous shoreline with scenic pullouts and beaches to explore. Named the Ka Iwi Coast (*iwi*, "ee-vee," are bones—sacred to Hawaiians and full of symbolism) for the channel just offshore, this area was once home to a ranch and small fishing enclave that were destroyed by a tidal wave in the 1940s.

GETTING HERE AND AROUND

Driving straight from Waikiki to Makapuu Point takes from a half to a full hour, depending on traffic. There isn't a huge number of sights per se in this corner of Oahu, so a couple of hours should be plenty of exploring time, unless you make a lengthy stop at a particular point.

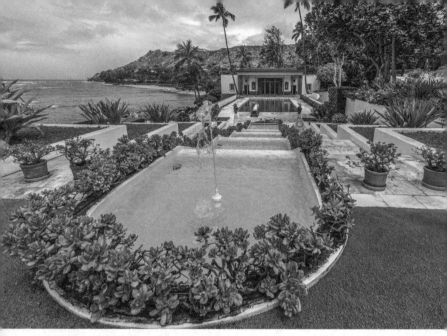

When Doris Duke died in 1993, her estate, Shangri La, became a museum of Islamic culture and art. Tours leave from the Honolulu Museum of Art in downtown Honolulu.

👁 Sights

Halona Blowhole

VIEWPOINT | Below a scenic turnout along the Koko Head shoreline, this oft-photographed lava tube sucks the ocean in and spits it out. Don't get too close, as conditions can get dangerous. ■**TIP→ Look to your right to see the tiny beach below that was used to film the wave-washed love scene in** *From Here to Eternity*. In winter, this is a good spot to watch whales at play. Offshore, the island of Molokai calls like a distant siren, and every once in a while Lanai is visible in blue silhouette. Take your valuables with you, and lock your car, because this scenic location is overrun with tourists and therefore a hot spot for petty thieves. ⊠ *Kalanianaole Hwy., Hawaii Kai* ✛ *1 mile east of Hanauma Bay.*

Koko Crater Botanical Gardens

GARDEN | If you've visited any of Oahu's other botanical gardens, this one will stand in stark contrast. Inside the tallest tuff cone on Oahu, in one of the hottest and driest areas on the island, Koko Crater Botanical Garden allows visitors the opportunity to see dryland species of plants including baobab trees, cacti, plumeria, and bougainvillea. ■**TIP→ Be sure to bring plenty of water, sunscreen, and a hat. This is the driest, hottest side of the island.** ⊠ *7491 Kokonani St., Hawaii Kai* ✛ *Entrance at end of Kokonani St.* ☎ *808/522–7066* ⊕ *www.honolulu.gov/parks/hbg.html* 🎟 *Free.*

Lanai Lookout

VIEWPOINT | A little more than half a mile past Hanauma Bay as you head toward Makapuu Point, you'll see a turnout on the ocean side with some fine views of the coastline. In winter, you'll have an opportunity to see storm-generated waves crashing against lava cliffs. This is also a popular place for winter whale-watching, so bring your binoculars, some sunscreen, and a picnic lunch, and join the small crowd scanning for telltale white spouts of water only a few hundred yards away. On clear days, you should be able to see the islands of Molokai and Lanai off in the distance, hence the name. ✉ *Kalanianaole Hwy., Hawaii Kai* ✛ *Just past Hanauma Bay.*

★ Shangri La Museum of Islamic Art, Culture & Design

HOUSE | In 1936, heiress Doris Duke bought 5 acres at Black Point, down the coast from Waikiki, and began to build and furnish the first home that would be all her own. She called it Shangri La. For more than 50 years, the home was a work in progress as Duke traveled the world, buying art and furnishings, picking up ideas for her Mughal Garden, for the Playhouse in the style of a 17th-century Irani pavilion, and for the water terraces and tropical gardens. When she died in 1993, Duke left instructions that her home was to become a public center for the study of Islamic art.

Outside of minor conservation-oriented changes and more extensive 2017 renovations to the courtyard and pool, the house and gardens have remained much as Duke left them. To walk through them is to experience the personal style of someone who saw everything as raw material for her art. With her trusted houseman, Jin de Silva, she helped build the elaborate Turkish Room, trimming tiles and painting panels to retrofit the existing space (including raising the ceiling and lowering the floor) and building a fountain of her own design. Among many aspects of the home inspired by the Muslim tradition is the entry: an anonymous gate, a blank white wall, and a wooden door that bids you, "Enter herein in peace and security" in Arabic script. Inside, tiles glow, fountains tinkle, and shafts of light illuminate artwork through arches and high windows. In 2014, after years of renovation, Duke's bedroom (the Mughal Suite) opened to the public. This was her private world, entered only by trusted friends.

The house is open by guided tour only, and reservations are required. Book your spot as early as possible, as tours fill up very quickly. Tours take 2½ hours including transportation from the Honolulu Museum of Art (*900 S. Beretania St., downtown Honolulu*), where all tours begin. Children under eight are not admitted. ✉ *Hawaii Kai* ☎ *808/532–3853 for Honolulu Museum of Art* ⊕ *www.shangrilahawaii.org* 🎫 *Tour $25 ($2 fee for online reservations, $2 for phone reservations)* ⊗ *Closed Sun.–Tues. and Sept.*

🌊 Beaches

Much of Southeast Oahu is surrounded by reef, making most of the coast uninviting to swimmers, but the spots where the reef opens up are true gems. The drive along this side of the island is amazing, with its sheer lava-rock walls on one side and deep-blue ocean on the other. There are plenty of restaurants in the suburb of Hawaii Kai so you can make a day of it, knowing that food isn't far away.

Halona Cove

BEACH—SIGHT | Also known as *From Here to Eternity* Beach and "Pounders," this little beauty is never crowded due to the short, treacherous climb down to the sand. But for the intrepid, what a treat this spot can be. It's in a break in the ocean cliffs, with the surrounding crags providing protection from the wind. Open-ocean waves roll up onto the beach (thus the second nickname), but unlike at Sandy Beach, a gently sloping sand bottom takes much of the punch out of them before they hit the shore. Turtles frequent the small cove, seeking respite from the otherwise blustery coast. It's great for packing a lunch and holing up for the day. ⚠ **The current is mellow inside the cove but dangerous once you get outside it. Amenities:** parking (no fee). **Best for:** sunrise. ✉ *8699 Kalanianaole Hwy., Hawaii Kai* ✛ *Below Halona Blow Hole Lookout parking lot.*

If you're a snorkeler, head straight for Hanauma Bay, the best and most popular place to snorkel on Oahu.

★ Hanauma Bay Nature Preserve

BEACH—SIGHT | FAMILY | Picture this as the world's biggest open-air aquarium. You go here to see fish, and fish you'll see. Due to their exposure to thousands of visitors every week, these fish are more like family pets than the skittish marine life you might expect. An old volcanic crater has created a haven from the waves where the coral has thrived. There's an educational center where you must watch a nine-minute video about the nature preserve before being allowed down to the bay. ■ TIP➔ **The bay is best early in the morning (around 7), before the crowds arrive; it can be difficult to park later in the day.**

Snorkel equipment and lockers are available for rent, and there's an entry fee for nonresidents. Smoking is not allowed, and the beach is closed on Tuesday. Wednesday to Monday, the beach is open 6 am–6 pm (until 7 pm June–August). There's a tram from the parking lot to the beach, or you can walk the short distance. Need transportation? Take TheBus each way from anywhere on the island. Alternatively, Hanauma Bay Tours runs snorkeling tours to Hanauma Bay, with equipment and transportation from Waikiki hotels. **Amenities:** food and drink; lifeguards; parking (fee); showers; toilets. **Best for:** snorkeling; swimming. ✉ *7455 Kalanianaole Hwy., Hawaii Kai* ☎ *808/768–6861* ⊕ *www.honolulu.gov/cms-dpr-menu/site-dpr-sitearticles/1716-hanauma-bay-home.html* 🖾 *Nonresidents $8; parking $1; mask and snorkel from $12; tram from parking lot to beach $3 round-trip* ☉ *Closed Tues.*

Sandy Beach Park

BEACH—SIGHT | Probably the most popular beach with locals on this side of Oahu, the broad, sloping beach is covered with sunbathers there to watch the "Show" and soak up rays. The Show is a shore break that's like no other in the Islands. Monster ocean swells rolling into the beach combined with the sudden rise in the ocean floor causes waves to jack up and crash magnificently on the shore. Expert surfers and body boarders young and old brave this danger to get some of the biggest barrels you can find for bodysurfing. ⚠ **But keep in mind that the beach is nicknamed Break-Neck Beach for a reason: many neck and back injuries are sustained here each year.** Use extreme caution when swimming here, or just kick back and watch the drama unfold from the comfort of your beach chair. **Amenities:** lifeguards; parking (no fee); showers; toilets. **Best for:** body boarding; walking. ⊠ *7850 Kalanianaole Hwy., Hawaii Kai* ⊹ *Makai (toward ocean) of Kalanianaole Hwy., 2 miles east of Hanauma Bay.*

 Restaurants

Roy's Hawaii Kai

$$$ | **MODERN HAWAIIAN** | Roy Yamaguchi is one of the 12 founding chefs of Hawaiian regional cuisine, a culinary movement that put Hawaii on the food map back in 1991. Opened in 1988, his flagship restaurant across the highway from Maunalua Bay is still packed every night with food-savvy visitors mixing with well-heeled residents. **Known for:** spectacular sunset views and a tiki torch–lit lanai and bar area; small and large portions available for many dishes; signature menu items like blackened ahi with a cultlike following. Ⓢ *Average main: $34* ⊠ *Hawaii Kai Corporate Plaza, 6600 Kalanianaole Hwy., Hawaii Kai* ☎ *808/396–7697* ⊕ *www.royshawaii.com* ☽ *No lunch.*

☕ Coffee and Quick Bites

Kokonuts Shave Ice & Snacks

$ | **CAFÉ** | **FAMILY** | Why not stop for shave ice like President Barack Obama did while visiting the island after the 2008 election? This spot in Koko Marina Center serves fluffy shave ice, açai bowls, ice cream, and more. **Known for:** shave ice with syrup flavors such as strawberry,

coconut, and lilikoi (passionfruit); an Obama connection; açai bowls. Ⓢ *Average main: $4* ⊠ *7192 Kalanianaole Hwy., Hawaii Kai* ☎ *808/396–8809* ▭ *No credit cards.*

Uncle Clay's House of Pure Aloha

$ | **HAWAIIAN** | **FAMILY** | Located in a strip mall in the residential neighborhood of Aina Haina, Uncle Clay's is a happy place. This shave-ice stand specializes in house-made all-natural syrups made from cane sugar and locally sourced fruits, including "kalespin"—a combination of kale and spinach. **Known for:** shave ice that's gone trendy; fun, and kids love it; uninspiring location. Ⓢ *Average main: $4* ⊠ *Aina Haina Shopping Center, 820 W. Hind Dr., right off Kalanianaole Hwy., Hawaii Kai* ☎ *808/373–5111* ⊕ *www.houseofpurealoha.com.*

🍸 Nightlife

BARS

Kona Brewing Co.

BARS/PUBS | This massive restaurant and bar on the docks of Koko Marina has long been a hot spot in east Honolulu. In addition to serving the company's signature brews, this authentic pub offers live music Thursday to Sunday nights. It's a lively spot, especially on the weekends when it's standing-room only at the bar. ⊠ *Koko Marina Center, 7192 Kalanianaole Hwy., Honolulu* ☎ *808/396–5662* ⊕ *www.konabrewingco.com.*

Waimanalo

14 miles northeast of Honolulu, 11 miles north of Hawaii Kai.

This modest little seaside town flanked by chiseled cliffs is worth a visit. Home to more Native Hawaiian families than Kailua to the north or Hawaii Kai to the south, Waimanalo's biggest draws are its beautiful beaches, offering glorious views to the windward side. Bellows Beach is great for swimming, bodysurfing, and camping, and Waimanalo Beach Park is also safe for swimming. Down the side roads, as you head *mauka* (toward the mountains), are little farms that grow a variety of fruits and flowers. Toward the back of the valley are small ranches with grazing horses. ■TIP→ **If you see any trucks selling corn, and you're staying at a place where you can cook it, be sure to get some in Waimanalo. It may be the sweetest you'll ever eat, and prices are the lowest on Oahu.**

GETTING HERE AND AROUND
The drive from Honolulu takes approximately 30 minutes from Waikiki.

◉ Sights

Makapuu Point
VIEWPOINT | This spot has breathtaking views of the ocean, mountains, and the windward Islands. The point of land jutting out in the distance is Mokapu Peninsula, site of a U.S. Marine base. The spired mountain peak is Mt. Olomana. On the long pier is part of the Makai Undersea Test Range, a research facility that's closed to the public. Offshore is Manana Island (Rabbit Island), a picturesque cay said to resemble a swimming bunny with its ears pulled back. Ironically enough, Manana Island was once overrun with rabbits, thanks to a rancher who let a few hares run wild on the land. They were eradicated in 1994 by biologists who grew concerned that the rabbits were destroying the island's native plants.

Nestled in the cliff face is the **Makapuu Lighthouse,** which became operational in 1909 and has the largest lighthouse lens in America. The lighthouse is closed to the public, but near the Makapuu Point turnout you can find the start of a paved mile-long road (it's closed to vehicular traffic). Hike up to the top of the 647-foot bluff for a closer view of the

lighthouse and, in winter, to do some whale-watching. For the more adventurous, at the whale-watching sign on the main path, head down a switchback trail to the Makapuu tide pools below. ⊠ *Ka Iwi State Scenic Shoreline, Kalanianaole Hwy., Kaneohe* ✛ *At Makapuu Beach* ⊕ *dlnr.hawaii.gov/dsp/hiking/oahu/ makapuu-point-lighthouse-trail.*

Sea Life Park
ZOO | FAMILY | Dolphins leap and spin and penguins frolic at this marine-life attraction 15 miles from Waikiki at scenic Makapuu Point. The park has a 300,000-gallon Hawaiian reef aquarium, a breeding sanctuary for Hawaii's endangered *honu* sea turtles, penguin and Hawaiian monk seal habitats, an aviary, a seabird sanctuary, and many more marine attractions. Sign up for a dolphin, sea lion, or shark encounter to get up close and personal in the water with these sea creatures. ⊠ *41-202 Kalanianaole Hwy., Waimanalo* ☎ *808/259–2500* ⊕ *www.sealifeparkhawaii.com* 🎟 *$40 (parking $5).*

⊕ Beaches

★ Bellows Field Beach Park
BEACH—SIGHT | Bellows is the same beach as Waimanalo, but it's under the auspices of the military, making it more friendly for visitors—though that also limits public access to weekends. The park area is excellent for camping, and ironwood trees provide plenty of shade. ■TIP→ **The beach is best before 2 pm. After 2, trade winds bring clouds that get hung up on steep mountains nearby, causing overcast skies.** There are no food concessions, but McDonald's and other takeout options are right outside the entrance gate. **Amenities:** lifeguards; parking (no fee); showers; toilets. **Best for:** solitude; swimming; walking. ⊠ *520 Tinker Rd., Waimanalo* ✛ *Enter on Kalanianaole Hwy. near Waimanalo town center.*

Makapuu Beach Park

BEACH—SIGHT | A magnificent beach protected by Makapuu Point welcomes you to the windward side. Hang gliders circle above, and the water is filled with body boarders. Just off the coast you can see Bird Island, a sanctuary for aquatic fowl, jutting out of the blue. The currents can be heavy, so check with a lifeguard if you're unsure of safety. Before you leave, take the prettiest (and coldest) outdoor shower available on the island. Being surrounded by tropical flowers and foliage while you rinse off that sand will be a memory you will cherish from this side of the rock. **Amenities:** lifeguards; parking (no fee); showers; toilets. **Best for:** sunrise; walking. ⊠ *41-095 Kalanianaole Hwy., Waimanalo* ✛ *Across from Sea Life Park, 2 miles south of Waimanalo.*

Waimanalo Beach Park

BEACH—SIGHT | FAMILY | One of the most beautiful beaches on the island, Waimanalo is a local pick, busy with picnicking families and active sports fields. Expect a wide stretch of sand; turquoise, emerald, and deep blue seas; and gentle shore-breaking waves that are fun for all ages. Theft is an occasional problem, so lock your car. **Amenities:** lifeguards; parking (no fee); showers; toilets. **Best for:** sunrise; swimming; walking. ⊠ *41-849 Kalanianaole Hwy., Waimanalo* ✛ *South of Waimanalo town center.*

Kailua

13 miles northeast of Honolulu, 6 miles north of Waimanalo.

Upscale Kailua is the most easily accessed town on the windward side. With two of Oahu's best beaches, Kailua town also offers great shopping and dining opportunities in its central core. You could easily spend a day visiting the stunning beaches, kayaking, exploring a hidden *heiau* (shrine), picnicking, or dining out with locals.

GETTING HERE AND AROUND

The easiest way to reach Kailua from Waikiki is to take the H1 interstate to Highway 61 (best know as the Pali Highway). On your way, stop for a breathtaking view at the Pali Lookout. Emerging from the tunnels, you'll immediately see what all of the fuss is about—a turquoise bay lies to your left while you hug the emerald green serrated Pali Mountains.

◉ Sights

Ulupo Heiau State Historic Site

ARCHAEOLOGICAL SITE | Although they may look like piles of rocks to the uninitiated, *heiau* are sacred stone platforms for the worship of the gods and date from ancient times. *Ulupo* means "night inspiration," referring to the legendary Menehune, a mythical race of diminutive people who are said to have built the heiau under the cloak of darkness. Find this spot, with signs near the heiau also explaining Kailua's early history, tucked next to the Windward YMCA. ⊠ *Kalanianaole Hwy. and Kailua Rd., Kailua* ✛ *Behind Windward YMCA* ⊕ *dlnr.hawaii.gov/dsp/parks/oahu/ulupo-heiau-state-historic-site.*

⊕ Beaches

★ Kailua Beach Park

BEACH—SIGHT | FAMILY | A cobalt-blue sea and a wide continuous arc of powdery sand make Kailua Beach Park one of the island's best beaches, illustrated by the crowds of local families who spend their weekend days here. This is like a big Lanikai Beach, but a little windier and a little wider, and a better spot for spending a full day. Kailua Beach has calm water, a line of palms and ironwoods that provide shade on the sand, and a huge park with picnic pavilions where you can escape the heat. This is the "it" spot if you're looking to try your hand at windsurfing or kiteboarding. You can rent kayaks nearby at Kailua Beach Adventures (130 Kailua

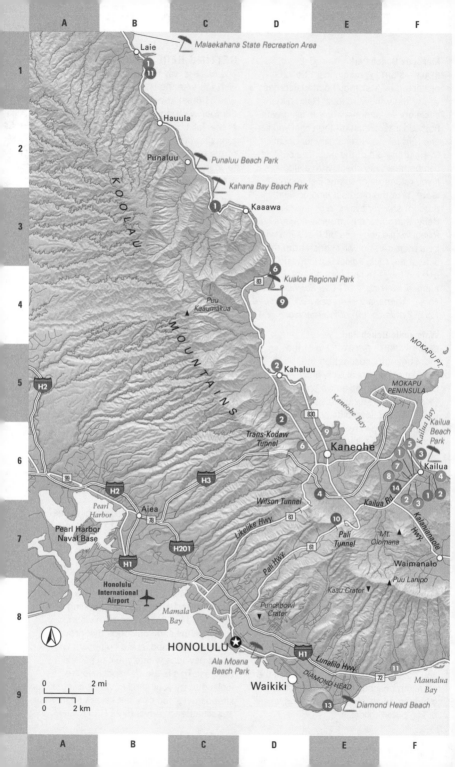

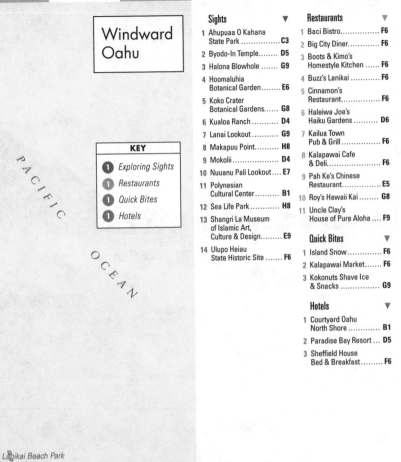

Windward Oahu

KEY

- ① Exploring Sights
- ① Restaurants
- ① Quick Bites
- ① Hotels

Sights ▼

1. Ahupuaa O Kahana State Park **C3**
2. Byodo-In Temple **D5**
3. Halona Blowhole **G9**
4. Hoomaluhia Botanical Garden **E6**
5. Koko Crater Botanical Gardens **G8**
6. Kualoa Ranch **D4**
7. Lanai Lookout **G9**
8. Makapuu Point **H8**
9. Mokolii **D4**
10. Nuuanu Pali Lookout **E7**
11. Polynesian Cultural Center **B1**
12. Sea Life Park **H8**
13. Shangri La Museum of Islamic Art, Culture & Design **E9**
14. Ulupo Heiau State Historic Site **F6**

Restaurants ▼

1. Baci Bistro **F6**
2. Big City Diner **F6**
3. Boots & Kimo's Homestyle Kitchen **F6**
4. Buzz's Lanikai **F6**
5. Cinnamon's Restaurant **F6**
6. Haleiwa Joe's Haiku Gardens **D6**
7. Kailua Town Pub & Grill **F6**
8. Kalapawai Cafe & Deli **F6**
9. Pah Ke's Chinese Restaurant **E5**
10. Roy's Hawaii Kai **G8**
11. Uncle Clay's House of Pure Aloha **F9**

Quick Bites ▼

1. Island Snow **F6**
2. Kalapawai Market **F6**
3. Kokonuts Shave Ice & Snacks **G9**

Hotels ▼

1. Courtyard Oahu North Shore **B1**
2. Paradise Bay Resort ... **D5**
3. Sheffield House Bed & Breakfast **F6**

PACIFIC OCEAN

Lanikai Beach Park

Bellows Field Beach Park

Waimanalo Beach Park

72

MANANA ISLAND (RABBIT ISLAND)

Makapuu Beach Park

⑫ ⑤ ⑧

⑩ Hawaii Kai ▼ Koko Crater ③

Sandy Beach Park

③ ⑦

Halona Cove

Hanauma Bay Nature Preserve

Hanauma Bay

KOKO HEAD

Did You Know?

Windward Oahu's Makapuu Beach is protected by Makapuu Point, but currents are still strong, so take caution when in the water.

Windward Oahu Villages

Tiny villages—generally consisting of a sign, store, a beach park, possibly a post office, and not much more—are strung along Kamehameha Highway on the windward side. Each has something to offer. In **Waiahole,** look for fruit stands and an ancient grocery store. In **Kaaawa,** there's a convenience store–gas station. In **Punaluu,** get a plate lunch at Keneke's, or visit venerable Ching General Store. Kim Taylor Reece's photo studio, featuring haunting portraits of hula dancers, is between Punaluu and Hauula. **Hauula** has the gallery of fanciful landscape artist Lance Fairly; the Shrimp Shack; Hauula Gift Shop & Art Gallery, formerly yet another Ching Store, now a clothing shop where sarongs wave like banners; and, at Hauula Kai Shopping Center, Tamura's Market, with excellent seafood and the last liquor before Mormon-dominated Laie.

Road) and take them to the Mokulua Islands for the day. **Amenities:** lifeguards; parking (no fee); showers; toilets; water sports. **Best for:** swimming; walking; windsurfing. ✉ *437 Kawailoa Rd., Kailua* ✥ *Near Kailua town, turn right on Kailua Rd. After Kalapawai Market, cross bridge, then turn left into beach parking lot.*

Lanikai Beach Park

BEACH—SIGHT | Think of the beaches you see in commercials: peaceful jade-green waters, powder-soft white sand, families and dogs frolicking mindlessly, and offshore islands in the distance. It's an ideal spot for camping out with a book. Though the beach hides behind multimillion-dollar houses, by state law there is public access every 400 yards. Street parking is available but difficult to find (and prohibited on holiday weekends). **TIP→ Look for walled or fenced pathways every 400 yards, leading to the beach. Be sure not to park in the marked bike/jogging lane.** There are no shower or bathroom facilities here—but you'll find both a two-minute drive away at Kailua Beach Park. **Amenities:** none. **Best for:** sunrise; swimming; walking. ✉ *974 Mokulua Dr., Kailua* ✥ *Past Kailua Beach Park.*

🍴 Restaurants

Baci Bistro

$$ | **ITALIAN** | A long time local favorite, Baci Bistro is a classic Italian restaurant offering an extensive range of pastas, antipasti, mains, and really excellent desserts. Elegant and inviting, Baci is the perfect spot for a romantic dinner. **Known for:** a wide variety of antipasti; homemade pasta; romantic ambience. [$] *Average main: $23* ✉ *30 Aulike St., Kailua* ☎ *808/262–7555* 🌐 *www.bacibistro.com.*

Big City Diner

$ | **AMERICAN** | **FAMILY** | This outlet of the popular retro diner chain has outdoor lanai seating and a bar and is across the street from a small bird sanctuary. It's a hot spot for breakfast and Sunday football; popular dinner items include grilled steak with onions and mushrooms, baby back ribs, meat loaf, and salads. **Known for:** happy families returning again and again; nice indoor and outdoor bar; big portions. [$] *Average main: $16* ✉ *108 Hekili St., Kailua* ☎ *808/263–8880* 🌐 *bigcitydinerhawaii.com.*

Boots & Kimo's Homestyle Kitchen

$ | **AMERICAN** | Sometimes you wait an hour for a table here since the restaurant's fervent followers come back again and again for the banana pancakes topped with thick macadamia-nut sauce. And it's no wonder: brothers Ricky and Jesse Kiakona treat their guests like family. **Known for:** macadamia nut pancakes; long lines of patient regulars; new location offering a nicer waiting area (but still the long waits). $ *Average main: $13* ✉ *151 Hekili St., Suite 102, Kailua* ☎ *808/263–7929* ⊕ *www.bootsnkimos. com* ⊗ *No dinner.*

Buzz's Lanikai

$$$ | **STEAKHOUSE** | Virtually unchanged since owners Bobby Lou and Buzz opened it in 1967, this neighborhood institution opposite Kailua Beach Park is filled with the aroma of grilling steaks and plumeria blooms. Sadly, Buzz has passed on, but you can now enjoy a predinner drink on Stan's Deck, a salute to Bobby Lou's second husband. **Known for:** local institution; the views from the lanai at lunch; excellent fruity beach cocktails. $ *Average main: $35* ✉ *413 Kawailoa Rd., Kailua* ☎ *808/261–4661* ⊕ *www. buzzsoriginalsteakhouse.com.*

Cinnamon's Restaurant

$ | **AMERICAN** | Known for uncommon variations on common breakfast themes (pancakes, eggs Benedict, French toast, home fries, and eggs), this neighborhood favorite is tucked into a hard-to-find Kailua office park (call for directions). Local-style lunch plates are good, but the main attraction is breakfast. **Known for:** endless variations on pancakes, eggs Benedict, and waffles; cinnamon rolls (of course); long waits. $ *Average main: $14* ✉ *315 Uluniu St., Kailua* ☎ *808/261–8724* ⊕ *www.cinnamons808.com.*

Kailua Town Pub & Grill

$ | **AMERICAN** | Looking for pub grub? This is the spot in Kailua for enormous gourmet hamburgers, fish 'n' chips, and, of course, an ever-changing selection of craft beers on tap. **Known for:** happy hour; craft beer; friendly atmosphere. $ *Average main: $14* ✉ *26 Hoolai St., Suite 1100, Kailua* ☎ *808/230–8444* ⊕ *www. kailuatownpub.com.*

Kalapawai Cafe & Deli

$$ | **ECLECTIC** | This one-stop, green-and-white, Mediterranean-leaning café, wine bar, bakery, and gourmet deli is the creation of the Dymond family, two generations of restaurateurs who have shaken up the windward food scene. Come in on your way to the beach for a cup of coffee and bagel, and stop back for a gourmet pizza or bruschetta (how does eggplant confit, sweet peppers, honey, and goat cheese sound?) for lunch or a candlelight dinner at night. **Known for:** signature dishes by night; good coffee and sandwiches by day; impressive wine list for such a small spot. $ *Average main: $19* ✉ *750 Kailua Rd., Kailua* ☎ *808/262–3354* ⊕ *www.kalapawaimarket.com.*

☕ Coffee and Quick Bites

Island Snow

$ | **HAWAIIAN** | This hole in the wall has been creating shave ice perfection in its tiny original spot since 1979, but when two young girls named Obama discovered the luscious flavors in 2008, it was really put on the map. A favorite spot for both locals and storied visitors (and these days lots of regular tourists), they make a mean shave ice, whether you stick with standard flavors like cherry or go for lilikoi guava with a snowcap on top. **Known for:** the best shave ice on the windward side; the Obama girls, who grew up on this stuff (look for their photos on the wall); long lines of local kiteboarders and surfers. $ *Average main: $5* ✉ *130 Kailua Rd., Kailua* ☎ *808/263–6339* ⊕ *islandsnow.com.*

Kalapawai Market

$ | DELI | Generations of children have purchased their beach snacks and sodas at Kalapawai Market, near Kailua Beach. A Windward Oahu landmark since 1932, the green-and-white market has distinctive charm. **Known for:** take-out deli sandwiches; good coffee; a great selection of wine. $ *Average main: $7* ✉ *306 S. Kalaheo Ave., Kailua* ☎ *808/262–4359* ⊕ *www.kalapawaimarket.com.*

Hotels

Sheffield House Bed & Breakfast

$$ | B&B/INN | Literally 10 houses from Kailua Beach, this cozy bed-and-breakfast has been around since the 1990s. **Pros:** Windward Oahu offers a uniquely local experience; best beaches on the island; boutiques and dining abound in Kailua. **Cons:** B&Bs aren't for everybody; don't expect luxury; rental car a must. $ *Rooms from: $180* ✉ *131 Kuulei Rd., Kailua* ☎ *808/262–0721* ⊕ *www.hawaiisheffieldhouse.com* ⌂ *2 rooms* ❚❍❙ *Free Breakfast.*

Nightlife

BARS

Boardrider's Bar & Grill

BARS/PUBS | Tucked away in Kailua Town, Boardrider's has long been the place for local bands to strut their stuff. Look for live music—reggae to rock and roll—every Friday and Saturday night. The space includes a pool table, dartboards, and eight TVs for watching the game. ✉ *201-A Hamakua Dr., Kailua* ☎ *808/261–4600.*

🛍 Shopping

Shopping on the windward side is one of Oahu's best-kept secrets. The trip here takes a half hour by car or about an hour on TheBus. The real treats lie in the small boutiques and galleries in the heart of Kailua—the perfect place to find unique gifts. After shopping, enjoy the outdoors in one of the most beautiful beach towns in the world. Kailua is also the best place to rent kayaks and paddle out to the Mokulua Islands with a guide, take a windsurfing lesson, or watch the expert kiteboarders sailing across the bay.

■ **TIP→ Stop by Kalapawai Market at Kailua Beach near the entrance to Lanikai—for sandwiches and cold drinks and souvenirs, and finish the day relaxing on a sparsely populated white-sand beach.** The surf here is minimal, making it a perfect picnic spot with the kids. It is not, however, the place to learn to ride waves. Save that for Waikiki.

BOOKS
★ Bookends

BOOKS/STATIONERY | Shop for gifts, or just take a break with the family at this independent bookstore, which feels more like a small-town library, welcoming browsers to linger for hours. It sells new and secondhand books, and its large children's section is filled both books and toys. ✉ *600 Kailua Rd., Kailua* ☎ *808/261–1996.*

CLOTHING
★ Global Village

CLOTHING | Tucked into a tiny strip mall near Maui Tacos, this boutique features clothing, accessories, gifts, and handcrafted jewelry from the islands and around the globe. ✉ *Kailua Village Shops, 539 Kailua Rd., No. 104, Kailua* ☎ *808/262–8183* ⊕ *www.globalvillagehawaii.com.*

HEALTH AND BEAUTY PRODUCTS

Lanikai Bath and Body

PERFUME/COSMETICS | Take home the fragrances of the Islands with this shop's organic body lotions, hand creams, soaps, sprays, bath salts, and scrubs. Botanical extracts such as papaya, mango, sea kelp, and calendula are combined with essential oils including macadamia and kukui nuts to produce fine bath and body products. Try Naupaka, a blend of coconut, lime, and verbena that suits both men and women. ⊠ *Kailua Shopping Center, 600 Kailua Rd., Kailua* ☎ *808/262–3260* ⊕ *www.lanikaibathand-body.com.*

HOME DECOR

★ Under a Hula Moon

HOUSEHOLD ITEMS/FURNITURE | Exclusive tabletop items and Pacific home decor, such as shell wreaths, shell night-lights, Hawaiian beach sheets, frames, and unique one-of-a-kind gifts with an Islands influence, define this eclectic shop. ⊠ *Kailua Shopping Center, 600 Kailua Rd., Kailua* ☎ *808/261–4252.*

Kaneohe

11 miles northeast of Oahu, 6 miles west of Kailua.

The largest community on Oahu's windward side, Kaneohe (meaning "bamboo man" in Hawaiian) is a sprawling community with malls, car dealerships, and a few worthwhile restaurants. At the base of the Koolau Mountains, Kaneohe sees a lot more rain than neighboring Kailua and is the greener for it. Kaneohe doesn't see a lot of tourists, but there are two worthwhile sights, which take advantage of their proximity to the mountains—the Byodo-In Temple and Hoomaluhi Botanical Garden.

GETTING HERE AND AROUND

Kaneohe is a 30-minute drive or one-hour bus ride from Waikiki. If driving, you can take any of the three highways across the Koolau Mountains: the H3, the Pali, or the Like Like.

◉ Sights

★ Byodo-In Temple

RELIGIOUS SITE | Tucked away in the back of the Valley of the Temples cemetery is a replica of the 11th-century Temple at Uji in Japan. A 2-ton, carved-wood statue of the Buddha presides inside the main building. Next to the temple are a meditation pavilion and gardens set dramatically against the sheer, green cliffs of the Koolau Mountains. You can ring the 5-foot, 3-ton brass bell for good luck and feed some of the hundreds of koi, ducks, and swans that inhabit the garden's 2-acre pond. Or, you can enjoy the peaceful surroundings and just relax. Call ahead to schedule a guided tour. ⊠ *47-200 Kahekili Hwy., Kaneohe* ☎ *808/239–9844* ⊕ *www.byodo-in.com* ☒ *$4 (cash only).*

Hoomaluhia Botanical Garden

GARDEN | The name, which means "a peaceful refuge," describes the serenity and feeling of endless space you find in this verdant garden framed by the stunning Koolau Mountain range. Open daily 9–4, its 400 acres contain plant collections from such tropical areas as the Americas, Africa, Melanesia, the Philippines, and Hawaii. Not just for the botanist, Hoomaluhia also has a 32-acre lake and open lawns ideal for picnicking and camping by permit. Families can also take advantage of the park's catch-and-release tilapia fishing program; staff provides free bamboo poles at the visitor center. ⊠ *45-680 Luluku Rd., Kaneohe* ☎ *808/233–7323* ⊕ *www.honolulu.gov/parks/hbg.html* ☒ *Free.*

Kualoa Point is in Kualoa Regional Park in Kaaawa, a beautiful but windy area overlooking Kaneohe Bay and the towering Koolau Mountains.

★ Nuuanu Pali Lookout

VIEWPOINT | This panoramic perch looks out to expansive views of Windward Oahu. It was in this region that King Kamehameha I drove defending forces over the edges of the 1,200-foot-high cliffs, thus winning the decisive battle for control of Oahu. From here, views stretch from Kaneohe Bay to a small island off the coast called Mokolii ("little lizard," also known as Chinaman's Hat). Temperatures at the summit are several degrees cooler than in warm Waikiki, so bring a jacket along. Hang on tight to any loose possessions, and consider wearing pants; it gets extremely windy at the lookout, which is part of the fun. And be sure to lock your car in the pay-to-park lot; break-ins have occurred here (this wayside is in the most trafficked state park in Hawaii). ⌂ *Pali Hwy., Kaneohe* ⌖ *at very top of Pali Hwy.* ⊕ *hawaiistateparks.org/parks/oahu/nu%-CA%BBuanu-pali-state-wayside/* ⛬ *Free* ☞ *Parking $3 per car.*

🏖 Beaches

Kahana Bay Beach Park

BEACH—SIGHT | **FAMILY** | Local parents often bring their children here to wade in safety in the very shallow, protected waters. This pretty beach cove, surrounded by mountains, has a long arc of sand that is great for walking and a cool, shady grove of tall ironwood and pandanus trees that is ideal for a picnic. An ancient Hawaiian fishpond, which was in use until the 1920s, is visible nearby. The water here is not generally a clear blue due to the runoff from heavy rains in the valley. **Amenities:** parking (no fee); showers; toilets. **Best for:** swimming; walking. ⌂ *52-201 Kamehameha Hwy., Kaneohe* ⌖ *North of Kualoa Park.*

🍴 Restaurants

Haleiwa Joe's Haiku Gardens

$$$ | **AMERICAN** | The Haleiwa location may be the namesake and claim the surf, but this windward-side spot offers all the same friendly vibe and grilled seafood with knock-'em-dead views and a tiki torch–lit atmosphere after dark. The chef promotes a daily special preparation for the day's catch delivered straight from the Honolulu Fish Auction, along with the signature turf favorites. **Known for:** stunning views of Haiku Gardens; reliable for both seafood and meat; excellent daily specials. [$] *Average main: $28* ✉ *44-336 Haiku Rd., Kaneohe* ☎ *808/274–6671* 🌐 *www.haleiwajoes.com.*

Pah Ke's Chinese Restaurant

$ | CHINESE | If you happen to be on the windward side at dinner time, this out-of-the-ordinary Chinese restaurant—named for the local pidgin term for Chinese (literally translated, this is "Chinese's Chinese Restaurant")—is a good option. Ebullient owner and chef Raymond Siu, a former hotel pastry chef, focuses on healthier cooking techniques and local ingredients. **Known for:** dependable spot for the family; house specials that are usually better than standard menu fare; a big dining room with bright lights and not much atmosphere. [$] *Average main: $12* ✉ *46-018 Kamehameha Hwy., Kaneohe* ☎ *808/235–4505* 🌐 *www.pahke.com.*

Hotels

Paradise Bay Resort

$$$ | RESORT | Located right on picturesque Kaneohe Bay amidst the junglelike fauna of the windward side, this resort offers apartment-style units ranging from cozy studios to spacious two-bedroom suites with breathtaking views of the majestic Koolau Mountains; there's also one stand-alone cottage in a remote area not generally frequented by tourists. **Pros:** local, authentic experience; beautiful views over the bay; pet-friendly (but $25 per night charge). **Cons:** remote location not near most other attractions; neighborhood is a bit run-down; rental car a necessity (but parking included in $35 nightly resort fee). [$] *Rooms from: $300* ✉ *47-039 Lihikai Dr., Kaneohe* ☎ *800/735–5071, 808/239–5711* 🌐 *www.paradisebayresort.com* 🛏 *46 rooms* 🍴 *Free Breakfast.*

Shopping

HOME DECOR

Jeff Chang Pottery & Fine Crafts

HOUSEHOLD ITEMS/FURNITURE | This family-owned and-operated gallery offers the artist's functional and decorative pottery as well as the works of approximately 200 other American artisans. Jeff has worked with clay for more than 40 years and his wife, Karon, operates the gallery and selects other works including jewelry, glass pieces, metal sculpture, wall art, wooden items, musical instruments, chimes, suncatchers, sand globes and pictures, holiday decor, and ornaments. ✉ *Windward Mall, 46-056 Kamehameha Hwy., 2nd fl., Theatre Wing, Kaneohe* ☎ *808/235–5150* 🌐 *www.windwardmall.com/stores/jeff-chang-pottery.*

Kaaawa

14 miles north of Kaneohe, 23 miles northeast of Honolulu.

Less a village than a collection of homes and bookended by its elementary school and fire station, Kaaawa consists of little more than a post office, bus stop, gas station, and, of course, a beach park.

GETTING HERE AND AROUND

With its location on Kamehameha Highway, you'll pass through Kaaawa immediately before or after you pass Kualoa Ranch.

Sights

Ahupuaa O Kahana State Park

NATIONAL/STATE PARK | FAMILY | This park offers the true Hawaiian experience: a beautiful windward bay sits a short

The 4,000-acre Kualoa Ranch may look familiar to you; a popular film site, it's been featured in several *Jurassic Park* movies, as well as other films and TV shows (you can take a film sites tour of the ranch).

walk away from the Huilua Fishpond, a national historic landmark (note that it's undergoing restoration to reinforce the rock walls). There are rain-forest hikes chock-full of local fruit trees, a hunting area for pigs, and a coconut grove for picnicking. The water is suitable for swimming and bodysurfing, though it's a little cloudy for snorkeling. ⊠ *52-222 Kamehameha Hwy., near Kahana Bay, Kaaawa* ⊕ *dlnr.hawaii.gov/dsp/parks/ oahu/ahupuaa-o-kahana-state-park.*

★ Kualoa Ranch

FARM/RANCH | FAMILY | Encompassing 4,000 acres, about 45 minutes by car from Waikiki, this working ranch offers a wide range of activities—from ATV and horseback tours to ziplining or expeditions into the valley on an electric bike. The mountainsthat serve as the backdrop here may seem familiar: the ranch has served as the set for movies such as *Jurassic Park* and *Wind Talkers,* as well as TV shows like *Magnum, P.I.* and *Lost* (and you can take a movie sites tour). From the grounds, you'll have a wonderful view of the ocean and Chinaman's Hat. You can drop by the visitor center anytime, but it's best to book activities and tours two or three days in advance. ⊠ *49-560 Kamehameha Hwy., Kaaawa* ☎ *808/237– 7321* ⊕ *www.kualoa.com* ✉ *From $48.*

Mokolii

NATURE SITE | As you drive the windward and northern shores along Kamehameha Highway, you'll note a number of interesting geological features. At Kualoa, look to the ocean and gaze at the uniquely shaped little island of Mokolii ("little lizard"), a 206-foot-high sea stack also known as Chinaman's Hat. According to Hawaiian legend, the goddess Hiiaka, sister of Pele, slew the dragon Mokolii and flung its tail into the sea, forming the distinct islet. Other dragon body parts—in the form of rocks, of course— were scattered along the base of nearby Kualoa Ridge. ⊠ *49-479 Kamehameha Hwy., Kaaawa.*

Beaches

Kualoa Regional Park

BEACH—SIGHT | Grassy expanses border a long, narrow stretch of sand with spectacular views of Kaneohe Bay and the Koolau Mountains, making Kualoa one of the island's most beautiful picnic, camping, and beach areas. Dominating the view is an islet called Mokolii, better known as Chinaman's Hat, which rises 206 feet above the water. You can swim in the shallow areas of this rarely crowded beach year-round. The one drawback is that it's usually windy here, but the wide-open spaces are ideal for kite flying. **Amenities:** lifeguards; showers; toilets. **Best for:** solitude; swimming. ⊠ *49-479 Kamehameha Hwy., Kaaawa ✛ North of Waiahole.*

Punaluu Beach Park

BEACH—SIGHT | If you're making a circle of the island, this is a great stopping point to jump out of your car and stretch your legs and get your toes wet. It's easy, because the sand literally comes up to your parked car, and nice, because there is a sandy bottom and mostly calm conditions. Plus there are full facilities, shops for picnic supplies, and lots of shade trees. Often overlooked, and often overcast, Punaluu can afford you a moment of fresh air before you get back to your sightseeing. **Amenities:** parking (no fee); showers; toilets. **Best for:** solitude; swimming. ⊠ *53-400 Kamehameha Hwy., Hauula.*

Laie

10 miles north of Kaaawa, 33 miles north of Honolulu.

Visiting Laie—over an hour by car and a world away from bustling Waikiki and Honolulu—is like taking a trip to another island. Home to a Mormon temple and the Mormon-founded Polynesian Cultural Center, Laie is a "dry town."

GETTING HERE AND AROUND

From Waikiki, it will take a little more than an hour by car or up to two hours by bus. By car you can take interstate H2 past Haleiwa, until it joins Kamehameha Highway. Along the route you'll pass Haleiwa town and world-famous North Shore surf spots. Alternatively, take any of the highways going over the Koolau Mountains (Like Like, Pali, or H3) to Kaneohe and follow Highway 83 north. This road will then meet up with the two-lane Kamehameha Highway, which leads you to all points north.

◉ Sights

★ **Polynesian Cultural Center**

ARTS VENUE | FAMILY | Re-created individual villages showcase the lifestyles and traditions of Hawaii, Tahiti, Samoa, Fiji, the Marquesas Islands, New Zealand, and Tonga. Focusing on individual islands within its 42-acre center, 35 miles from Waikiki, the Polynesian Cultural Center was founded in 1963 by the Church of Jesus Christ of Latter-day Saints. It houses restaurants, hosts luau, and demonstrates cultural traditions such as hula, fire dancing, and ancient customs and ceremonies. The Hukilau Marketplace carries Polynesian handicrafts. There are multiple packages available, from basic admission to an all-inclusive deal. Every May, the PCC hosts the World Fireknife Dance Competition, an event that draws the top fire-knife dance performers from around the world. Get tickets for that event in advance. ■TIP→ **If you're staying in Honolulu, see the center as part of a van tour so you won't have to drive home late at night after the two-hour evening show.** ⊠ *55-370 Kamehameha Hwy., Laie* ☎ *800/367–7060* ⊕ *www.polynesia.com* ⊠ *From $70* ☉ *Closed Sun.*

Beaches

Malaekahana State Recreation Area
BEACH—SIGHT | The big attraction here is tiny Goat Island, a bird sanctuary just offshore. At low tide the water is shallow enough—never more than waist-high—so that you can wade out to it. Wear sneakers or aqua socks so you don't cut yourself on the coral. The beach itself is fairly narrow but long enough for a 20-minute stroll, one-way. The waves are never too big, and sometimes they're just right for the beginning bodysurfer. The entrance gates, which close at 7:45 pm in summer and 6:45 pm the rest of the year, are easy to miss, and you can't see the beach from the road. It's a great rural getaway: families love to camp in the groves of ironwood trees at Malaekahana State Park, and there are also cabins here. **Amenities:** parking (no fee); showers; toilets. **Best for:** swimming; walking. ✉ *56-207 Kamehameha Hwy., Laie* ✣ *Enter at gates ½ mile north of Laie on Kamehameha Hwy.* 🌐 *dlnr.hawaii.gov/dsp/parks/oahu/malaekahana-state-recreation-area.*

Hotels

Courtyard Oahu North Shore
$$$ | **HOTEL** | This property offers reliable and affordable accommodations close to the Polynesian Cultural Center and a short drive to some of the North Shore's most iconic beaches and surfing spots. **Pros:** best bet for North Shore exploring; reliable, modern, and clean; near the beach. **Cons:** a long drive to the rest of Oahu's attractions; no alcohol served in the hotel or nearby establishments; a car is needed, and parking is not free. [$] *Rooms from: $270* ✉ *55-400 Kamehameha Hwy., Laie* ☎ *808/293–4900* 🌐 *www.marriott.com/hotels/travel/hnloa-courtyard-oahu-north-shore* 🛏 *144 rooms* 🍴 *No meals.*

Chapter 7

ACTIVITIES AND TOURS

Updated by
Cheryl Crabtree

Although much is written about the water surrounding this little rock known as Oahu, there is as much to be said for the rock itself. It's a wonder of nature, thrust from the ocean floor thousands of millennia ago by a volcanic hot spot that is still spitting out islands today.

Hawaii is the most remote island chain on Earth, and there are creatures and plants that can be seen here and nowhere else. And there are dozens of ways for you to check them all out.

From the air, you can peer down into nooks and crannies in the mountains—where cars cannot reach and hikers don't dare. Whether flitting here and there amid a helicopter's rush and roar, or sailing by in the silence of a glider's reverie, you glimpse sights that few have experienced. Or, if you would rather, take a step back in time and take off from the waters of Keehi Lagoon in a World War II–era seaplane. Follow the flight path flown by the Japanese Zeros as they attempted to destroy Pearl Harbor and the American spirit.

Would you prefer the ground tour, where you and gravity are no longer at odds? Oahu is covered in hiking trails that vary from tropical rain forest to arid desert. Even when in the bustling city of Honolulu, you are but minutes from hidden waterfalls and bamboo forests. Out west, you can wander a dusty path that has long since given up its ability to accommodate cars but is perfect for hikers. You can splash in tidal pools, admire sea arches, and gape at caves opened by the rock slides that closed the road. You can camp out on many of these treks and beaches.

If somewhat less rugged and less vigorous exploration is more your style, how about letting horses do your dirty work? You can ride them on the beaches and in the valleys, checking out ancient holy sites, movie sets, and brilliant vistas.

Finally, there is the ancient sport of Scotland. Why merely hike into the rain forest when you can slice a 280-yard drive through it and then hunt for your Titleist in the bushy leaves instead? Almost 40 courses cover this tiny expanse, ranging from the target jungle golf of the Royal Hawaiian Golf Club to the pro-style links of Turtle Bay. There is no off-season in the tropics, and no one here knows your real handicap.

Aerial Tours

Taking an aerial tour of the Islands opens up a world of perspective. Look down from the sky at the outline of the USS *Arizona*, where it lies in its final resting place below the waters of Pearl Harbor, or get a glimpse of the vast carved expanse of a volcanic crater—here are views only seen by an "eye in the sky." Don't forget your camera. △ **All helicopter tour companies in Hawaii are under**

Take a helicopter tour for a unique perspective of the island.

increasing legislative and regulatory scrutiny due to multiple fatal accidents since 2018, so it's possible that they will undergo further regulations and limitations in the near future.

HONOLULU

Blue Hawaiian Helicopters

FLYING/SKYDIVING/SOARING | This company stakes its claim as Hawaii's largest helicopter company, with tours on all the major Islands and more than two-dozen choppers in its fleet. The 45-minute Oahu tour seats up to six passengers and includes narration from your friendly pilot along with sweeping views of Waikiki, the beautiful Windward Coast, and the North Shore. If you like to see the world from above or are just pinched for time and want to get a quick overview of the whole island without renting a car, this is the way to go. Discounts are available if you book online in advance. ⊠ *99 Kaulele Pl., Airport Area* ☎ *808/831–8800, 800/745–2583* ⊕ *www.bluehawaiian.com* ⌕ *From $284.*

Magnum Helicopters

FLYING/SKYDIVING/SOARING | For the adventurous, this Magnum PI doors-off helicopter tour offers sweeping views of Keehi Lagoon through urban Honolulu and the harbor, including the Aloha Tower and Waikiki Beach. Soar past and over Diamond Head Crater and up the scenic coast by Makapuu Lighthouse, Sandy Beach, and over Windward Oahu's iconic Lanikai and Kailua beaches. The breathtaking finale takes you inland to Sacred Falls, known for its stunning, 1,000-foot falls and its starring role in Jurassic Park, before returning to the airport via North Shore surf spots and a bird's-eye view of Pearl Harbor and the USS *Arizona* Memorial. ⊠ *130 Iolana Pl., Airport Area* ☎ *808/833–4354* ⊕ *www.magnumheli-copters.com* ⌕ *From $269.*

NORTH SHORE

Most aerial tour and skydiving operators on the North Shore work out of Dillingham Airfield. Controversially, the airfield is scheduled to close for most of these operators; both the activity and tour outfitters object to the closures, but the issue is likely to drag out over the coming months, so, if you have booked a glider or skydiving adventure, definitely reconfirm with your activity outfitter closer to the time of any reservation to ensure that it is operational..

The Original Glider Rides

FLYING/SKYDIVING/SOARING | "Mr. Bill" has been offering piloted glider (sailplane) rides over the northwest end of Oahu's North Shore since 1970. Choose from piloted scenic rides for one or two passengers in sleek, bubble-top, motorless aircraft with aerial views of mountains, shoreline, coral pools, windsurfing sails, and, in winter, humpback whales. Seeking more thrills? You can also take a more acrobatic ride or take control yourself in a mini lesson. Flights run 15–60 minutes long and depart continuously, daily 10–5. Reservations are requested. ⊠ *Dillingham Airfield, 69-132 Farrington Hwy., Waialua* ☎ *808/637–0207* ⊕ *www.honolulusoaring.com* ⊠ *From $85.*

Paradise Helicopters

FLYING/SKYDIVING/SOARING | Paradise offers tours on several islands, with Oahu tours departing from two helipads: Kalaeloa (at the Ko Olina resorts on the west side) and Turtle Bay Resort on the North Shore. Kalaeloa options range from a one-hour scenic tour over Diamond Head to a two-hour island circle (daytime and sunset) to specialized trips that focus on WW II history. Turtle Bay choices include several 1½-hour North Shore adventures, offering scenic vistas of beaches as well as inland waterfalls. ☎ *866/300–2294* ⊕ *paradisecopters.com* ⊠ *From $295.*

Animal Encounters

Pods of dolphins surround the Islands, and spotting them can be as easy as just getting yourself out in the ocean. They are wild animals, of course, and do not follow a schedule, but a catamaran sail off Waikiki will usually net you a sighting. Dolphins also generally make appearances shortly after sunrise on the West Shore and can be clearly observed from beaches like Makua and Makaha. And while they won't have the peppy music of Sea World in the background, their jumping and spinning is even more awe-inspiring when you realize they are just doing it as a natural part of their lives rather than for a reward.

Some tour operators offer opportunities to swim with dolphins, but keep in mind that these are federally protected marine mammals, so you should always follow the instructions given by the tour operator if you take one of these trips. The National Oceanographic and Atmospheric Administration (NOAA) provides specific guidelines for tour operators encountering dolphins through their Dolphin Safe program. The cost for dolphin encounters ranges from $130 for a chance to swim with wild dolphins on a snorkel cruise to $700 for getting in the pool with them as trainer-for-a-day. ⇨ *Both Sea Life Park in Waimanalo and Dolphin Quest at The Kahala offer opportunities to view and interact with captive dolphins. See Chapter 3, Honolulu, and Chapter 4, Windward Oahu, for more information.*

Similarly, you can also swim with sharks, though you do so in a protective cage.

LEEWARD (WEST) OAHU
Dolphin Excursions Hawaii

WILDLIFE-WATCHING | FAMILY | Oahu's leeward coast offers an abundance of spinner dolphins, whales in the winter months, and other marine wildlife that's perfect for those who want a naturalist and guide to lead them through these waters. The company's three-hour Dolphin Adventure departs from Waianae Boat Harbor and includes round-trip transportation from Waikiki and Ko Olina. ⊠ *Waianae Boat Harbor, 85-491 Farrington Hwy., Waianae* ⊹ *Check in at Spinners Café* ☎ *808/239–5579* ⊕ *www. dolphinexcursions.com* ⊠ *From $140.*

NORTH SHORE
North Shore Shark Adventures

WILDLIFE-WATCHING | "You go in the cage, cage goes in the water, you go in the water, shark's in the water." You remember this line from *Jaws*, and now you get to play the role of Richard Dreyfus, as North Shore Shark Adventures provides you with an interactive experience out of your worst nightmare. The tour allows you to swim and snorkel in a cage as dozens of sharks lurk just feet below and around you in the open ocean off the North Shore. No swimming required. They'll provide transportation from Waikiki for an additional charge. Discounts are available if you book online. ■TIP→ **If you go, go early: the sea is calmer and clearer in the morning, and the sitings are more plentiful.** ⊠ *Haleiwa Small Boat Harbor, 66-105 Haleiwa Rd., Haleiwa* ✛ *Check in at Shark Shack in harbor* ☎ *808/228–5900* ⊕ *www.sharktourshawaii.com* ✉ *From $96.*

Biking

Oahu's coastal roads are flat, well-paved, and, unfortunately, awash in vehicular traffic. Frankly, biking is no fun in either Waikiki or Honolulu, but things are a bit better outside the city. Your best bet is to cycle early in the morning or get off the road to check out the island's bike trails.

Honolulu City and County Bike Coordinator

BICYCLING | This office can answer all your biking questions concerning trails, permits, and state laws. ☎ *808/768–8335* ⊕ *www.honolulu.gov/bicycle.html.*

BEST SPOTS
HONOLULU
Maunawili Demonstration Trail

BICYCLING | Locals favor biking this 10-mile trail that has breathtaking views as you descend into Waimanalo. There are many flat portions but also some uneven ground to negotiate unless you're willing to carry your bike for small stretches. The main trailhead is at the Pali Lookout on the blacktop of Old Pali Road. Be aware that the trail is also popular with hikers and dog walkers. ⊠ *Nuuanu Pali Dr., at Pali Lookout, Honolulu.*

NORTH SHORE
Kaena Point Trail

BICYCLING | If going up a mountain is not your idea of mountain biking, then perhaps Kaena Point Trail is better suited to your needs. A longer ride (10 miles) but much flatter, this trail takes you oceanside around the westernmost point on the island. You pass sea arches and a mini-blowhole, then finish up with some motocross jumps right before you turn around. There's no drinking water available on this ride, so remember to bring your own, and then cool off at the Yokohama Beach showers. ⊠ *69-385 Farrington Hwy., Waialua.*

North Shore Bike Park

BICYCLING | Wind around 12 miles of trails plus seven professionally designed, single-track loops at the North Shore's Turtle Bay Resort. Trails lead to protected wildlife areas and ancient Hawaiian sites, a WWII pillbox, a giant banyan tree, and secluded beaches and bays. Purchase day passes at the Hele Huli Adventure Center and rent bikes right on site. ⊠ *57-091 Kuilima Dr., Kahuku* ☎ *808/293–6024* ⊕ *www.turtlebayresort.com* ✉ *Rates vary depending on season, trails, and bikes rented.*

West Kaunala Trail

BICYCLING | Biking the North Shore may sound like a great idea, but the two-lane road is narrow and traffic-heavy. Consider trying the West Kaunala Trail. It's a little tricky at times, but with the rain-forest surroundings and beautiful ocean vistas, you'll hardly notice your legs burning on the steep ascent at the end. It's about 5½ miles round-trip. Bring water because there's none on the trail unless it comes from the sky. (Also remember it gets really muddy and slippery after heavy rains.) ⊠ *59-777 Pupukea Rd., at the end of Pupukea Rd., Haleiwa ⬦ Pupukea Rd. is next to Foodland, the only grocery store on North Shore.*

EQUIPMENT AND TOURS
HONOLULU
Bike Hawaii

BICYCLING | Whether it's road tours of the North Shore or muddy off-road adventures in the Koolau Mountains, this is the company to get you there. There are combination packages that pair cycling with snorkeling, sailing, or hiking. Their rain forest to reef tour (for either a half- or full day) is often mentioned as one of the best outings on the island, taking you 2,000 feet up into the Koolau Mountains so you can coast downhill through lush rain forests before getting on a catamaran to swim and snorkel with turtles. The company offers both three-hour road tours and a six-hour mountain-biking foray. Tours include equipment, transportation, and water; some also include lunch. The company will pick you up at central locations in Waikiki. ☎ 808/734–4214 ⊕ *www.bikehawaii.com* ⊠ *From $62.*

Biki

BICYCLING | In late 2017, nonprofit Bikeshare Hawaii launched a Honolulu bike-sharing system equipped with 1,300 bikes docked at solar-powered kiosks throughout urban Honolulu. The comfortable, easy-to-maneuver bikes are designed to accommodate riders of all sizes and even include a basket to carry your farmers market goodies. The procedure is easy: pay at the kiosk, hop on the bike, and dock it at the kiosk closest to your destination. You can do a one-time rental for 30 or 60 minutes or prepurchase a pool of minutes to use during the course of your trip. Helmets are not required by law, but you can purchase or rent one. ⊠ *Honolulu* ☎ 888/340–2454 ⊕ *gobiki.org* ⊠ *From $4.*

Hawaii Bicycling League

BICYCLING | Don't want to go cycling by yourself? Visit this shop online, and you can get connected with rides and contests, including the annual circle island ride. ☎ 808/735–5756 ⊕ *www.hbl.org.*

NORTH SHORE
North Shore Explorers

BICYCLING | Rent cruisers, fat-tire bikes, mountain bikes, or mopeds at this outfitter's three North Shore and Laie locations: Hele Huli Adventure Center at Turtle Bay Resort, Polynesian Cultural Center, and the Courtyard Marriott hotel. The company also runs an array of guided adventure tours, plus disc and foot golf, tennis, and mountain bike lessons. If you want to do it, they probably offer it. ⊠ *Kahuku* ☎ 808/293–6024 ⊕ *northshore-explorers.com* ⊠ *Bike rentals from $50.*

Birding

Victor Emanuel Nature Tours, the largest company in the world specializing in birding tours, has two 10-day Fall Hawaii and Spring Hawaii trips to Oahu, Kauai, and the Big Island that cost $4,895 (fall), including double-occupancy accommodations, meals, interisland air, ground transportation, and guided excursions.

Victor Emanuel Nature Tours

SPECIAL-INTEREST | This mainland-based tour company offers periodic bird-watching tours in Hawaii, usually in February and October. ☎ 800/328–8368 ⊕ *www.ventbird.com.*

Boat Tours and Charters

Being on the water can be the best way to enjoy the Islands. Whether you want to see the fish in action or experience how they taste, there is a tour for you.

For a sailing experience in Oahu, you need go no farther than the beach in front of your hotel in Waikiki. Strung along the sand are several beach catamarans that will provide you with one-hour rides during the day and 90-minute sunset

Camping in Oahu

If you are looking for a more rugged escape from the resorts of Waikiki, consider pitching a tent on the beach or in the mountains, where you have easy access to hiking trails and the island's natural features. ■TIP➔ **Camping here is not as highly organized as it is on the mainland: expect few marked sites, scarce electrical outlets, and nary a ranger station.** What you find instead are unblemished spots in the woods and on the beach. Both the Division of Forestry and Wildlife and the State Park Service offer recreation areas at which you can camp, both in the mountains and on the beach. All such campsites can now be reserved up to a year in advance online at ⊕ *www. hawaiistateparks.org.* The fee is $18 per night per campsite for up to six people.

As for the county spots, there are 17 currently available, and all require a permit. The good news is that the permits are only $32 for three nights over the weekend or $52 for five days at the site. They are also easy to obtain, as long as you're not trying to go on a holiday weekend. Visit ⊕ *camping.honolulu.gov* for more information.

sails. Look for $35 for day sails and $49–$120 for sunset rides. ■TIP➔ **Feel free to haggle, especially with the smaller boats.** Some provide drinks for free, some charge for them, and some let you pack your own, so keep that in mind when pricing the ride. Or choose to go the ultraluxe route and charter a boat for a day or week. These run from less than $100 per person per day to more than $1,000 *(see Deep-Sea Fishing).*

HONOLULU

Hawaii Duck Tours

BOATING | FAMILY | These unique tours in amphibious vehicles take advantage of the ducks' dual means of travel by navigating the streets of Waikiki and then gliding into the waters of Waikiki. The tour starts in Waikiki and then travels on land to Kapiolani Park, Diamond Head, and the Ala Wai Canal. Then it's out to sea for views of Waikiki's famous beaches and landmarks from the water. Tours last approximately 75 minutes and run throughout the day and at sunset. On Friday night there's a special evening fireworks tour. All tours start at the Illikai Hotel. ✉ *Illikai Hotel, 1777 Ala Moana Blvd., Waikiki* ☎ *808/988–3825* ⊕ *www. hawaiiducktours.com* 🖅 *From $35.*

Hawaii Nautical

BOATING | With two locations—one in Waikiki and one on the Waianae Coast— this outfit offers a wide variety of cruise options, including guaranteed-sighting dolphin and whale-watching (in season), gourmet dinners, lunches, snorkeling, scuba diving, and sunset viewing. Three-hour cruises, including lunch and two drinks, depart from the Kewalo Basin Harbor just outside Waikiki. (The company's Port Waikiki Cruises sail from the Hilton Pier off the Hilton Hawaiian Village in Waikiki.) For those interested in leaving from the Waianae Coast, snorkel tours are available from the Waianae Boat Harbor on Farrington Highway (85-471 Farrington Hwy.). Prices include all gear, food, and two alcoholic beverages. The dock in the Waianae Boat Harbor is a little more out of the way, but this is a much more luxurious option than what is offered in Waikiki. Both morning and afternoon snorkel tours include stops for observing dolphins from the boat and visit to a snorkel spot well populated with fish. All gear, snacks, sandwiches, and two alcoholic beverages make for a more complete experience. Pickup in Ko Olina is free. ⊠ *Kewalo Basin Harbor, 1125 Ala Moana Blvd., Waikiki* ☎ *808/234–7245* ⊕ *www.hawaiinautical.com* ⊴ *From $97.*

Honolulu Sailing Company

BOATING | With a small fleet of mono- and multihull sail and power boats, the Honolulu Sailing Company offers both boat charters and sailing instruction opportunities. Itineraries include private chartered day or sunset sails, snorkeling adventures, powerboating around Oahu as well as multiday interisland cruises. Remember that these are all private, full-ship charters, so you need at least a small group to make them affordable. ⊠ *Kewalo Basin Harbor, 1125 Ala Moana Blvd., Honolulu* ☎ *808/239–3900* ⊕ *www. honsail.com* ⊴ *From $450.*

Maitai Catamaran

BOATING | Taking off from the stretch of sand behind the Sheraton Waikiki, this 44-foot cat is the fastest and sleekest on the beach. There are a variety of tours to choose from, including a sunset sail and a snorkel excursion. If you have a need for speed and want a more upscale experience, this is the boat for you. ⊠ *Sheraton Waikiki, 2255 Kalakaua Ave., Waikiki* ✛ *On beach behind hotel* ☎ *808/922–5665, 800/462–7975* ⊕ *www. maitaicatamaran.net* ⊴ *From $39.*

Makani Catamaran

BOATING | This 65-foot *Makani* is the top catamaran in Hawaii for luxury, from its Bose stereo system to its LCD TVs to its freshwater bathrooms. It sails out of Kewalo Basin four times daily, offering snorkel cruises that include lunch, afternoon "fun" sails, "Honolulu City Lights/ Sunset" dinner cruises, and Friday night fireworks-viewing cruises. ⊠ *Kewalo Basin Harbor, 1125 Ala Moana Blvd., Ala Moana* ☎ *808/591–9000* ⊕ *www. sailmakani.com* ⊴ *From $85.*

Star of Honolulu Cruises

BOATING | FAMILY | Founded in 1957, this company's fleet includes two family-friendly vessels. The 232-foot *Star of Honolulu,* which casts off at Pier 8 in the **Aloha Tower harbor** (*1 Aloha Tower Dr., downtown Honolulu*) offers seasonal whale-watching as well as sunset gourmet dinner cruises with live entertainment. Some cruises even teach you how to string lei, play ukulele, or dance hula. Moored at the **Waianae Boat Harbor** (85-491 Farrington Hwy., Waianae ⊕ *www.dolphin-star.com*), the 65-foot *Dolphin Star* catamaran, offers either dolphin-viewing or snorkeling cruises with optional barbecue lunches. Because of its size, this cat provides a comfortable way for three generations of family members to enjoy the water together. Transportation from all hotels on the island can be arranged. ⊠ *Honolulu* ☎ *808/983–7827, 800/334–6191* ⊕ *www. starofhonolulu.com* ⊴ *From $42.*

Tradewind Charters

BOATING | This company's half-day private excursions can include sailing, snorkeling, reef fishing, sunset dinner cruises, or whale-watching excursions and can accommodate from 2 to 49 people. Traveling on these luxury yachts not only gets you away from the crowds but also gives you the opportunity to take the helm if you wish. The cruises may include snorkeling at an exclusive anchorage, as well as hands-on snorkeling and sailing instruction. All charters are for the full ship. ⊠ *Kewalo Basin Harbor, 1125 Ala Moana Blvd., Ala Moana* ☎ *808/227– 4956, 800/829–4899* ⊕ *www.tradewind- charters.com* ⊴ *From $495.*

Body Boarding and Bodysurfing

Body boarding (or sponging) has long been a popular alternative to surfing for a couple of reasons. First, the start-up cost is much less—a usable board can be purchased for $30–$40 or can be rented on the beach for $5 an hour. Second, it's a whole lot easier to ride a body board than to tame a surfboard. All you have to do is paddle out to the waves, then turn toward the beach as the wave approaches and kick like crazy.

Most grocery and convenience stores sell body boards. Though these boards don't compare to what the pros use, beginners won't notice a difference in their handling on smaller waves.

Though they are not absolutely necessary for body boarding, fins do give you a tremendous advantage when you're paddling. If you plan to go out into bigger surf, we would also suggest getting a leash, which reduces the chance you'll lose your board. The smaller, sturdier versions of dive fins used for body boarding sell for $25–$60 at surf and sporting-goods stores. Most beach stands don't rent fins with the boards, so if you want them, you'll probably need to buy them.

Bodysurfing requires far less equipment—just a pair of swim fins with heel straps—but it can be a lot more challenging to master. Typically, surf breaks that are good for body boarding are good for bodysurfing.

If the direction of the current or dangers of the break are not readily apparent to you, don't hesitate to ask a lifeguard for advice.

BEST SPOTS

Body boarding and bodysurfing can be done anywhere there are waves, but due to the paddling advantage surfers have over spongers, it's usually more fun to go to surf breaks exclusively for body boarding. ⇨ *For more information on Oahu beaches, see the individual regional chapters.*

Bellows Beach. On Oahu's windward side, Bellows Field Beach has shallow waters and a consistent break that makes it an ideal spot for body boarders and bodysurfers. (Surfing isn't allowed between the two lifeguard towers.) But take note: the Portuguese man-of-war, a blue jellyfishlike invertebrate that delivers painful and powerful stings, is often seen here. ⊠ *41-043 Kalanianaole Hwy., Waimanalo.*

Kuhio Beach Park. This beach is an easy spot for first-timers to check out the action. The Wall, a break near the large pedestrian walkway called Kapahulu Groin, is the quintessential body-boarding spot. The soft, rolling waves make it perfect for beginners. Even during summer's south swells, it's relatively tame because of the outer reefs. ⊠ *Waikiki Beach, between Sheraton Moana Surfrider Hotel and Kapahulu Groin, Honolulu.*

Makapuu Beach. With its extended waves, Makapuu Beach is a sponger's dream. If you're a little more timid, go to the far end of the beach to **Keiki's,** where the waves are mellowed by Makapuu Point. Although the main break at Makapuu is much less dangerous than Sandy's, check out the ocean floor—the sands are always shifting, sometimes exposing coral heads and rocks. Always check (or ask lifeguards about) the currents, which can get pretty strong. ⊠ *41-095 Kalanianaole Hwy., across from Sea Life Park.*

Sandy Beach. The best spot—and arguably one of the most dangerous—on the island for advanced body boarding is

The windward side has many good spots for body boarding.

Sandy Beach, located on Oahu's eastern shore. Dubbed one of the most treacherous shore breaks in the nation, the break can be extremely dangerous even when it's small. As lifeguards will attest, there are more neck injuries suffered here than at any other surf break in the United States. It's awesome for the advanced, but know its danger before paddling out. ⊠ *8800 Kalanianaole Hwy., 2 miles east of Hanauma Bay, Honolulu.*

Waimanalo Beach Park. With the longest sand beach on Oahu's windward side, Waimanalo Bay has a shallow sandbar at the water's edge that provides good waves for body boarding and bodysurfing. It's an ideal break for novices because of its soft waves. Like Walls in Waikiki, this area is protected by an outer reef. And like Bellows, it's favored by the dangerous Portuguese man-of-war. ⊠ *Aloiloi St., Waimanalo.*

EQUIPMENT

There are more than 30 rental spots along Waikiki Beach, all offering basically the same prices. But if you plan to body board for more than just an hour, consider buying an inexpensive board for $20–$40 at an ABC Store—there are more than 30 in the Waikiki area—and giving it to a kid at the end of your vacation. It will be more cost-effective for you, and you'll be passing along some aloha spirit in the process.

Deep-Sea Fishing

Fishing isn't just a sport in Hawaii, it's a way of life. A number of charter boats with experienced crews can take you on a sportfishing adventure throughout the year. Sure, the bigger yellowfin tuna (ahi) are generally caught in summer, and the coveted spearfish are more frequent in winter, but you can still hook them any day of the year. You can also find dolphinfish (mahimahi), wahoo (ono), skipjacks, and the king—Pacific blue marlin—ripe for the picking on any given day. The largest marlin ever caught, weighing in at 1,805 pounds, was reeled in along Oahu's coast.

When choosing a fishing boat in the Islands, keep in mind the immensity of the surrounding ocean. Look for veteran captains who have decades of experience. Better yet, find those who care about Hawaii's fragile marine environment. Many captains now tag and release their catches to preserve the state's fishing grounds.

The general rule for the catch is an even split with the crew. Unfortunately, there are no "freeze-and-ship" providers in the state, so unless you plan to eat the fish while you're here, you'll probably want to leave it with the boat. Most boats do offer mounting services for trophy fish; ask your captain.

Prices vary greatly, but expect to pay from around $65 per person for a spot on a boat with more than 20 people to $2,000 for an overnight trip for up to 6 people. Besides the gift of fish, a gratuity of 10%–20% is standard, but use your own discretion depending on how you feel about the overall experience.

BOATS AND CHARTERS
HONOLULU
Maggie Joe Sport Fishing
FISHING | The oldest sportfishing company on Oahu boasts landing one of the largest marlins ever caught out of Kewalo Basin. With a fleet of three boats, including the 53-foot custom *Maggie Joe* (which can hold up to 15 anglers and has air-conditioned cabins, hot showers, and cutting-edge fishing equipment), they offer a variety of offshore fishing packages. A marine taxidermist can mount the monster you reel in. Half-day exclusives on the 41-foot *Sea Hawk* or the 38-foot *Ruckus* can accommodate up to six people and are the cheapest options for daytime fishing. The larger *Maggie Joe* embarks on three-quarter or full-day (but not half-day) sails. ⌧ *Kewalo Basin, 1025 Ala Moana Blvd., Ala Moana* ☎ *808/591–8888, 877/806–3474* ⊕ *www. maggiejoe.com* ⌲ *From $190.*

Magic Sportfishing
FISHING | This 50-foot Pacifica fishing yacht, aptly named *Magic,* boasts a slew of sportfishing records, including some of the largest marlins caught in local tournaments and the most mahimahi hooked during a one-day charter. This yacht is very comfortable, with twin diesel engines that provide a smooth ride, air-conditioning, and a cozy seating area. The boat can accommodate up to six passengers and offers both shared and full charters, inviting both skilled anglers and first-timers to experience deep-sea fishing in Hawaii. ⌧ *Kewalo Basin Harbor, 1125 Ala Moana Blvd., Slip G, Ala Moana* ☎ *808/596–2998* ⊕ *www.magicsportfishing.com* ⌲ *From $220 per person for a shared charter; from $1,190 for a private charter.*

Sashimi Fun Fishing
FISHING | With a luxury, 74-foot boat for sport fishing, a 65-footer for bottom fishing, and a 100-foot double-decker for dinner cruises, Sashimi Fun Fishing offers a variety of water activities. Choose a midnight shark hunt, head out in search of marlin, bottom fish near shore, or relax and enjoy live entertainment on the *Prince Kuhio's* sunset steak and seafood dinner cruise. Rates can include hotel transportation. ⌧ *Kewalo Basin Harbor, 1025 Ala Moana Blvd., Ala Moana* ☎ *808/955–3474* ⊕ *www.808955fish.com* ⊕ *www.princekuhiocruises.com* ⌲ *From $63 per person for shared trips; $69 for dinner cruises.*

Golf

Unlike on the other Hawaiian Islands, the majority of Oahu's golf courses are not associated with hotels and resorts. In fact, of the island's three dozen–plus courses, only five are tied to lodging; none is in the tourist hub of Waikiki.

Municipal courses are a good choice for budget-conscious golfers but are more

Tips for the Green

Before you head out to the first tee, there are a few things you should know about golf in Hawaii:

- All resort courses and many daily-fee courses provide rental clubs. In many cases, they're the latest lines from Titleist, Ping, Callaway, and the like. This is true for both men and women, as well as for left-handers, which means you don't have to schlep clubs across the Pacific.

- Most courses offer deals varying from twilight deep-discount rates to frequent-visitor discounts, even for tourists. Ask questions when calling pro shops, and don't just accept the first quote—deals abound if you persist.

- Pro shops at most courses are well stocked with balls, tees, and other accoutrements, so even if you bring your own bag, it needn't weigh a ton.

- Come spikeless—very few Hawaii courses still permit metal spikes.

- Sunscreen. Buy it, apply it (minimum 30 SPF). The subtropical rays of the sun are intense, even in December.

- Resort courses, in particular, offer more than the usual three sets of tees, sometimes four or five. So bite off as much or little challenge as you can chew. Tee it up from the tips, and you'll end up playing a few 600-yard par 5s and see a few 250-yard forced carries.

- In theory, you can play golf in Hawaii 365 days a year. But there's a reason the Hawaiian Islands are so green. Better to bring an umbrella and light jacket and not use them than not to bring them and get soaked.

- Unless you play a muni or certain daily-fee courses, plan on taking a cart. Riding carts are mandatory at most courses and are included in greens fees.

---

crowded and are not always maintained to the same standard as the private courses. Your best bet is to call the day you want to play and inquire about walk-on availability. Greens fees are standard at city courses: walking rate $66 for visitors, riding carts $20 for 18 holes, pull carts $4.

Greens fees listed here are the highest course rates per round on weekdays and weekends for U.S. residents. (Some courses charge non–U.S. residents higher prices.) Discounts are often available for resort guests and for those who book tee times online. Twilight fees are usually offered; call individual courses for information.

HONOLULU

There is only one spot to golf near Waikiki and it is the busiest course in America. Although not a very imaginative layout, the price is right and the advantage of walking from your hotel to the course is not to be overlooked. Unless you make a reservation, make sure you bring a newspaper because it will be a little while before you tee off.

Ala Wai Municipal Golf Course

GOLF | Just across the Ala Wai Canal from Waikiki, this municipal golf course is said to host more rounds than any other U.S. course—up to 500 per day. Not that it's a great course, just really convenient. The best bet for a visitor is to show up and expect to wait at least an hour or call up to three days in advance for a tee-time reservation. When reserving, the automated system will ask for an ID code—simply enter your phone number and give that number and your tee time when checking in. The course itself is flat; Robin Nelson did some redesign work in the 1990s, adding mounding, trees, and a lake. The Ala Wai Canal comes into play on several holes on the back nine, including the treacherous 18th. There's also an on-site restaurant and bar. ⊠ *404 Kapahulu Ave., Waikiki* ☎ *808/733–7387 for starter's office, 808/738–4652 for pro shop, 808/296–2000 for reservations only* ⊕ *www.honolulu.gov/des/golf/ala-wai.html* ☑ *$66* ↥ *18 holes, 5861 yards, par 70.*

Moanalua Golf Club

GOLF | Said to be (not without dispute) the oldest golf club west of the Rockies, this 9-holer is semiprivate, allowing public play except on weekend and holiday mornings. Near Pearl Harbor and nestled in the hardwoods, this course will remind you more of golf in Pennsylvania than in the tropics, but it offers the lowest greens fees in the area, and by the time you get here, you'll probably be over the whole palm tree theme anyway. The course is a bit quirky, but the final two holes, a par 3 off a cliff to a smallish tree-rimmed green and a par 4 with an approach to a green set snugly between stream and jungle, are classic. Although carts are not required, they are recommended, as this course is a bit steep in places. ⊠ *1250 Ala Aolani St., Salt Lake* ☎ *808/839–2411 for starter's office, 808/839–2311 for pro shop and clubhouse* ☑ *$41* ↥ *9 holes, 2972 yards, par 36.*

HAWAII KAI

Prepare to keep your ball down on this windy corner of Oahu. You'll get beautiful ocean vistas, but you may need them to soothe you once your perfect drive gets blown 40 yards off course by a gusting trade wind.

Hawaii Kai Golf Course

GOLF | The **Championship Golf Course** (William F. Bell, 1973) winds through a Honolulu suburb at the foot of Koko Crater. Homes (and the liability of a broken window) come into play on many holes, but they are offset by views of the nearby Pacific and a crafty routing of holes. With several lakes, lots of trees, and bunkers in all the wrong places, Hawaii Kai really is a "championship" golf course, especially when the trade winds howl. Greens fees for this course include a mandatory cart. The **Executive Course** (1962), a par-54 track, is the first of only three courses in Hawaii built by Robert Trent Jones Sr. Although a few changes have been made to his original design, you can find the usual Jones attributes, including raised greens and lots of risk-reward options. You may walk or use a cart on this course for an additional fee. ⊠ *8902 Kalanianaole Hwy., Hawaii Kai* ☎ *808/395–2358* ⊕ *hawaiikaigolf.com* ☑ *Championship Course $150, Executive Course $50* ↥ *Championship Course: 18 holes, 6207 yards, par 72. Executive Course: 18 holes, 2196 yards, par 54.*

WINDWARD OAHU

Windward Oahu is what you expect when you think of golfing in the Islands. Lush, tropical foliage will surround you, with towering mountains framing one shot and the crystal-blue Pacific framing the next. Although it's a bit more expensive to golf on this side, and a good deal wetter, the memories and pictures you take on these courses will last a lifetime.

Koolau Golf Club

GOLF | Koolau Golf Club is marketed as the toughest golf course in Hawaii and one of the most challenging in the country. Dick Nugent and Jack Tuthill (1992) routed 10 holes over jungle ravines that require at least a 110-yard carry. The par-4 18th may be the most difficult closing hole in golf. The tee shot from this hole's regular tees must carry 200 yards of ravine, 250 from the blue tees.

The approach shot is back across the ravine, 200 yards to a well-bunkered green. Set at the windward base of the Koolau Mountains, the course is as much beauty as beast. Kaneohe Bay is visible from most holes, orchids and yellow ginger bloom, the shama thrush (Hawaii's best singer since Don Ho) chirps, and waterfalls flute down the sheer, green mountains above. The greens fee includes a (required) cart. ⊠ 45-550 Kionaole Rd., Kaneohe ☎ 808/236–4653 ⊕ www.koolaugolfclub.com ☒ $165 ↥ 18 holes, 7310 yards, par 72.

Olomana Golf Links

GOLF | Bob and Robert L. Baldock are the architects of record for this layout, but so much has changed since it opened in 1969 that they would recognize little of it. A turf specialist was brought in to improve fairways and greens, tees were rebuilt, new bunkers added, and mangroves cut back to make better use of natural wetlands. But what really puts Olomana on the map is that this is where wunderkind Michelle Wie learned the game. A cart is required at this course and is included in the greens fee. ⊠ 41-1801 Kalanianaole Hwy., Waimanalo ☎ 808/259–7926 ⊕ www.olomanalinks.com ☒ $59 for 9 holes, $105 for 18 holes ↥ 18 holes, 6306 yards, par 72.

Pali Golf Course

GOLF | Panoramic views of the Koolau Mountains and Kaneohe Bay enhance the many challenges at this popular municipal course between Kaneohe and Kailua. ⊠ 45-050 Kamehameha Hwy., Kaneohe ☎ 808/266–7612 starter's office, 808/262–2911 pro shop ⊕ www.honolulu.gov/des/golf/pali.html ☒ $66 ↥ 18 holes, 6524 yards, par 72.

★ Royal Hawaiian Golf Club

GOLF | In the cool, lush Maunawili Valley, Pete and Perry Dye created what can only be called target jungle golf. In other words, the rough is usually dense jungle, and you may not hit a driver on three of the four par 5s, or several par 4s,

including the perilous 18th that plays off a cliff to a narrow green protected by a creek. Mt. Olomana's twin peaks tower over the course. ■TIP→ **The back nine wanders deep into the valley, and includes an island green (par-3 11th) and perhaps the loveliest inland hole in Hawaii (par-4 12th).** ⊠ 770 Auloa Rd., at Luana Hills Rd., Kailua ☎ 808/262–2139 ⊕ royalhawaiiangc.com ☒ $160 ↥ 18 holes, 5541 yards, par 72.

NORTH SHORE

The North Shore has both the cheapest and the most expensive courses on the island. You can play nine holes in your bare feet, and you can chunk up the course played by both the LPGA and Champions Tour here, too. Don't try to go the barefoot route on the LPGA course, or the only course in the Islands you may be allowed on will be the Kahuku muni.

Kahuku Municipal Golf Course

GOLF | The only true links course in Hawaii, this 9-hole municipal course is not for everyone. Maintenance is an ongoing issue, and in summer it can look a bit like the Serengeti. It's walking-only (a few pull-carts are available for rent); there's no pro shop, just a starter who sells lost-and-found balls; and the 19th hole is a soda machine and a covered picnic bench. And yet the course stretches out along the blue Pacific where surf crashes on the shore, the turf underfoot is spongy, sea mist drifts across the links, and wildflowers bloom in the rough. ⊠ 56-501 Kamehameha Hwy., Kahuku ☎ 808/293–5842 ⊕ www.honolulu.gov/des/golf/kahuku.html ☒ $22 ↥ 9 holes, 2699 yards, par 35.

Turtle Bay Resort & Spa

GOLF | When the Lazarus of golf courses, the **Fazio Course** (George Fazio, 1971), rose from the dead in 2002, Turtle Bay on Oahu's rugged North Shore became a premier golf destination. Two holes had been plowed under when the **Palmer Course** (Arnold Palmer and Ed Seay, 1992) was built, while the other seven

The North Shore's Turtle Bay Resort attracts golfers who come for the prized Palmer Course.

lay fallow, and the front nine remained open. Then new owners came along and re-created holes 13 and 14 using Fazio's original plans, and the Fazio became whole again. It's a terrific track with 90 bunkers. The gem at Turtle Bay, though, is the Palmer. The front nine is mostly open as it skirts Punahoolapa Marsh, a nature sanctuary, while the back nine plunges into the wetlands and winds along the coast. The short par-4 17th runs along the rocky shore, with a diabolical string of bunkers cutting diagonally across the fairway from tee to green. Carts are required for both courses and are included in the greens fee. ⊠ *57-049 Kuilima Dr., Kahuku* ☎ *808/293–8574* ⊕ *www.turtlebaygolf. com* 🖃 *Fazio Course: $69 for 9 holes, $129 for 18 holes. Palmer Course: $99 for 9 holes, $199 for 18 holes* 🏌️. *Fazio Course: 18 holes, 6600 yards, par 72. Palmer Course: 18 holes, 7200 yards, par 72.*

CENTRAL OAHU

Golf courses are densest here in Central Oahu, where plantations morphed into tract housing, and golf courses were added to anchor communities. The vegetation is much sparser, but some of the best greens around can be found here. Play early to avoid the hot afternoons, but if you can handle the heat, note that most courses offer substantial discounts for twilight hours.

Hawaii Country Club

GOLF | Also known as Kunia—but not to be confused with Royal Kunia a few miles away—this course is in the middle of former sugarcane fields and dates from plantation times. Several par 4s are drivable, including the 9th and 18th holes. This is a fun course, but it's a bit rough around the edges. You can walk the course on weekdays only. Reservations can be made online two weeks in advance. ⊠ *94-1211 Kunia Rd., Waipahu* ☎ *808/621–5654* 🖃 *$45* 🏌️. *18 holes, 5910 yards, par 71.*

Mililani Golf Club

GOLF | Located on Oahu's central plain, Mililani is usually a few degrees cooler than downtown, 25 minutes away. The eucalyptus trees through which the course plays add to the cool factor, and stands of Norfolk pines give Mililani a "mainland course" feel. Bob and Robert L. Baldock (1966) make good use of an old irrigation ditch reminiscent of a Scottish burn. Carts are required and are included in the greens fee. ✉ 95-176 Kuahelani Ave., Mililani ☎ 808/623–2222 ⊕ www.mililanigolf.com ⛳ $160 ⛳ 18 holes, 6274 yards, par 72.

Pearl Country Club

GOLF | Carved in the hillside high above Pearl Harbor, the 18 holes here are really two courses. The front nine rambles out along gently sloping terrain, while the back nine zigzags up and down a steeper portion of the slope as it rises into the Koolau Mountains. The views of Pearl Harbor are breathtaking. Hawaii residents consistently rank it their #1 choice in the *Honolulu Star Advertiser* annual rankings of state courses. Carts are required and are included in the greens fee. ✉ 98-535 Kaonohi St., Aiea ☎ 808/487–3802 ⊕ www.pearlcc.com ⛳ $120 ⛳ 18 holes, 6232 yards, par 72.

Royal Kunia Country Club

GOLF | At one time, the PGA Tour considered buying the Royal Kunia Country Club and hosting the Sony Open here. It's that good. ■ TIP→ **Every hole offers fabulous views from Diamond Head to Pearl Harbor to the nearby Waianae Mountains.** Robin Nelson's eye for natural sight lines and his dexterity with water features add to the visual pleasure. Carts are required and are included in the greens fee. ✉ 94-1509 Anonui St., Waipahu ☎ 808/688–9222 ⊕ www.royalkuniacc.com ⛳ From $85 ⛳ 18 holes, 6507 yards, par 72.

Ted Makalena Golf Course

GOLF | The flat layout of this bare-bones municipal course with Bermuda grass fairways appeals to all levels of players, but especially those just starting to learn the sport. ✉ 93-059 Waipio Point Access Rd., Waipahu ☎ 808/675–6052 ⊕ www. honolulu.gov/des/golf/makalena.html ⛳ $66 ⛳ 18 holes, 5976 yards, par 71.

Waikele Country Club

GOLF | Outlet stores are not the only bargain in Waikele. The adjacent, daily-fee golf course offers a private club–like atmosphere and a terrific Ted Robinson (1992) layout. Robinson's water features are less distinctive here but define the short par-4 4th hole—with a lake running down the left side of the fairway and guarding the green—and the par-3 17th, which plays across a lake. The par-4 18th is a terrific closing hole, with a lake lurking on the right side of the green. Carts are required and are included in the greens fee. ✉ 94-200 Paioa Pl., Waipahu ☎ 808/676–9000 ⊕ www.golfwaikele. com ⛳ $170 ⛳ 18 holes, 6261 yards, par 72.

LEEWARD (WEST) OAHU

On the leeward side of the mountains, shielded from the rains that drench the Kaneohe side, West Oahu is arid and sunny and has a unique kind of beauty. The Ewa area is dotted with golf courses and new development, so you'll have your pick of a number of options—golfers generally choose courses in Ewa and Kapolei because they provide a totally different landscape from Waikiki or the North Shore. The resort courses on the west side are a long drive from town, but the beaches are magnificent, and you can find deals if you're combining a room with a round or two on the greens.

Coral Creek Golf Course

GOLF | On the Ewa Plain, 4 miles inland, Coral Creek is cut from ancient coral left from when this area was still underwater. Robin Nelson (1999) did some of his best work in making use of the coral—and of some dynamite, blasting out portions to create dramatic lakes and tee and green sites. They could just as easily call it Coral Cliffs, because of the 30- to 40-foot cliffs

Nelson created. They include the par-3 10th green's grotto and waterfall, and the vertical drop-off on the right side of the par-4 18th green. An ancient creek meanders across the course, but there's not much water, just enough to be a babbling nuisance. Carts are required and are included in the greens fee. ✉ *91-1111 Geiger Rd., Ewa Beach* ☎ *808/441–4653* ⊕ *www.coralcreekgolfhawaii.com* 🏷 *$75 for 9 holes, $150 for 18 holes* 🏌 *18 holes, 6347 yards, par 72.*

Ewa Beach Golf Club

GOLF | A private course open to the public, Ewa is one of the delightful products of the too-brief collaboration of Robin Nelson and Rodney Wright (1992). Trees are very much part of the character here, but there are also elements of links golf, such as a double green shared by the 2nd and 16th holes. Carts are required and are included in the greens fee. ✉ *91-050 Fort Weaver Rd., Ewa Beach* ☎ *808/689–6565* ⊕ *www.ewabeachgc. com* 🏷 *$165* 🏌 *18 holes, 5861 yards, par 72.*

Hawaii Prince Golf Course

GOLF | Affiliated with the Hawaii Prince Hotel in Waikiki, the Hawaii Prince Golf Course (not to be confused with the Prince Course at Princeville, Kauai) has a links feel to it, and it is popular with local-charity fund-raiser golf tournaments. Arnold Palmer and Ed Seay (1991) took what had been flat, featureless sugar-cane fields and sculpted 27 challenging, varied holes. Mounding breaks up the landscape, as do 10 lakes. Water comes into play on six holes of the A course, three of B, and seven of C. The most difficult combination is A and C (A and B from the forward tees). Carts are required and are included in the greens fee. ✉ *91-1200 Fort Weaver Rd., Ewa Beach* ☎ *808/944–4567* ⊕ *www.hawaiiprincegolf.com* 🏷 *$149 for 18 holes; $170 for 18 holes including rental clubs* 🏌 *A Course: 9 holes, 3138 yards, par 36.*

B Course: 9 holes, 3099 yards, par 36. C Course: 9 holes, 3076 yards, par 36.

Kapolei Golf Course

GOLF | This is a Ted Robinson water wonderland with waterfalls and four lakes—three so big they have names—coming into play on 10 holes. Set on rolling terrain, Kapolei is a serious golf course, especially when the wind blows. Carts are required and are included in the greens fee. ✉ *91-701 Farrington Hwy., Kapolei* ☎ *808/674–2227* ⊕ *www.kapoleigolf.com* 🏷 *$185* 🏌 *18 holes, 6586 yards, par 72.*

Ko Olina Golf Club

GOLF | Hawaii's golden age of golf-course architecture came to Oahu when Ko Olina Golf Club opened in 1989. Ted Robinson, king of the water features, went splash-happy here, creating nine lakes that come into play on eight holes, including the par-3 12th, where you reach the tee by driving behind a Disney-like waterfall. Tactically, though, the most dramatic is the par-4 18th, where the approach is a minimum 120 yards across a lake to a two-tiered green guarded on the left by a cascading waterfall. Today Ko Olina has matured into one of Hawaii's top courses. You can niggle about routing issues—the first three holes play into the trade winds (and the morning sun), as do two consecutive par 5s on the back nine play—but Robinson does enough solid design to make those of passing concern. ■ **TIP→ The course provides free transportation from Waikiki hotels.** ✉ *92-1220 Aliinui Dr., Ko Olina* ☎ *808/676–5300* ⊕ *www.koolinagolf.com* 🏷 *$115 for 9 holes, $225 for 18 holes* 🏌 *18 holes, 6432 yards, par 72.*

Makaha Valley Country Club

GOLF | This course (William F. Bell, 1968), known locally as Makaha East, is indeed a valley course, taking great advantage of the steep valley walls and natural terrain. The double-dogleg, downhill-up-hill, par-5 18th is a doozy of a closer. Carts are required and are included in the greens fee. ✉ *84-627 Makaha Valley Rd., Waianae* ☎ *808/695–7111* ⊕ *www. makahavalleycc.com* 🖘 *$37 for 9 holes, $89 for 18 holes* ✠. *18 holes, 6260 yards, par 71.*

★ West Loch Municipal Golf Course

GOLF | The best of Honolulu's municipal courses, this Robin Nelson (1991) design plays along Pearl Harbor's West Loch. In the process of building the course, wetlands were actually expanded, increasing bird habitat. ✉ *91-1126 Okupe St., Ewa Beach* ☎ *808/675–6076* ⊕ *www.honolulu. gov/des/golf/westloch.html* 🖘 *$66* ✠. *18 holes, 6335 yards, par 72.*

Hiking

The trails of Oahu cover a full spectrum of environments: desert walks through cactus, slippery paths through bamboo-filled rain forest, and scrambling rock climbs up ancient volcanic calderas. The only thing you won't find is an overnighter, as even the longest of hikes won't take you more than half a day. In addition to being short in length, many of the prime hikes are within 10 minutes of downtown Waikiki, meaning that you won't have to spend your whole day getting back to nature.

Hawaii State Department of Land and Natural Resources

HIKING/WALKING | Go to the website for information on all major hiking trails on Oahu. You can also obtain camping permits for state parks here. ■TIP→ **Make sure to follow DLNR recommendations regarding personal safety and environmental impact in these fragile areas.** ✉ *1151 Punchbowl St., Room 310, Downtown* ☎ *808/587–0300* ⊕ *dlnr.hawaii.gov/dsp/ hiking/oahu.*

Na Ala Hele Trails and Access

HIKING/WALKING | Contact the Na Ala Hele ("Trails to Go On") folks for a free hiking-safety guide and trail information. The interactive website has maps and

information about the current status of trails on all of the Islands. You can also stop in their office for free printed maps and information. ✉ *1151 Punchbowl St., Room 325, Downtown* ☎ *808/587–0166* ⊕ *hawaiitrails.hawaii.gov.*

BEST SPOTS
HONOLULU
Aiea Loop Trail

HIKING/WALKING | This 4.8-mile loop begins and ends in the Keaiwa Heiau State Recreation Area, running along the ridge on the west side of Halawa Valley. It's a fairly easy hike that lasts about 2½ to 3 hours and brings many rewards, including views of the southern coastline of Oahu from Pearl Harbor and the Waianae Range to Honolulu and Diamond Head. Foresters replanted this area with various trees in the 1920s, so scents of lemon eucalyptus, pine, koa, and other trees enhance the trek. There's ample parking near the trailhead, close to restrooms and a picnic pavilion. ✉ *Aiea District Park, 99-350 Aiea Heights Dr., Aiea* ⊕ *At upper east corner of park, at top of Aiea Heights Rd.* ☎ *808/587–0300* ⊕ *dlnr. hawaii.gov/dsp/hiking/oahu/aiea-loop-trail.*

Diamond Head Crater

HIKING/WALKING | Every vacation has requirements that must be fulfilled, so that when your neighbors ask, you can say, "Yeah, did it." Climbing Diamond Head is high on that list of things to do on Oahu. It's a moderately easy hike if you're in good physical condition, but be prepared to climb many stairs along the way. Also be sure to bring a water bottle, because it's hot and dry. Only a mile up, a clearly marked trail with handrails scales the inside of this extinct volcano. At the top, the fabled final 99 steps take you up to the pillbox overlooking the Pacific Ocean and Honolulu. It's a breathtaking view and a lot cheaper than taking a helicopter ride for the same photo op. Last entry for hikers is 4:30 pm. ✉ *Diamond Head Rd. at 18th Ave., Diamond Head* ⊕ *Enter on east side of crater;*

there's limited parking inside, so most park on street and walk in ☎ *808/587– 0300* ⊕ *dlnr.hawaii.gov/dsp/parks/oahu/ diamond-head-state-monument* ⌫ *$1 per person, $5 to park.*

★ Manoa Falls Trail

HIKING/WALKING | Travel up into the valley beyond Honolulu to make the Manoa Falls hike. Though only a mile long, this well-trafficked path, visited by an estimated 100,000 hikers a year, passes through so many different ecosystems that you feel as if you're in an arboretum—and you're not far off. (The beautiful Lyon Arboretum is right near the trailhead, if you want to make another stop.) Walk among the elephant ear ape plants, ruddy fir trees, and a bamboo forest straight out of China. At the top is a 150-foot waterfall, which can be an impressive cascade or, if rain has been sparse, little more than a trickle. This hike is more about the journey than the destination; make sure you bring some mosquito repellent because they grow 'em big up here. ⚠ **The trail is undergoing renovations, which were supposed to finish in the first half of 2020 but which have been extended, so there are sometimes unscheduled and unexpected closures.** ✉ *3998 Manoa Rd., Manoa* ⊹ *West Manoa Rd. is behind Manoa Valley in Paradise Park. Take West Manoa Rd. to end, park on side of road or in parking lot for a small fee, follow trail signs* ⊕ *www.hawaiitrails.org/trails/#/ trail/manoa-falls-trail/225.*

LEEWARD (WEST) OAHU
★ Kaena Point Trail

HIKING/WALKING | Kaena Point is one of the island's last easily accessible pockets of nature left largely untouched. For more than a quarter century, the state has protected nearly 60 acres of land at the point, first as a nature preserve and, more recently, as an ecosystem restoration project for endangered and protected coastal plants and seabirds. The uneven 5-mile trail around the point can be entered from two locations—Keawaula

Beach (aka Yokohama Bay) at the end of Farrington Highway on Oahu's western coastline, or Mokuleia at the same highway's northern coast endpoint. It's a rugged coastline hike without much shade, so bring lots of water and sunscreen (or better yet, start early!). ■**TIP→ Keep a lookout for the Laysan albatrosses; these enormous birds have recently returned to the area. Don't be surprised if they come in for a closer look at you, too.** ✉ *81-780 Farrington Hwy., Waianae* ⊹ *Take Farrington Hwy. to its end at Yokohama. Hike in on old 4x4 trail* ⊕ *dlnr.hawaii.gov/dsp/hiking/ oahu/kaena-point-trail.*

HAWAII KAI
Makapuu Lighthouse Trail

HIKING/WALKING | For the less adventurous hiker and anyone looking for a great view, this paved trail that runs up the side of Makapuu Point in Southeast Oahu fits the bill. Early on, the trail is surrounded by lava rock but, as you ascend, foliage—the tiny white *koa haole* flower, the cream-tinged spikes of the *kiawe,* and, if you go early enough, the stunning night-blooming *cereus*—begins taking over the barren rock. At the easternmost tip of Oahu, where the island divides the sea, this trail gives you a spectacular view of the cobalt ocean meeting the land in a cacophony of white caps. To the south are several tide pools and the lighthouse, while the eastern view looks down upon Manana (Rabbit Island) and Kaohikaipu islets, two bird sanctuaries just off the coast. The 2-mile round-trip hike is a great break on a circle-island trip. From late December to early May, this is a great perch to see migrating humpback whales. ■**TIP→ Be sure not to leave valuables in your car, as break-ins, even in the parking lot, are common.** ✉ *Makapuu Lighthouse Rd., Hawaii Kai* ⊹ *Take Kalanianaole Hwy. to base of Makapuu Point, then look for parking lot* ⊕ *dlnr.hawaii.gov/dsp/hiking/oahu/ makapuu-point-lighthouse-trail.*

Did You Know?

Manoa Falls is about 150 feet high and is the gem at the end of a mile-long hike. At its top, you'll find a small pool perfect for wading.

Tips for the Trail

- When hiking the waterfall and rain-forest trails, use insect repellent. The dampness draws huge swarms of bloodsuckers that can ruin a walk in the woods.

- Volcanic rock is very porous and therefore likely to be loose. Rock climbing is strongly discouraged, as you never know which little ledge is going to go.

- Avoid hiking after heavy rains and check for flash-flood warnings. Keep in mind that those large boulders in the idyllic pools beneath the waterfalls were carried by torrential flows high up in the mountains.

- Always let someone know where you're going, and never hike alone. The foliage gets very dense, and, small as the island is, hikers have been known to get lost for a week or longer.

7

Activities and Tours

HIKING

NORTH SHORE
Maunawili Falls

HIKING/WALKING | Want to find a waterfall that you can actually swim in? Then Maunawili Falls is your trip. In fact, even if you don't want to get wet, you're going to have to cross Maunawili Stream several times to get to the falls, and the route is pretty muddy. Along the 1½-mile trek enjoy the ginger, vines, and heliconia before greeting fern-shrouded falls that are made for swimming. The water is not the clearest, but it's cool and refreshing after battling the bugs to get here.
■ **TIP→ On weekends, the trail can be very crowded. Prepare to park far from the trailhead as regulations are strictly enforced. Be sure to bring mosquito repellant. Walking sticks are helpful—if you don't have any, use the loaner sticks often left by hikers at the trailhead.** ⊠ 1221 Kelewina St., Kailua ⊹ Take Pali Hwy. (Rte. 61) from Honolulu through tunnels, then take 3rd right onto Auloa Rd., then take left fork immediately. At dead end, climb over vehicle gate to find trailhead.

Trails at Turtle Bay Resort

HIKING/WALKING | When on the North Shore, check out the Turtle Bay Resort, which has more than 12 miles of trails and oceanside pathways. You can pick up a map of the resort property, which includes trail and coastal jogging paths. ⊠ 57-091 Kamehameha Hwy., Kahuku ☎ 808/293–8811 ⊕ www.turtlebayresort. com.

GOING WITH A GUIDE
HONOLULU
Hawaii Nature Center

HIKING/WALKING | **FAMILY** | A good choice for families, the center in upper Makiki Valley conducts a number of programs for both adults and children. There are guided hikes into tropical settings that reveal hidden waterfalls and protected forest reserves. They don't run tours every day, so it's a good idea to get advance reservations. ⊠ 2131 Makiki Heights Dr., Makiki Heights ☎ 808/955–0100 ⊕ www.hawaiinaturecenter.org.

Oahu Nature Tours

HIKING/WALKING | Guides explain the native flora and fauna and history that are your companions on the various walking and hiking tours of the North Shore, Diamond Head, and Windward Oahu. The company also offers much more expensive private birding tours, perfect for those interested in spotting one of Hawaii's native honeycreepers. Tours include pickup at centralized Waikiki locations and are discounted if booked online in advance. ☎ 808/924–2473 ⊕ www. oahunaturetours.com ⊠ From $36.

NORTH SHORE
North Shore Eco Tours

HIKING/WALKING | Native Hawaiians own and operate this business, the only one allowed to lead guided small-group adventures in private conservation lands. Options range from 2-mile and 3½-mile round-trip hikes to pools and waterfalls (lunch included) to an off-road expedition in all-terrain vehicles. Hiking adventures begin at a pickup point in Haleiwa town at North Shore Marketplace; off-road tours begin in Waimea Valley. ✉ *North Shore Marketplace, 56-250 Kamehameha Hwy., Haleiwa* ☎ *877/521–4453* ⊕ *www. northshoreecotours.com* 🎟 *From $95.*

Horseback Riding

A great way to see the island is atop a horse, leaving the direction to the pack while you drink in the views of mountains or the ocean. It may seem like a cliché, but there really is nothing like riding a horse with spectacular ocean views to put you in a romantic state of mind.

WINDWARD OAHU
Gunstock Ranch

HORSEBACK RIDING | This working cattle ranch encompasses nearly 800 acres on the northeastern shore of Oahu, in the foothills of the Koolau range. Choose among 5 to 10 small-group guided trail rides a day (one to 2½ hours or longer) for riders of all skill levels. Rides are designed to replicate the experience of the *paniolo*, or Hawaiian cowboy. Some climb high enough to view (on clear days) 30 miles of coastline, and sometimes as far as Maui and Molokai. The ranch also offers private 30-minute horse experiences for ages two to seven, private and group advanced trail rides, and private romantic couples tours with picnics. Reservations are required. ✉ *56-250 Kamehameha Hwy., Laie* ✛ *2 miles North of the Polynesian Cultural Center, between Laie and Kahuku.* ☎ *808/341–3995* ⊕ *www.gunstockranch.com* 🎟 *Trail rides from $82.*

Kualoa Ranch

HORSEBACK RIDING | FAMILY | This 4,000-acre working ranch across from Kualoa Beach Park on Windward Oahu offers two-hour trail rides in the breathtaking Kaaawa Valley, which was the site of such movie back lots as *Jurassic Park, Godzilla,* and *50 First Dates,* as well as numerous television shows, including *Lost.*   There is an hour-long option, but it doesn't take you into the valley. Instead, this tour takes you to the scenic northern section of the ranch with its WWII-era bunkers. Kualoa has other activities— bus, boat, and Jeep tours; electric mountain bike tours; kayak adventure tours; ATV trail rides; canopy zipline tours; and children's activities—that may be combined for full-day package rates. The minimum age for horseback rides is 10. ✉ *49-479 Kamehameha Hwy., Kaneohe* ☎ *800/231–7321, 808/237–7321* ⊕ *www. kualoa.com* 🎟 *From $88.*

LEEWARD (WEST) OAHU
Happy Trails Hawaii

HORSEBACK RIDING | FAMILY | Take a guided horseback ride above the North Shore's Waimea Bay along trails that offer panoramic views from Kaena Point to the famous surfing spots. Groups are no larger than 10, and instruction is provided. The rides are particularly family-friendly, and children six and older are welcome. You can take either a 1½- or a 2-hour ride, which includes a 15-minute minilesson. Reservations are required. ✉ *59-231 Pupukea Rd., Pupukea* ✛ *Go 1 mile mauka (toward mountain) up Pupukea Rd.; the office is on right* ☎ *808/638–7433* ⊕ *www.happytrailshawaii.com* 🎟 *From $99.*

NORTH SHORE
Turtle Bay Stables

HORSEBACK RIDING | FAMILY | Trail rides follow the 12-mile-long coastline and even step out onto sandy beaches fronting this luxe resort on Oahu's fabled North Shore. The stables here are part of the resort but can be utilized by nonguests.

The sunset ride is a definite must. A basic trail ride lasts 45 minutes and visits filming sites for ABC's *Lost* and the film *Pirates of the Caribbean.* ⊠ *Turtle Bay Resort, 57-091 Kamehameha Hwy., Kahuku* ☎ *808/293–6024* ⊕ *www.turtle-bayresort.com/things-to-do/sports-recreation/horse-riding* 🖵 *From $86.*

Jet Skiing and Waterskiing

HONOLULU

Aloha Jet Ski

JET SKIING | Skip across the surface of the immense Keehi Lagoon as planes from Honolulu International Airport soar above you. After an instructional safety course, you can try your hand at navigating the buoyed course. The Yamaha deluxe waverunners can either be operated tandem or solo. Reservations are required. ⊠ *Keehi Lagoon, Sand Island Access Rd., Honolulu* ☎ *888/538–6248, 808/721–1754* ⊕ *www.alohajetski.com* 🖵 *From $69.*

Hawaii Water Sports Center

JET SKIING | **FAMILY** | This company transforms Maunalua Bay into a water park with activities for all ages. You can bounce around in a bumper tube, zoom around on Jet Skis, wakeboard, scuba dive, or ride the six-person banana boats. Jet Ski rentals can be as short as 30 minutes. ⊠ *Koko Marina Center, 7192 Kalanianaole Hwy., Honolulu* ☎ *808/395–3773* ⊕ *www.hawaiiwatersportscenter.com* 🖵 *From $39.*

HAWAII KAI

H2O Sports Hawaii

WATER SPORTS | **FAMILY** | Parasailing, banana boats, bumper boats, jetskiing, snorkeling, and scuba diving: this company offers a wide variety of tours and activities on the water. But the Jet Pack is H2O's most famous program. Pumping 1,000 gallons of seawater per minute

through the pack gets you airborne like a character in a sci-fi film. With a 90% success rate for first-time flyers, this safety-conscious outfitter allows you to rocket into the air or walk on water. Launches for first-timers last 15 minutes and depart from a floating platform in Maunalua Bay near Hawaii Kai. ■TIP➔ **Make your reservations early, as flights book up more than a week in advance, and note that the Jet Pack is only available on weekdays.** ⊠ *Hawaii Kai Shopping Center, 377 Keahole St., near Longs Drugs, Hawaii Kai* ☎ *808/396–0100* ⊕ *www.h2osportshawaii.com* 🖵 *From $199 for Jet Pack; other options from $50.*

Kayaking

Kayaking is an easy way to explore the ocean—and Oahu's natural beauty—without much effort or skill. It offers a vantage point not afforded by swimming or surfing and a workout you won't get lounging on a catamaran. Even novices can get in a kayak and enjoy the island's scenery.

The ability to travel long distances can also get you into trouble. ■TIP➔ **Experts agree that rookies should stay on the windward side.** Their reasoning is simple: if you get tired, break or lose an oar, or just plain pass out, the onshore winds will eventually blow you back to the beach. The same cannot be said for the offshore breezes of the North Shore and West Oahu.

Kayaks are specialized: some are better suited for riding waves while others are designed for traveling long distances. Your outfitter can address your needs depending on your skill level. Sharing your plans with your outfitter can lead to a more enjoyable—and safer—experience. Expect to pay from $35 for a half-day single rental to $139 for a guided kayak tour with lunch. Some kayaking outfitters also rent stand-up paddleboards (⇨ *see Stand-Up Paddleboarding*).

BEST SPOTS

If you want to try your hand at surfing kayaks, **Bellows Field Beach** (near Waimanalo Town Center, entrance on Kalanianaole Highway) on the windward side and **Mokuleia Beach** (across from Dillingham Airfield) on the North Shore are two great spots. Hard-to-reach breaks, the ones that surfers exhaust themselves trying to reach, are easily accessed by kayak. The buoyancy of the kayak also allows you to catch the wave earlier and get out in front of the white wash. One reminder on these spots: if you're a little green, stick to Bellows Field Beach with those onshore winds. Generally speaking, you don't want to be catching waves where surfers are; in Waikiki, however, pretty much anything goes.

The perennial favorite of kayakers is **Lanikai Beach,** on the island's windward side. Tucked away in an upscale residential area, this award-winning beach has become a popular spot for amateur kayakers because of its calm waters and onshore winds. More adventurous paddlers can head to the Mokulua Islands, two islets less than 1 mile from the beach. You can land on Moku Nui, which has surf breaks and small beaches great for picnicking. Take a dip in Queen's Bath, a small saltwater swimming hole.

For something a little different, try Windward Oahu's Kahana River, which empties into the ocean at **Kahana Bay Beach Park.** The river may not have the blue water of the ocean, but the majestic Koolau Mountains, with waterfalls during rainy months, make for a picturesque backdrop. It's a short jaunt, about 2 miles round-trip from the beach, but it's tranquil and packed with rain-forest foliage. Bring mosquito repellent.

Kayaking to The Mokes

The Mokulua Islands (aka The Mokes) are two islets off Lanikai Beach. The larger Moku Nui is a perfect kayaking destination and a popular place for picnics. The islands are state-protected bird sanctuaries, and sometimes you can glimpse one of the 11 different kinds of seabirds that nest there. Some outfitters offer guided tours. But as it would be impossible to miss the islets and the water between them is typically calm, spend your money on sunscreen and snacks instead, and enjoy the paddle.

EQUIPMENT, LESSONS, AND TOURS

HONOLULU

Go Bananas

KAYAKING | Staffers make sure that you rent the appropriate kayak for your abilities and can also outfit your rental car with soft racks to transport your boat to the beach. (Racks are included in the rental fee.) You can rent either a single or double kayak. The store also carries clothing and kayaking accessories and rents stand-up paddleboards. (There's a second location in Aiea, which is closer to the North Shore.) ⊠ *799 Kapahulu Ave., Kapahulu* ☎ *808/737–9514* ⊕ *www.gobananaskayaks.com* ⌕ *From $35.*

WINDWARD OAHU

Hawaiian Water Sports

KAYAKING | **FAMILY** | This multifaceted outfitter emphasizes ocean safety with fully guided 90-minute or 3-hour tours to the Mokes and Flat Island that include both instruction and equipment rental. Experienced paddlers can also rent a single or double kayak and venture out on their own. In addition, the company rents windsurfing equipment, surf and body boards, snorkel equipment, and stand-up paddleboards. Discounts are available if you reserve online. ✉ *171 Hamakua Dr., Kailua* ☎ *808/262–5483* ⊕ *www.hawaiianwatersports.com* 🚣 *Rentals from $29, tours from $74.*

Kailua Beach Adventures

KAYAKING | One of the best places for beginners to rent kayaks is Kailua Beach, and Kailua Beach Adventures has an ideal location just across the street. The company offers two- and five-hour guided kayak tours (the longer tour includes lunch, time for kayaking, and time for the beach). More adventurous visitors can rent a kayak (double or single for a half or full day) and venture to the Mokulua Islands off Lanikai. You can also rent snorkeling equipment, stand-up paddleboards, and bikes. (Discounts are given if booked online.) ✉ *Kailua Beach Shopping Center, 130 Kailua Rd., Kailua* ☎ *808/262–2555* ⊕ *www.kailuasailboards.com* 🚣 *From $59 for rental, $139 for tours.*

Twogood Kayaks Hawaii

KAYAKING | The outfitter offers kayak rentals (single or double), lessons, and guided tours. Guides are trained in the history, geology, and birds of the area. Fully guided kayak excursions are either 2½ or 5 hours and include lunch, snorkeling gear, and transportation to and from Waikiki. For those who want to create their own itinerary, owner Bob Twogood offers custom "Elite" tours. The outfitter has also recently added rental bikes as well as guided hikes to its offerings. ✉ *134B Hamakua Dr., Kailua* ☎ *808/262–5656* ⊕ *www.twogoodkayaks.com* 🚣 *Rentals from $60, tours from $115.*

NORTH SHORE
Surf 'N Sea

KAYAKING | This outfitter is located in a rustic wooden building on the beach, so in minutes you can start paddling on a single or double kayak. ■ **TIP→ Keep in mind that these plastic boats are great from spring to fall, but winter weather can be hazardous for even veteran kayakers. This outfitter's proximity to a protected stream makes kayaking in any sea conditions possible.** The company also offers just about any surf-related activity you can imagine on the North Shore in addition to kayaking. ✉ *62-595 Kamehameha Hwy., Haleiwa* ☎ *800/899–7873* ⊕ *www.surfnsea.com* 🚣 *From $60 for a full-day rental.*

Running

In Honolulu, the most popular places to jog are the two parks, **Kapiolani** and **Ala Moana,** at either end of Waikiki. In both cases, the loop around the park is just less than 2 miles. You can run a 4-mile ring around **Diamond Head Crater,** past scenic views, luxurious homes, and herds of other joggers.

BEST SPOTS
HONOLULU
Hawaii State Department of Health Community Resources Section

RUNNING | **FAMILY** | This department provides a free downloadable Fitness Fun Map, which lists a dozen walking and jogging routes and suggested itineraries. ✉ *1250 Punchbowl St., Room 422, Downtown* ☎ *808/586–4488* ⊕ *www.healthyhawaii.com/wp-content/uploads/2015/05/fun_map.pdf.*

Honolulu Marathon

RUNNING | The Honolulu Marathon is a thrilling event to watch as well as to participate in. Join the throngs who cheer at the finish line at Kapiolani Park as internationally famous and local runners tackle the 26.2-mile challenge. It's held on the second Sunday in December and is sponsored by the Honolulu Marathon Association. ☎ *808/734–7200* ⊕ *www.honolulumarathon.org.*

Running Room

RUNNING | Once you leave Honolulu, it gets trickier to find places to jog that are both scenic and safe. It's best to stick to the well-traveled routes, or ask the experienced folks at this store for advice. Their website includes information about local races as well as a list of jogging routes complete with maps. ⊠ *819 Kapahulu Ave., Kapahulu* ☎ *808/737–2422* ⊕ *www. runningroomhawaii.com.*

Scuba Diving

Not all of Hawaii's beauty is above water. What lurks below can be just as magnificent.

Although snorkeling provides adequate access to this underwater world, nothing gives you the freedom—or depth, quite literally—as scuba.

The diving on Oahu is comparable with any you might do in the tropics, but its uniqueness comes from the isolated environment of the Islands. There are literally hundreds of species of fish and marine life that you can find only in this chain. In fact, about 25% of Hawaii's marine life can be seen here only—nowhere else in the world. Adding to the singularity of diving off Oahu is the human history of the region. Military activities and tragedies of the 20th century filled the waters surrounding Oahu with wreckage that the ocean creatures have since turned into their homes.

Although instructors certified to license you in scuba are plentiful in the Islands, it's best to get your PADI certification before coming, as a week of classes may be a bit of a commitment on a short vacation. Expect to pay around $100 for a two-tank boat dive (provided that you are certified). ■ TIP→ **You can go on short, shallow introductory dives without the certification, but the best dives require it and cost a bit more.**

BEST SPOTS

Hanauma Bay Nature Preserve. On Oahu's southeast shore, about a 30-minute drive east of Waikiki, Hanauma Bay Nature Preserve is home to more than 250 different species of fish, of which a quarter can be found nowhere else in the world. This has made this volcanic crater bay one of the most popular dive sites in the state. It's a long walk from the parking lot to the beach—even longer lugging equipment—so consider hooking up with a licensed dive-tour operator. Preservation efforts have aided the bay's delicate ecosystem, so expect to see various butterfly fish, surgeonfish, tangs, parrot fish, and endangered Hawaiian sea turtles. ⊠ *7455 Kalanianaole Hwy., Hawaii Kai* ☎ *808/396–4229* $7.50 per person and $1 parking.

Hundred Foot Hole. Once an ancient Hawaiian fishing ground reserved for royalty, the Hundred Foot Hole is a cluster of volcanic boulders that have created ledges, caves, and a large open-ended cavern perfect for diving. Accessible from shore, this spot near Diamond Head attracts octopus, manta rays, and the occasional white-tip shark. ⊠ *Off Diamond Head, Honolulu.*

Mahi Waianae. Hawaii's waters are littered with shipwrecks, but one of the most intact and accessible is the *Mahi Waianae,* a 165-foot minesweeper that was sunk in 1982 off the Waianae Coast. It lies upright in about 90 feet of calm and clear water, encrusted in coral and patrolled by white spotted eagle rays and millet seed butterfly fish. The wreck serves as an artificial reef for such Hawaii aquatic residents as blue-striped snappers, puffer fish, lionfish, moray eels, and octopus. Visibility averages about 100 feet, making this one of the most popular dives on the island. ⊠ *Waianae.*

Maunalua Bay. The bay stretches about 7 miles, from Portlock Point to Black Point on Oahu's southeastern shore. Teeming with marine life, this spot has several accessible dive sites of varying difficulty. The shallow-water Turtle Canyon is home to endangered Hawaiian green sea turtles. Fantasy Reef is another shallow dive with three plateaus of volcanic rock lined with coral that is home to fish, eels, and sea turtles. In about 85 feet of water, *Baby Barge* is an easy-to-penetrate sunken vessel encrusted in coral. An advanced dive, the wreck of a Vought F4U Corsair gives you a close-up look at garden eels and stingrays. ⊠ *Southeast Oahu.*

Sharks Cove. Oahu's best shore dive is accessible only during the summer months. Sharks Cove, on Oahu's North Shore, churns with monster surf during the winter, making this popular snorkeling and diving spot extremely dangerous. In summer, the cavernous lava tubes and tunnels are great for both novices and experienced divers. Some dive-tour companies offer round-trip transportation from Waikiki. ⊠ *Haleiwa.*

Three Tables. A short walk from Sharks Cove is Three Tables, named for a trio of flat rocks running perpendicular to shore. There are lava tubes to the right of these rocks that break the surface and then extend out about 50 feet. Although this area isn't as active as Sharks Cove, you can still spot octopus, moray eels, parrot fish, green sea turtles, and the occasional shark. ⊠ *Haleiwa.*

EQUIPMENT, LESSONS, AND TOURS
NORTH SHORE
Surf 'N Sea
SCUBA DIVING | The North Shore headquarters for all things water-related is also great for diving. One interesting perk: upon request, their dive guides can shoot a video of you diving. It's hard to see facial expressions under the water, but it still might be fun for those who want to prove that they took the plunge. Two-tank shore dives are the most economical

choice (prices for noncertified divers are higher), but the company also offers boat dives, and in the summer, night dives are available for only slightly more. ⊠ *62-595 Kamehameha Hwy., Haleiwa* ☎ *800/899–7873* ⊕ *www.surfnsea.com* ⤳ *From $120 (2-tank shore dives).*

LEEWARD (WEST) OAHU
Hawaii Nautical
SCUBA DIVING | With operations throughout the islands, this eco-focused operator follows strict guidelines to protect marine mammals and wildlife. Their full-service offerings include refresher and introductory dives as well as more advanced dives. Transportation from the Ko Olina hotels is free and is available to/from Waikiki at an additional charge. All equipment is included. The dive trips depart from the Waianae Boat Harbor. ⊠ *Waianae Boat Harbor, 85-491 Farrington Hwy., Waianae* ☎ *808/234–7245* ⊕ *www.hawaiinautical. com* ⤳ *From $159 for 2-tank dives.*

WINDWARD OAHU
Aaron's Dive Shop
SCUBA DIVING | This friendly and well-equipped dive shop caters to everyone. Take an "introductory" dive if you're not certified; get certified; or sign up for an offshore day or night dive excursion if you're experienced. In addition to organized group dives, the company's "Dive Concierge" can arrange private charters for those who want a completely customized experience. Snorkelers can go along on many dives as well. ⊠ *307 Hahani St., Kailua* ☎ *808/262–2333* ⊕ *aaronsdiveshop.com* ⤳ *From $140 for 2-tank dive.*

Snorkeling

If you can swim, you can snorkel. And you don't need any formal training, either.

Snorkeling is a favorite pastime for both visitors and residents and can be done anywhere there's enough water to stick

Here, in the warm waters off the coast of Oahu, there's a good chance you'll find yourself swimming alongside a green sea turtle.

your face in. You can pick up a mask and snorkel at a corner ABC store for around $35, including fins, and get going on your own or pay up to $175 for a luxurious snorkel cruise including lunch and drinks. Each spot will have its great days depending on the weather and time of year, so consult with the purveyor of your gear for tips on where the best viewing is that day. Keep in mind that the North Shore should be attempted only when the waves are calm, namely in the summertime.

Make sure you put plenty of sunscreen on your back (or better yet, wear a T-shirt) because once you start gazing below, your head may not come back up for hours.

BEST SPOTS

Electric Beach. On the western side of the island, directly across from the electricity plant—hence the name—Electric Beach is a haven for tropical fish, making it a great snorkeling spot. The expulsion of hot water from the plant raises the temperature of the ocean, attracting Hawaiian green sea turtles, spotted moray eels, and spinner dolphins. Although visibility is not always the best, the crowds are small and the fish are guaranteed. ⊠ *Farrington Hwy., 1 mile west of Ko Olina Resort, Kapolei.*

Hanauma Bay Nature Preserve. What Waimea Bay is to surfing, Hanauma Bay in Southeast Oahu is to snorkeling. Easily the most popular snorkeling spot on the island, it's home to more than 250 different species of marine life. Due to the protection of the narrow mouth of the cove and the prodigious reef, you will be hard-pressed to find a place you will feel safer while snorkeling. ⊠ *7455 Kalanianaole Hwy., Honolulu* ☎ *, 808/396–4229 $7.50 per person and $1 parking.*

Queen's Surf Beach. On the edge of Waikiki, Queen's Surf is a marine reserve located between Kapahulu Groin and the Waikiki Aquarium. It's not as chock-full of fish as Hanauma Bay, but it has its share of colorful reef fish and the occasional

Hawaiian green sea turtle. Just yards from shore, it's a great spot for an escape if you're stuck in Waikiki and have grown weary of watching the surfers. ⊠ *Kalakaua Ave., Honolulu.*

Sharks Cove. Great shallows protected by a huge reef make Sharks Cove on the North Shore a prime spot for snorkelers, even young ones, in the summer. You'll find a plethora of critters, from crabs to octopus, in water that's no more than waist deep. When the winter swells come, this area can turn treacherous. ⊠ *Kamehameha Hwy., across from Foodland, Haleiwa.*

EQUIPMENT AND TOURS
HONOLULU
Snorkel Bob's
SNORKELING | This place has all the stuff you'll need—and more—to make your water adventures more enjoyable. Bob makes his own gear and is active in protecting reef fish species. Feel free to ask the staff about good snorkeling spots, as the best ones can vary with weather and the seasons. You can either rent or buy gear (and reserve it in advance online). ⊠ *700 Kapahulu Ave., Kapahulu* ☎ *808/735–7944, 800/262–7725* ⊕ *www.snorkelbob.com* ⊠ *Rentals from $38 per wk.*

HAWAII KAI
★ Hanauma Bay Rental Stand
SNORKELING | **FAMILY** | You can rent masks, fins, and snorkels here. The stand also has small lockers available right at the park that are large enough for your valuables. Bring ID or car keys as a deposit for rental. ⊠ *Hanauma Bay Nature Preserve, 7455 Kalanianaole Hwy., Hawaii Kai* ☎ *808/396–3483* ⊠ *Rentals from $20, lockers from $10.*

Hanauma Bay Snorkeling Excursions
SNORKELING | If you're going to Hanauma Bay, you have three options: take a chance with limited parking spaces at the park, take TheBus, or contact Hanauma Bay Snorkeling Excursions. They provide transportation to and from Waikiki hotels, equipment, and instruction on how to use the equipment for a reasonable price that does not include the $7.50 park entrance fee. ☎ *808/306–3393* ⊕ *www.hanaumabaysnorkel.com* ⊠ *From $25.*

Stand-Up Paddleboarding

From the lakes of Wisconsin to the coast of Lima, Peru, stand-up paddleboarding (or SUP, for short) is taking the sport of surfing to the most unexpected places. Still, the sport remains firmly rooted in the Hawaiian Islands.

Back in the 1960s, Waikiki beach boys would paddle out on their longboards using a modified canoe paddle. It was longer than a traditional paddle, enabling them to stand up and stroke. It was easier this way to survey the ocean and snap photos of tourists learning how to surf. Eventually it became a sport unto itself, with professional contests at world-class surf breaks and long-distance races across treacherous waters.

Stand-up paddleboarding is easy to learn—though riding waves takes some practice—and most outfitters on Oahu offer lessons for all skill levels starting at about $55. It's also a great workout; you can burn off yesterday's dinner buffet, strengthen your core, and experience the natural beauty of the island's coastlines all at once. Once you're ready to head out on your own, half-day rentals start at $50.

If you're looking to learn, go where there's already a SUP presence. Avoid popular surf breaks, unless you're an experienced stand-up paddle surfer, and be wary of ocean and wind conditions. You'll want to find a spot with calm waters, easy access in and out of the ocean, and a friendly crowd that doesn't mind the occasional stand-up paddleboarder.

Did You Know?

Sharks Cove is a wonderful place for young snorkelers to spend time exploring the ocean's bottom in shallow waters, as the area is protected by a huge reef just offshore.

BEST SPOTS

Ala Moana Beach Park. About a mile west of Waikiki, Ala Moana is the most SUP-friendly spot on the island. In fact, the state installed a series of buoys in the flat-water lagoon to separate stand-up paddlers and swimmers. There are no waves here, making it a great spot to learn, but beware of strong trade winds, which can push you into the reef.

Anahulu Stream. Outfitters on the North Shore like to take SUP beginners to Anahulu Stream, which empties into Waialua Bay near the Haleiwa Boat Harbor. This area is calm and protected from winds, plus there's parking at the harbor, and surf shops nearby rent boards.

Waikiki. There are a number of outfitters on Oahu's South Shore that take beginners into the waters off Waikiki. **Canoes,** the surf break fronting the Duke Kahanamoku statue, and the channels between breaks are often suitable for people learning how to maneuver their boards in not-so-flat conditions. But south swells here can be menacing, and ocean conditions can change quickly. Check with lifeguards before paddling out, and be mindful of other surfers in the water.

White Plains. If you've got a car with racks, you might want to venture to White Plains, a fairly uncrowded beach about 27 miles west of Waikiki. It's a long, sandy beach with lots of breaks, and plenty of room for everyone. There are lifeguards, restrooms, and lots of parking, making this a great spot for beginners and those just getting comfortable in small waves.

EQUIPMENT AND LESSONS
HONOLULU
Hans Hedemann Surf School

WATER SPORTS | Get professional instruction in stand-up paddleboarding right in Waikiki, where the sport originated. This school offers group lessons, semiprivate lessons, and private training. Lessons are also offered through locations at the Park Shore Hotel in Waikiki and Turtle Bay Resort in Kahuku. ⊠ *Park Shore Waikiki, 2586 Kalakaua Ave., Honolulu* ☎ *808/924–7778, 808/447–6755* ⊕ *www. hhsurf.com* 🖃 *From $85.*

WINDWARD OAHU
Hawaiian Watersports

WATER SPORTS | FAMILY | Paddle off the shore of picturesque Kailua Beach. This safety-conscious outfitter offers both equipment rentals and 90-minute and 3-hour group or individual lessons. A one-stop shop for water sports, they also offer kiteboarding, surfing, and windsurfing lessons as well as kayak tours and equipment rentals. Discounts are available online if you book ahead. ⊠ *171 Hamakua Dr., Kailua* ☎ *808/262–5483* ⊕ *www.hawaiianwatersports.com* 🖃 *Rentals from $59.*

HONOLULU
Paddle Core Fitness

WATER SPORTS | Paddling is a way of life for Reid Inouye, who now shares his passion for the sport with students. (He's also the publisher of *Standup Paddle Magazine.*) His company offers introductory classes as well as fitness programs for serious paddlers. Lessons and workout programs are held in the flat waters of Ala Moana Beach, where there's a designated area for paddling, and you can have either group or private lessons. ⊠ *Ala Moana Beach Park, Ala Moana Blvd., Ala Moana* ☎ *808/200–0574* ⊕ *www.paddlecorefitness.com* 🖃 *Workout programs from $25, lessons from $135.*

NORTH SHORE
Rainbow Watersports Adventures

WATER SPORTS | When you spot this company's colorful Rainbow Watersports van at the bay near Haleiwa Beach Park, you'll know you're in the right place. You can get a two-hour private or group lesson on Oahu's North Shore. All lessons are held in a spot popular with the resident green sea turtles. The company also offers a 3½-hour coastal eco-adventure trip including snorkeling and lunch. Their Twilight Glow Paddle lets you glide through calm waters illuminated by lights mounted to your board. ⊠ *Haleiwa Beach Park, Kamehameha Hwy., Haleiwa* ☎ *800/470–4964, 808/372–9304* ⊕ *www. rainbowwatersports.com* ⊠ *Lessons from $79.*

Surf 'N Sea

WATER SPORTS | FAMILY | With stand-up paddleboarding lessons for every skill level, Surf 'N Sea is a great place to start. Beginners can take the introductory lesson to learn proper paddling technique. A one-hour session focuses on honing your skills. More advanced paddlers can book surf trips that take you out to several North Shore breaks. ⊠ *62-595 Kamehameha Hwy., Haleiwa* ☎ *808/637–3008, 800/899–7873* ⊕ *www.surfnsea.com* ⊠ *Rentals from $60 (includes paddle).*

Submarine Tours

HONOLULU

Atlantis Submarines

TOUR—SPORTS | This is the underwater adventure for the unadventurous. Not fond of swimming, but want to see what you've been missing? Board this high-tech 64-passenger vessel for a ride past shipwrecks, turtle breeding grounds, and coral reefs. The tours, which depart from the pier at the Hilton Hawaiian Village, are available in several languages. (Discounts are available if booked online.) ⊠ *Hilton Hawaiian Village Beach Resort & Spa, 2005 Kalia Rd., Honolulu* ☎ *808/973–9800, 800/381–0237 for reservations* ⊕ *www.atlantisadventures. com* ⊠ *From $133.*

Surfing

Perhaps no word is more associated with Hawaii than surfing. Every year, the best of the best gather on Oahu's North Shore to compete in their version of the Super Bowl: the prestigious Vans Triple Crown of Surfing. The pros dominate the waves for a month, but the rest of the year belongs to folks just trying to have fun.

Oahu is unique because it has so many famous spots: Banzai Pipeline, Waimea Bay, Kaiser Bowls, and Sunset Beach. These spots, however, require experience. Nonetheless, with the most dependable sets and access to lessons, Waikiki is still a great place for beginners to learn or for novice surfers to catch predictable waves. Group lessons on Waikiki Beach start at $50, but if you really want to fine-tune your skills, you can pay up to $500 for a daylong private outing with a former pro.

The island also has miles of coastline with surf spots that are perfect for everyday surfers. But remember this surfer's credo: when in doubt, don't go out. If you're unsure about conditions, stay on the beach and talk to locals to get more info about surf breaks before trying yourself.

⚠ **If you don't want to run the risk of a confrontation with local surfers, who can be very territorial about their favorite breaks, try some of the alternate spots listed below. They may not have the name recognition, but the waves can be just as great.**

BEST SPOTS

Makaha Beach Park. If you like to ride waves, try Makaha Beach on Oahu's west side. It has legendary, interminable rights that allow riders to perform all manner of stunts: from six-man canoes with everyone doing headstands to Bullyboards (oversize body boards) with whole families along for the ride. Mainly known as a longboarding spot, it's predominantly

This surfer is doing a stellar job of riding the infamous Banzai Pipeline on Oahu's North Shore.

local but respectful to outsiders. Use caution in winter, as the surf can get huge. It's not called Makaha—which means "fierce"—for nothing. ☒ *84-369 Farrington Hwy., Waianae.*

Sunset Beach. If you want to impress your surfing buddies back home, catch a wave at the famous Sunset Beach on Oahu's North Shore. Two of the more manageable breaks are **Kammie Land** (or Kammie's) and **Sunset Point.** For the daring, Sunset is part of the Vans Triple Crown of Surfing for a reason. Thick waves and long rides await, but you're going to want to have a thick board and a thicker skull. Surf etiquette here is a must, as it's mostly local. ☒ *59-104 Kamehameha Hwy., 1 mile north of Ehukai Beach Park, Haleiwa.*

Ulukou Beach. In Waikiki you can paddle out to **Populars,** a break at Ulukou Beach. Nice and easy, Populars—or Pops—never breaks too hard and is friendly to both newbies and veterans. It's one of the best places to surf during pumping south swells, as this thick wave breaks in open ocean, making it more rideable. The only downside is the long paddle out to the break from Kuhio Beach, but that keeps the crowds manageable. ☒ *Waikiki Beach, in front of Sheraton Waikiki hotel, Honolulu.*

White Plains Beach. Known among locals as "mini Waikiki," the surf at White Plains breaks in numerous spots, preventing the logjams that are inevitable at many of Oahu's more popular spots. It's a great break for novice to intermediate surfers, though you do have to keep a lookout for wayward boards. From the H1, take the Makakilo exit. ☒ *Off H1, Kapolei.*

EQUIPMENT AND LESSONS
HONOLULU
Aloha Beach Services

SURFING | It may sound like a cliché, but there's no better way to learn to surf than from a beach boy in Waikiki. And there's no one better than Harry "Didi" Robello, a second-generation beach boy and owner of Aloha Beach Services. Learn to surf in an hour-long group lesson, a semiprivate lesson, or with just you and an instructor. You can also rent a board here. ✉ *2365 Kalakaua Ave., on beach near Moana Surfrider, Waikiki* ☎ *808/922–3111* ⊕ *www.alohabeachservices.com* 🔁 *Lessons from $50, board rentals from $20.*

Faith Surf School

SURFING | Professional surfer Tony Moniz started his own surf school in 2000, and since then, he and his wife, Tammy, have helped thousands of people catch their first waves in Waikiki. The 90-minute group lessons include all equipment and are the cheapest option. You can pay more (sometimes a lot more) for semiprivate lessons with up to three people or for private lessons. You can also book an all-day surf tour with Moniz, riding waves with him at his favorite breaks. ✉ *Outrigger Waikiki Beach Resort, 2335 Kalakaua Ave., Waikiki* ☎ *808/931–6262* ⊕ *www.faithsurfschool.com* 🔁 *Lessons from $65, board rental from $20.*

NORTH SHORE
Hans Hedemann Surf School

SURFING | Hans Hedemann spent 17 years on the professional surfing circuit. He and his staff offer surfing, bodysurfing, and stand-up paddleboarding instruction; multiday intensive surf camps; and fine-tuning courses with Hedemann himself. Two-hour group lessons are the cheapest option, but private lessons are also available. There are also locations at Turtle Bay Resort in Kahuku and at Kahala Hotel & Resort in Kahala. ✉ *Park Shore Waikiki, 2586 Kalakaua Ave., Waikiki* ☎ *808/924–7778 for Park Shore Waikiki, 808/447–6755 for Turtle Bay Resort* ⊕ *www.hhsurf.com* 🔁 *From $78.*

Surf 'N Sea

SURFING | This is a one-stop shop for surfers (and other water-sports enthusiasts) on the North Shore. Rent a short or long board by the hour or for a full day. Two-hour group lessons are offered, as

are four- to five-hour surf safaris for experienced surfers. ✉ *62-595 Kamehameha Hwy., Haleiwa* ☎ *800/899–7873* ⊕ *www.surfnsea.com* 🔁 *Lessons from $85, rentals from $35 per day.*

WINDWARD OAHU
Hawaiian Water Sports

SURFING | FAMILY | Although the shop is located in Kailua, this jack-of-all-trades outfitter conducts surf lessons on storied Waikiki Beach. Choose from a 1½- or 3-hour group or private lesson. There are discounts if you book online in advance. This safety-conscious company also offers windsurfing, stand-up paddleboarding, kayaking, and kitesurfing lessons and equipment rental. ✉ *171 Hamakua Dr., Kailua* ☎ *808/262–5483* ⊕ *www.hawaiianwatersports.com* 🔁 *Group lessons from $74 (online booking only).*

Whale-Watching

December is marked by the arrival of snow in much of America, but in Hawaii it marks the return of the humpback whale. These migrating behemoths move south from their North Pacific homes during the winter months for courtship and calving, and they put on quite a show. Watching males and females alike throwing themselves out of the ocean and into the sunset awes even the saltiest of sailors. Newborn calves riding gently next to their 2-ton mothers will stir you to your core. These gentle giants can be seen from the shore as they make a splash, but there is nothing like having your boat rocking beneath you in the wake of a whale's breach.

HONOLULU
Atlantis Majestic Cruises

WHALE-WATCHING | FAMILY | The 150-foot cruise vessel *Majestic* bills itself as the smoothest whale-watching tour on Oahu and guarantees a whale sighting. Because of the boat's size—it has three decks—you can choose from indoor or outdoor viewing while listening to Hawaiian music and an onboard naturalist who provides information as you search for the leviathans. Included among the offerings are 2½-hour lunch cruises. Departures are from the historic Aloha Tower Marketplace at Pier 6. Transportation from Waikiki can be arranged. ■TIP→ **Check-in begins 30 minutes before departure. Arrive early to get a table near a window for the best views while you dine.** ⊠ *Aloha Tower Marketplace, 1 Aloha Tower Dr., Pier 6, Downtown* ☎ *800/381–0237* ⊕ *www.atlantisadventures.com* ⊠ *From $69.*

LEEWARD (WEST) OAHU
Wild Side Specialty Tours

WHALE-WATCHING | Boasting a marine-biologist/naturalist crew, this company takes you to undisturbed snorkeling areas. Along the way you may see dolphins and turtles. The company promises a sighting of migrating whales year-round on some itineraries. Tours may depart as early as 8 am from Waianae, so it's important to plan ahead. The three-hour deluxe wildlife tour is the most popular option. ⊠ *Waianae Boat Harbor, 85-471 Farrington Hwy., Waianae* ☎ *808/306–7273* ⊕ *www.sailhawaii.com* ⊠ *From $175.*

Windsurfing and Kiteboarding

Those who call windsurfing and kiteboarding cheating because they require no paddling have never tried hanging on to a sail or kite. It will turn your arms to spaghetti quicker than paddling ever could, and the speeds you generate earn these sports the label of "extreme."

Windsurfing was born here in the Islands. For amateurs, the windward side is best because the onshore breezes will bring you back to land even if you're not

a pro. The newer sport of kiteboarding is tougher but more exhilarating, as the kite will sometimes take you in the air for hundreds of feet. ■TIP→ **Recent changes to local laws restrict lessons on the beach, so outfitters offering lessons are few and far between.**

WINDWARD OAHU
Hawaiian Water Sports

WINDSURFING | Learn to kiteboard, windsurf, kayak, surf, or ride a stand-up paddleboard with this multifaceted outfitter. This is the only shop to offer kiteboarding and windsurfing lessons on Oahu, and the location of your lessons—off Kailua Beach—is one of the best and most beautiful on the island. The company also offers windsurfing, stand-up paddleboard, surf- and body board, snorkeling, and kayak equipment rentals. (For experienced kitesurfers, kitesurfing equipment rental is available.) You'll get a discount by booking your rental or lessons online in advance. ⊠ *171 Hamakua Dr., Kailua* ☎ *808/262–5483* ⊕ *www.hawaiianwatersports.com* ⊠ *Group lessons from $120, equipment rental from $100.*

Index

Photo Credits

Front Cover: Art Wager [Description:Aerial View of S Curve Freeway on Oahu.]. **Back cover, from left to right:** Elias/iStockphoto, Leigh Anne Meeks/Shutterstock, Rradams/Dreamstime. Spine: Bennyartist/Shutterstock. **Interior, from left to right:** santonius silaban/iStockphoto (1). Eddy Galeotti/Shutterstock (2). Rradams/Dreamstime (5). **Chapter 1: Experience Oahu:** tomas del amo/Shutterstock (6-7). Zhu_zhu/Dreamstime (8). O'ahu Visitor's Bureau (9). Dave/Flickr, [CC BY-NC 2.0] (9). Jennifer Boyer / Flickr [CC BY 2.0] (10). Eddygaleotti/Dreamstime.com (10). Hawaii Tourism Authority (HTA) / Dana Edmunds (10). RobertaLouise/Shutterstock (10). Luckydog1/Dreamstime(11). Pevans941/Dreamstime (11). Ashmephotography/Dreamstime (12). Mason Higa (12). Joshua Rainey Photography/Shutterstock (12). Shane Myers Photography/Shutterstock (12). 7maru/Shutterstock (13). Hawaii Tourism Authority (HTA) / Dana Edmunds (14). Westin Hotels & Resorts (14). Adeliepenguin/Dreamstime.com (14). Westin Hotels & Resorts (14). Mcdonojj/Dreamstime (15). Esusek/Dreamstime (15). Bhofack2/Dreamstime (16). Follow2find/Shutterstock (16). Phillip B. Espinasse/Shutterstock (16) (Bottom left & right). Nalukai/Dreamstime (17). Christian Mueller/Shutterstock (22). Leigh Anne Meeks/Shutterstock (23). dshumny/Shutterstock (24). Shane Myers Photography/Shutterstock (24). segawa7/iStockphoto (24). Cupertino10/Dreamstime (25). Norbert Turi/Shutterstock (25). Pr2is/Dreamstime (26). Ancha Chiangmai/Shutterstock (26). Marilyn Gould/Dreamstime (26). Tpower70/Dreamstime (26). Vfbjohn/Dreamstime (26). Big Island Visitors Bureau (BIVB) / Kirk Lee Aeder (27). Eddygaleotti/Dreamstime (27). Caner CIFTCI/Dreamstime (27). Elmar Langle/iStockphoto (27). Koondon/Shutterstock (27). Martinmark/Dreamstime (28). Dana Edmunds 2014 (28). Hawaii Tourism (28). Magdanatka/Shutterstock (29). Big Island Visitors Bureau (BIVB) / Kirk Lee Aeder (29). Temanu/Shutterstock (30). Hawaii Tourism Authority (HTA) / Brooke Dombroski (30). Lost Mountain Studio/Shutterstock (30). Alla Machutt/iStockphoto (30). Mongkolchon Akesin/Shutterstock (30). Hawaii Tourism Authority (HTA) / Heather Goodman (31). Hawaii Tourism Authority (HTA) / Heather Goodman (31). Hawaii Tourism Authority (HTA) / Dana Edmunds (31). Hawaii Tourism Authority (31). olgakr/iStockphoto (31). Cathy Locklear/Dreamstime (35). HVCB (36). Thinkstock LLC (37). Linda Ching/HVCB (39). Sri Maiava Rusden/HVCB (39). Leis Of Hawaii @ leisofhawaii.com (40). www.kellyalexanderphotography.com (40). Leis Of Hawaii @ leisofhawaii.com (40). Leis Of Hawaii @ leisofhawaii.com (40). Leis Of Hawaii @ leisofhawaii.com (40). www.kellyalexanderphotography.com(40). Tim Wilson/Flickr, [CC BY-NC 2.0] (41). Polynesian Cultural Center (42, 1-5). Dana Edmunds/Polynesian Cultural Center's/Alii Luau (43,1-3). Oahu Visitors Bureau (43). **Chapter 3: Honolulu and Pearl Harbor:** Izabela23/Shutterstock (71). Diamond Head (79). 7maru/iStockphoto (94). Memorial Association (113). Rradams/Dreamstime (115). NPS/ USS Arizona Memorial Photo Collection (115). Army Signal Corps Collection in the U.S. National Archives (116). USS Missouri Memorial Association (116). USS Bowfin Submarine Museum & Park (117). 7maru/Shutterstock (128). Rico Leffanta/Dreamstime (138). 7maru/Shutterstock.com (147). MH Anderson Photography/Shutterstock (152). **Chapter 4: West (Leeward) and Central Oahu:** Hpbfotos/Dreamstime (159). Harry Beugelink/Shutterstock (168). Dudarev Mikhail/Shutterstock (171). **Chapter 5: North Shore:** Phillip B. Espinasse (173). Malgorzata Litkowska/Shutterstock (180). MNStudio/Shutterstock (185). Photo Resource Hawaii / Alamy (187). **Chapter 6: Windward Oahu with Hawaii Kai:** SvetlanaSF/iStockphoto (189). Phillip B. Espinasse/Shutterstock (194). Eddygaleotti/Dreamstime (196). SuperStock/age fotostock (202). hipho/iStockphoto (204). Ppictures/Shutterstock (208). Malgorzata Litkowska/Shutterstock (210). **Chapter 7: Activities and Tours:** Anna Bryukhanova (213). Blue Hawaiian Helicopters (215). Photo Resource Hawaii / Alamy (222). Wellych/Dreamstime.com (227). Photo Resource Hawaii / Alamy (232). Photo Resource Hawaii / Alamy (240). Photo Resource Hawaii / Alamy (242). Karen Wilson (245). **About Our Writers:** All photos are courtesy of the writers.

Every effort has been made to trace the copyright holders, and we apologize in advance for any accidental errors. We would be happy to apply the corrections in the following edition of this publication.

Notes

Notes

Fodor's OAHU

Publisher: Stephen Horowitz, *General Manager*

Editorial: Douglas Stallings, *Editorial Director*; Jill Fergus, Jacinta O'Halloran, Amanda Sadlowski, *Senior Editors*; Kayla Becker, Alexis Kelly, Rachael Roth, *Editors*

Design: Tina Malaney, *Director of Design and Production*; Jessica Gonzalez, *Graphic Designer*; Mariana Tabares, *Design and Production Intern*

Production: Jennifer DePrima, *Editorial Production Manager*; Elyse Rozelle, *Senior Production Editor*; Monica White, *Production Editor*

Maps: Rebecca Baer, *Senior Map Editor*; David Lindroth, Mark Stroud (Moon Street Cartography), *Cartographers*

Photography: Viviane Teles, *Senior Photo Editor*; Namrata Aggarwal, Ashok Kumar, Carl Yu, *Photo Editors*; Rebecca Rimmer, *Photo Intern*

Business and Operations: Chuck Hoover, *Chief Marketing Officer*; Robert Ames, *Group General Manager*; Devin Duckworth, *Director of Print Publishing*; Victor Bernal, *Business Analyst*

Public Relations and Marketing: Joe Ewaskiw, *Senior Director Communications and Public Relations*

Fodors.com Jeremy Tarr, *Editorial Director*; Rachael Levitt, *Managing Editor*

Technology: Jon Atkinson, *Director of Technology*; Rudresh Teotia, *Lead Developer*; Jacob Ashpis, *Content Operations Manager*

Writers: Powell Berger, Marla Cimini, Cheryl Crabtree, Tiffany Hill, Trina Kudlacek, and Anna Weaver

Editor: Douglas Stallings

Production Editor: Jennifer DePrima

8th Edition

ISBN 978-1-64097-298-8

ISSN 1559–0771

All details in this book are based on information supplied to us at press time. Always confirm information when it matters, especially if you're making a detour to visit a specific place. Fodor's expressly disclaims any liability, loss, or risk, personal or otherwise, that is incurred as a consequence of the use of any of the contents of this book.

SPECIAL SALES

This book is available at special discounts for bulk purchases for sales promotions or premiums. For more information, e-mail SpecialMarkets@fodors.com.

PRINTED IN CANADA

10 9 8 7 6 5 4 3 2 1

About Our Writers

Powell Berger lives in the heart of Honolulu's Kakaako neighborhood, where she's ever in search of the best poke bowl. Her wanderlust has taken her to more than 50 countries around the world, and her writing appears in numerous state and regional publications, AAA magazines, *The Atlantic,* and various websites, in addition to Fodor's.

Marla Cimini is an award-winning writer with a passion for travel, beaches, music, and culinary adventures. As an avid globetrotter and frequent Oahu visitor, she has covered topics such as Hawaii's luxury hotels, fascinating and fun surf culture, and the innovative restaurant scene on the islands. She appreciates Oahu's unique dichotomy, and enjoys the bustling Waikiki neighborhood as much as exploring the island's quieter beaches. And she's always up for surfing or an outrigger canoe ride in Waikiki! Marla's articles have appeared in numerous publications worldwide, including *USA Today* and many others. Marla's website is *www.marlacimini. com.* She updated Waikiki and Diamond Head for this edition.

Cheryl Crabtree first visited Hawaii as a kindergartner, a trip that sparked a life-long passion for the islands and led to frequent visits. She spends months at a time in residence on the North Shore and updated The North Shore and West (Leeward) & Central Oahu chapters for this edition. Cheryl has also contributed to *Fodor's California* for nearly two decades and is a regular updater for *Fodor's National Parks of the West.* She also contributes to numerous regional and national publications.

Tiffany Hill has grew up on Oahu and has lived on both the Leeward and Windward sides, but today she calls Portland, Oregon home. She specializes in travel, culture, and business. Her work is regularly published in regional and national publications, as well as online. When she's not on assignment, you can find her playing roller derby.

Trina Kudlacek fell in love with Hawaii while on vacation 20 years ago. She now has the best of all possible worlds as she splits her time between her home in Hawaii, where she is a lecturer at the University of Hawaii, and Italy, where she is a tour guide.

Writer and multimedia journalist **Anna Weaver** is a sixth-generation *kamaaina,* born and raised in Kailua, Oahu. She can never get enough Spam *musubi, malassadas,* or hiking time in her home state. Anna has written for *Slate, Simplemost,* and such Hawaii publications as the *Honolulu Advertiser* (now *Star-Advertiser*), *Honolulu Magazine,* and *Pacific Business News.*